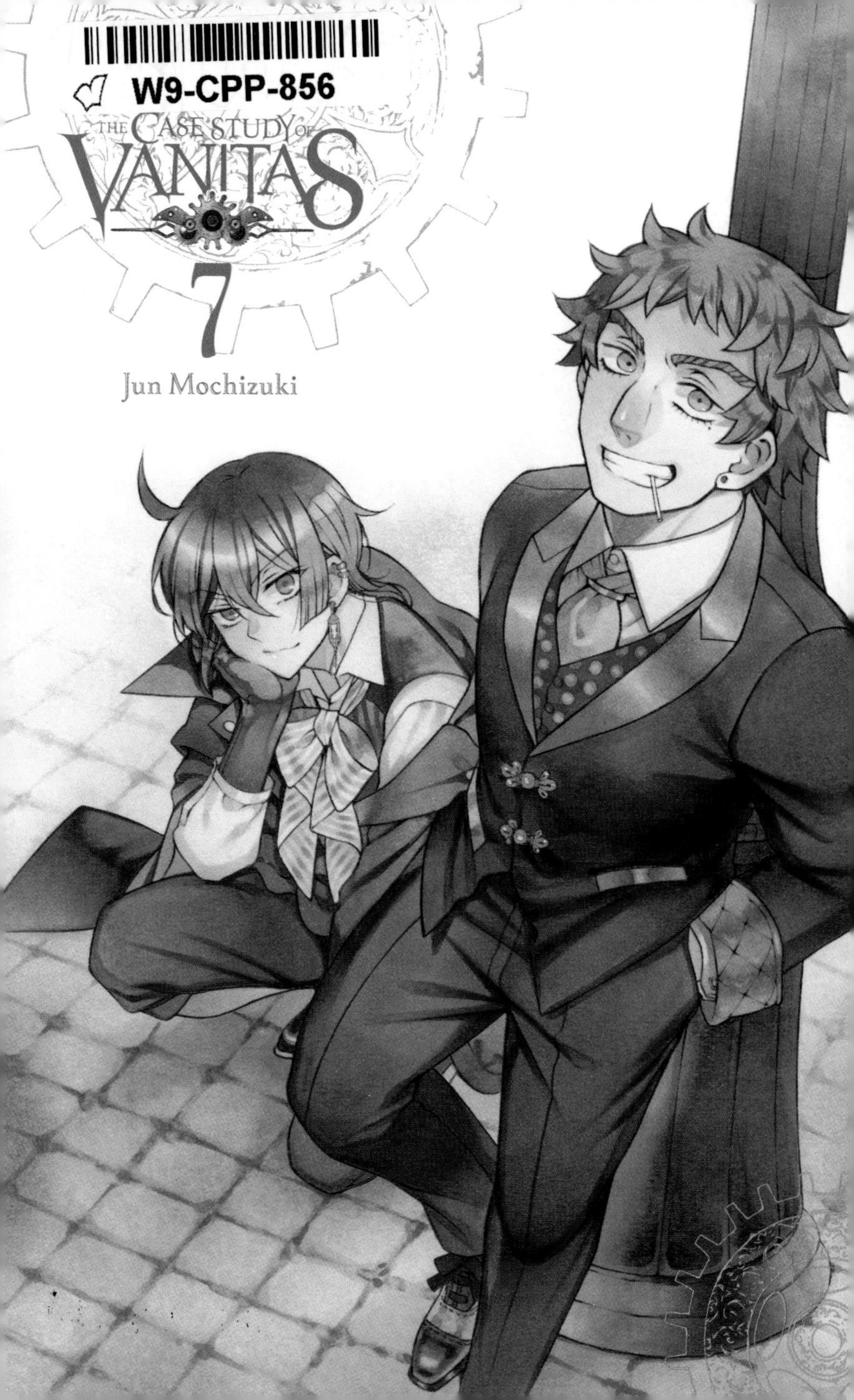
THE CASE STUDY OF
VANITAS
7
Jun Mochizuki

THE CASE STUDY OF VANITAS 7

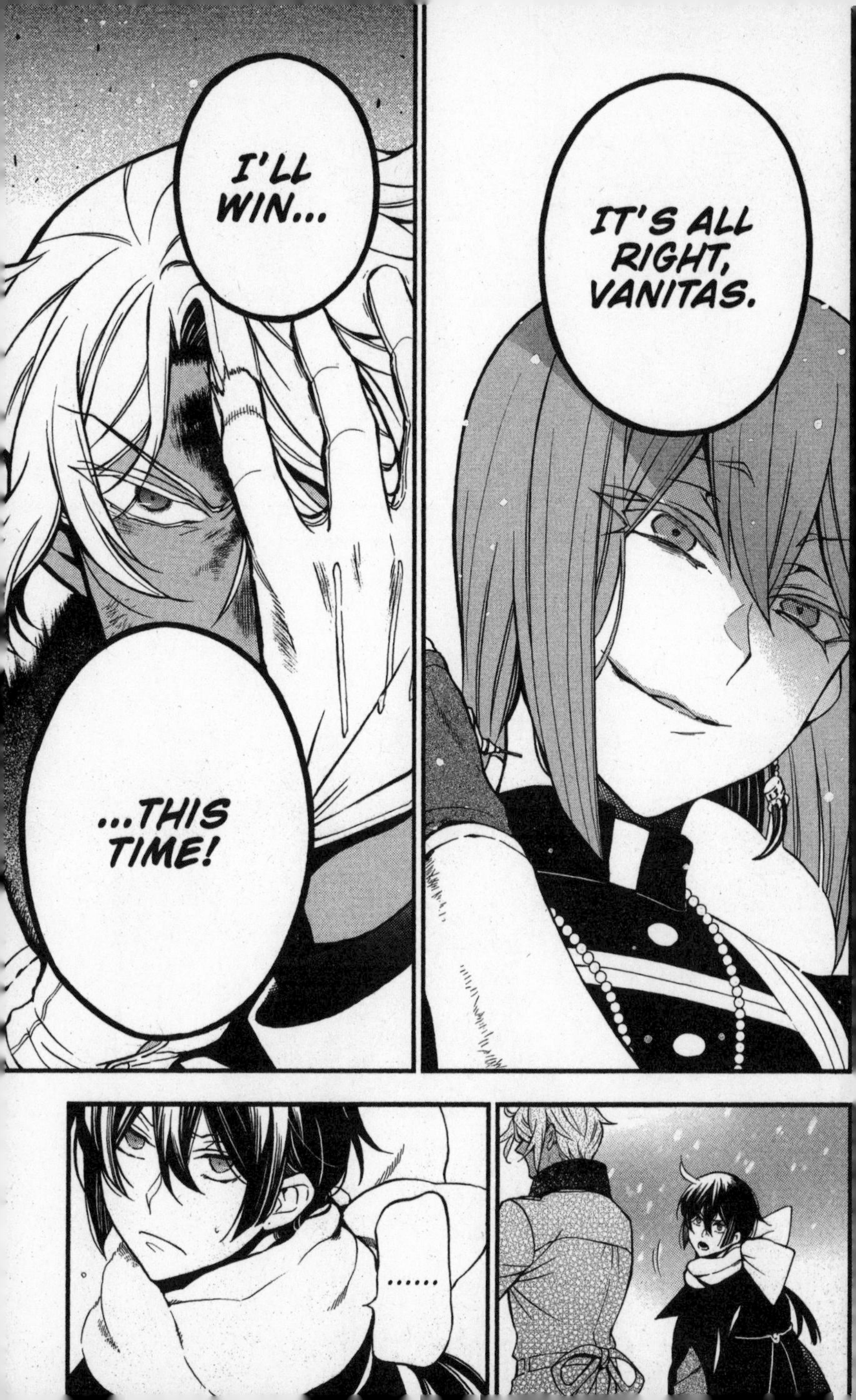
IT'S ALL RIGHT, VANITAS.
I'LL WIN...
...THIS TIME!
......

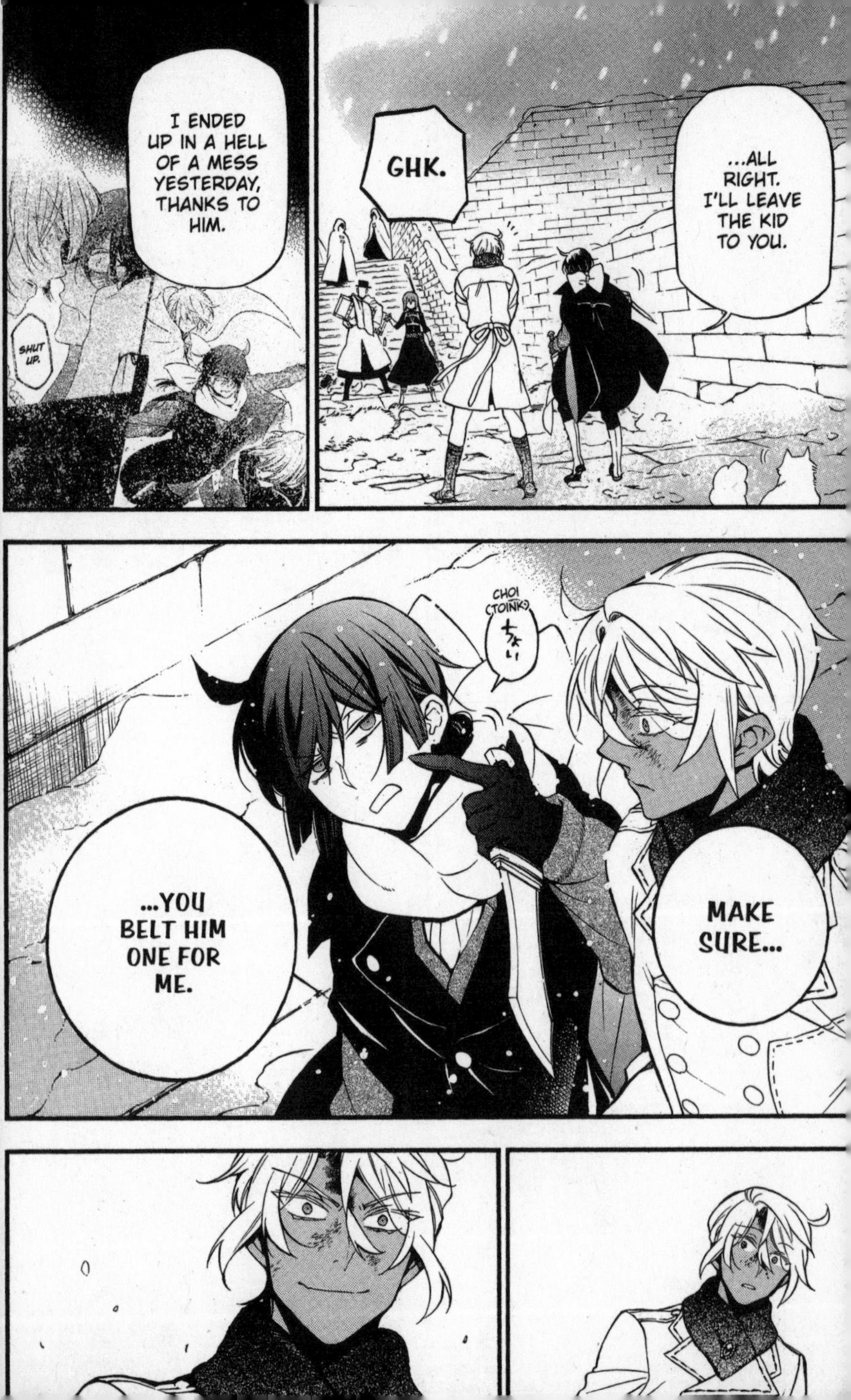

...ALL RIGHT. I'LL LEAVE THE KID TO YOU.
GHK.
I ENDED UP IN A HELL OF A MESS YESTERDAY, THANKS TO HIM.
SHUT UP.
CHOI (TOINK)
ちょい
MAKE SURE...
...YOU BELT HIM ONE FOR ME.

MÉMOIRE 35

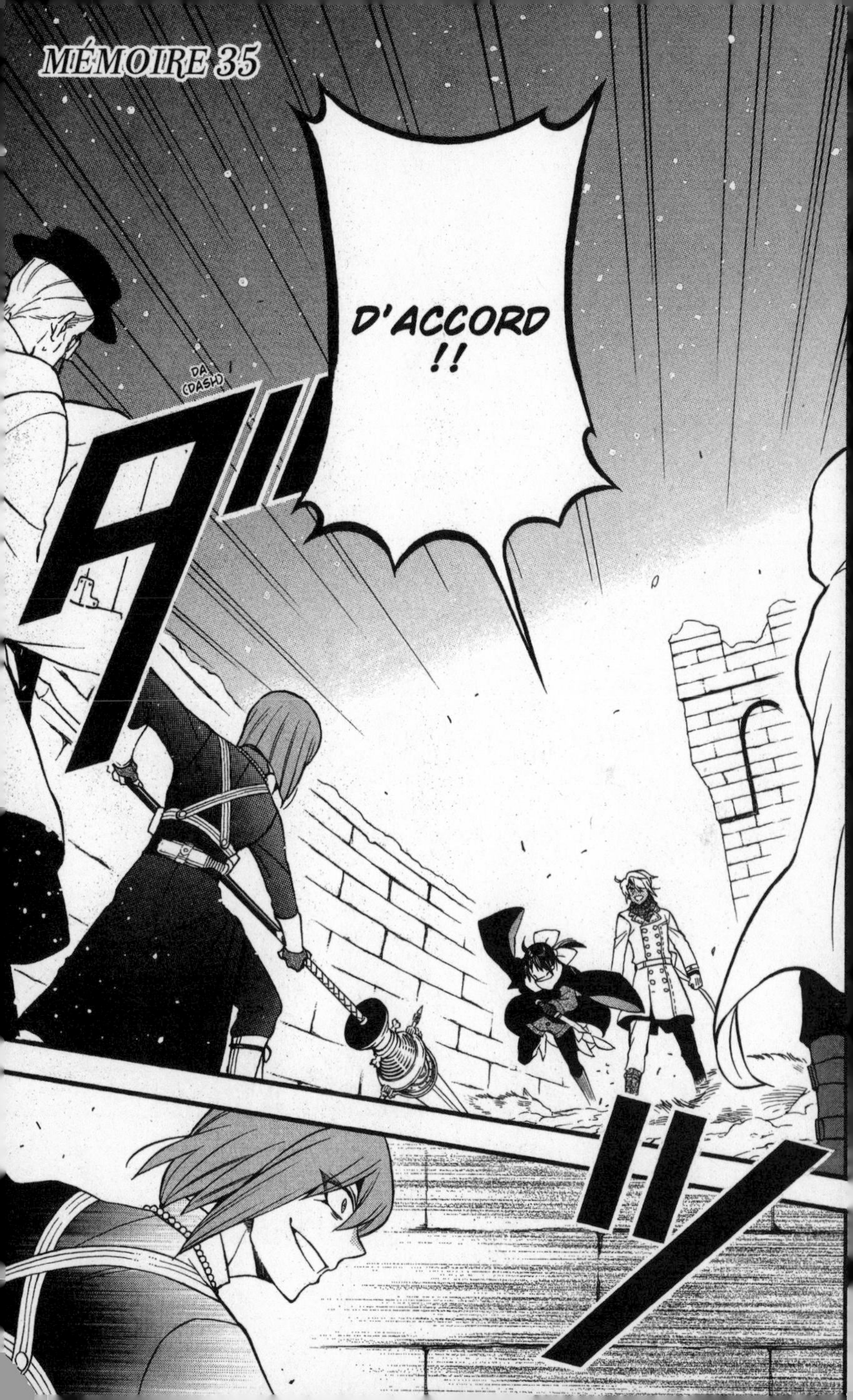
D'ACCORD !!
DA (DASH)

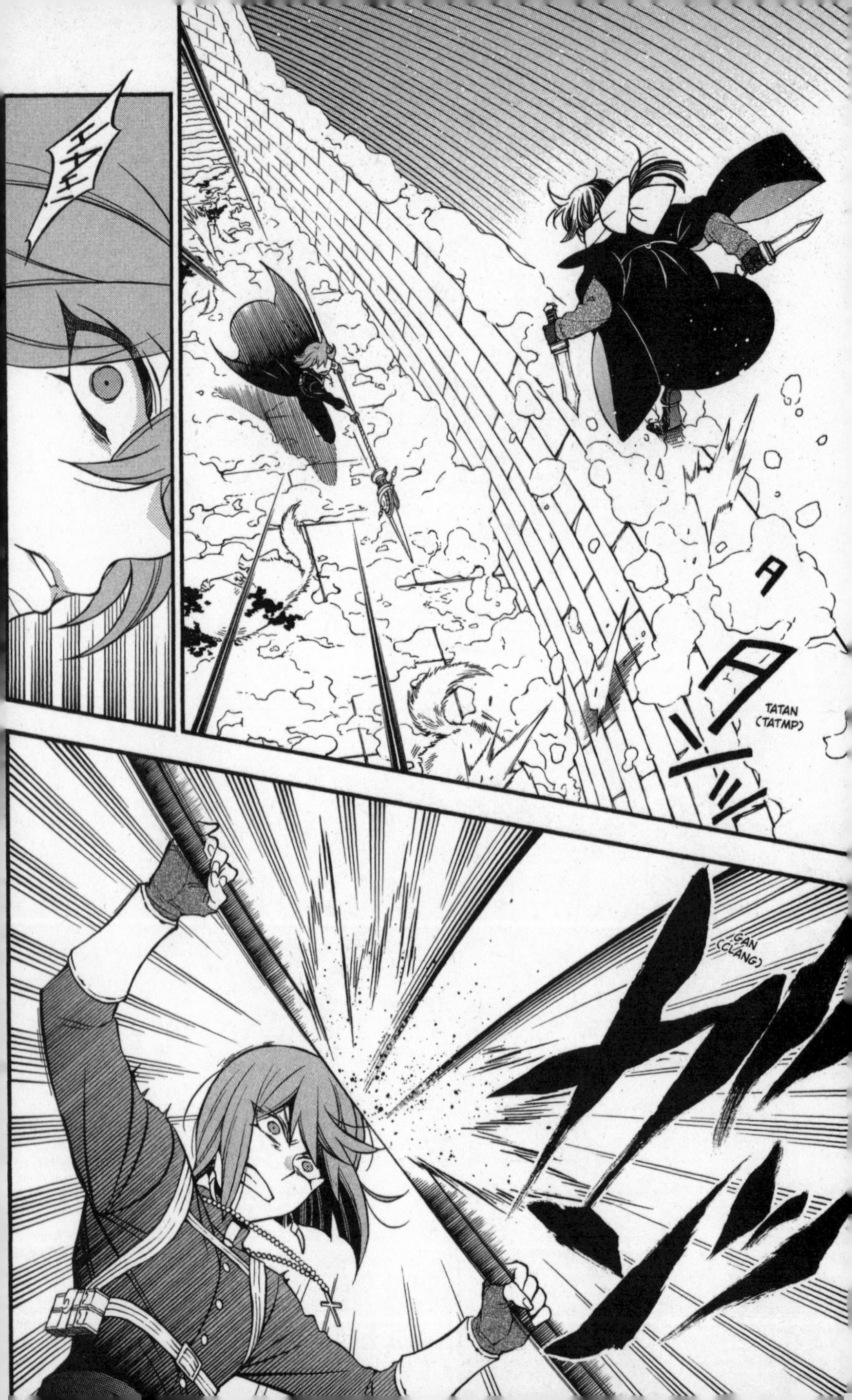
TATAN (TATMP)
HAH!
GAN (CLANG)

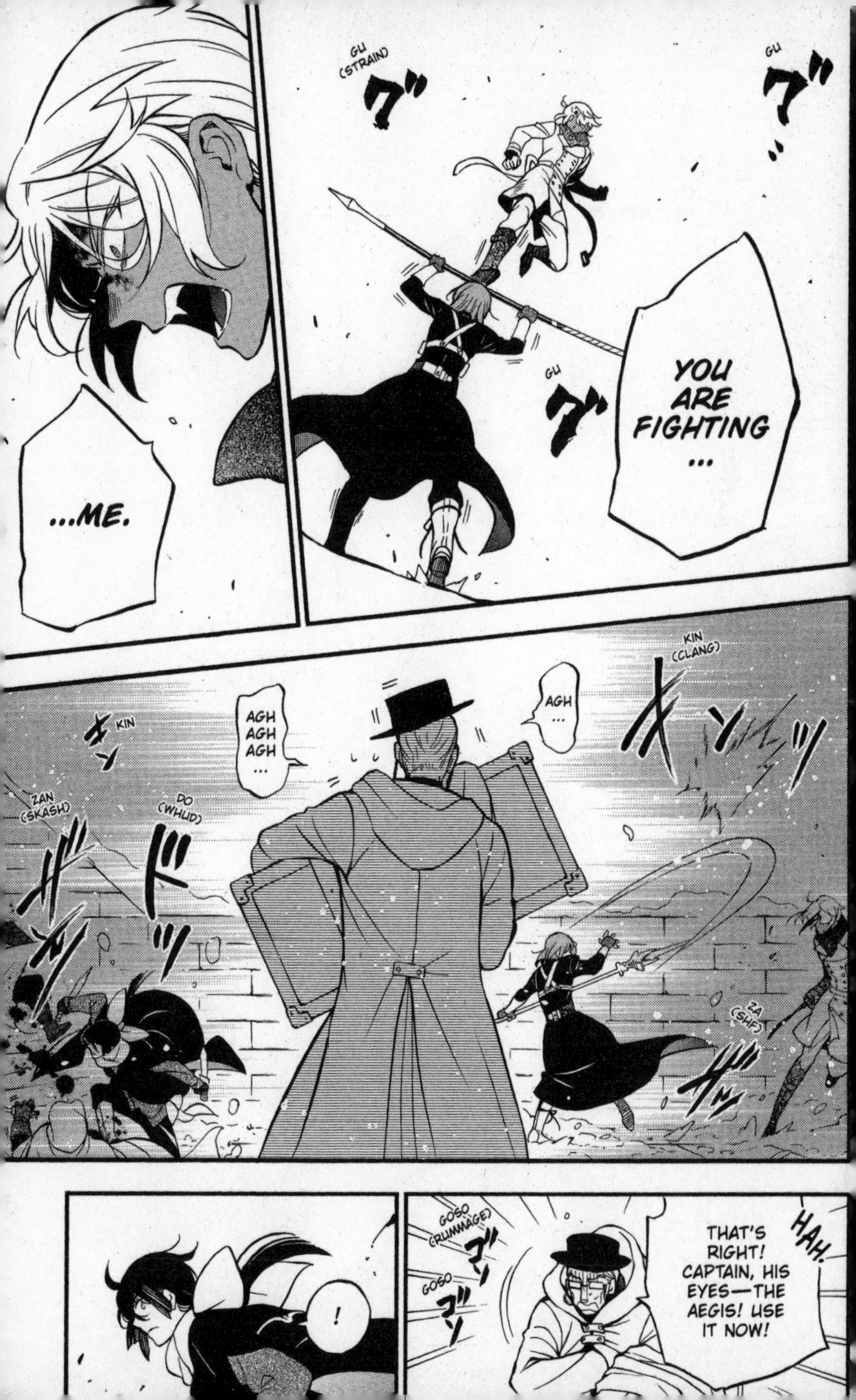
GU
GU (STRAIN)
YOU ARE FIGHTING ...
GU
...ME.
KIN (CLANG)
AGH ...
AGH AGH AGH ...
KIN
ZA (SHF)
DO (WHUD)
ZAN (SKASH)
HAH!
THAT'S RIGHT! CAPTAIN, HIS EYES—THE AEGIS! USE IT NOW!
GOSO (RUMMAGE)
GOSO
!

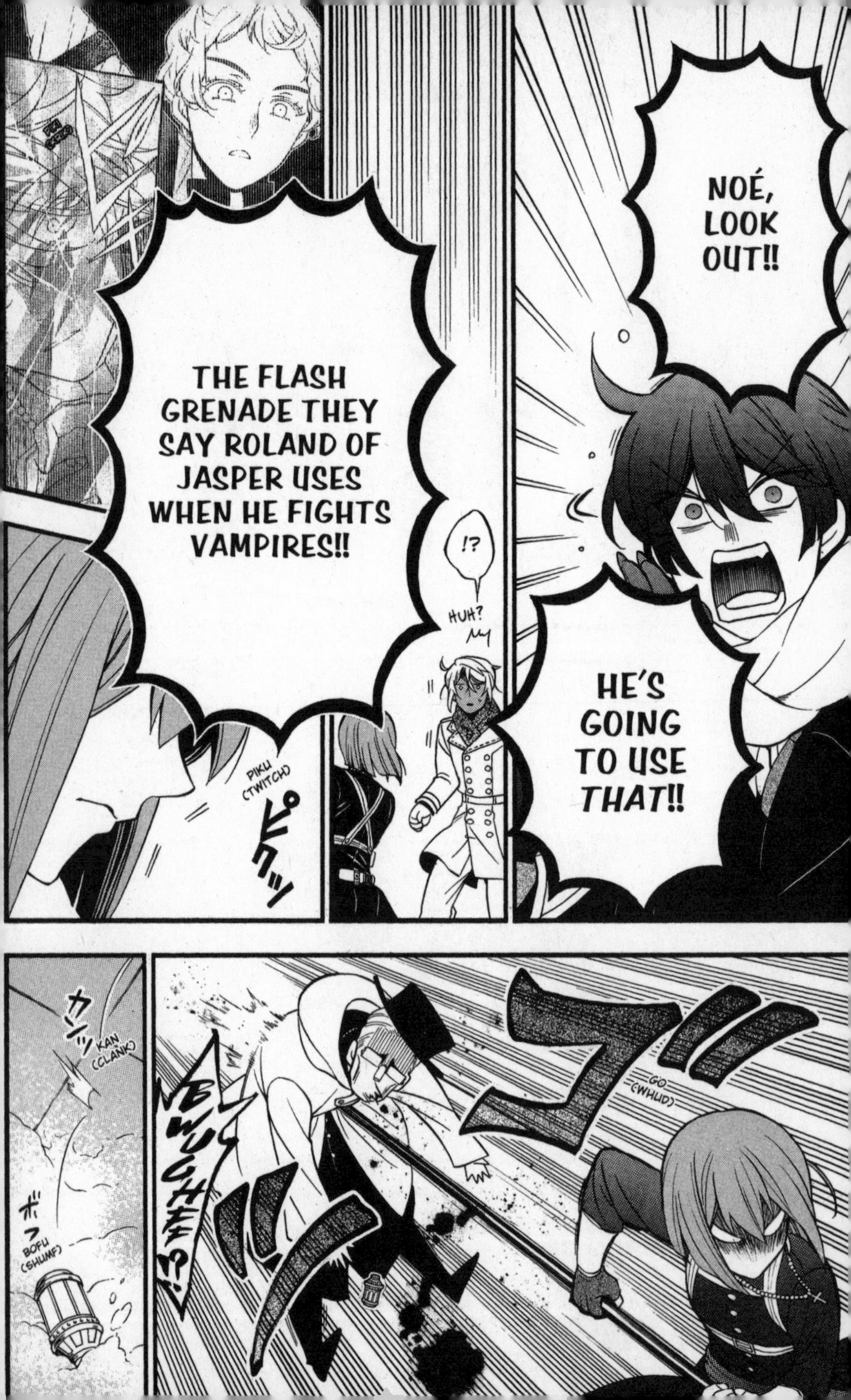
NOÉ, LOOK OUT!!
HE'S GOING TO USE THAT!!
!?
HUH?
THE FLASH GRENADE THEY SAY ROLAND OF JASPER USES WHEN HE FIGHTS VAMPIRES!!
PIKU (TWITCH)
GO (WHUD)
NGWUGHEE!?
KAN (CLANK)
BOFU (SHUMF)

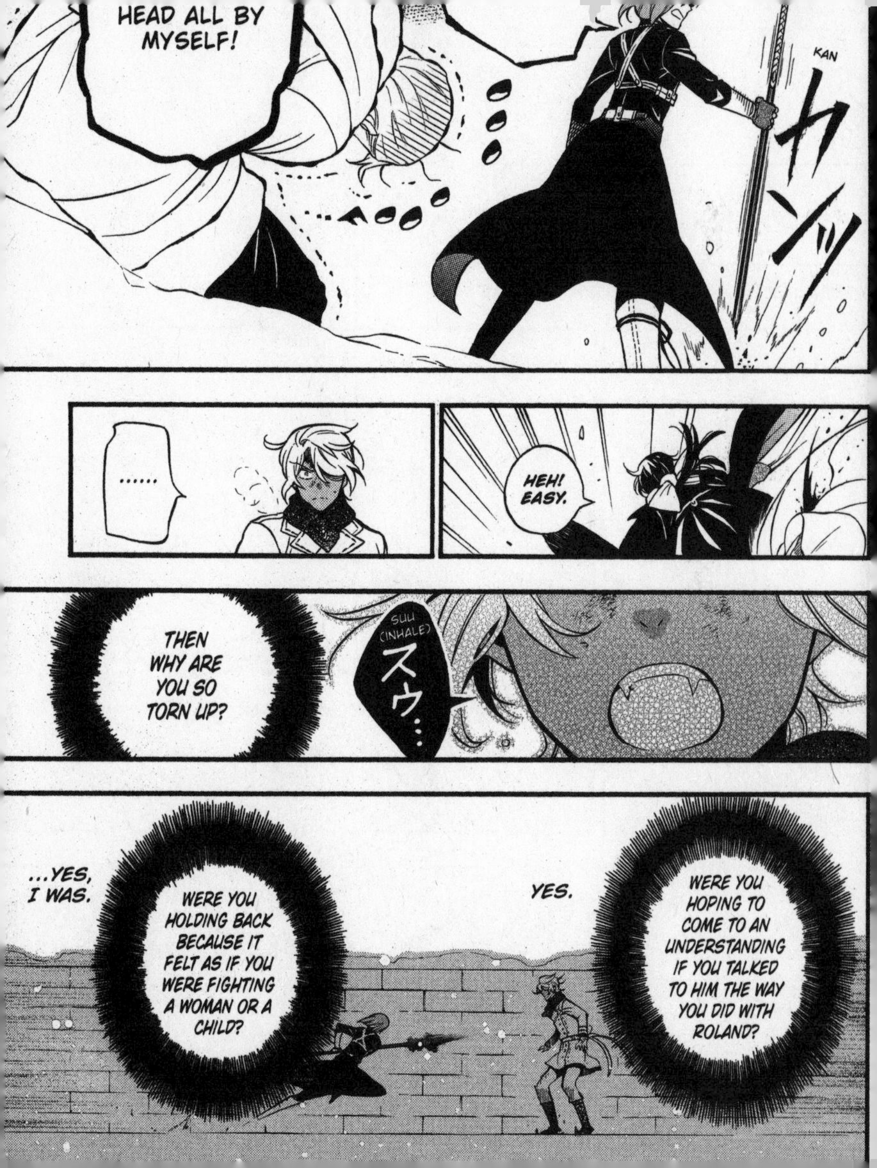

KAN
カーンッ
HEAD ALL BY MYSELF!
HEH! EASY.
......
SUU (INHALE)
スウ...
THEN WHY ARE YOU SO TORN UP?
WERE YOU HOPING TO COME TO AN UNDERSTANDING IF YOU TALKED TO HIM THE WAY YOU DID WITH ROLAND?
YES.
WERE YOU HOLDING BACK BECAUSE IT FELT AS IF YOU WERE FIGHTING A WOMAN OR A CHILD?
...YES, I WAS.

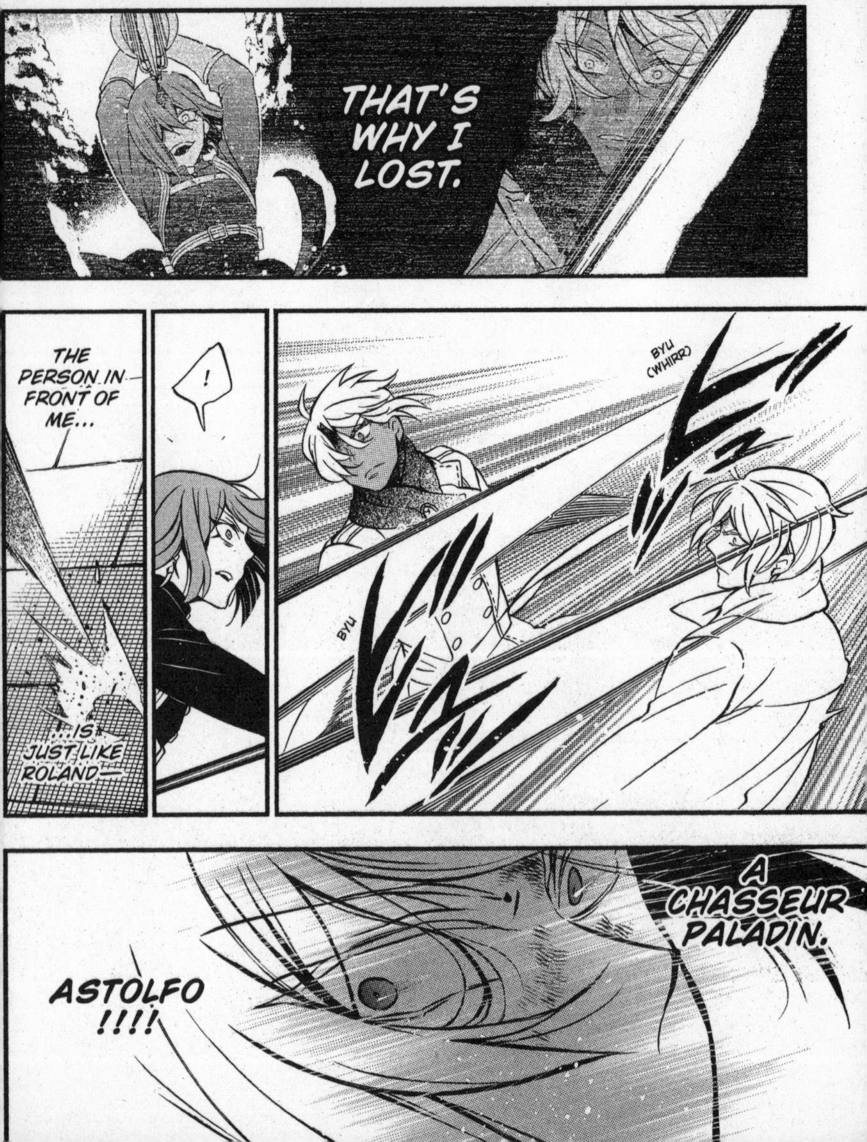
THAT'S WHY I LOST.
BYU (WHIRR)
BYU
!
THE PERSON IN FRONT OF ME...
...IS JUST LIKE ROLAND—
A CHASSEUR PALADIN.
ASTOLFO !!!!

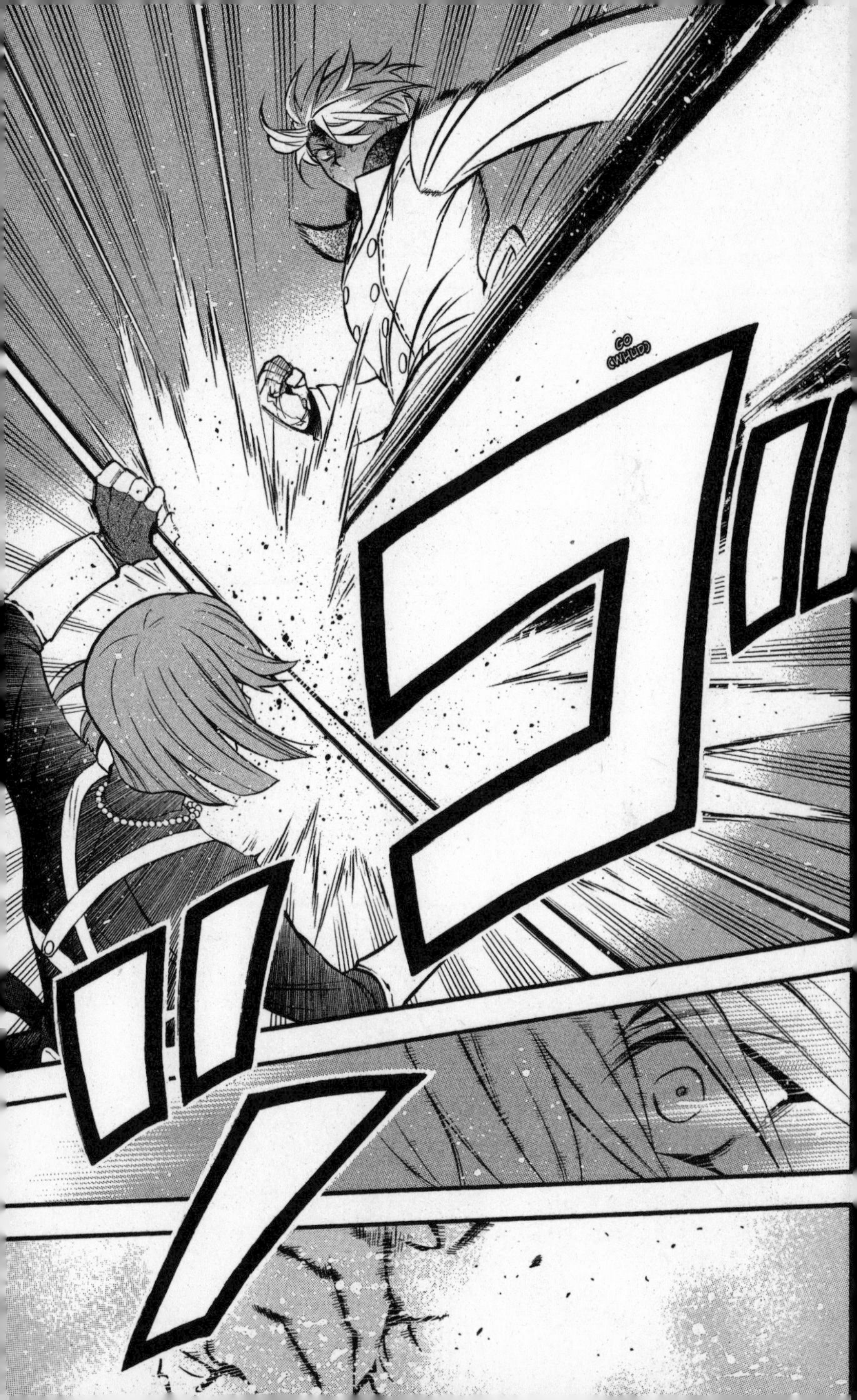
GO
(WHUD)

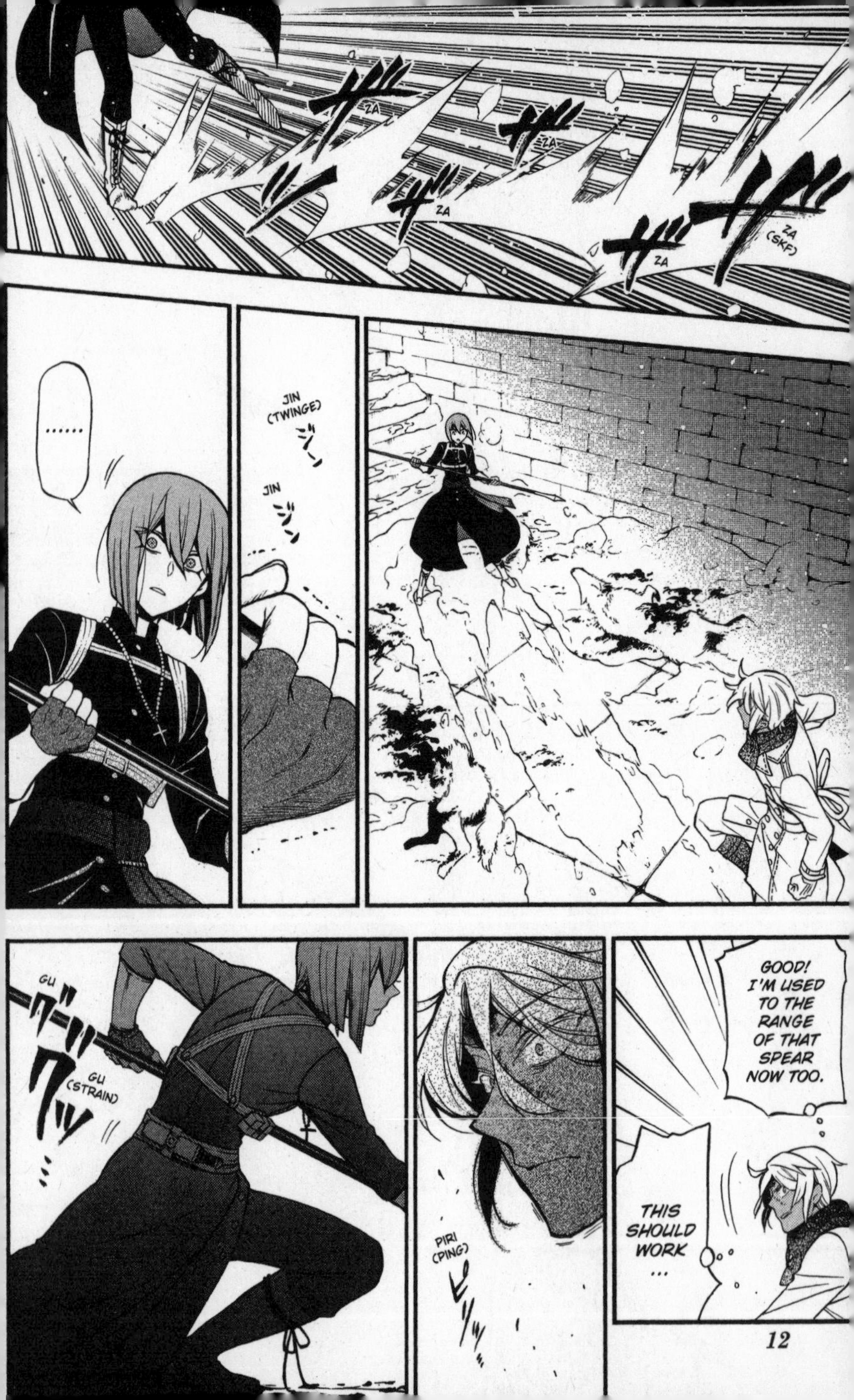
ZA
ZA
ZA
ZA
ZA (SKF)
JIN (TWINGE)
JIN
......
GOOD! I'M USED TO THE RANGE OF THAT SPEAR NOW TOO.
THIS SHOULD WORK ...
PIRI (PING)
GU
GU (STRAIN)

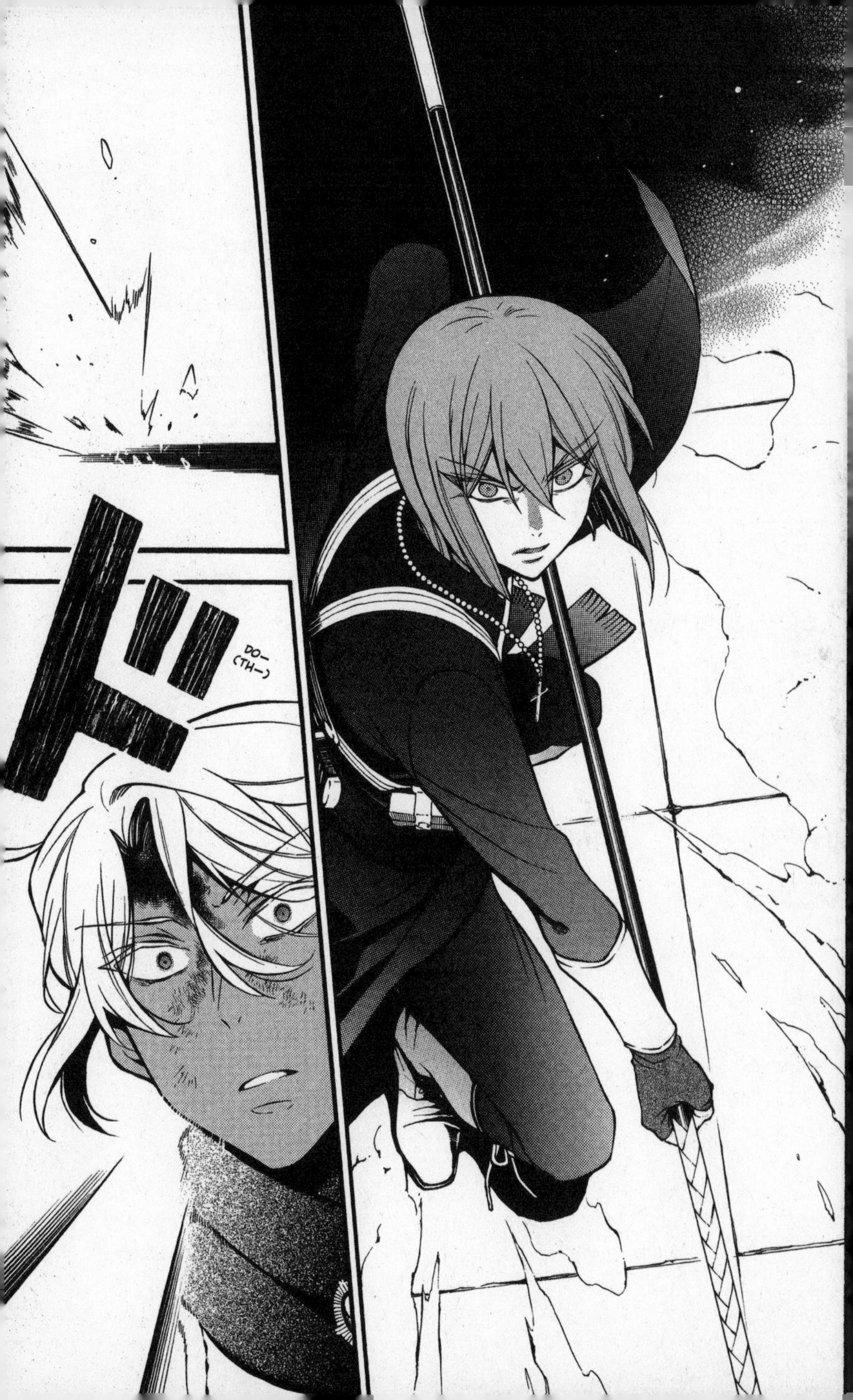
DO–
(TH–)

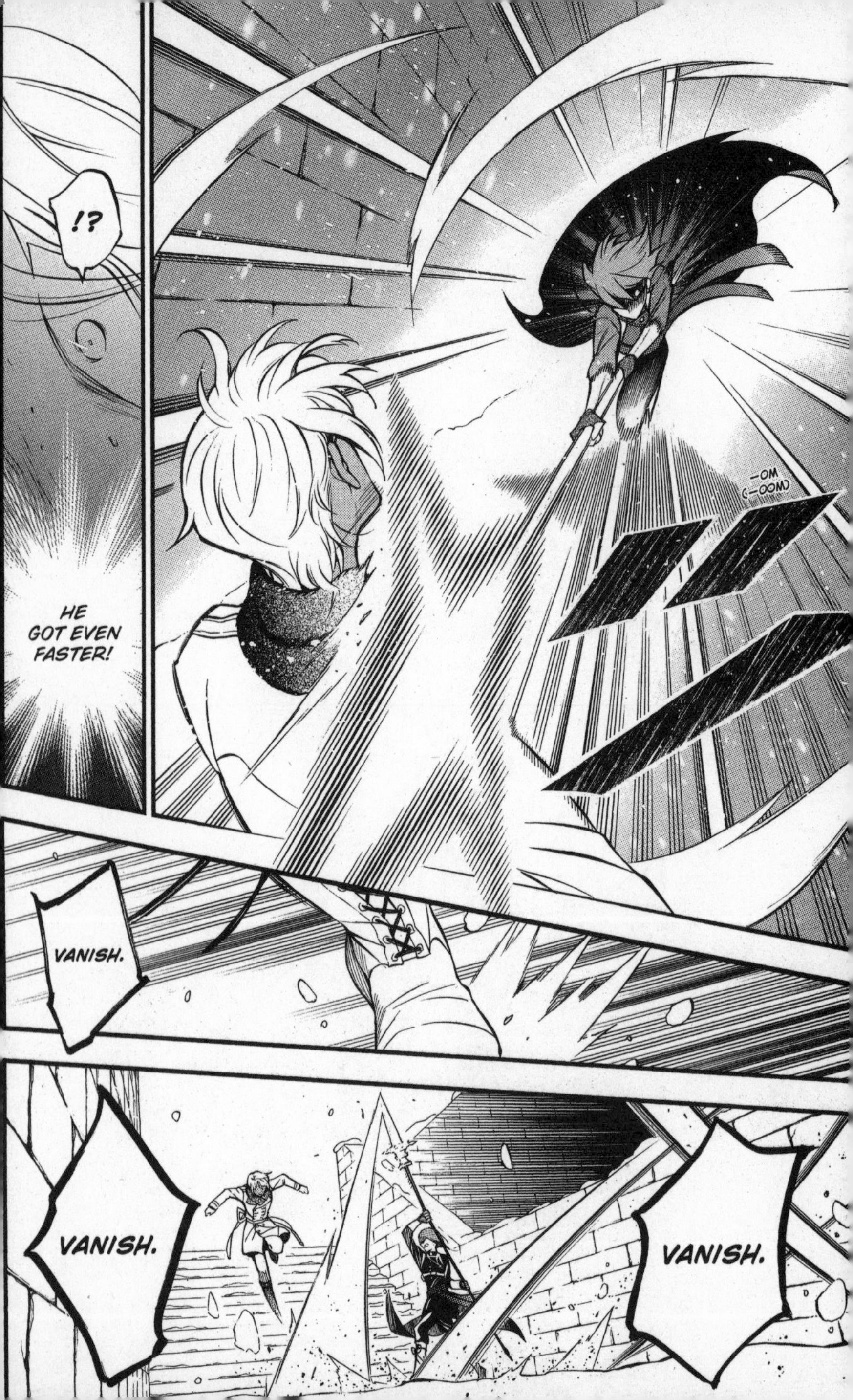
—OM
(—OOM)
!?
HE GOT EVEN FASTER!
VANISH.
VANISH.
VANISH.

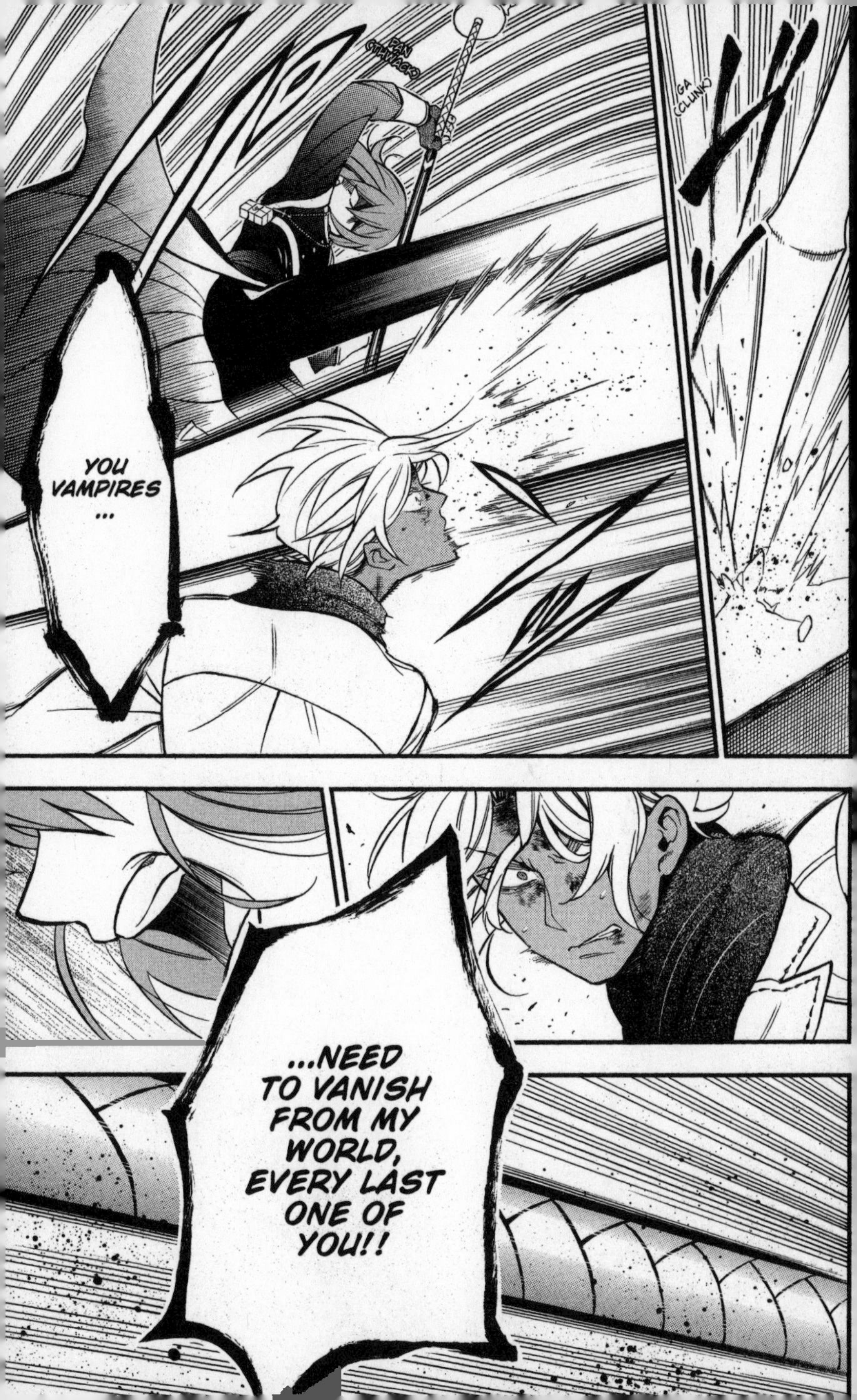
GA (CLUNK)
PAN (THWACK)
YOU VAMPIRES...
...NEED TO VANISH FROM MY WORLD, EVERY LAST ONE OF YOU!!

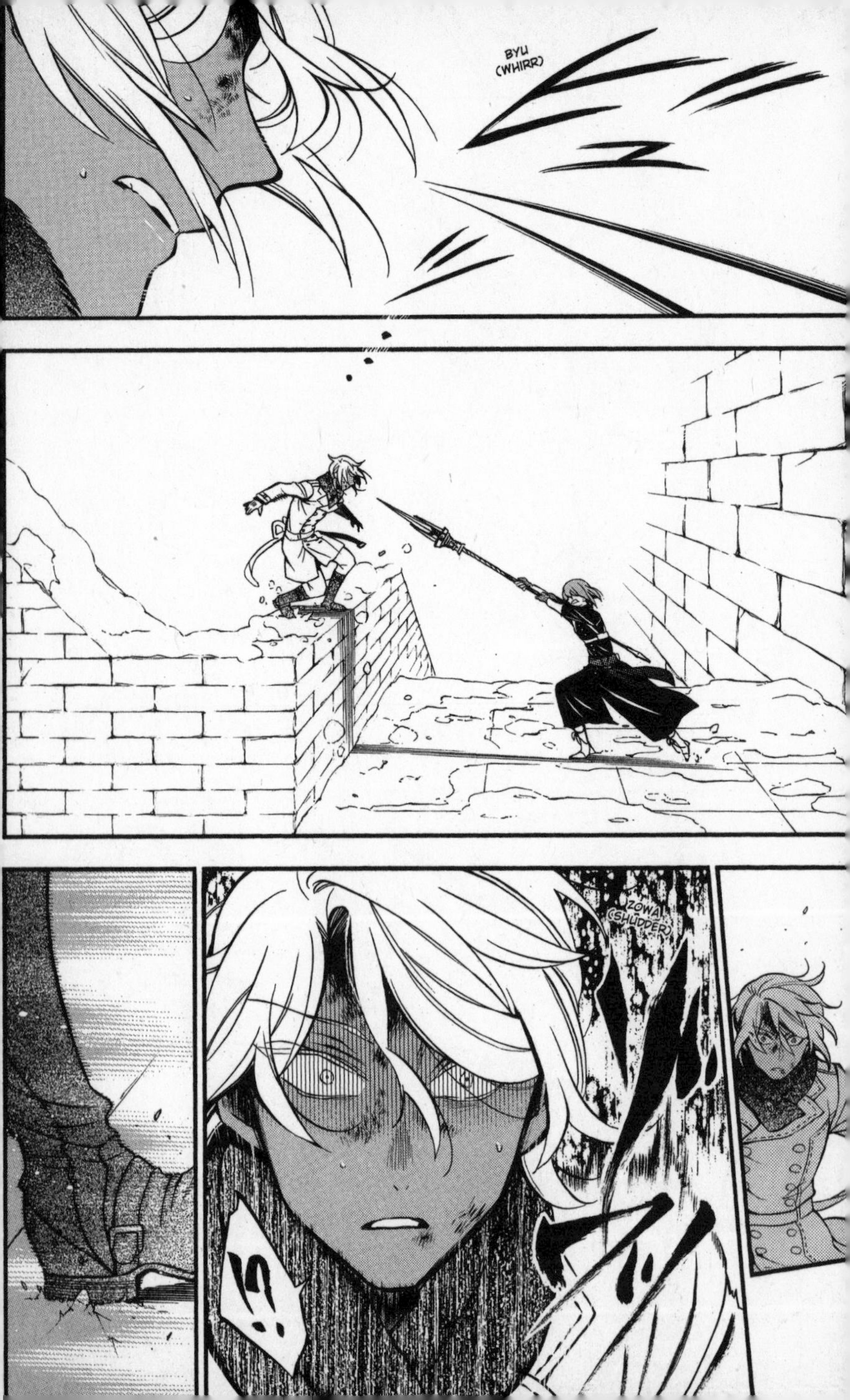
BYU
(WHIRR)
ZOWA
(SHUDDER)
!?

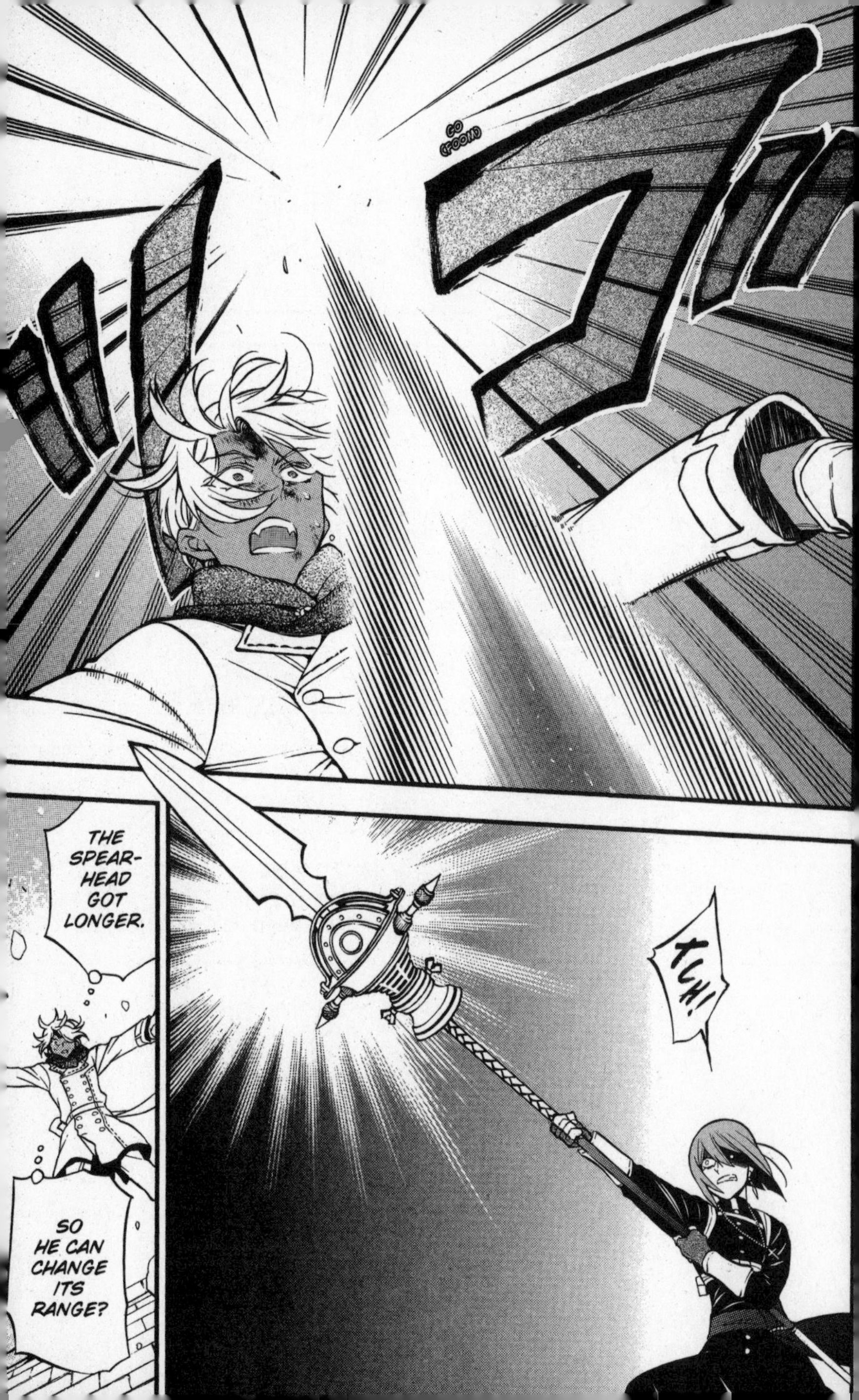
GO (FOOM)
KUH!
THE SPEAR-HEAD GOT LONGER.
SO HE CAN CHANGE ITS RANGE?

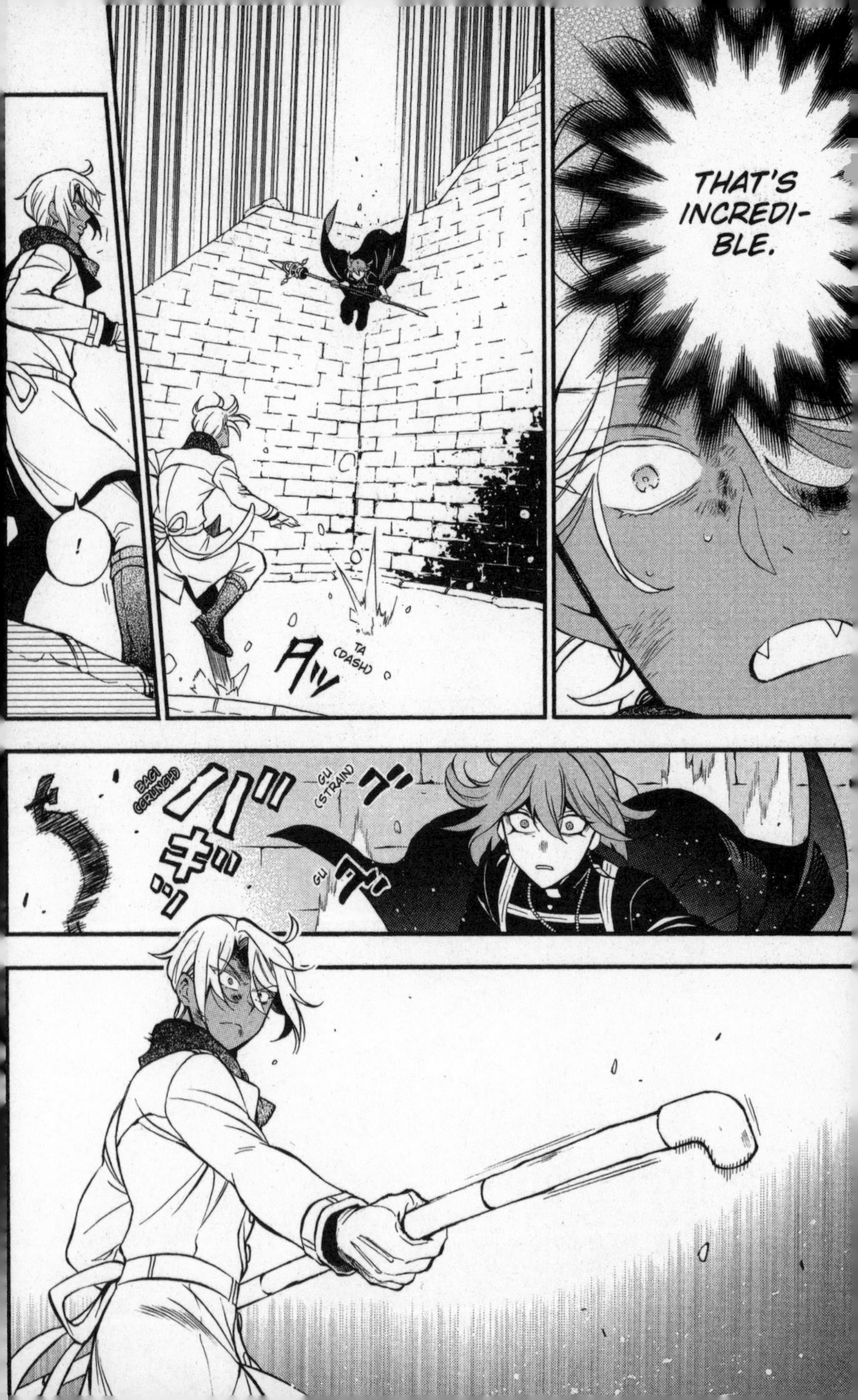
THAT'S INCREDIBLE.
TA (DASH)
!
GU (STRAIN)
GU
BAGI (CRUNCH)

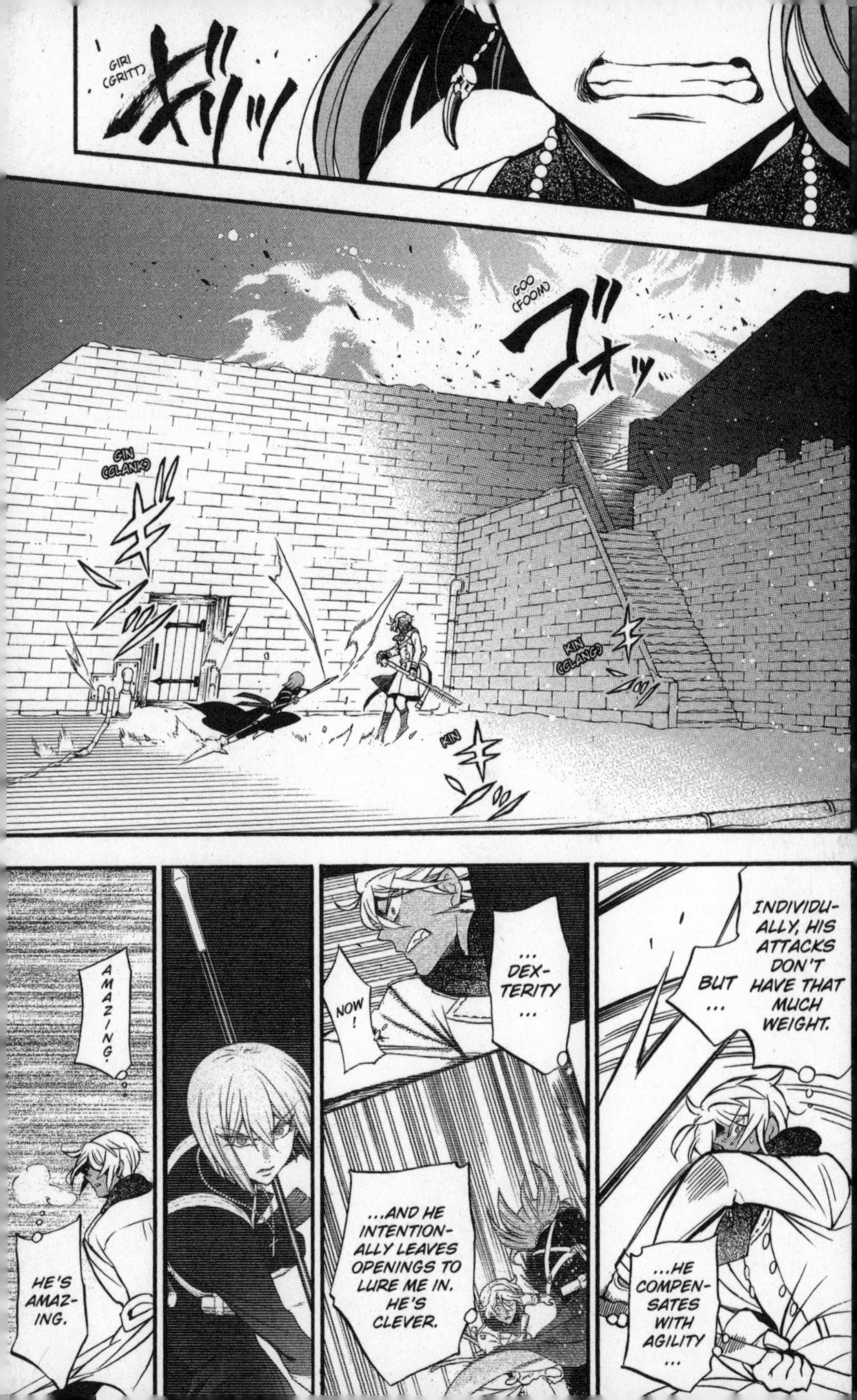
GIRI (GRITT)
GOO (FOOM)
KIN (CLANG)
GIN (CLANK)
KIN
INDIVIDU-ALLY, HIS ATTACKS DON'T HAVE THAT MUCH WEIGHT.
BUT...
...HE COMPEN-SATES WITH AGILITY...
...DEX-TERITY...
NOW!
...AND HE INTENTION-ALLY LEAVES OPENINGS TO LURE ME IN. HE'S CLEVER.
AMAZING.
HE'S AMAZ-ING.

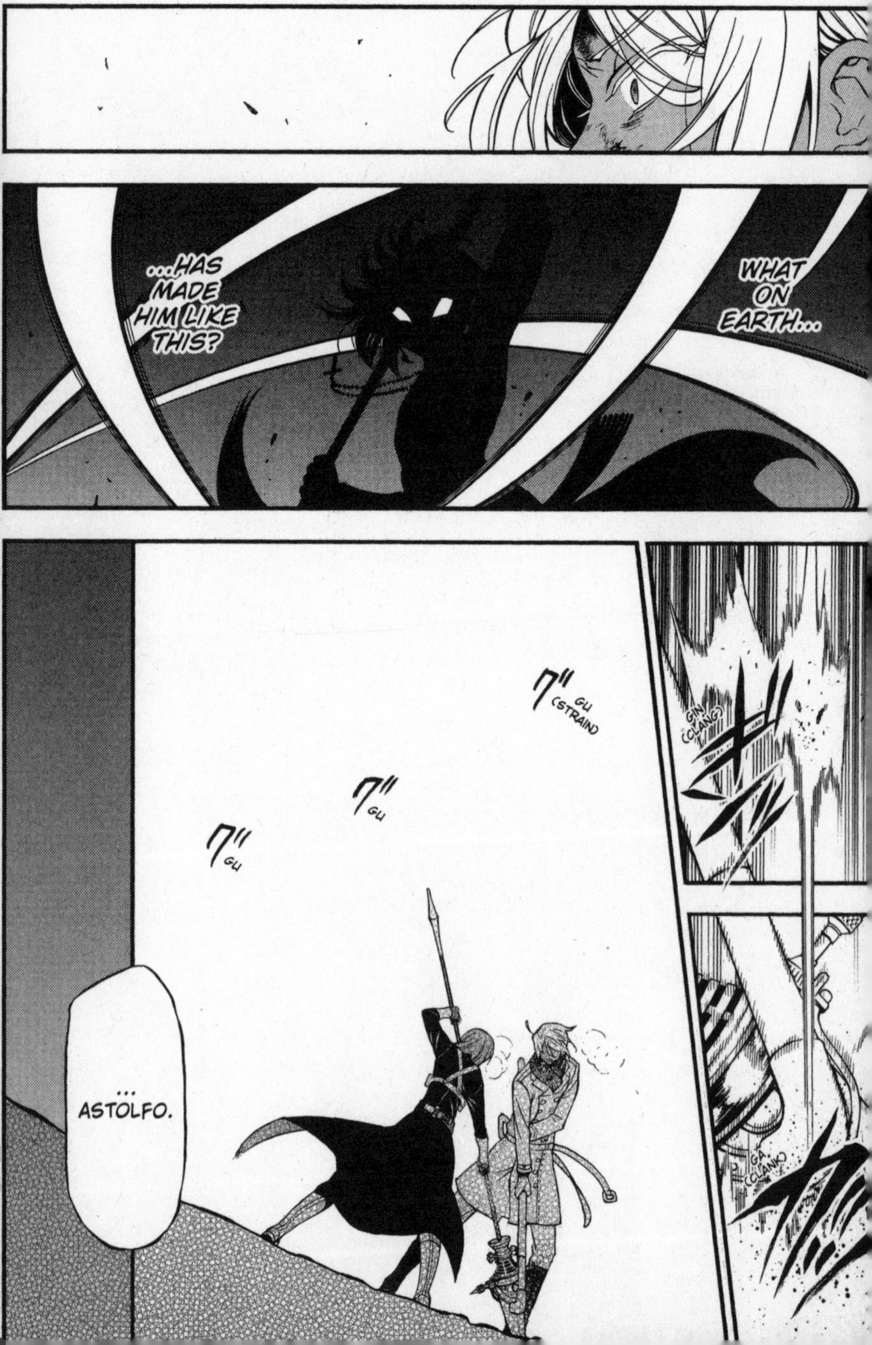
WHAT ON EARTH...
...HAS MADE HIM LIKE THIS?
GIN (CLANG)
GA (CLANK)
GU (STRAIN)
GU
GU
... ASTOLFO.

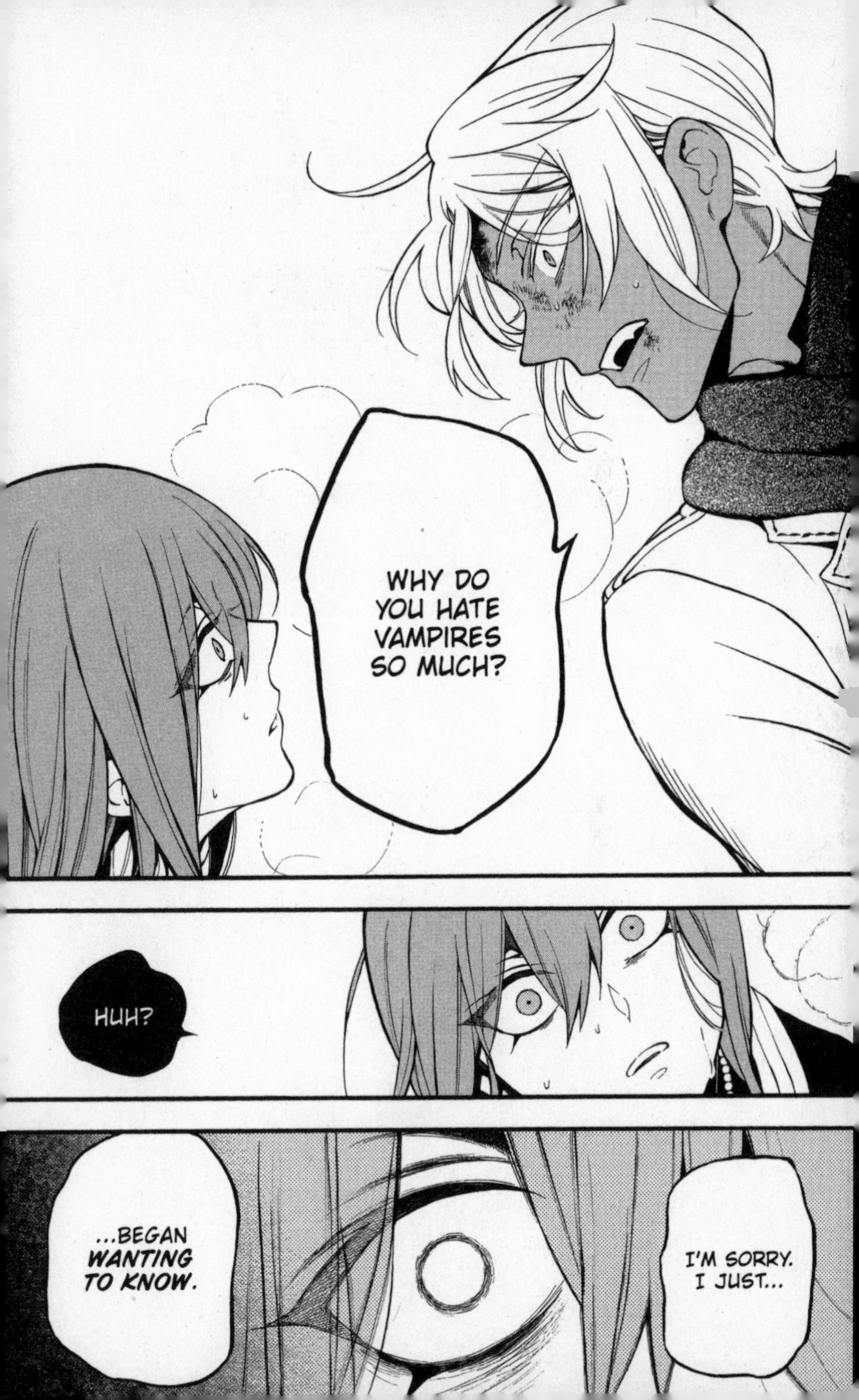
WHY DO YOU HATE VAMPIRES SO MUCH?
HUH?
I'M SORRY. I JUST...
...BEGAN WANTING TO KNOW.

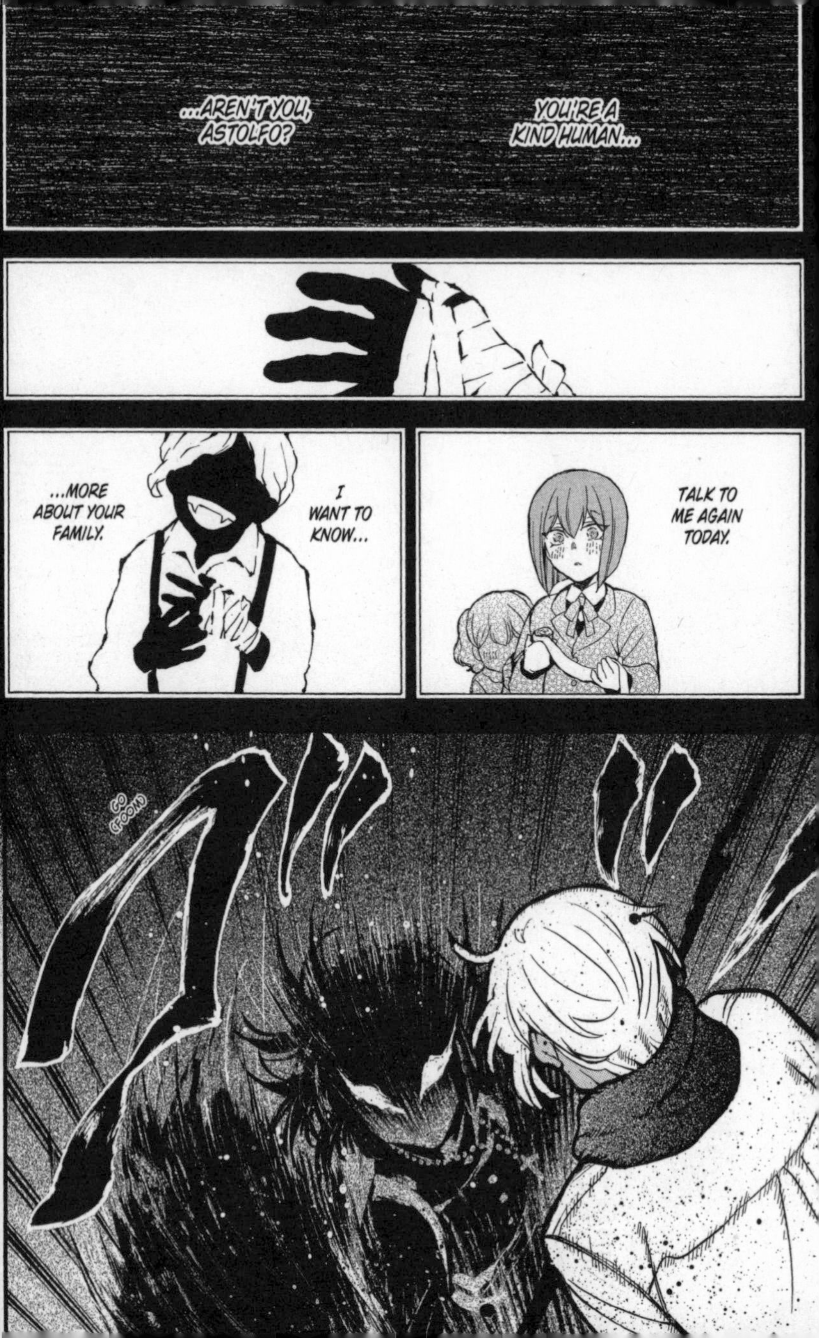
YOU'RE A KIND HUMAN...
...AREN'T YOU, ASTOLFO?
TALK TO ME AGAIN TODAY.
I WANT TO KNOW...
...MORE ABOUT YOUR FAMILY.
GO (GOOM)

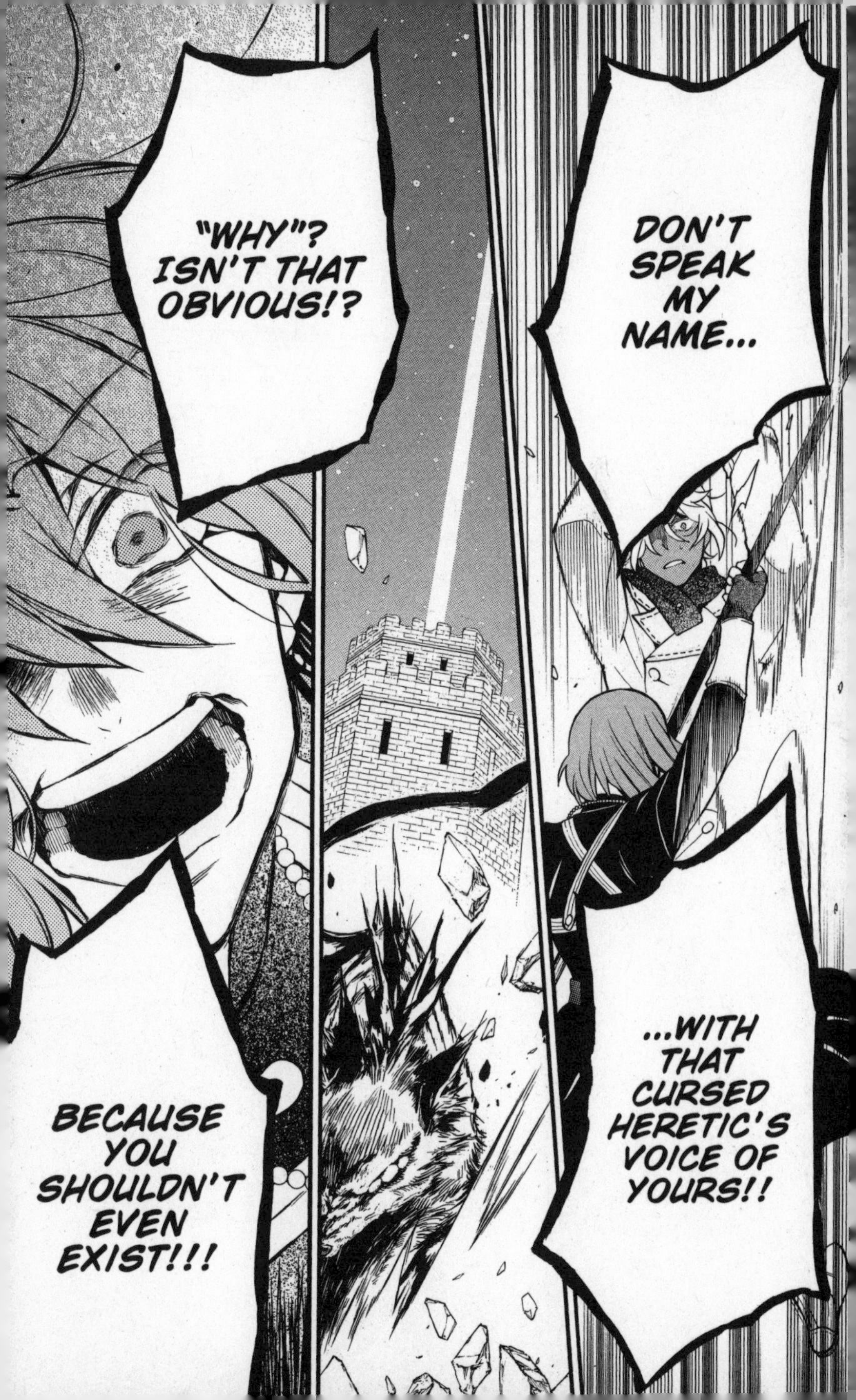
DON'T SPEAK MY NAME...
...WITH THAT CURSED HERETIC'S VOICE OF YOURS!!
"WHY"? ISN'T THAT OBVIOUS!?
BECAUSE YOU SHOULDN'T EVEN EXIST!!!

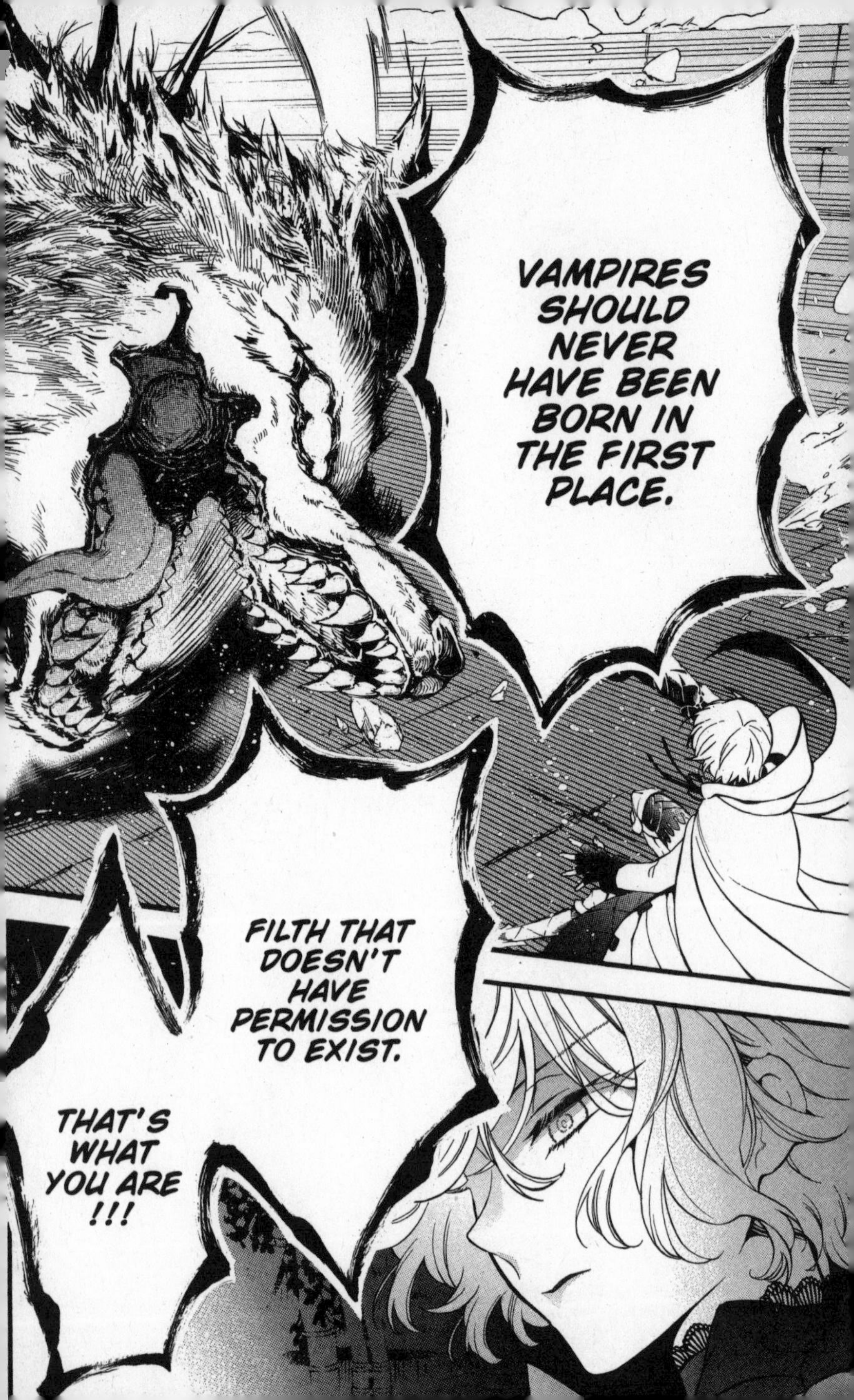
VAMPIRES SHOULD NEVER HAVE BEEN BORN IN THE FIRST PLACE.
FILTH THAT DOESN'T HAVE PERMISSION TO EXIST.
THAT'S WHAT YOU ARE !!!

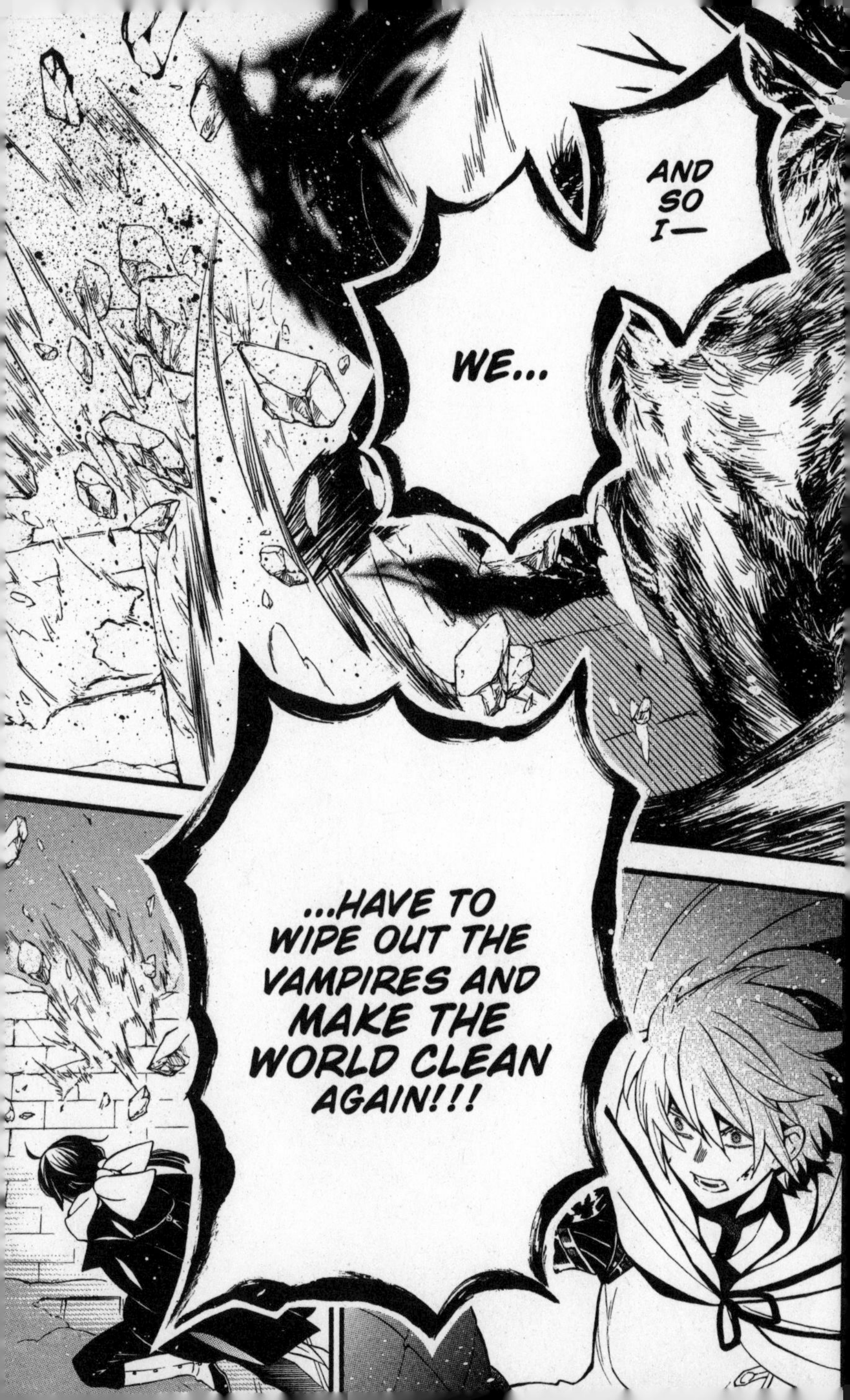
AND SO I—
WE...
...HAVE TO WIPE OUT THE VAMPIRES AND MAKE THE WORLD CLEAN AGAIN!!!

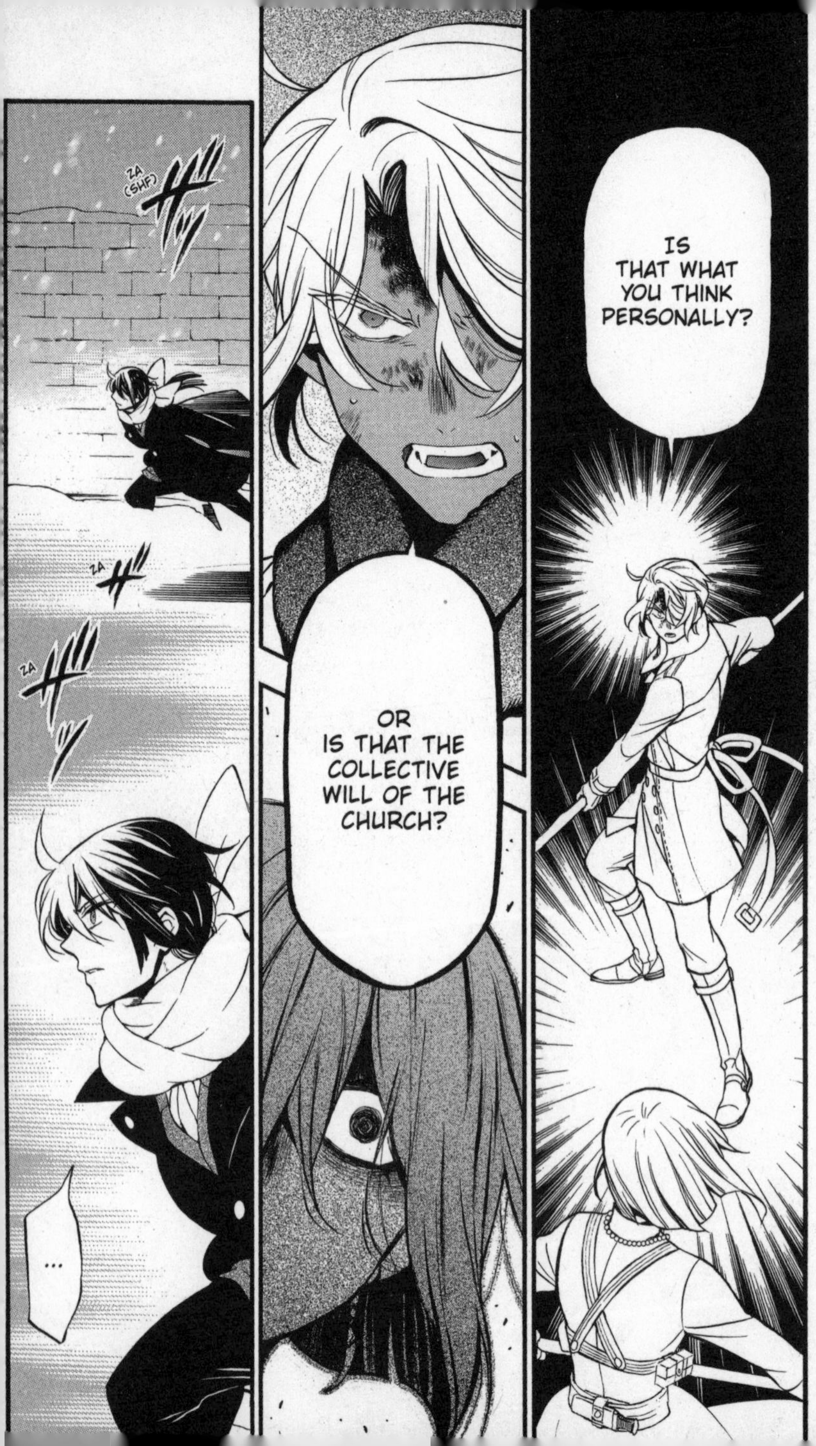
IS THAT WHAT YOU THINK PERSONALLY?
OR IS THAT THE COLLECTIVE WILL OF THE CHURCH?
ZA (SHF)
ZA
ZA
...

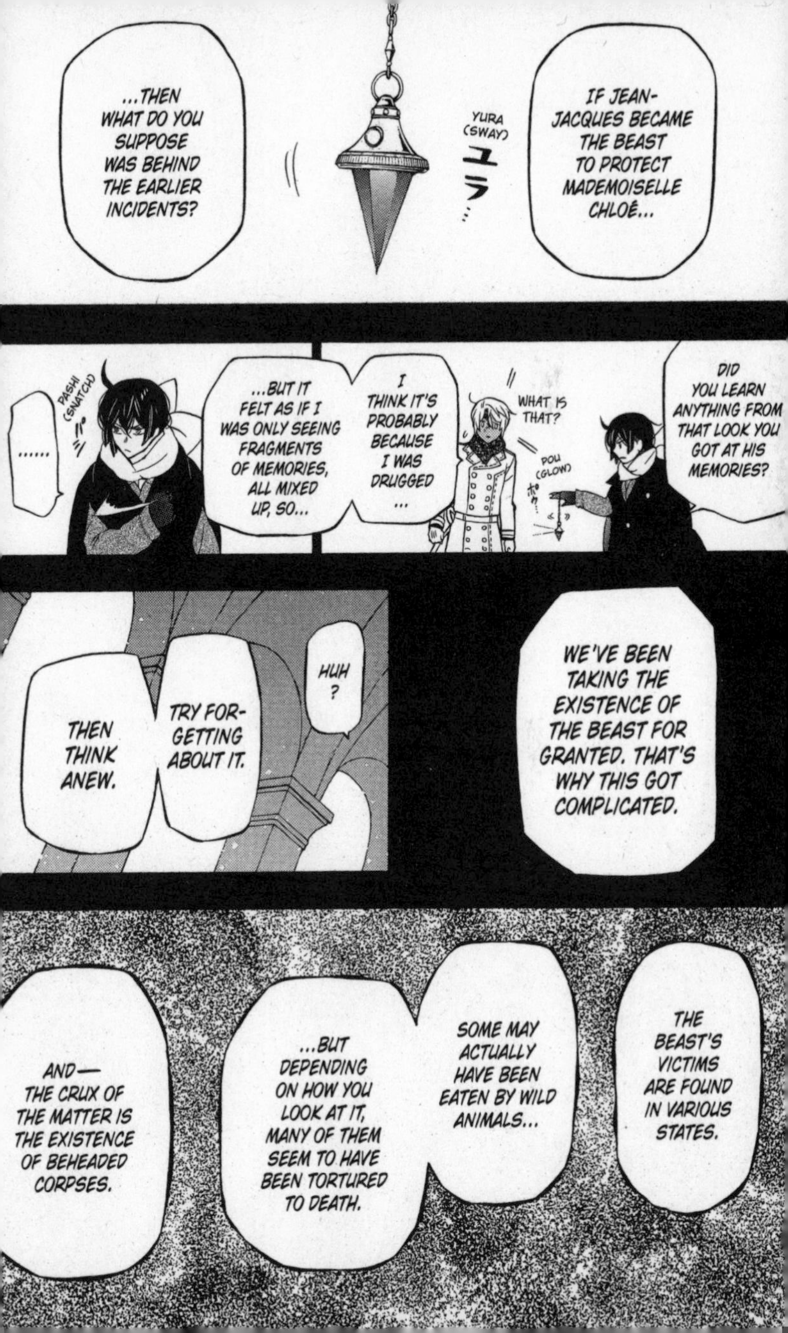
IF JEAN-JACQUES BECAME THE BEAST TO PROTECT MADEMOISELLE CHLOÉ...
YURA (SWAY)
ユラ…
...THEN WHAT DO YOU SUPPOSE WAS BEHIND THE EARLIER INCIDENTS?
DID YOU LEARN ANYTHING FROM THAT LOOK YOU GOT AT HIS MEMORIES?
POU (GLOW)
WHAT IS THAT?
I THINK IT'S PROBABLY BECAUSE I WAS DRUGGED...
...BUT IT FELT AS IF I WAS ONLY SEEING FRAGMENTS OF MEMORIES, ALL MIXED UP, SO...
PASHI (SNATCH)
......
WE'VE BEEN TAKING THE EXISTENCE OF THE BEAST FOR GRANTED. THAT'S WHY THIS GOT COMPLICATED.
HUH?
TRY FORGETTING ABOUT IT.
THEN THINK ANEW.
THE BEAST'S VICTIMS ARE FOUND IN VARIOUS STATES.
SOME MAY ACTUALLY HAVE BEEN EATEN BY WILD ANIMALS...
...BUT DEPENDING ON HOW YOU LOOK AT IT, MANY OF THEM SEEM TO HAVE BEEN TORTURED TO DEATH.
AND—THE CRUX OF THE MATTER IS THE EXISTENCE OF BEHEADED CORPSES.

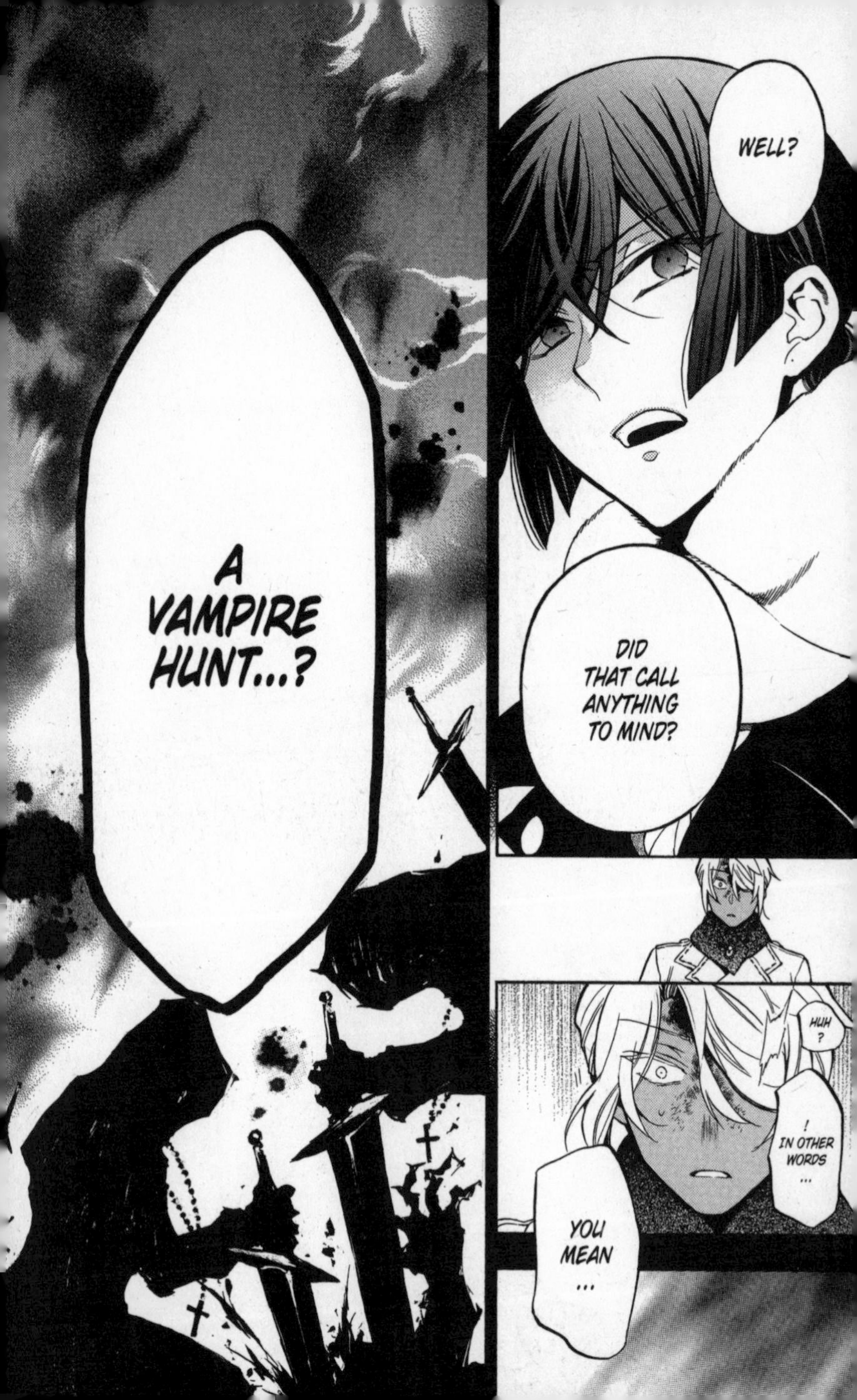
WELL?
DID THAT CALL ANYTHING TO MIND?
HUH?
! IN OTHER WORDS...
YOU MEAN...
A VAMPIRE HUNT...?

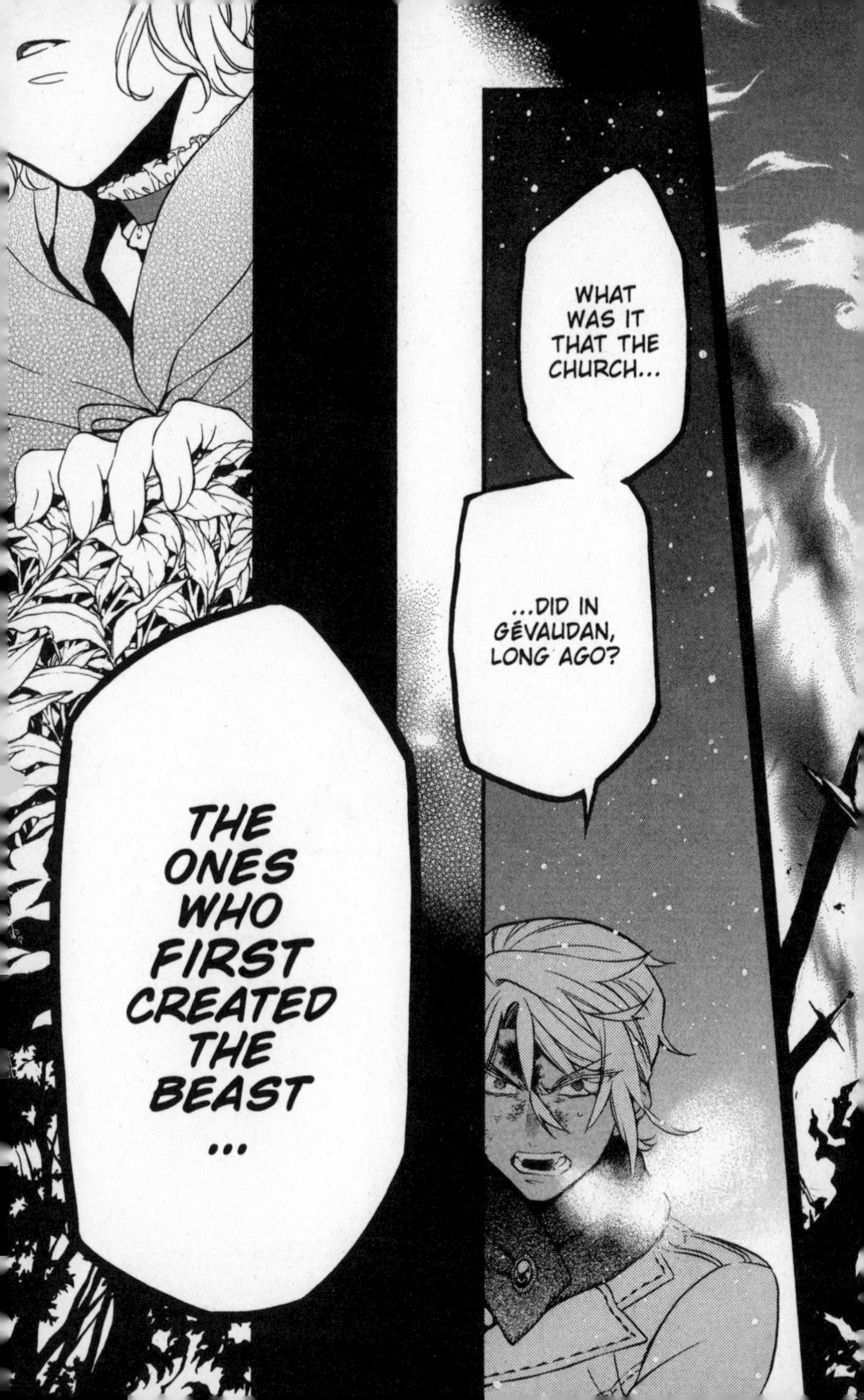
WHAT WAS IT THAT THE CHURCH...
...DID IN GÉVAUDAN, LONG AGO?
THE ONES WHO FIRST CREATED THE BEAST ...

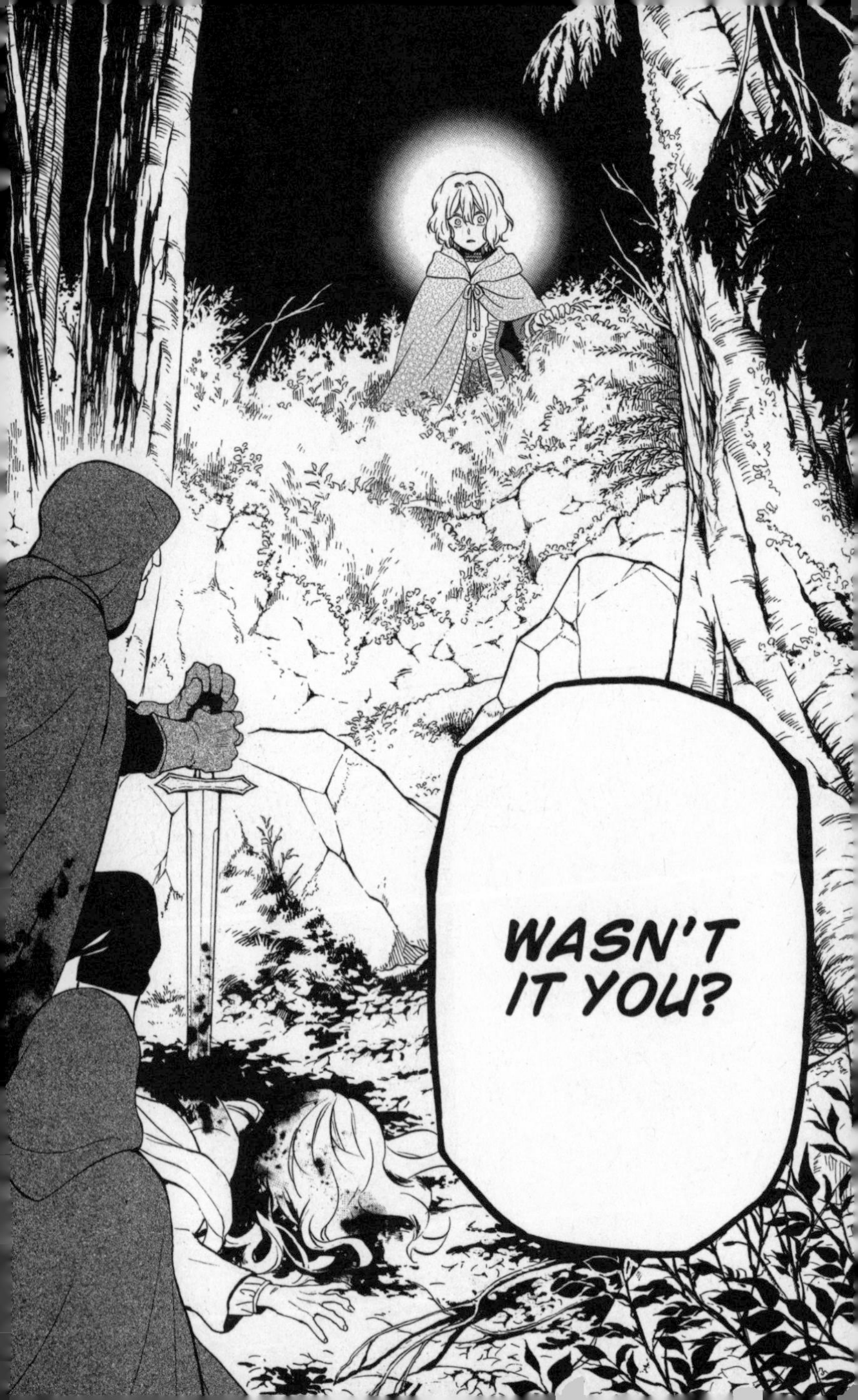
WASN'T IT YOU?

Mémoire 35 Louisette PILLAR OF JUSTICE

ASTOLFO AND MARCO

HAVE YOU SEEN MARCO?
UH-UH.
NO.
MARCO.
MARCO.
UNDER THE BED
MARCO.
I'M TERRIBLY SORRY, CAPTAIN! WHAT DID YOU NEED?
WAAAAAAGH!
DOTA (SCRAMBLE)
BATA (TROMP)
...HUH?
WHAT MADE YOU THINK I NEEDED SOME-THING?
TOTE (TUP)
TOTE

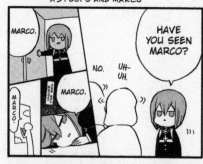

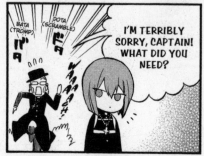

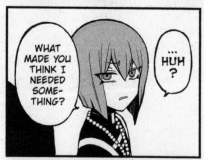

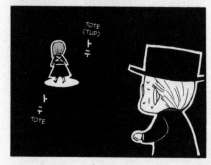

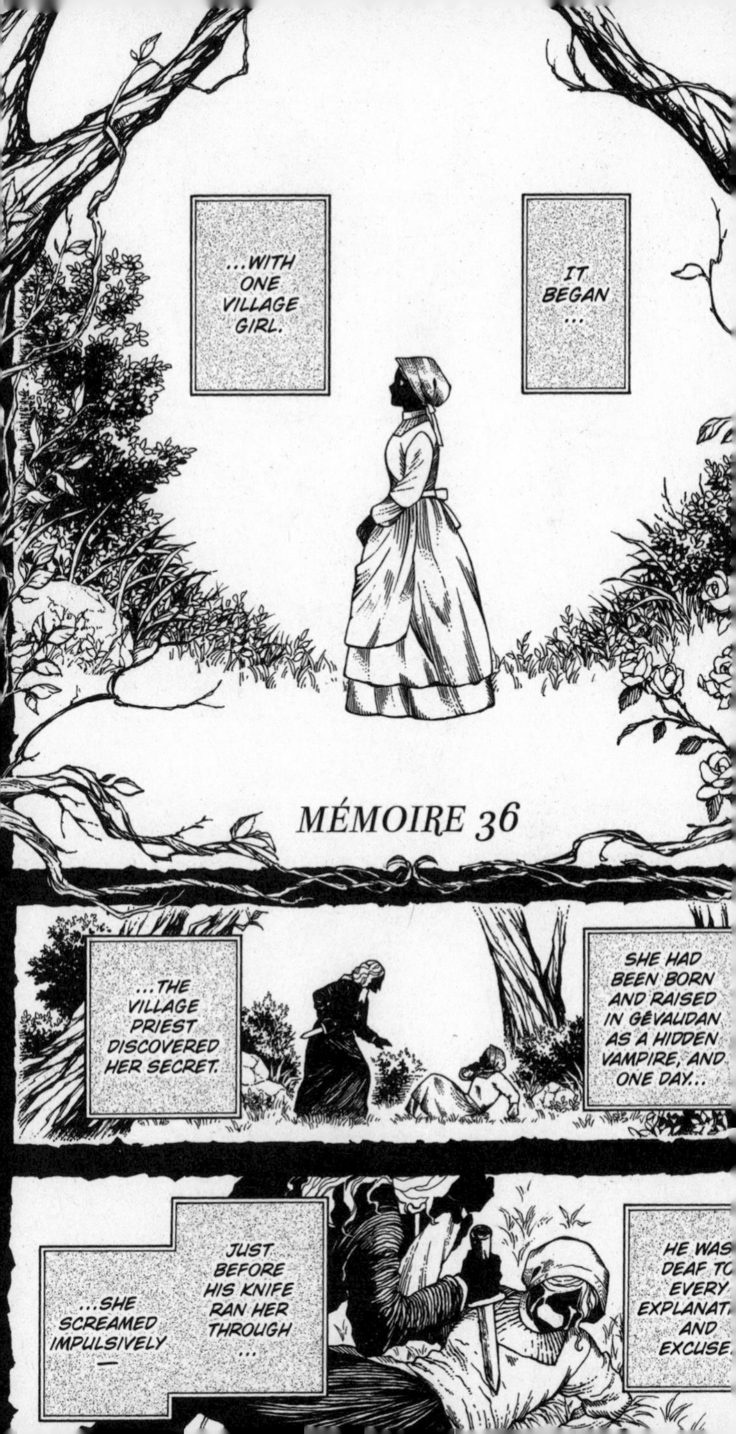
IT BEGAN...
...WITH ONE VILLAGE GIRL.
MÉMOIRE 36
SHE HAD BEEN BORN AND RAISED IN GÉVAUDAN AS A HIDDEN VAMPIRE, AND ONE DAY...
...THE VILLAGE PRIEST DISCOVERED HER SECRET.
HE WAS DEAF TO EVERY EXPLANAT AND EXCUSE
JUST BEFORE HIS KNIFE RAN HER THROUGH...
...SHE SCREAMED IMPULSIVELY—

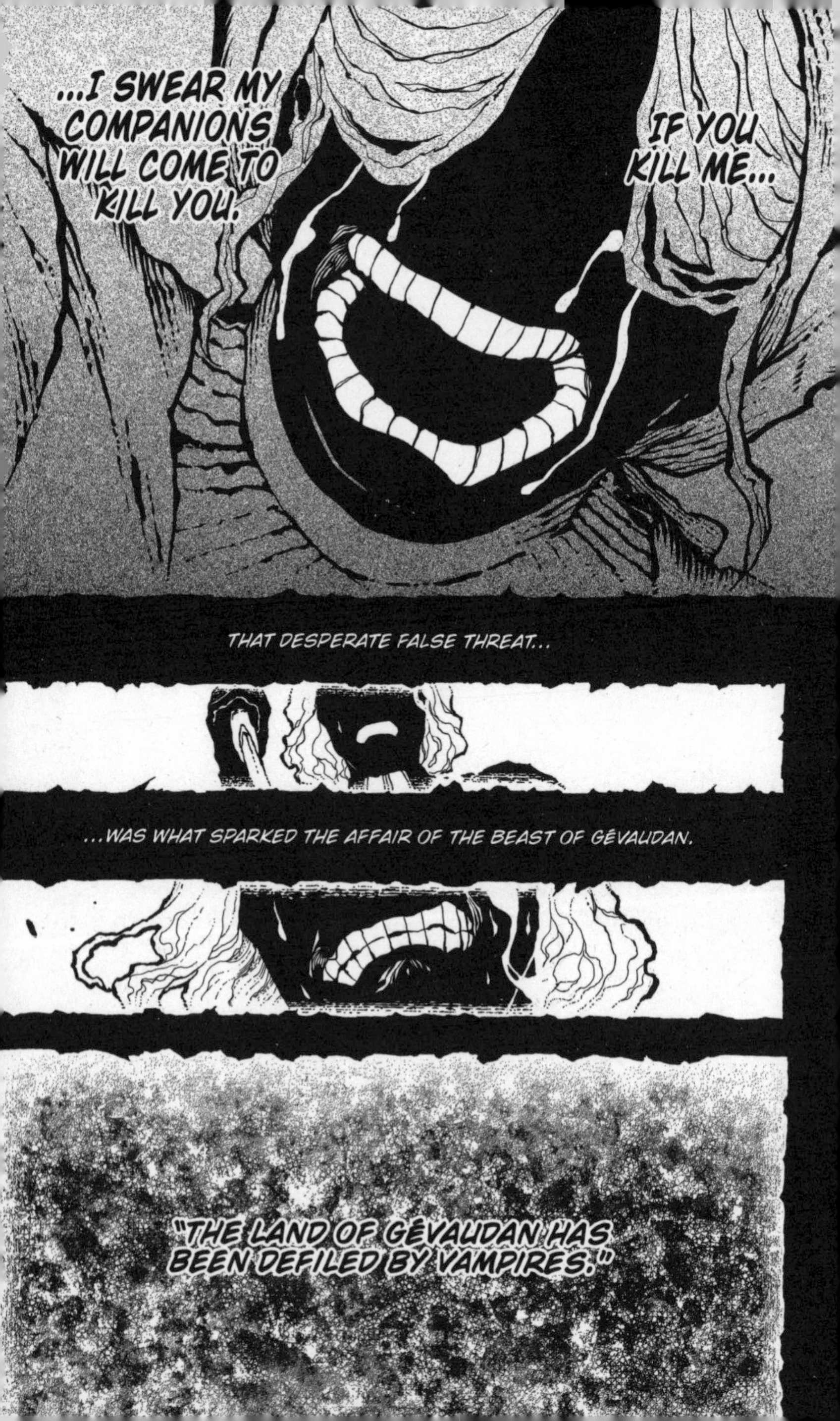
IF YOU KILL ME...
...I SWEAR MY COMPANIONS WILL COME TO KILL YOU.
THAT DESPERATE FALSE THREAT...
...WAS WHAT SPARKED THE AFFAIR OF THE BEAST OF GÉVAUDAN.
"THE LAND OF GÉVAUDAN HAS BEEN DEFILED BY VAMPIRES."

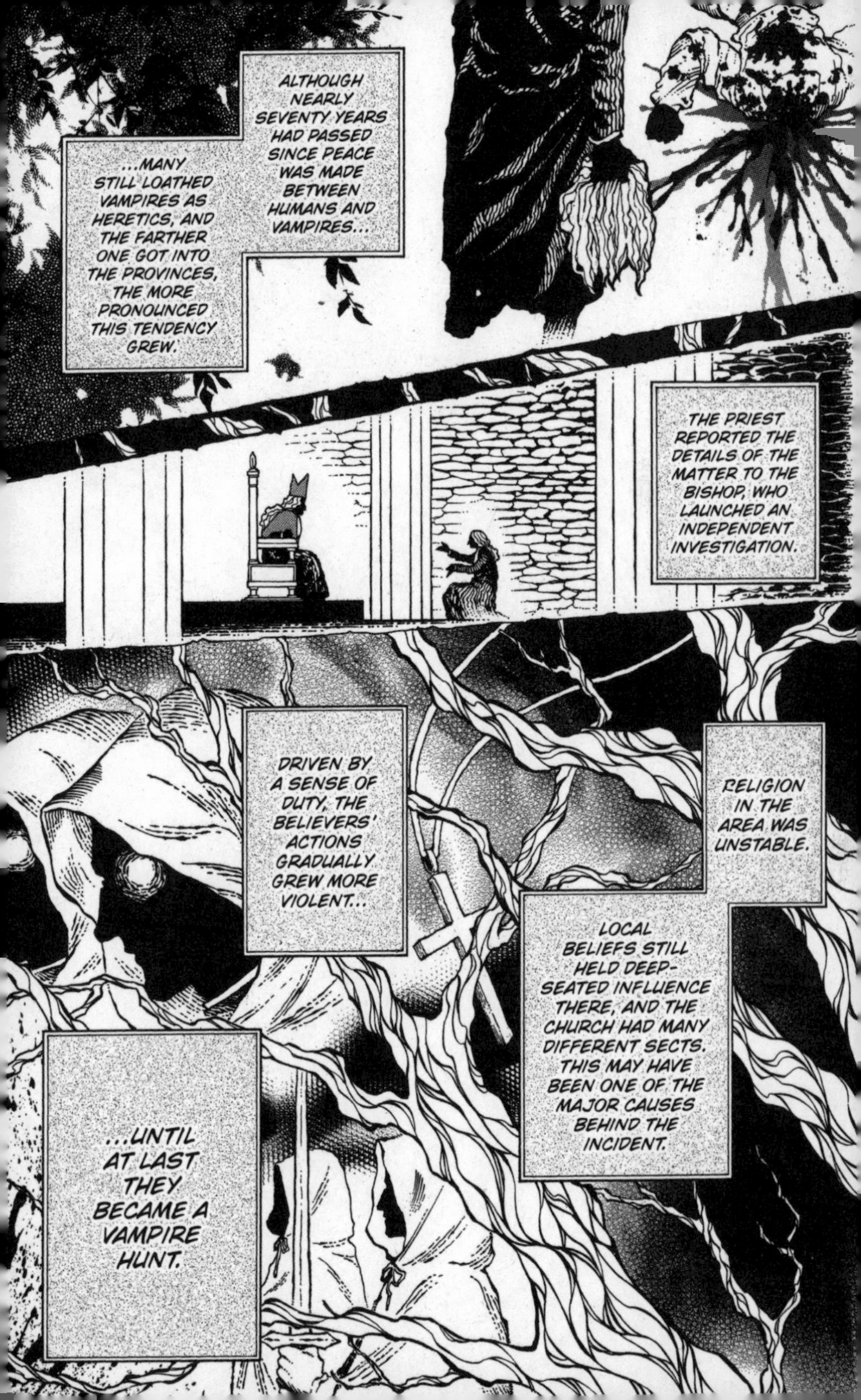
ALTHOUGH NEARLY SEVENTY YEARS HAD PASSED SINCE PEACE WAS MADE BETWEEN HUMANS AND VAMPIRES...
...MANY STILL LOATHED VAMPIRES AS HERETICS, AND THE FARTHER ONE GOT INTO THE PROVINCES, THE MORE PRONOUNCED THIS TENDENCY GREW.
THE PRIEST REPORTED THE DETAILS OF THE MATTER TO THE BISHOP, WHO LAUNCHED AN INDEPENDENT INVESTIGATION.
RELIGION IN THE AREA WAS UNSTABLE.
LOCAL BELIEFS STILL HELD DEEP-SEATED INFLUENCE THERE, AND THE CHURCH HAD MANY DIFFERENT SECTS. THIS MAY HAVE BEEN ONE OF THE MAJOR CAUSES BEHIND THE INCIDENT.
DRIVEN BY A SENSE OF DUTY, THE BELIEVERS' ACTIONS GRADUALLY GREW MORE VIOLENT...
...UNTIL AT LAST THEY BECAME A VAMPIRE HUNT.

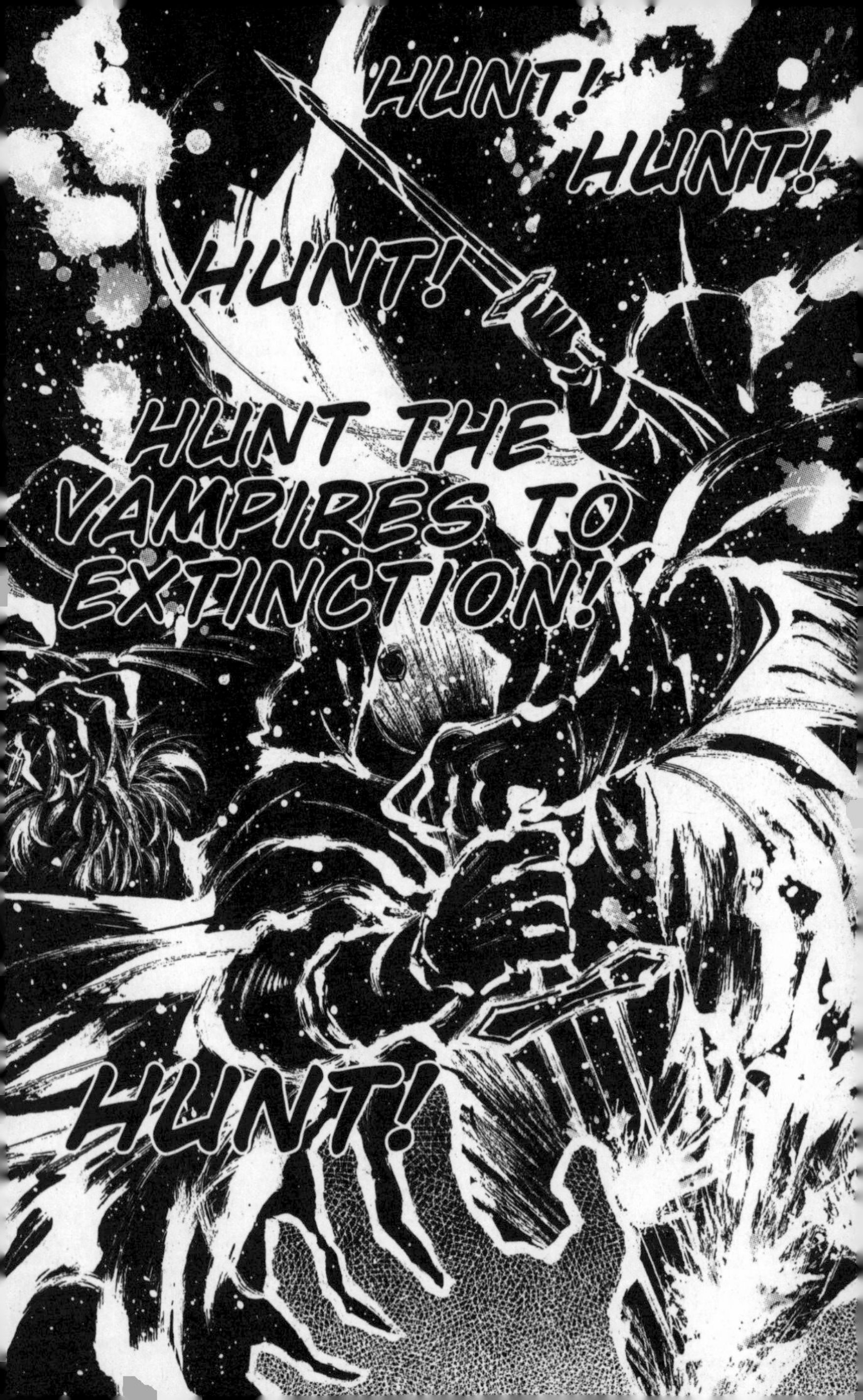
HUNT!
HUNT!
HUNT!
HUNT THE VAMPIRES TO EXTINCTION!
HUNT!

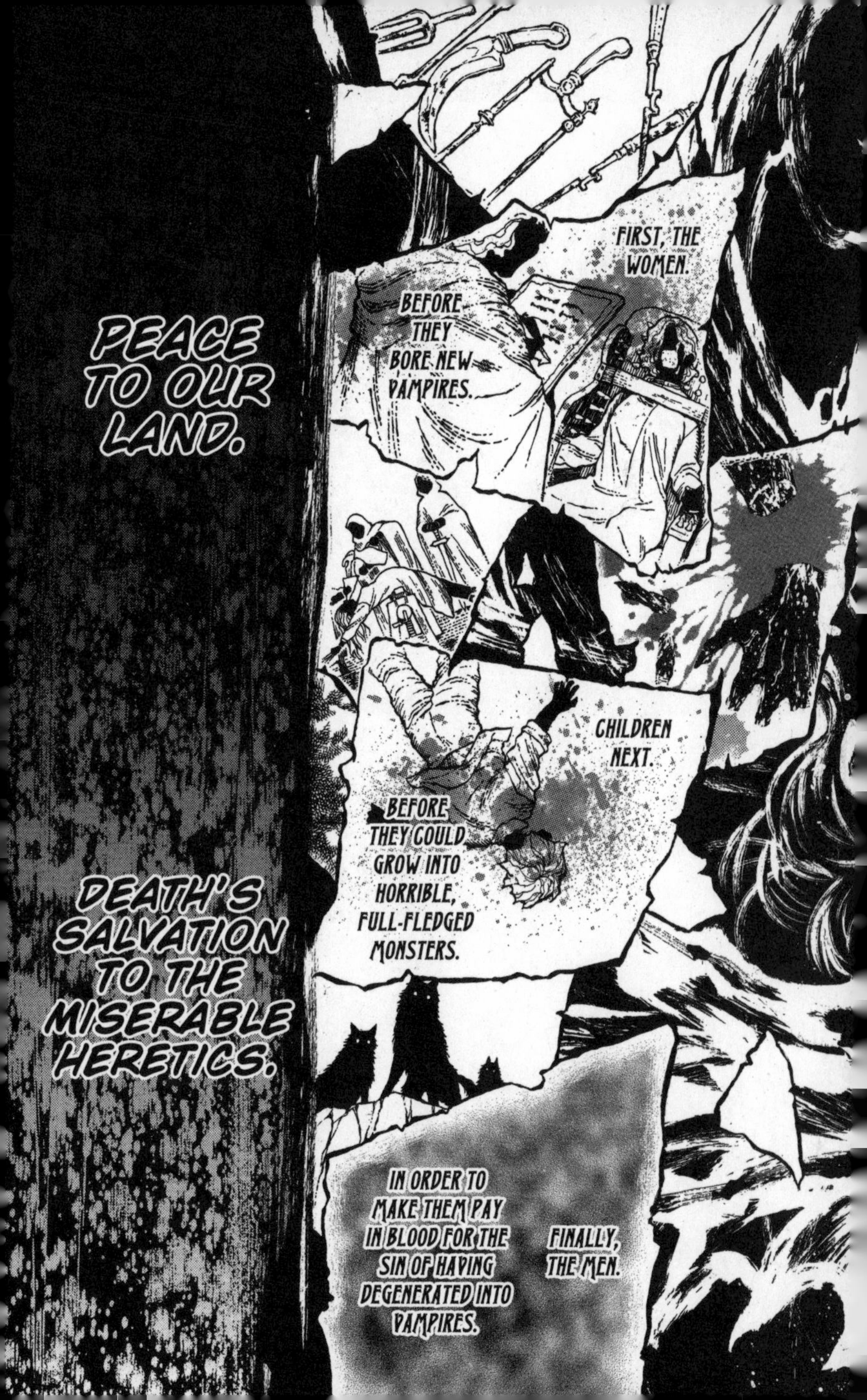
FIRST, THE WOMEN.
BEFORE THEY BORE NEW VAMPIRES.
CHILDREN NEXT.
BEFORE THEY COULD GROW INTO HORRIBLE, FULL-FLEDGED MONSTERS.
FINALLY, THE MEN.
IN ORDER TO MAKE THEM PAY IN BLOOD FOR THE SIN OF HAVING DEGENERATED INTO VAMPIRES.
PEACE TO OUR LAND.
DEATH'S SALVATION TO THE MISERABLE HERETICS.

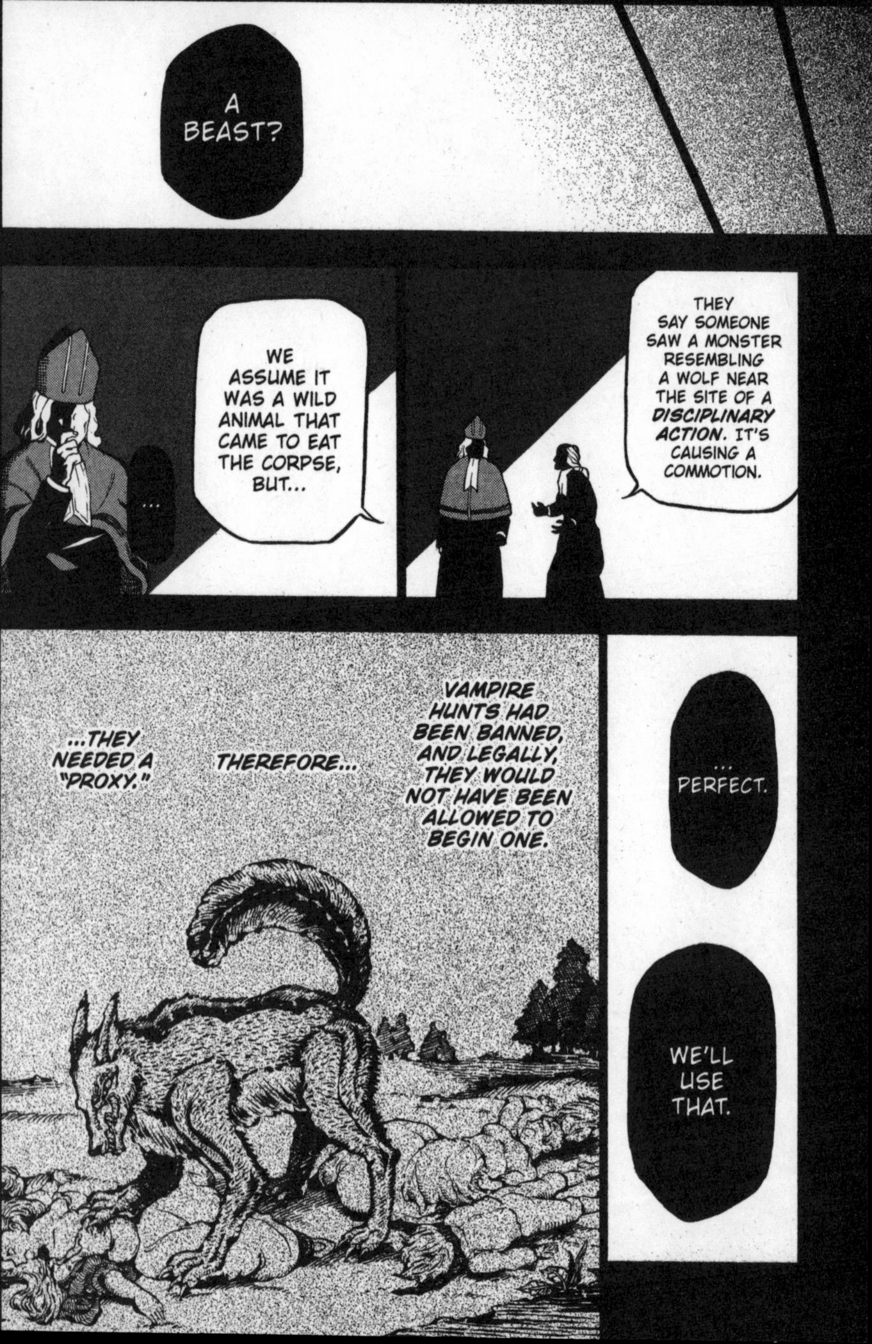
A BEAST?
THEY SAY SOMEONE SAW A MONSTER RESEMBLING A WOLF NEAR THE SITE OF A ***DISCIPLINARY ACTION***. IT'S CAUSING A COMMOTION.
WE ASSUME IT WAS A WILD ANIMAL THAT CAME TO EAT THE CORPSE, BUT...
...
...PERFECT.
WE'LL USE THAT.
VAMPIRE HUNTS HAD BEEN BANNED, AND LEGALLY, THEY WOULD NOT HAVE BEEN ALLOWED TO BEGIN ONE.
THEREFORE...
...THEY NEEDED A "PROXY."

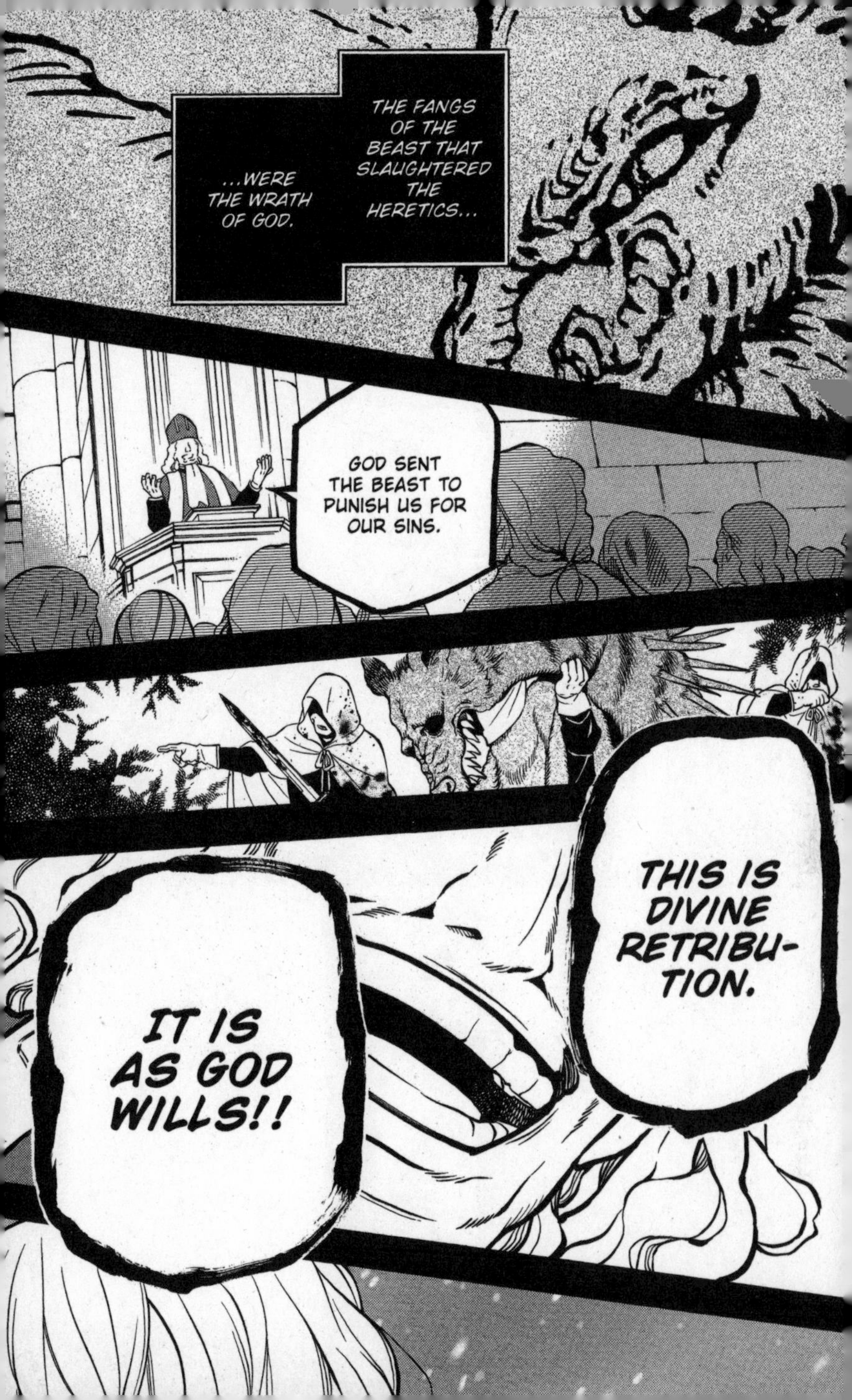
THE FANGS OF THE BEAST THAT SLAUGHTERED THE HERETICS...
...WERE THE WRATH OF GOD.
GOD SENT THE BEAST TO PUNISH US FOR OUR SINS.
THIS IS DIVINE RETRIBUTION.
IT IS AS GOD WILLS!!

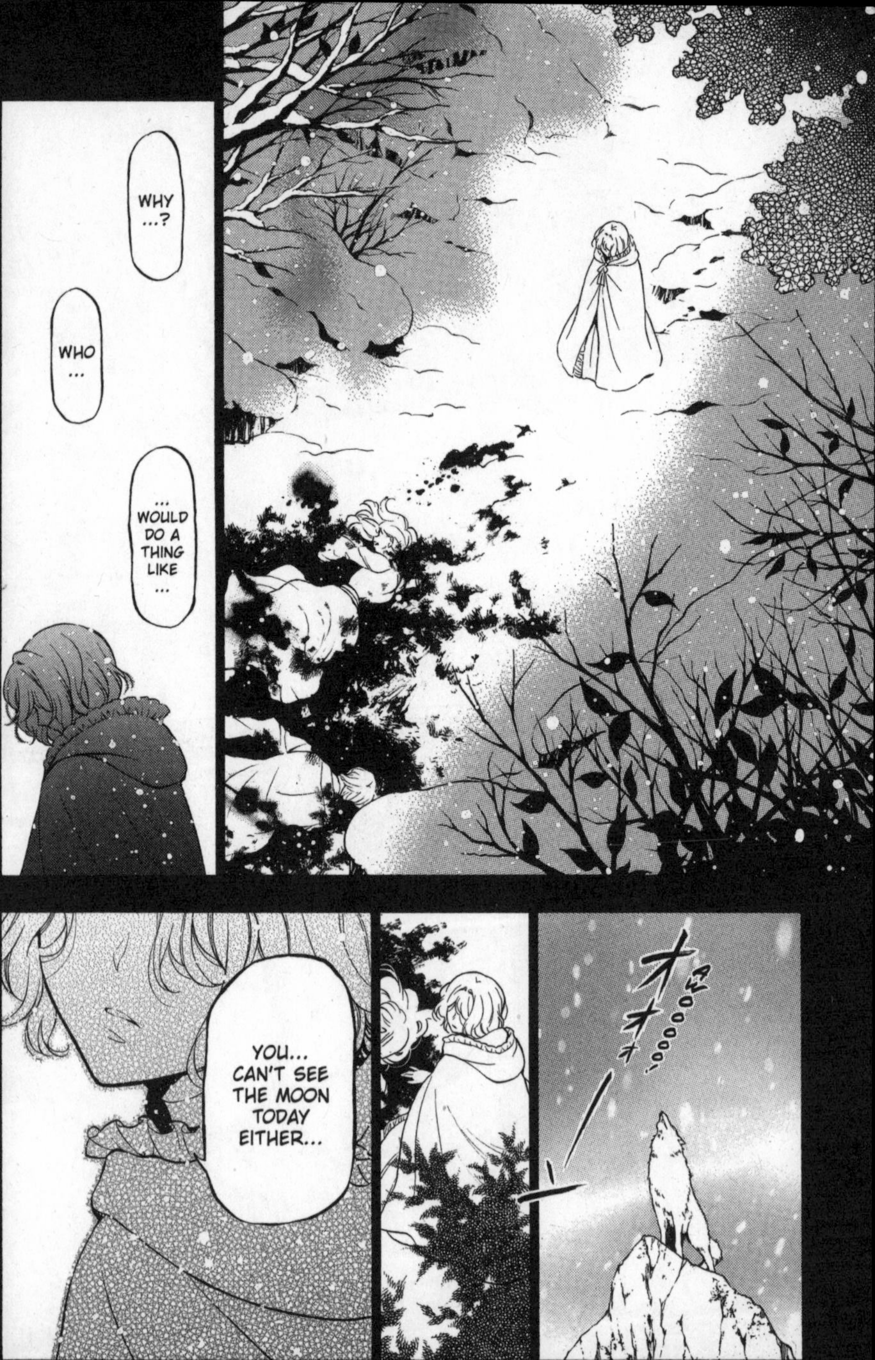
WHY ...?
WHO ...
... WOULD DO A THING LIKE ...
AWOOOOO!
YOU... CAN'T SEE THE MOON TODAY EITHER...

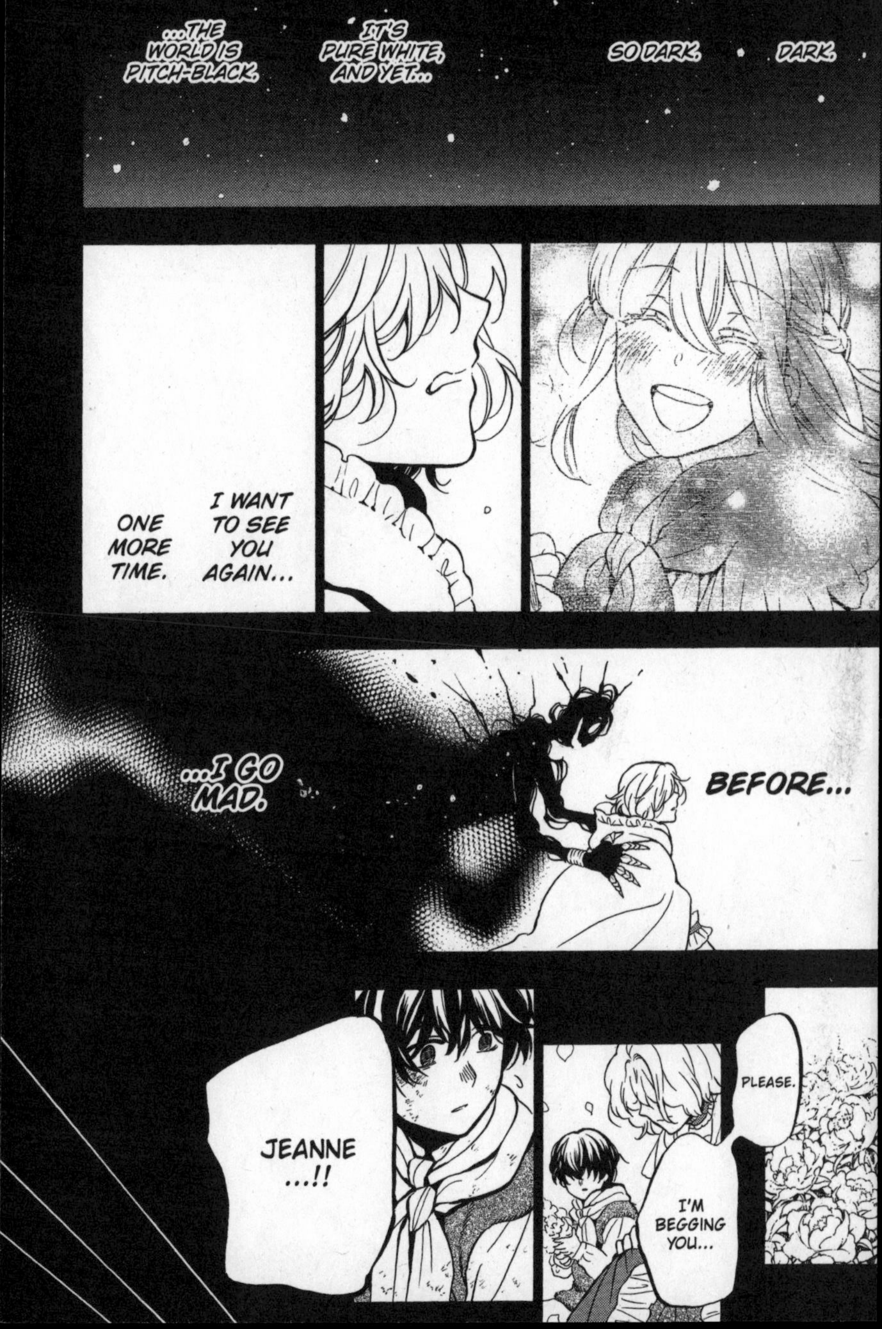
DARK.
SO DARK.
IT'S PURE WHITE, AND YET...
...THE WORLD IS PITCH-BLACK.
I WANT TO SEE YOU AGAIN...
ONE MORE TIME.
BEFORE...
...I GO MAD.
PLEASE.
I'M BEGGING YOU...
JEANNE ...!!

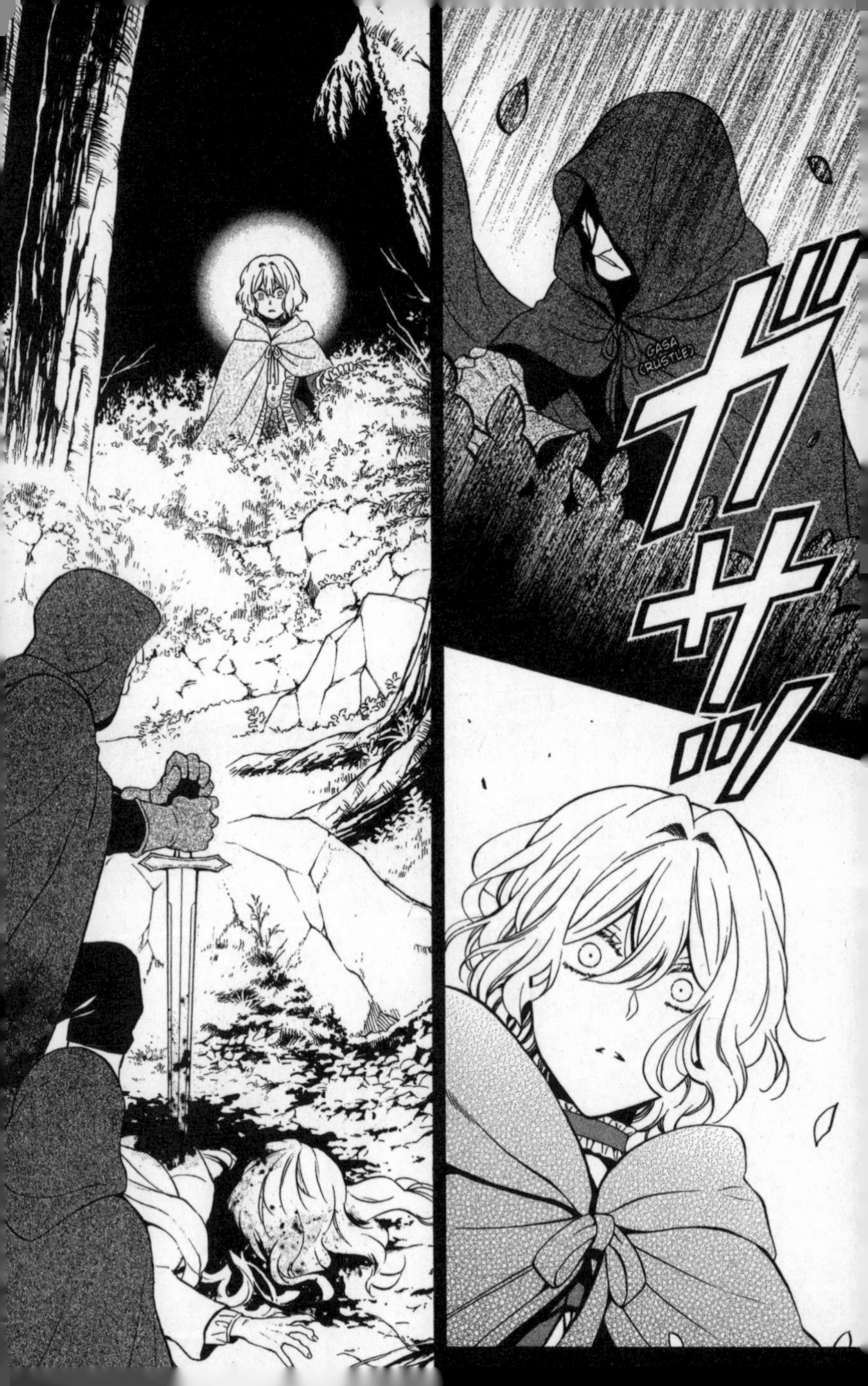
ガサッ
GASA (RUSTLE)

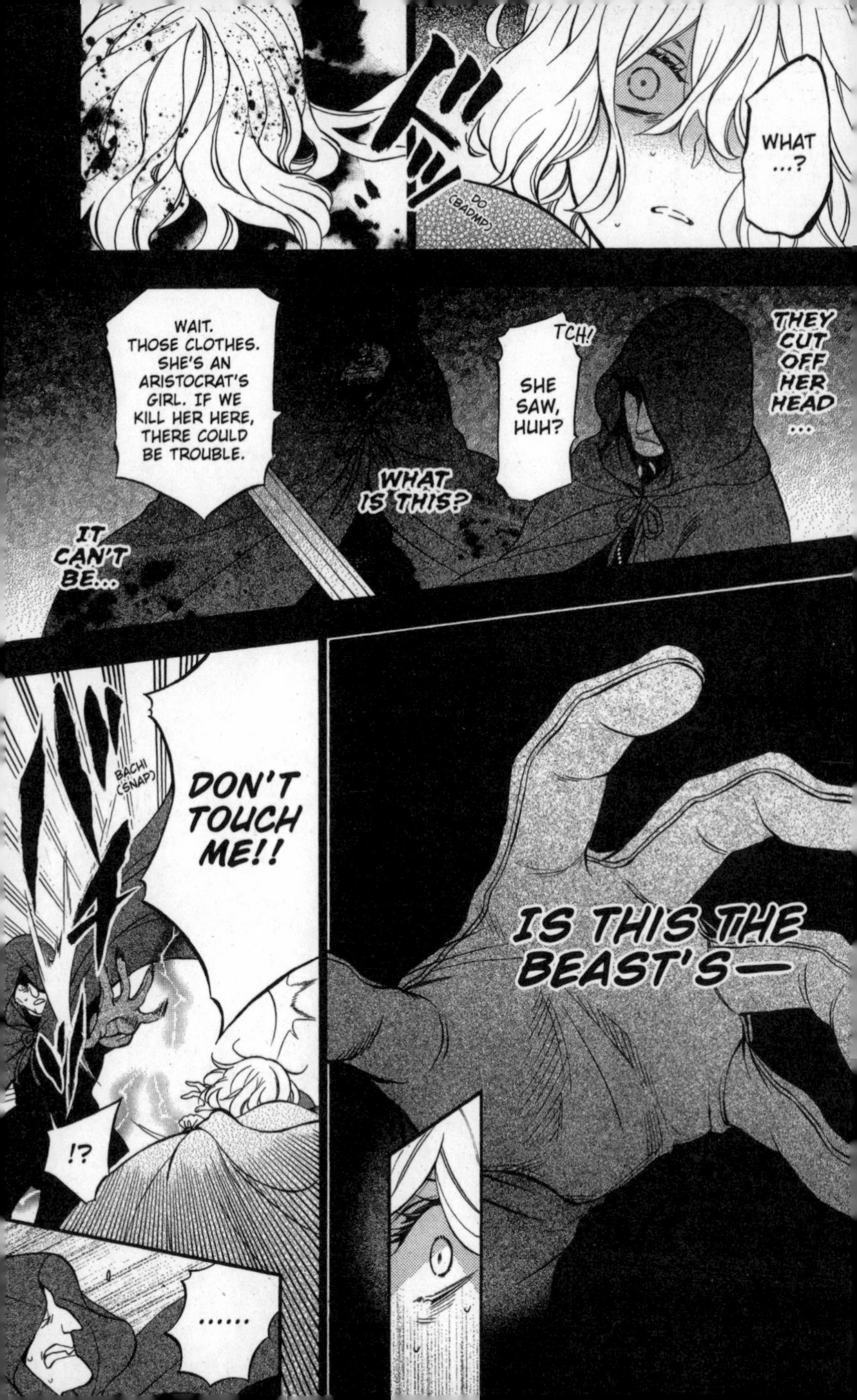
WHAT ...?
DO (BADMP)
THEY CUT OFF HER HEAD ...
TCH!
SHE SAW, HUH?
WHAT IS THIS?
WAIT. THOSE CLOTHES. SHE'S AN ARISTOCRAT'S GIRL. IF WE KILL HER HERE, THERE COULD BE TROUBLE.
IT CAN'T BE...
IS THIS THE BEAST'S—
BACHI (SNAP)
DON'T TOUCH ME!!
!?
......

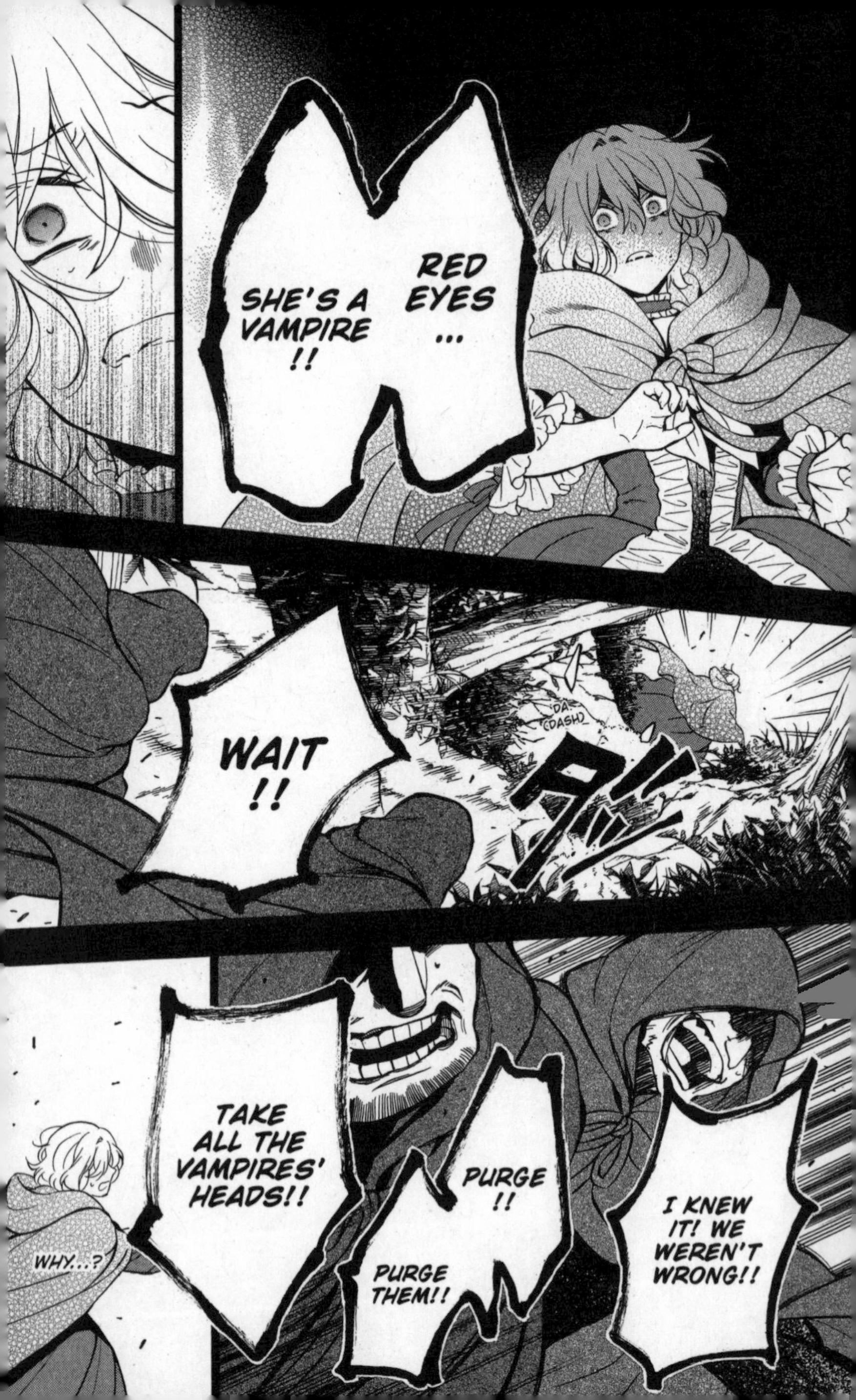

RED EYES ...
SHE'S A VAMPIRE !!
DA- (DASH)
WAIT !!
I KNEW IT! WE WEREN'T WRONG!!
PURGE !!
PURGE THEM!!
TAKE ALL THE VAMPIRES' HEADS!!
WHY...?

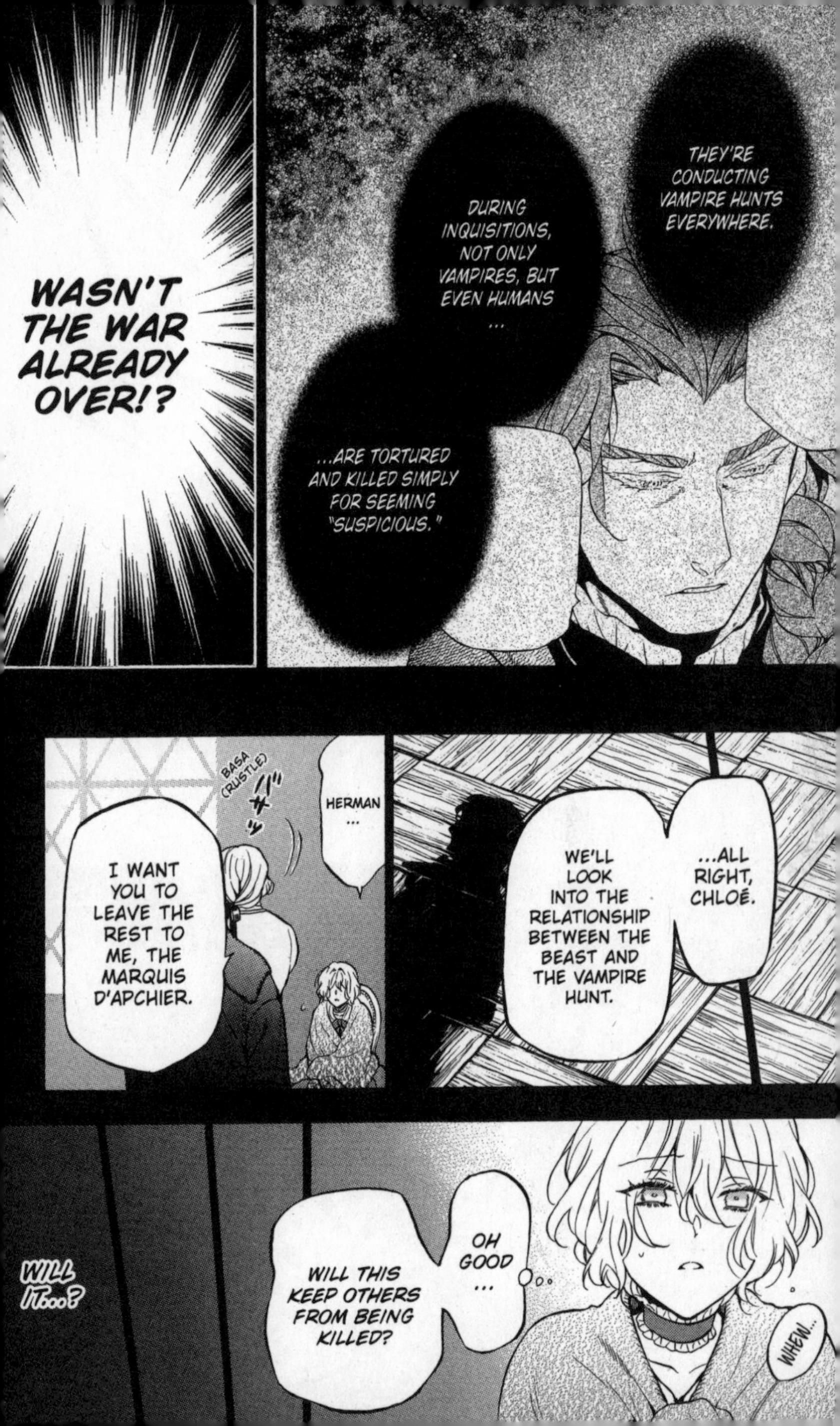
THEY'RE CONDUCTING VAMPIRE HUNTS EVERYWHERE.
DURING INQUISITIONS, NOT ONLY VAMPIRES, BUT EVEN HUMANS ...
...ARE TORTURED AND KILLED SIMPLY FOR SEEMING "SUSPICIOUS."
WASN'T THE WAR ALREADY OVER!?
...ALL RIGHT, CHLOÉ.
WE'LL LOOK INTO THE RELATIONSHIP BETWEEN THE BEAST AND THE VAMPIRE HUNT.
HERMAN ...
BASA (RUSTLE)
I WANT YOU TO LEAVE THE REST TO ME, THE MARQUIS D'APCHIER.
WHEW...
OH GOOD ...
WILL THIS KEEP OTHERS FROM BEING KILLED?
WILL IT...?

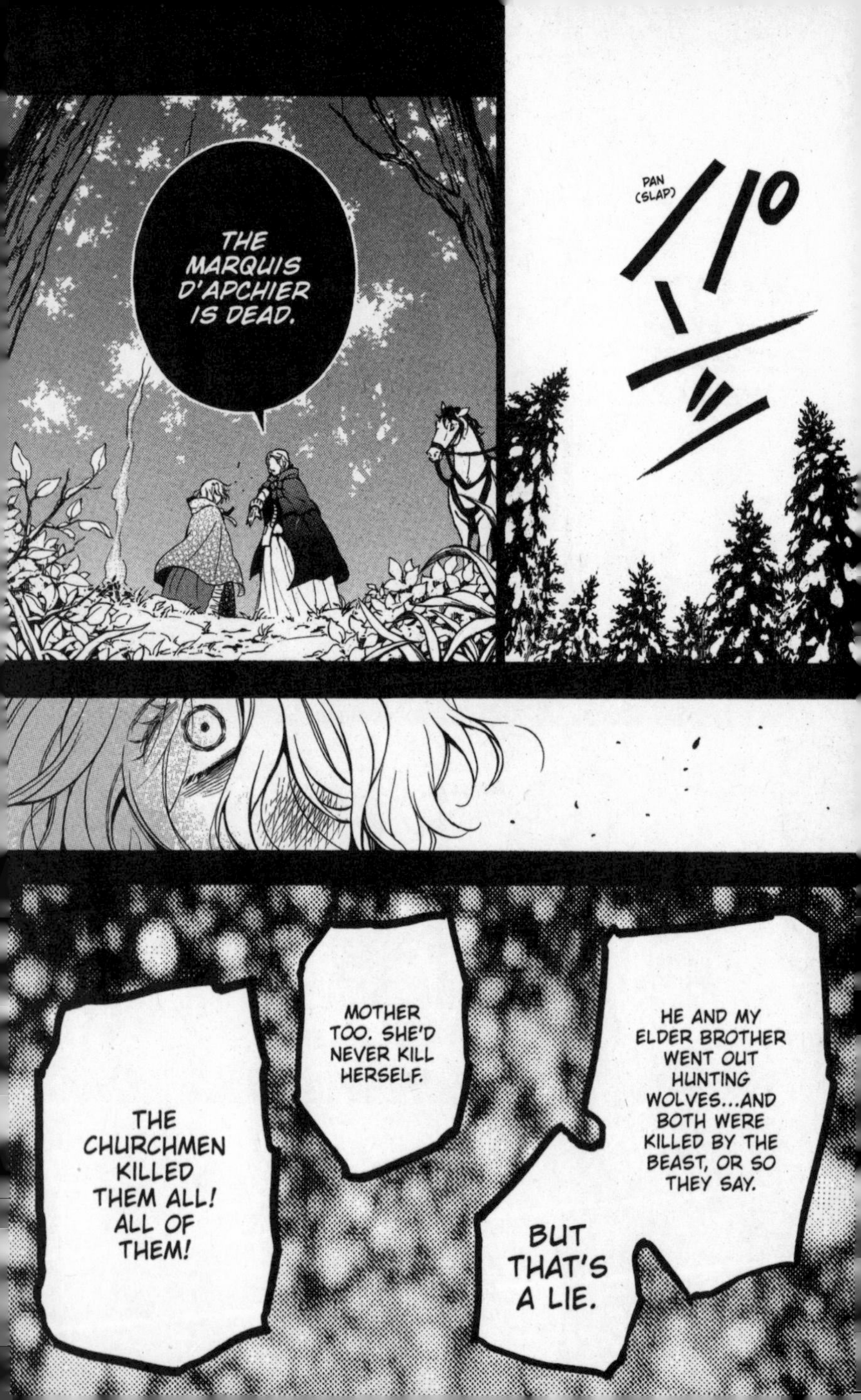
PAN (SLAP)
THE MARQUIS D'APCHIER IS DEAD.
HE AND MY ELDER BROTHER WENT OUT HUNTING WOLVES...AND BOTH WERE KILLED BY THE BEAST, OR SO THEY SAY.
BUT THAT'S A LIE.
MOTHER TOO. SHE'D NEVER KILL HERSELF.
THE CHURCHMEN KILLED THEM ALL! ALL OF THEM!

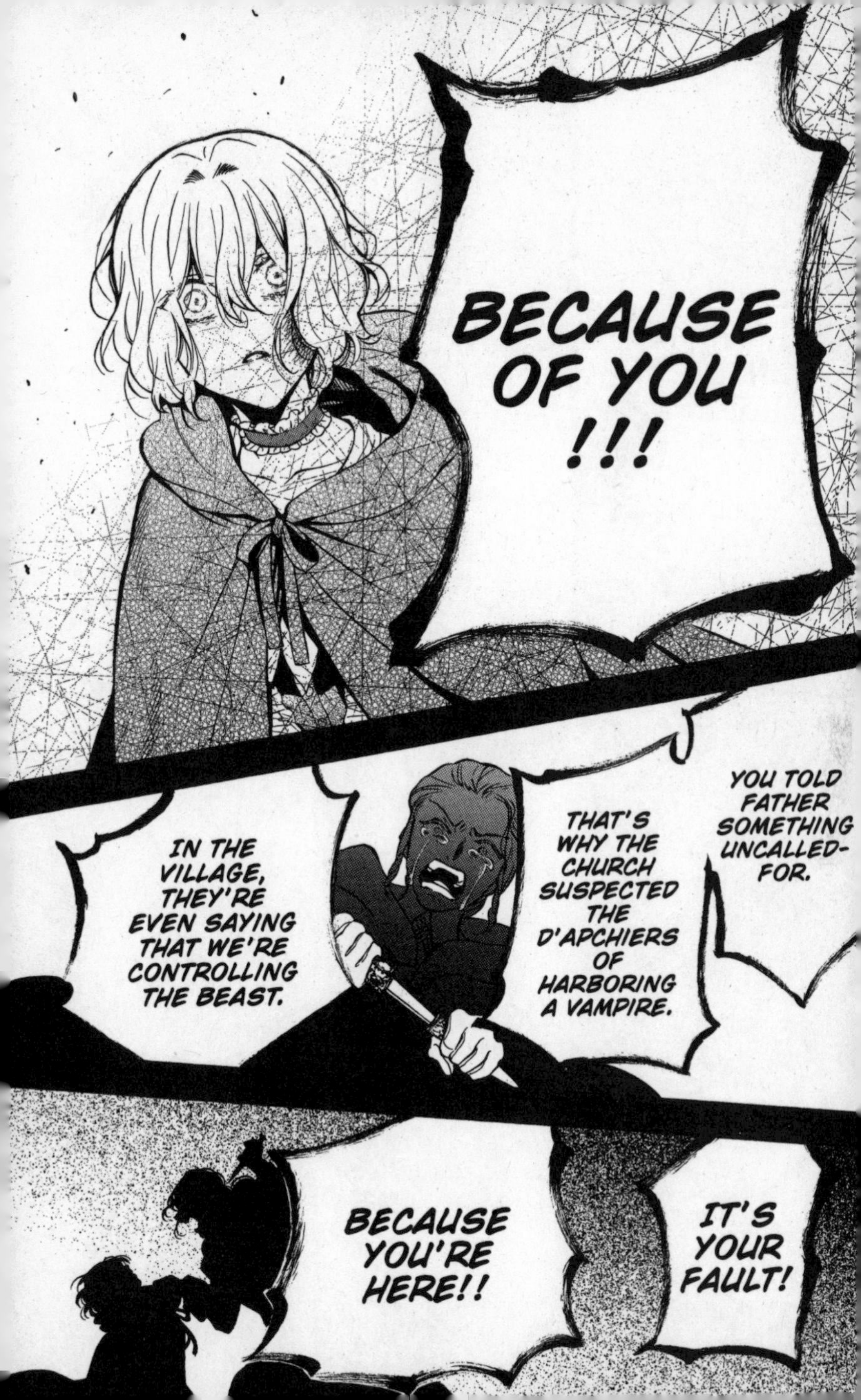
BECAUSE OF YOU !!!
YOU TOLD FATHER SOMETHING UNCALLED-FOR.
THAT'S WHY THE CHURCH SUSPECTED THE D'APCHIERS OF HARBORING A VAMPIRE.
IN THE VILLAGE, THEY'RE EVEN SAYING THAT WE'RE CONTROLLING THE BEAST.
IT'S YOUR FAULT!
BECAUSE YOU'RE HERE!!

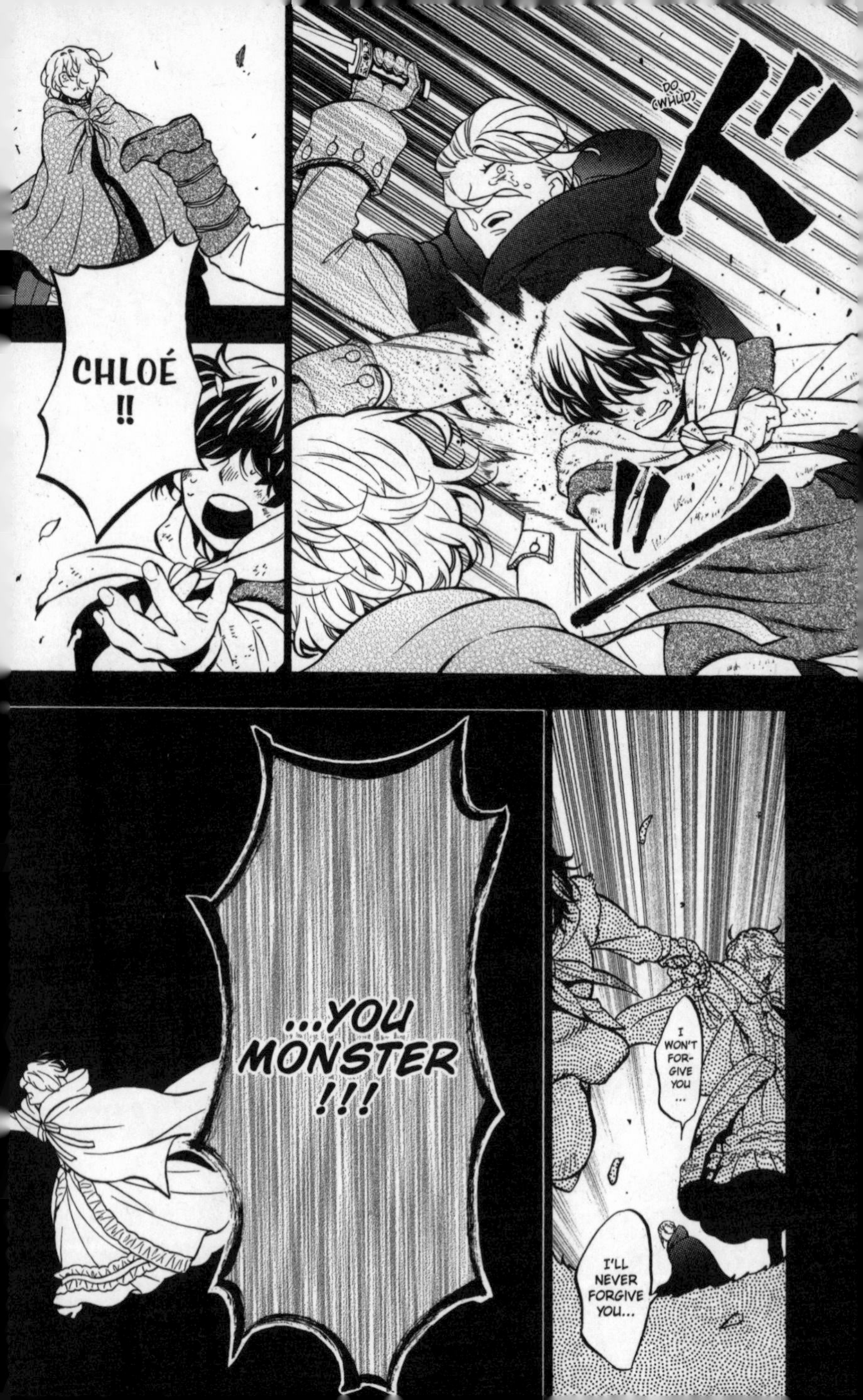
ド
DO (WHUD)
CHLOÉ !!
I WON'T FOR-GIVE YOU ...
I'LL NEVER FORGIVE YOU...
...YOU MONSTER !!!

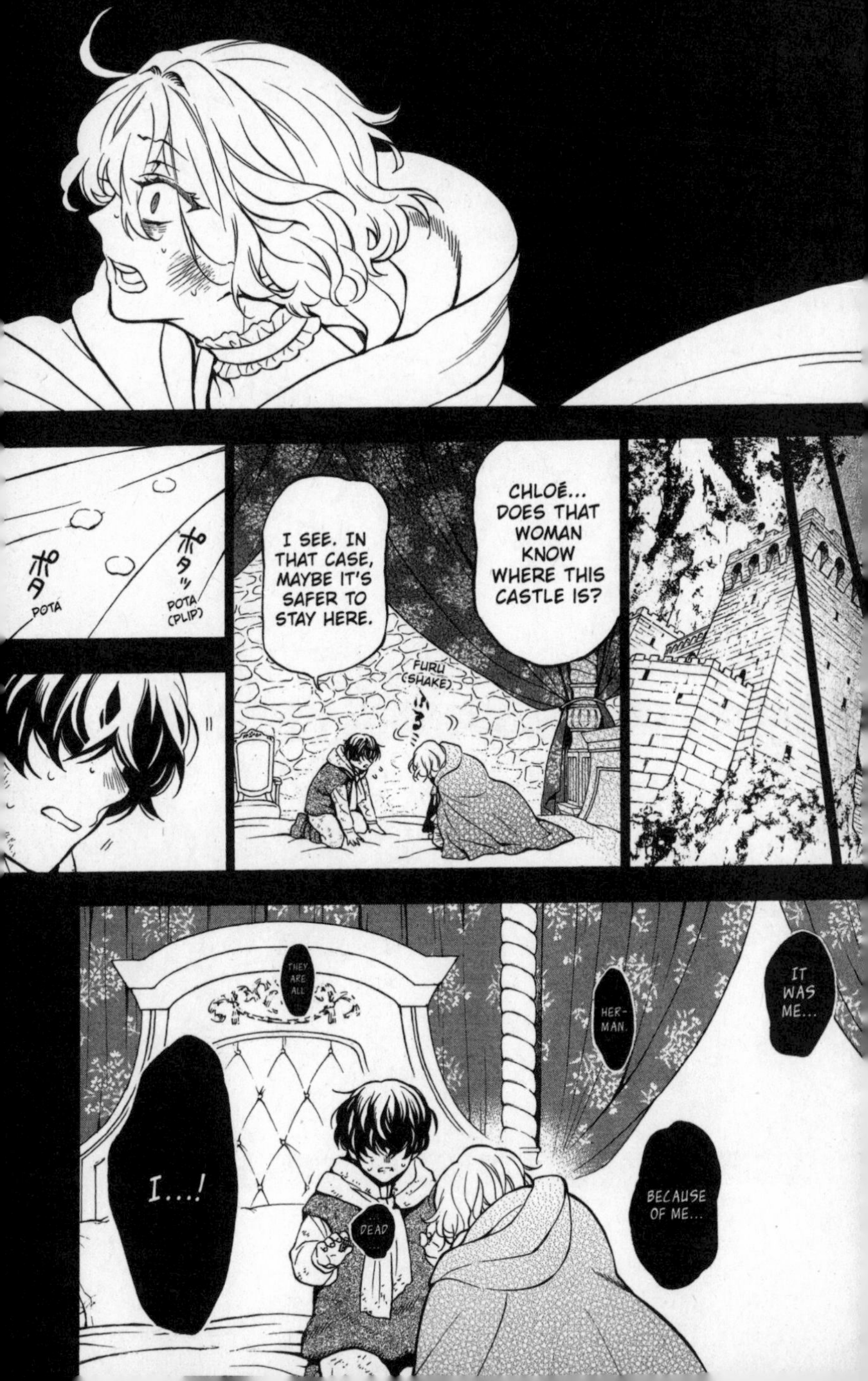
CHLOÉ... DOES THAT WOMAN KNOW WHERE THIS CASTLE IS?
FURU (SHAKE)
I SEE. IN THAT CASE, MAYBE IT'S SAFER TO STAY HERE.
ポタッ
POTA (PLIP)
ポタ
POTA
IT WAS ME...
HER-MAN.
THEY ARE ALL
BECAUSE OF ME...
DEAD...
I...!

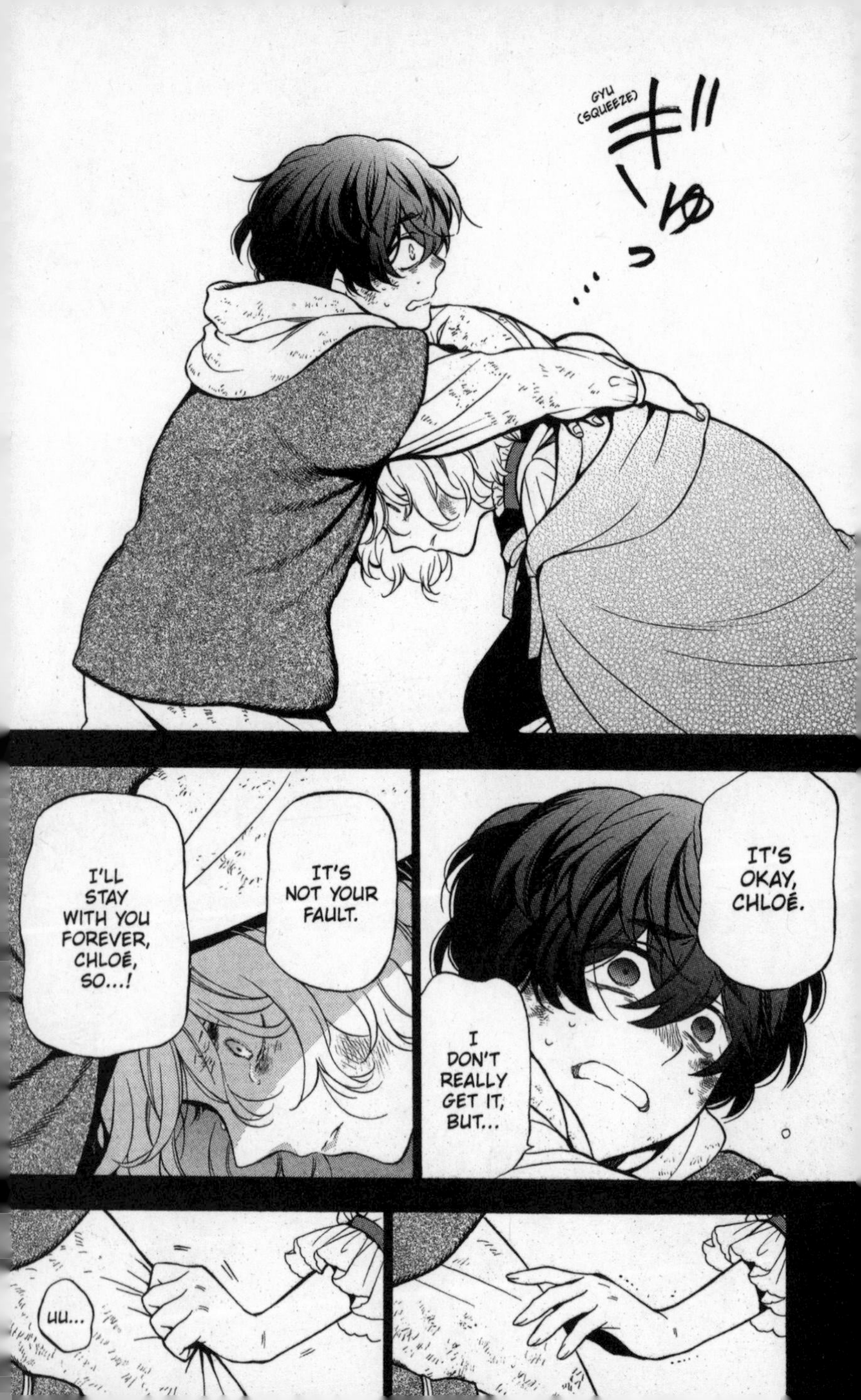
GYU (SQUEEZE)
ぎゅっ
...
IT'S OKAY, CHLOÉ.
I DON'T REALLY GET IT, BUT...
IT'S NOT YOUR FAULT.
I'LL STAY WITH YOU FOREVER, CHLOÉ, SO...!
UU...

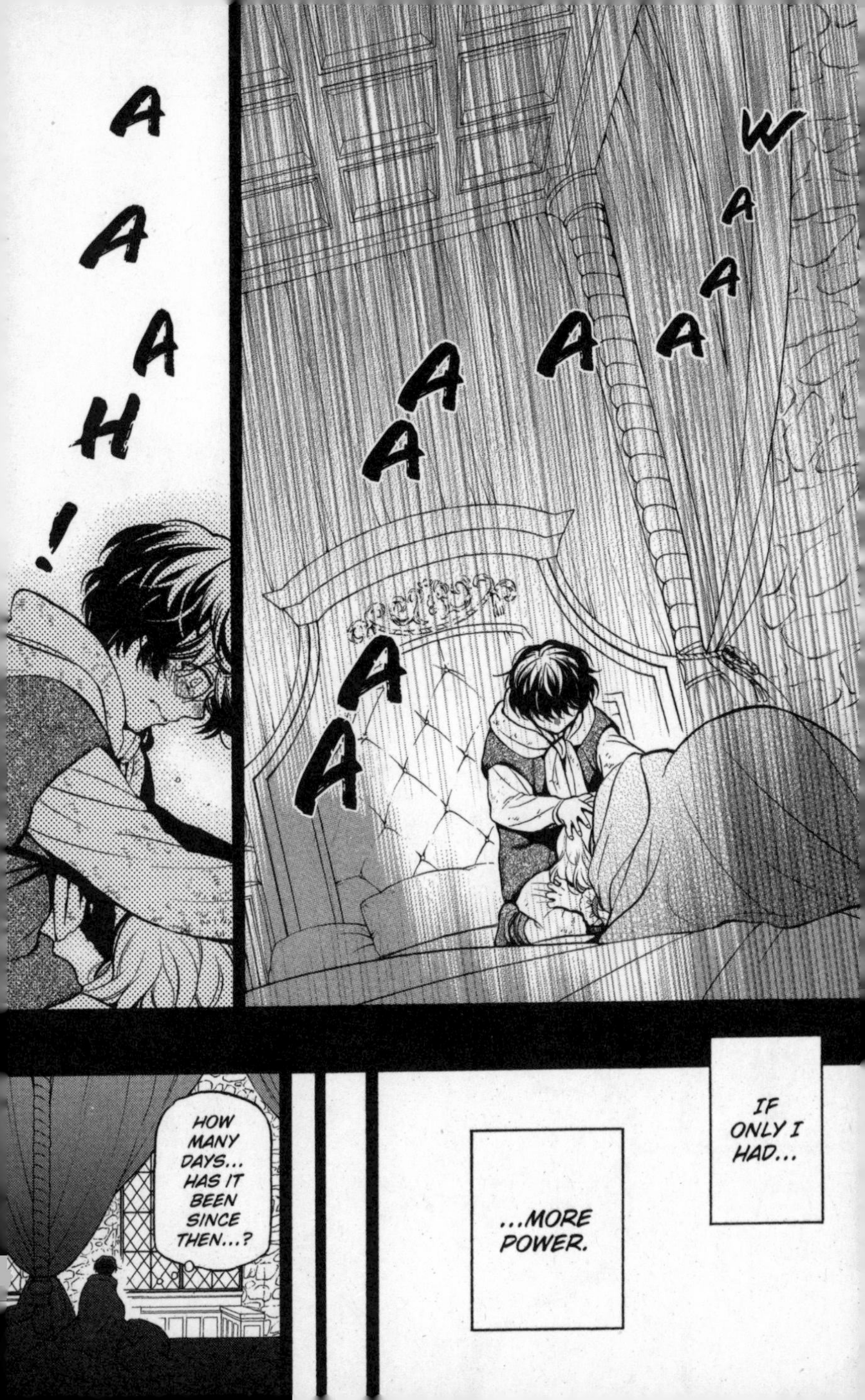
WAAAAAAAAA
AAAAH!
IF ONLY I HAD...
...MORE POWER.
HOW MANY DAYS... HAS IT BEEN SINCE THEN...?

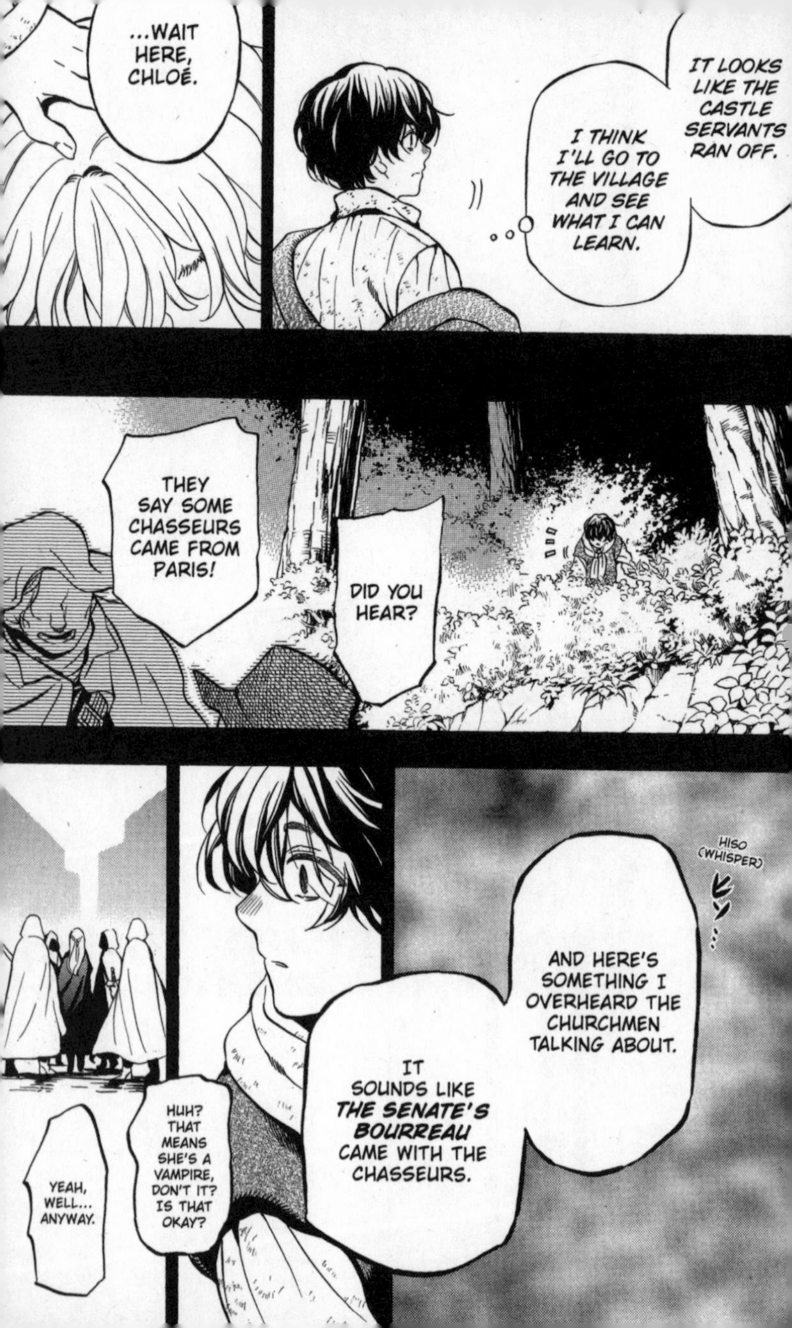
IT LOOKS LIKE THE CASTLE SERVANTS RAN OFF.
I THINK I'LL GO TO THE VILLAGE AND SEE WHAT I CAN LEARN.
...WAIT HERE, CHLOÉ.
DID YOU HEAR?
THEY SAY SOME CHASSEURS CAME FROM PARIS!
HISO (WHISPER)
AND HERE'S SOMETHING I OVERHEARD THE CHURCHMEN TALKING ABOUT.
IT SOUNDS LIKE *THE SENATE'S BOURREAU* CAME WITH THE CHASSEURS.
HUH? THAT MEANS SHE'S A VAMPIRE, DON'T IT? IS THAT OKAY?
YEAH, WELL... ANYWAY.

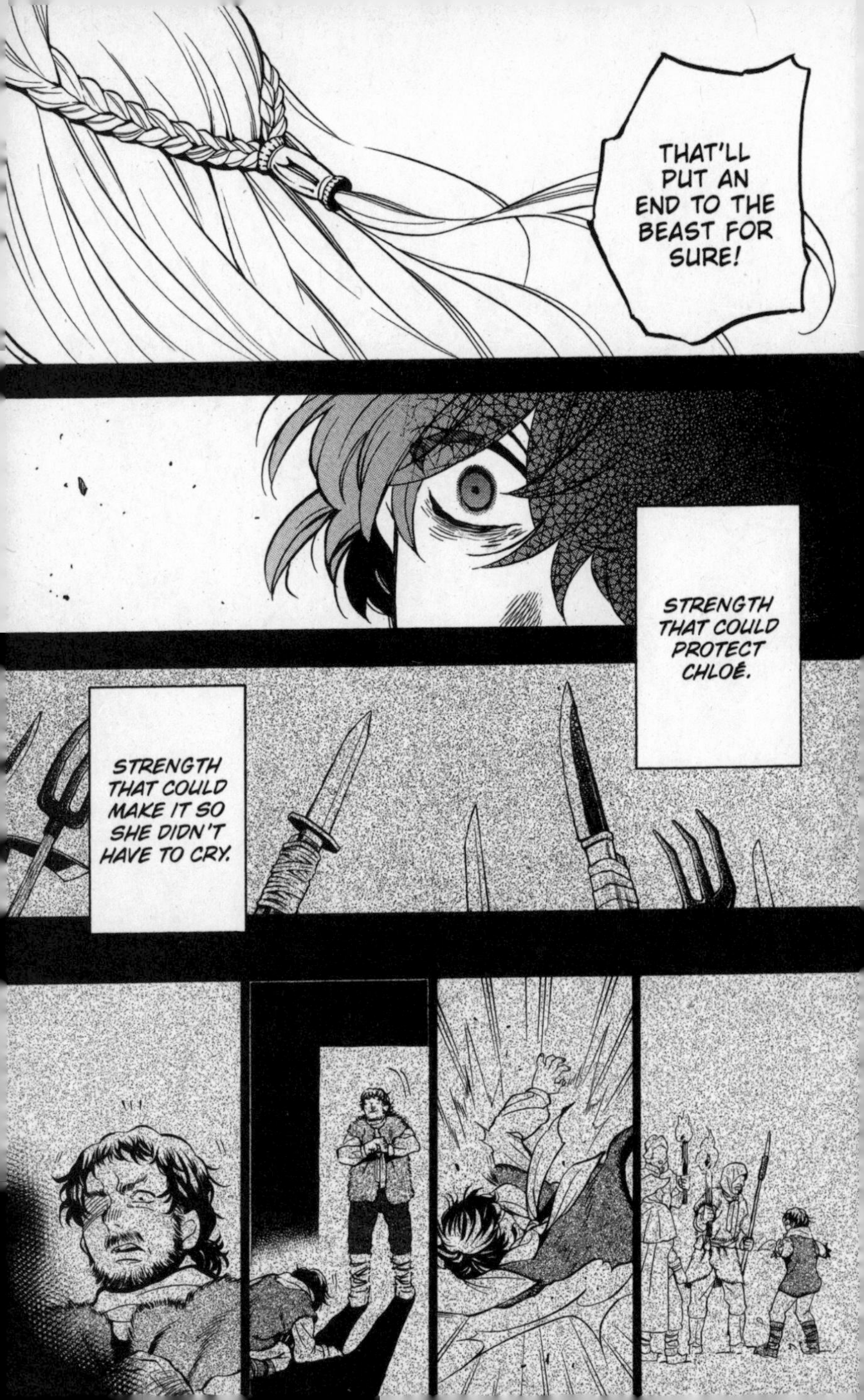
THAT'LL PUT AN END TO THE BEAST FOR SURE!
STRENGTH THAT COULD PROTECT CHLOÉ.
STRENGTH THAT COULD MAKE IT SO SHE DIDN'T HAVE TO CRY.

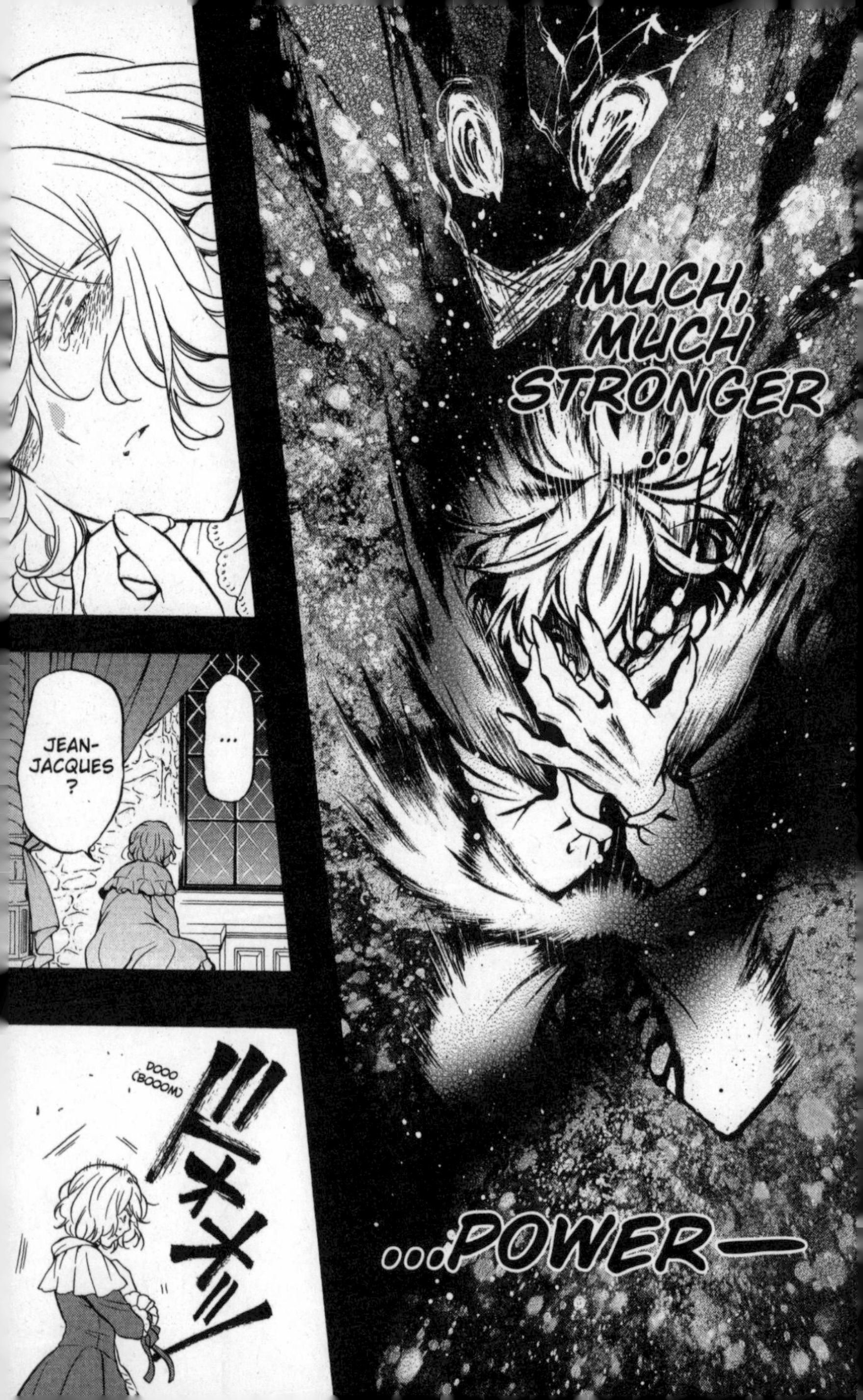
MUCH, MUCH STRONGER
...
...POWER—
...
JEAN-JACQUES?
DOOO (BOOOM)

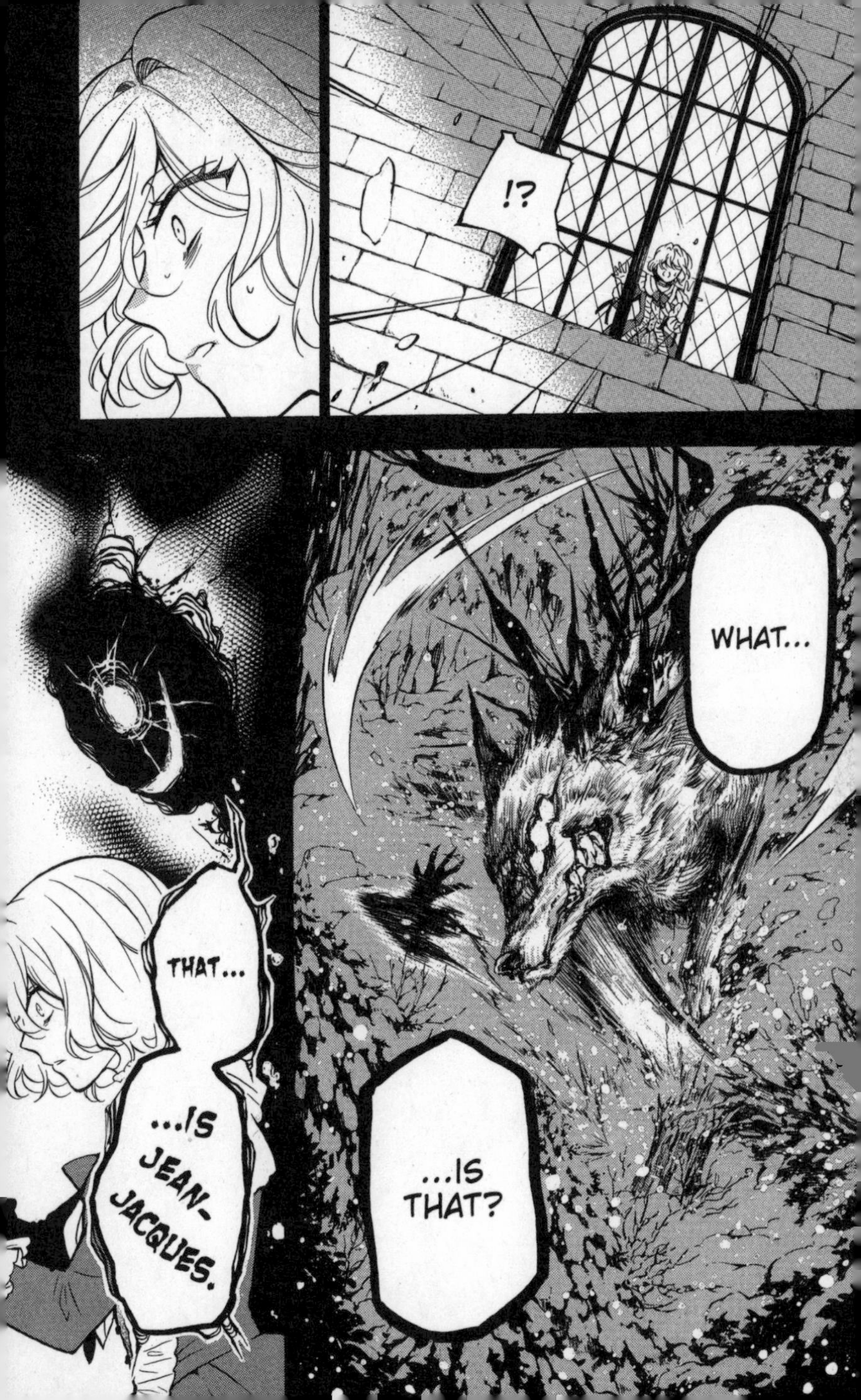
!?
WHAT...
...IS THAT?
THAT...
...IS JEAN-JACQUES.

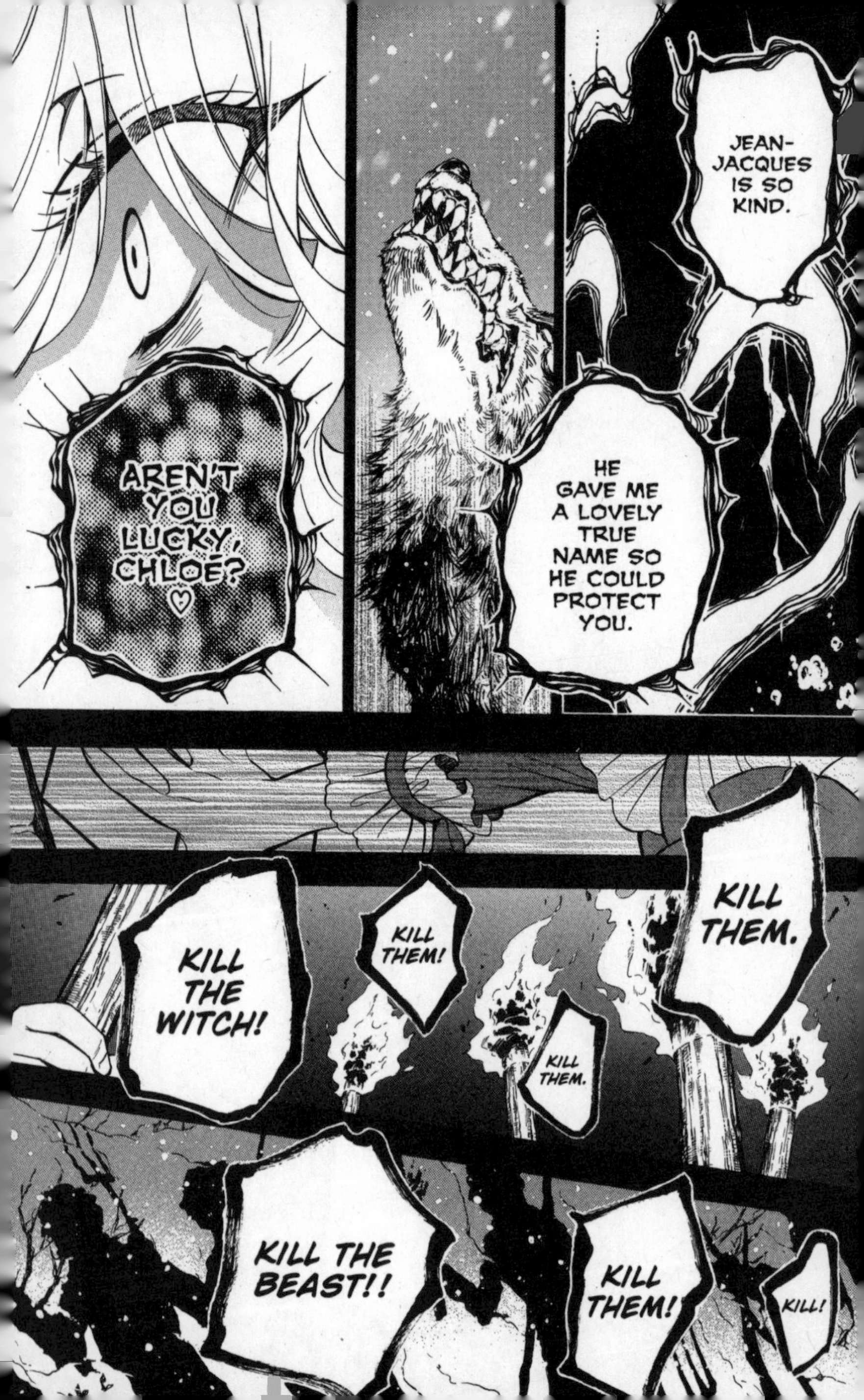
JEAN-JACQUES IS SO KIND.
HE GAVE ME A LOVELY TRUE NAME SO HE COULD PROTECT YOU.
AREN'T YOU LUCKY, CHLOÉ? ♡
KILL THEM.
KILL THEM.
KILL THEM!
KILL THE WITCH!
KILL!
KILL THEM!
KILL THE BEAST!!

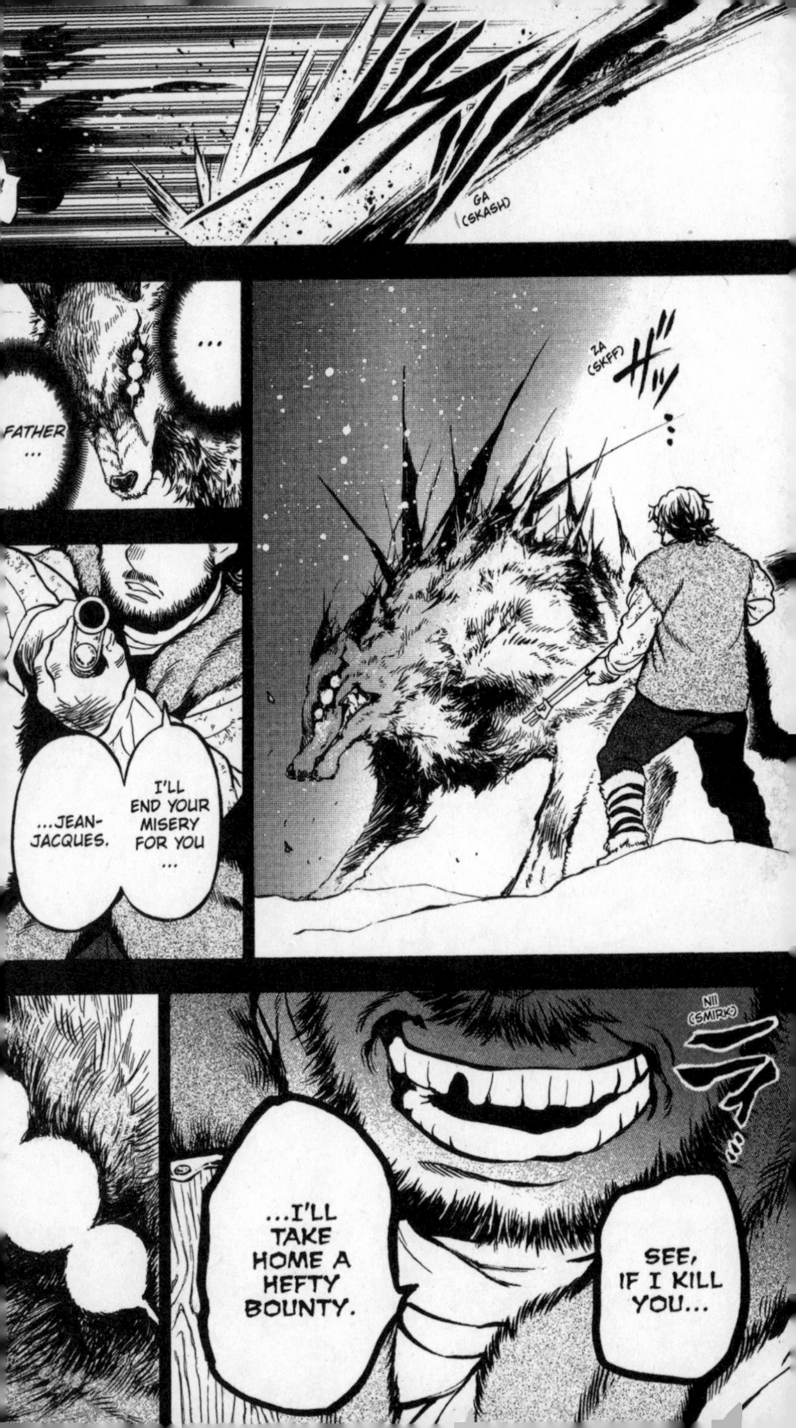
GA (SKASH)
ZA (SKFF)
...
FATHER ...
I'LL END YOUR MISERY FOR YOU ...
...JEAN-JACQUES.
NII (SMIRK)
SEE, IF I KILL YOU...
...I'LL TAKE HOME A HEFTY BOUNTY.

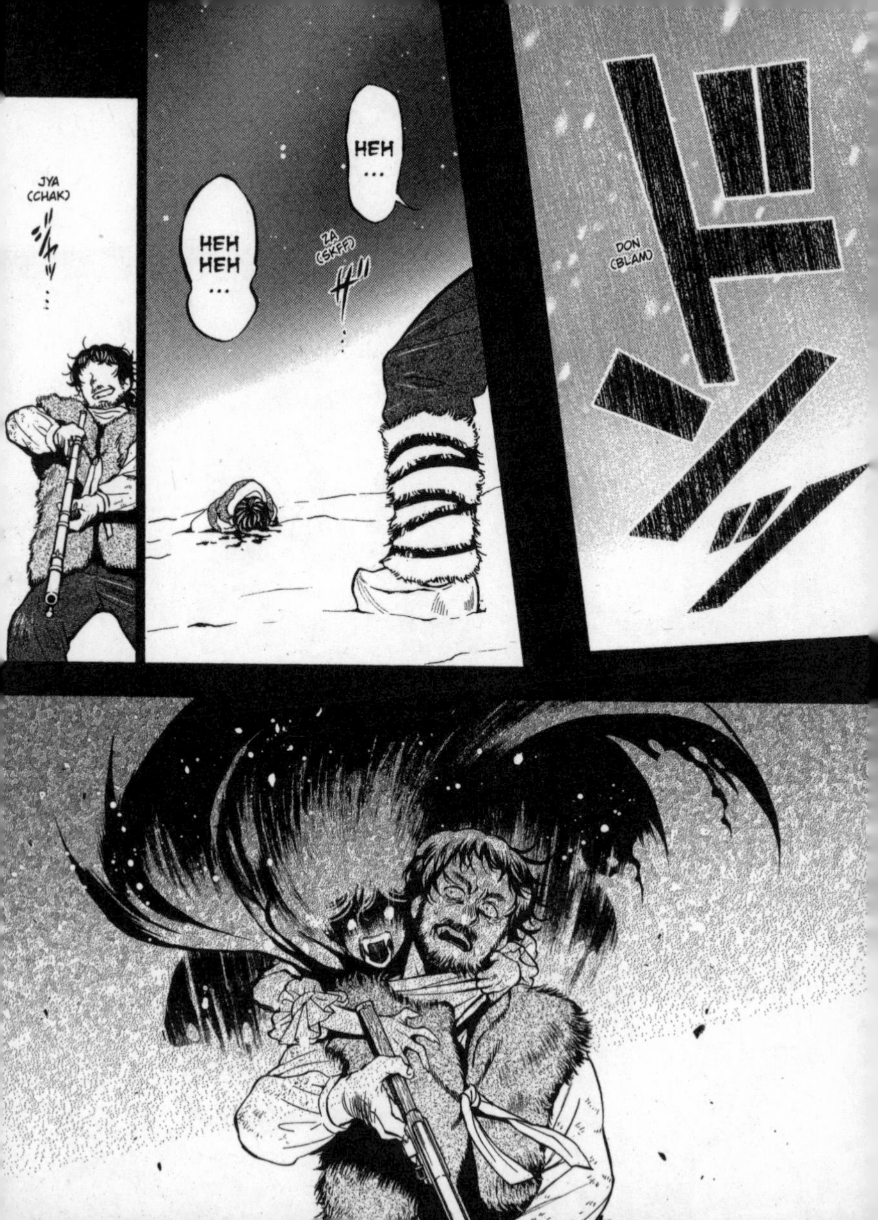
DON (BLAM)
HEH ...
HEH HEH ...
ZA (SKFF)
JYA (CHAK)

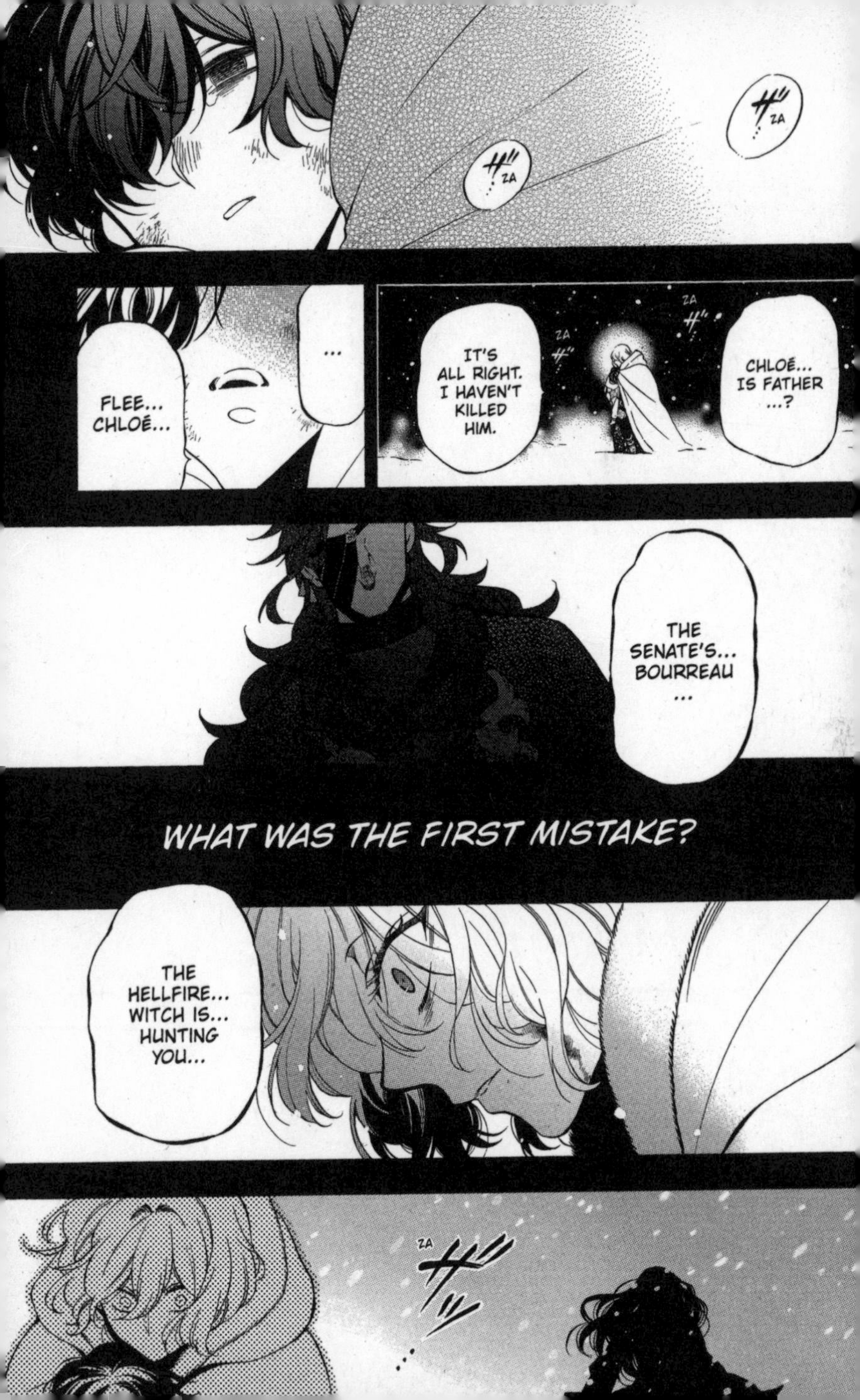
ZA
ZA
CHLOÉ... IS FATHER ...?
ZA
ZA
IT'S ALL RIGHT. I HAVEN'T KILLED HIM.
...
FLEE... CHLOÉ...
THE SENATE'S... BOURREAU ...
WHAT WAS THE FIRST MISTAKE?
THE HELLFIRE... WITCH IS... HUNTING YOU...
ZA

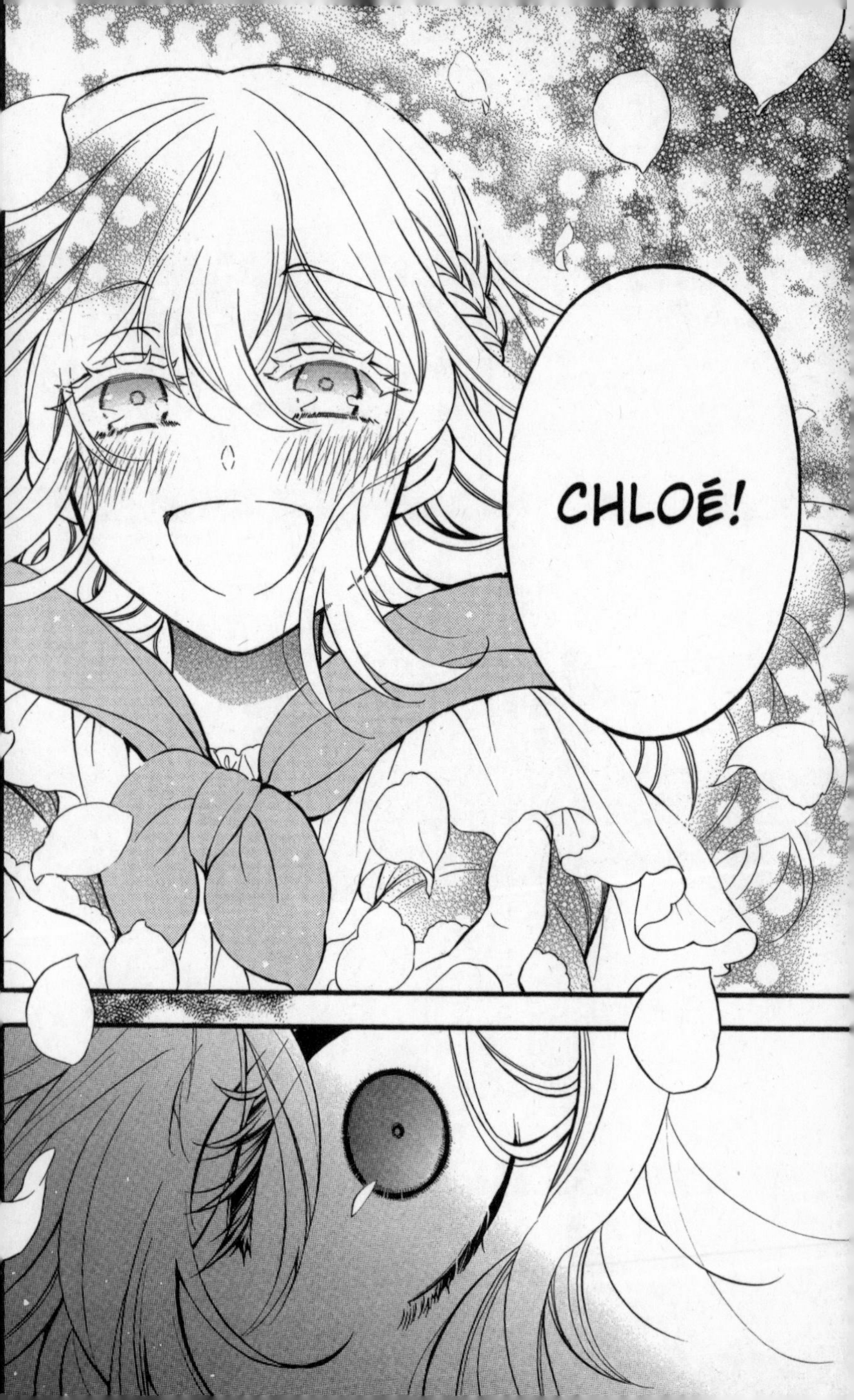
CHLOÉ!

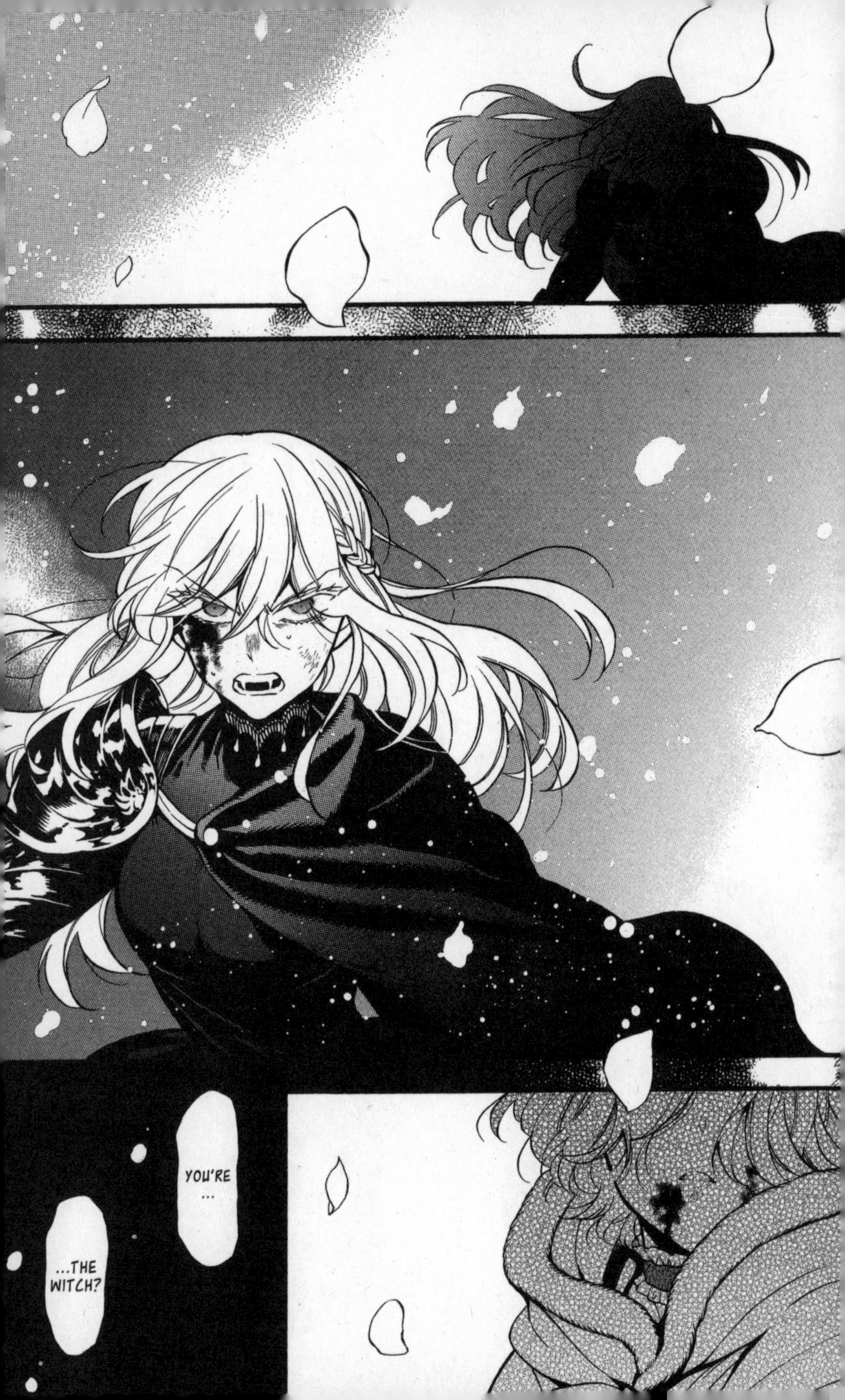
YOU'RE ...
...THE WITCH?

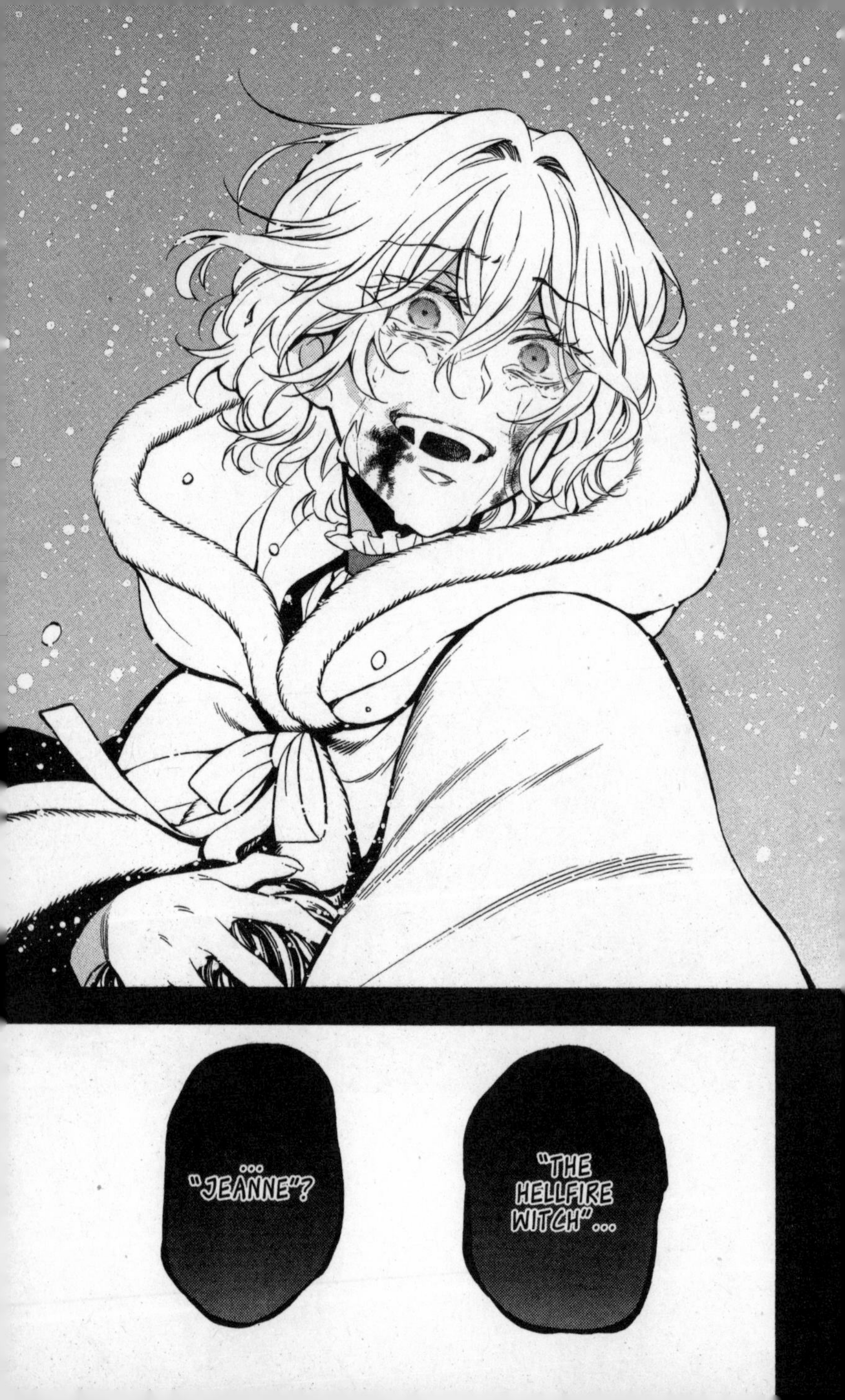
"THE HELLFIRE WITCH"...
... "JEANNE"?

Mémoire 56 Chasse aux Vampires THE BEAST

SHE INVITED JEAN-JACQUES TO THE CASTLE ON THE SLY.
WHOAAA! IT'S INCREDIBLE!!
DOYA (PROUD)
THIS IS MY BEDROOM.
HUH!?
IT'S OKAY IF I SEE?
BADMP BADMP
THANK YOU!
ぐっちゃあ……
GUCCHAA (TRASHED)
WHAT A MESS...
PUT OFF.

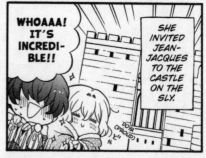

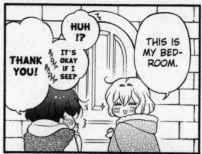

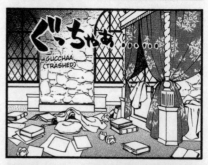

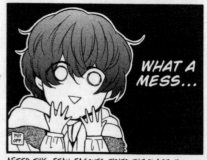

AFTER THIS, JEAN-JACQUES TIDIED THE PLACE UP.

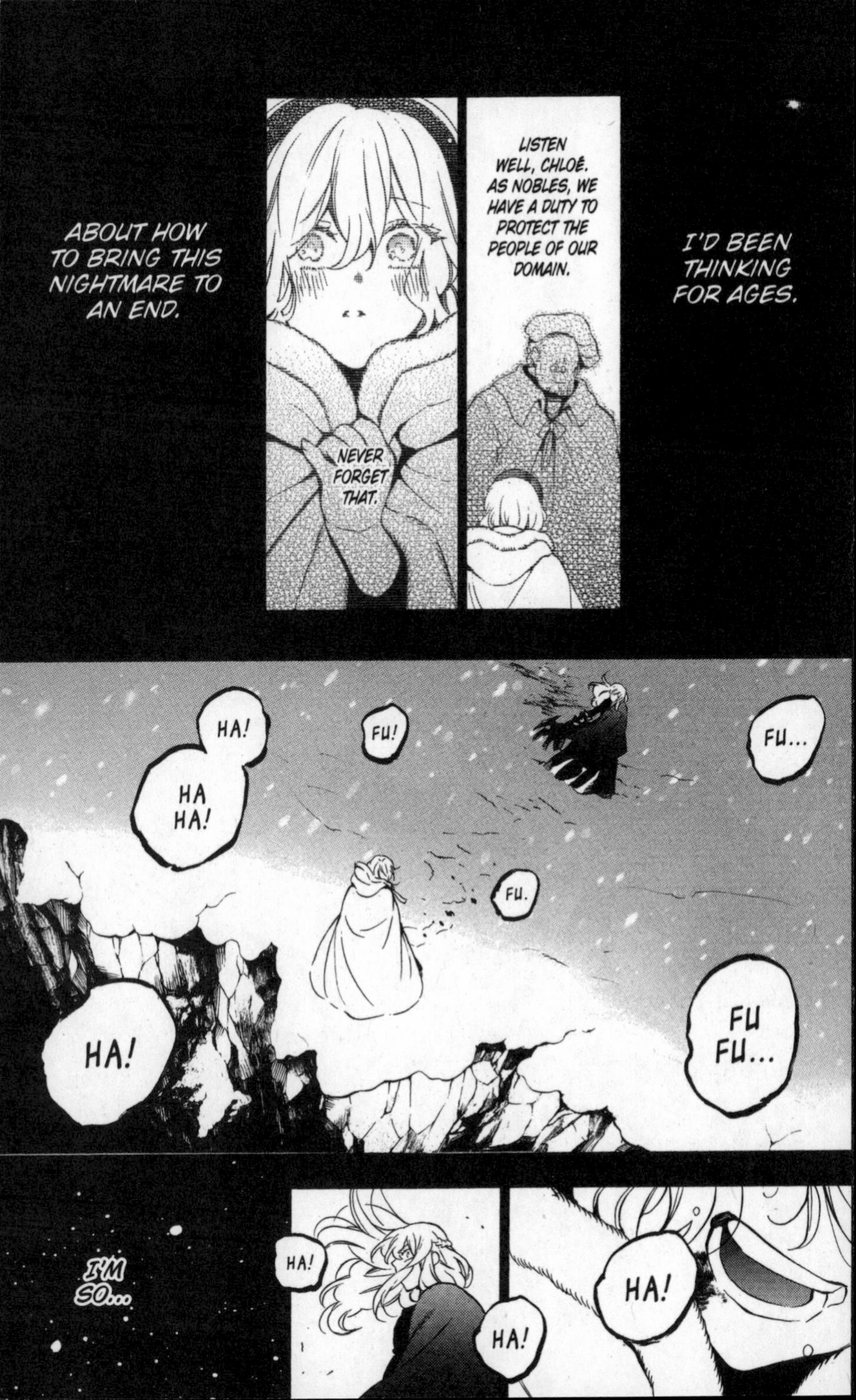
I'D BEEN THINKING FOR AGES.
LISTEN WELL, CHLOÉ. AS NOBLES, WE HAVE A DUTY TO PROTECT THE PEOPLE OF OUR DOMAIN.
NEVER FORGET THAT.
ABOUT HOW TO BRING THIS NIGHTMARE TO AN END.
FU...
FU!
HA!
HA HA!
FU.
FU FU...
HA!
HA!
HA!
HA!
I'M SO...

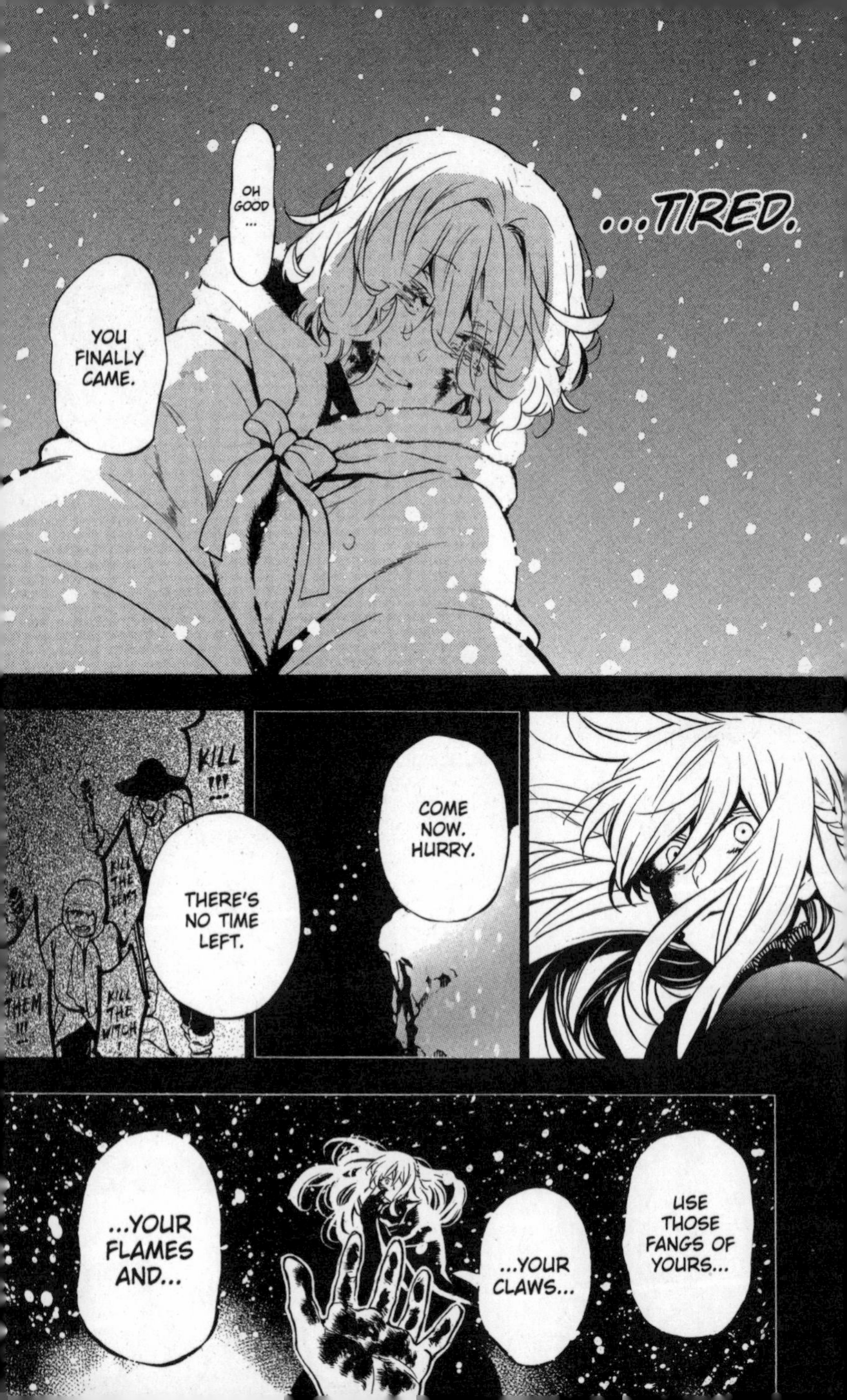
...TIRED.
OH GOOD...
YOU FINALLY CAME.
COME NOW. HURRY.
THERE'S NO TIME LEFT.
KILL!!!
KILL THE BEAST!
KILL THE WITCH!
KILL THEM!!!
USE THOSE FANGS OF YOURS...
...YOUR CLAWS...
...YOUR FLAMES AND...

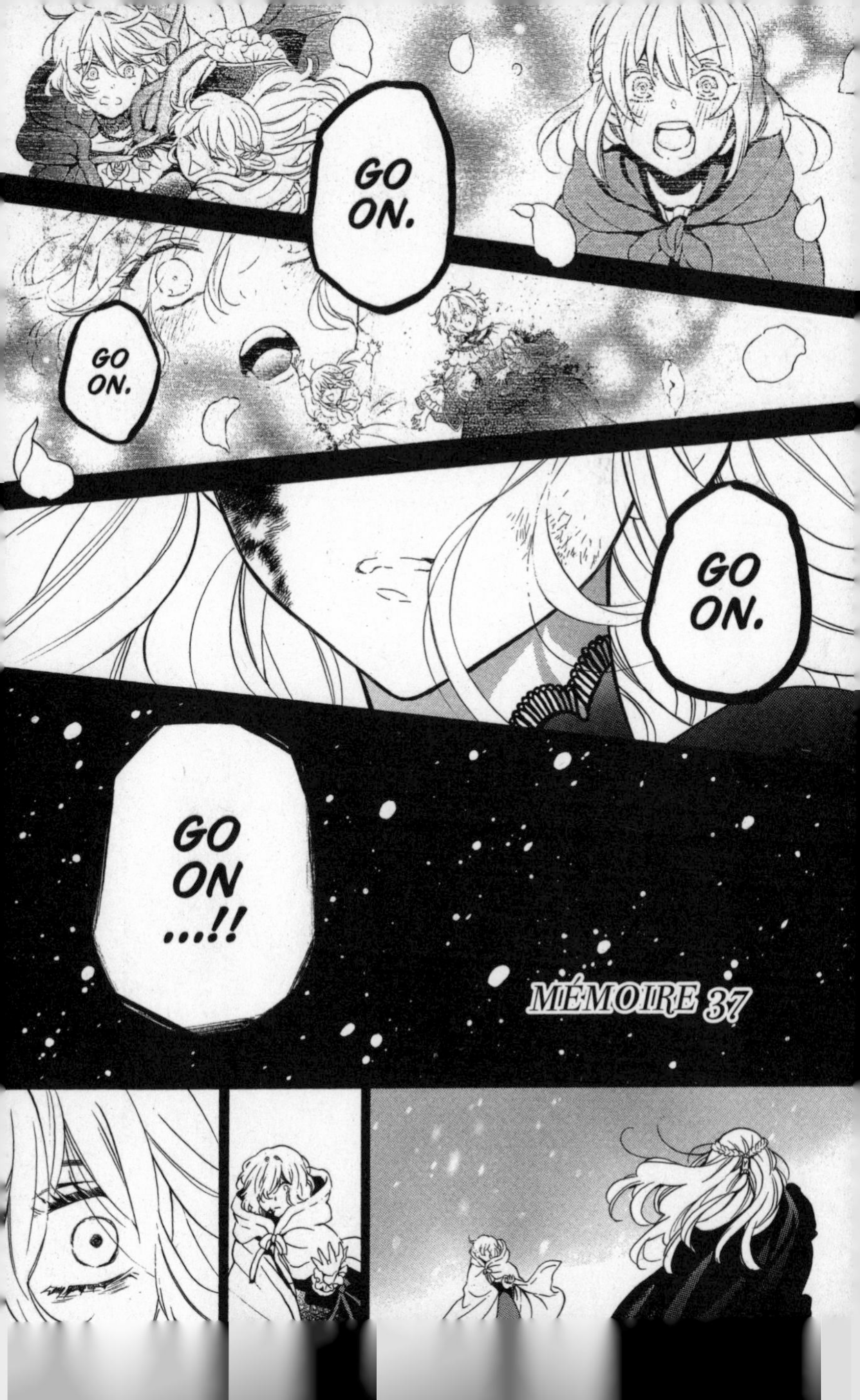
GO ON.
GO ON.
GO ON.
GO ON ...!!
MÉMOIRE 37

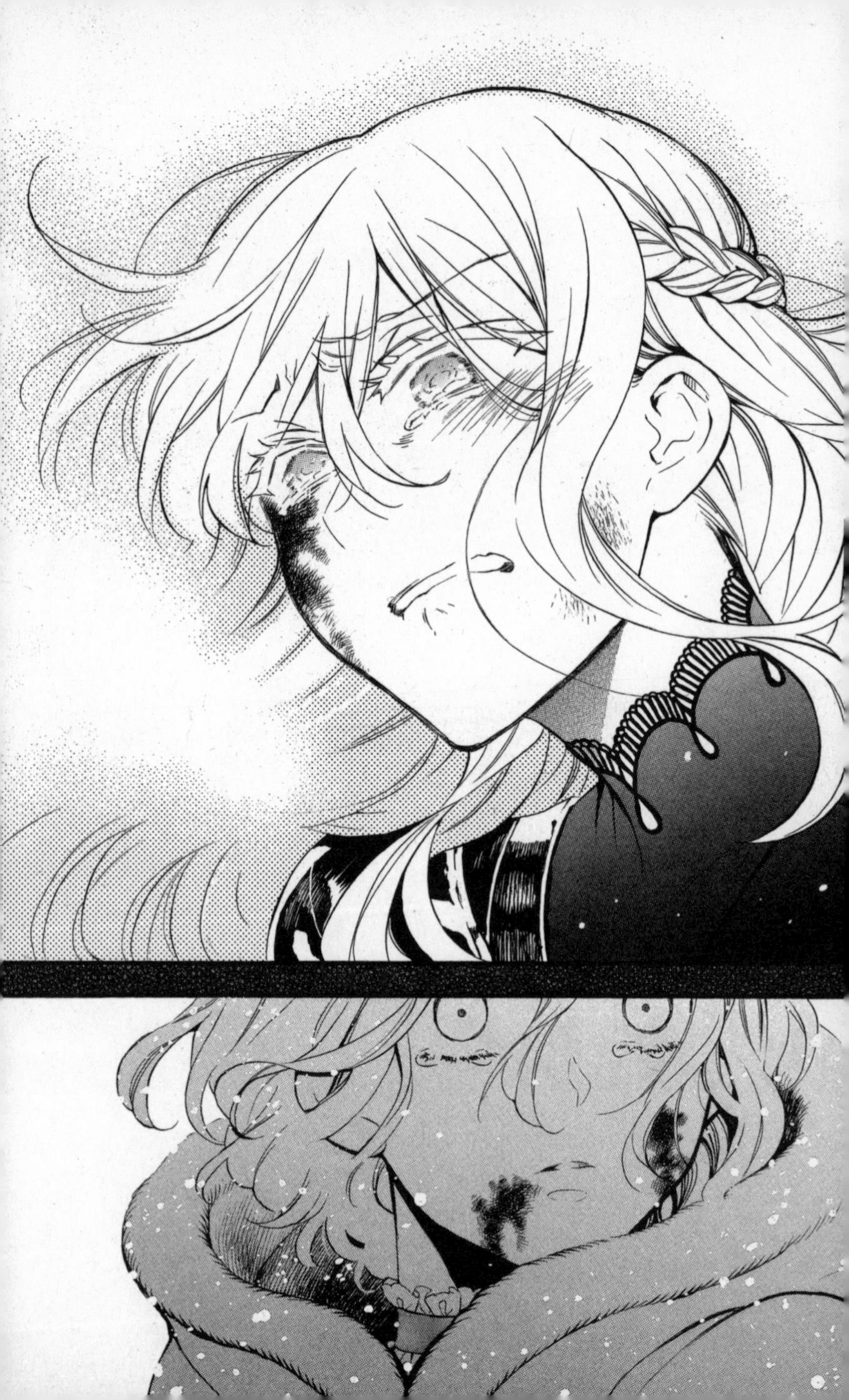

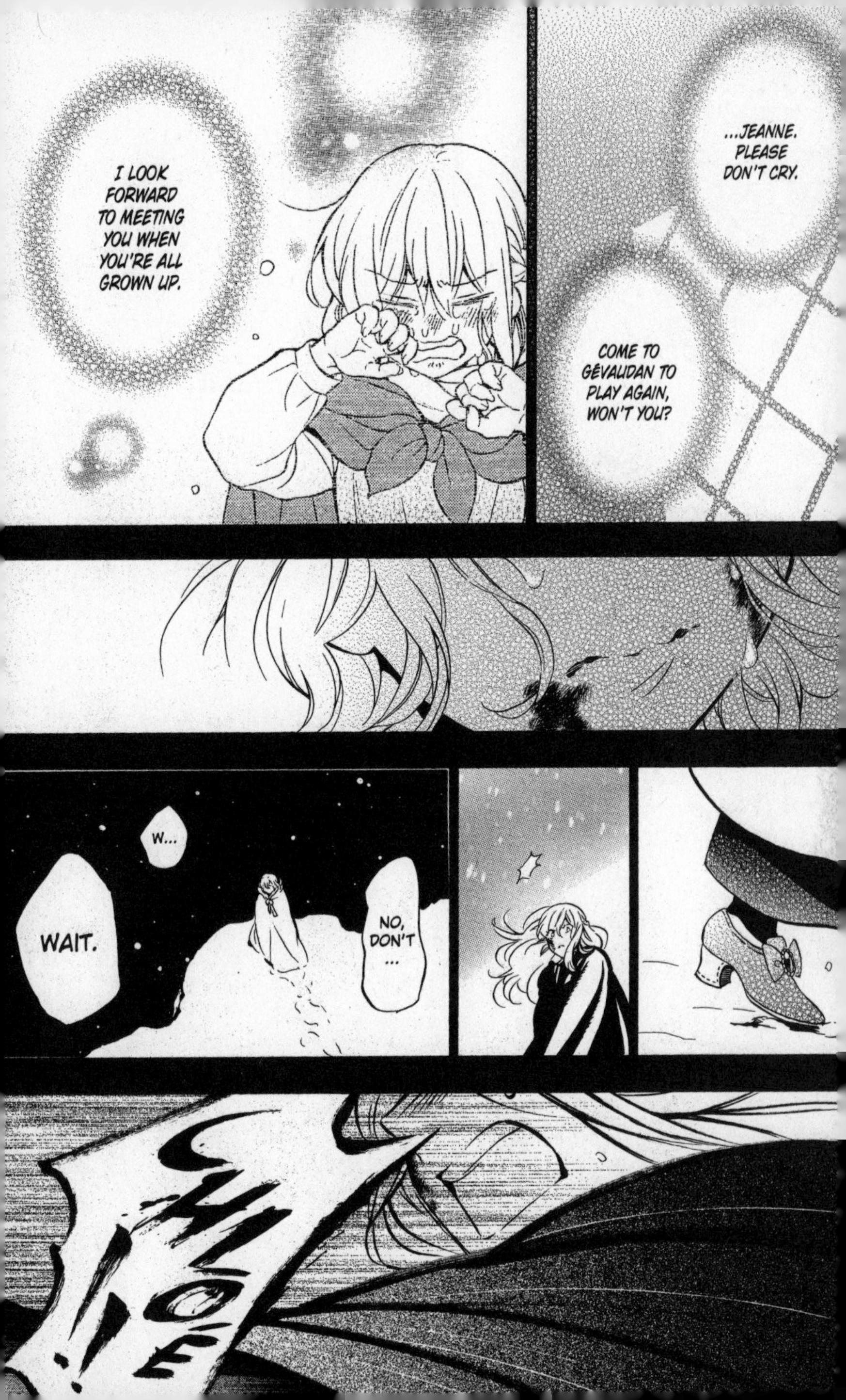
...JEANNE. PLEASE DON'T CRY.
COME TO GÉVAUDAN TO PLAY AGAIN, WON'T YOU?
I LOOK FORWARD TO MEETING YOU WHEN YOU'RE ALL GROWN UP.
NO, DON'T ...
W...
WAIT.
CHLOE!!

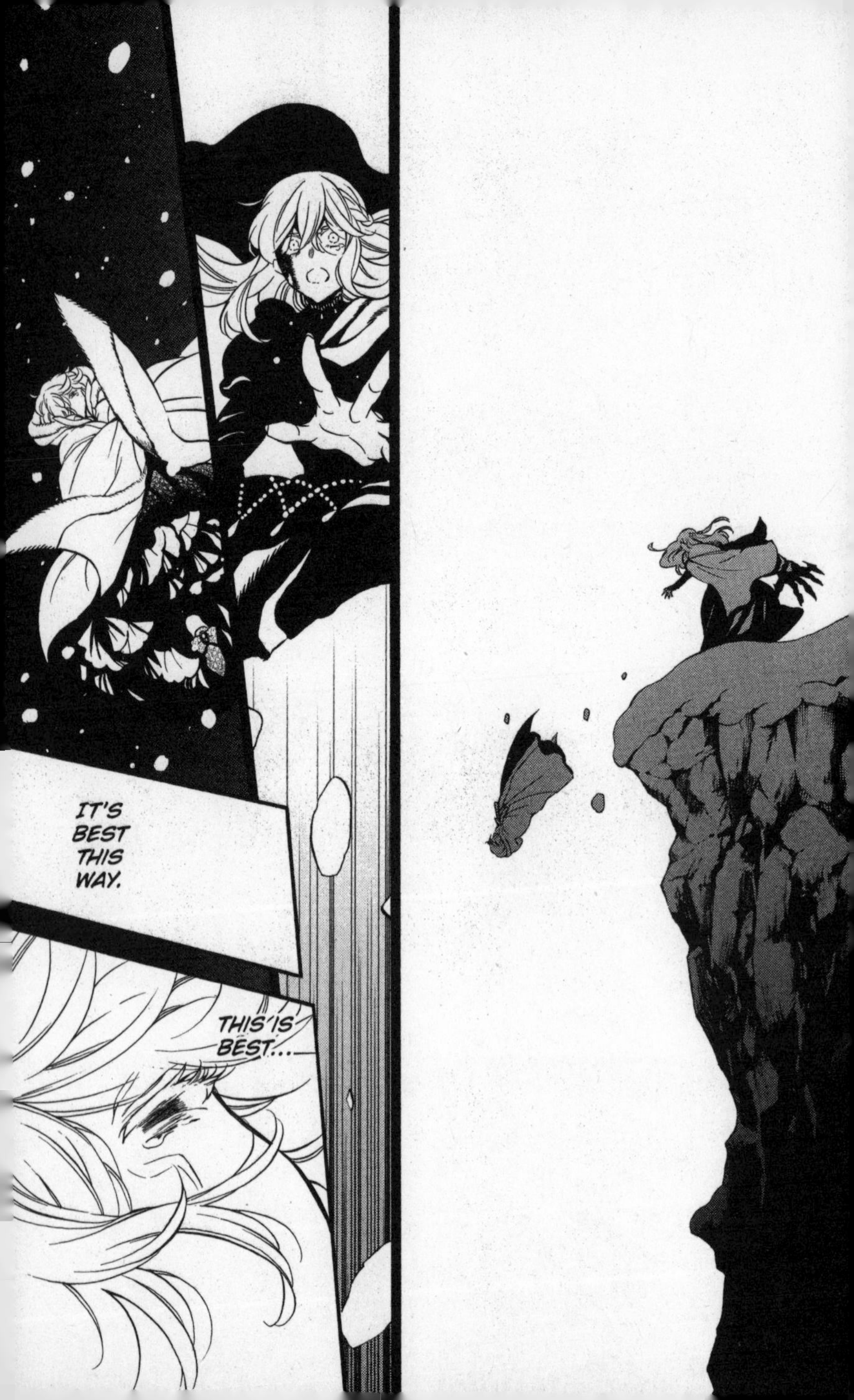
IT'S BEST THIS WAY.
THIS IS BEST....

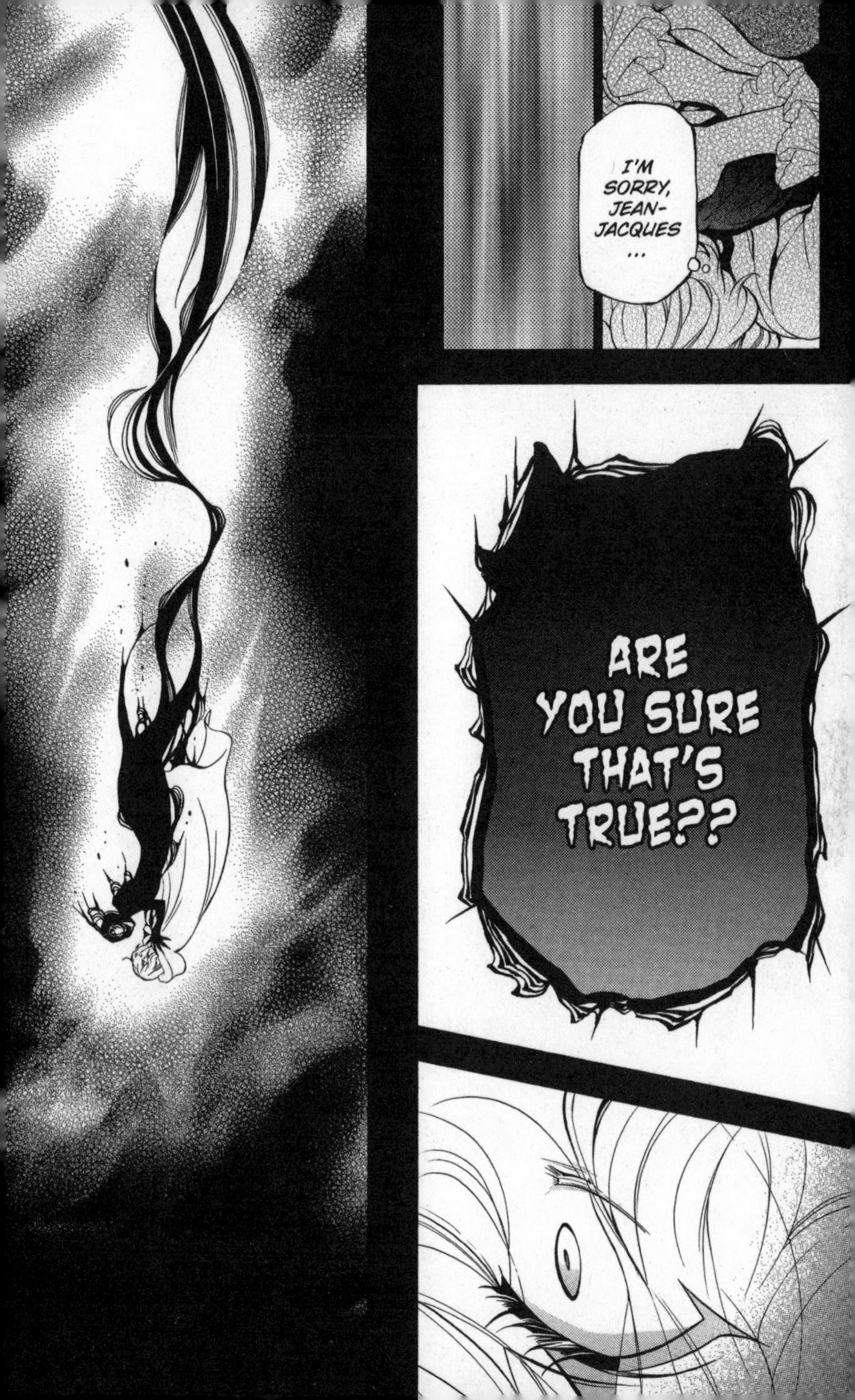
I'M SORRY, JEAN-JACQUES ...
ARE YOU SURE THAT'S TRUE??

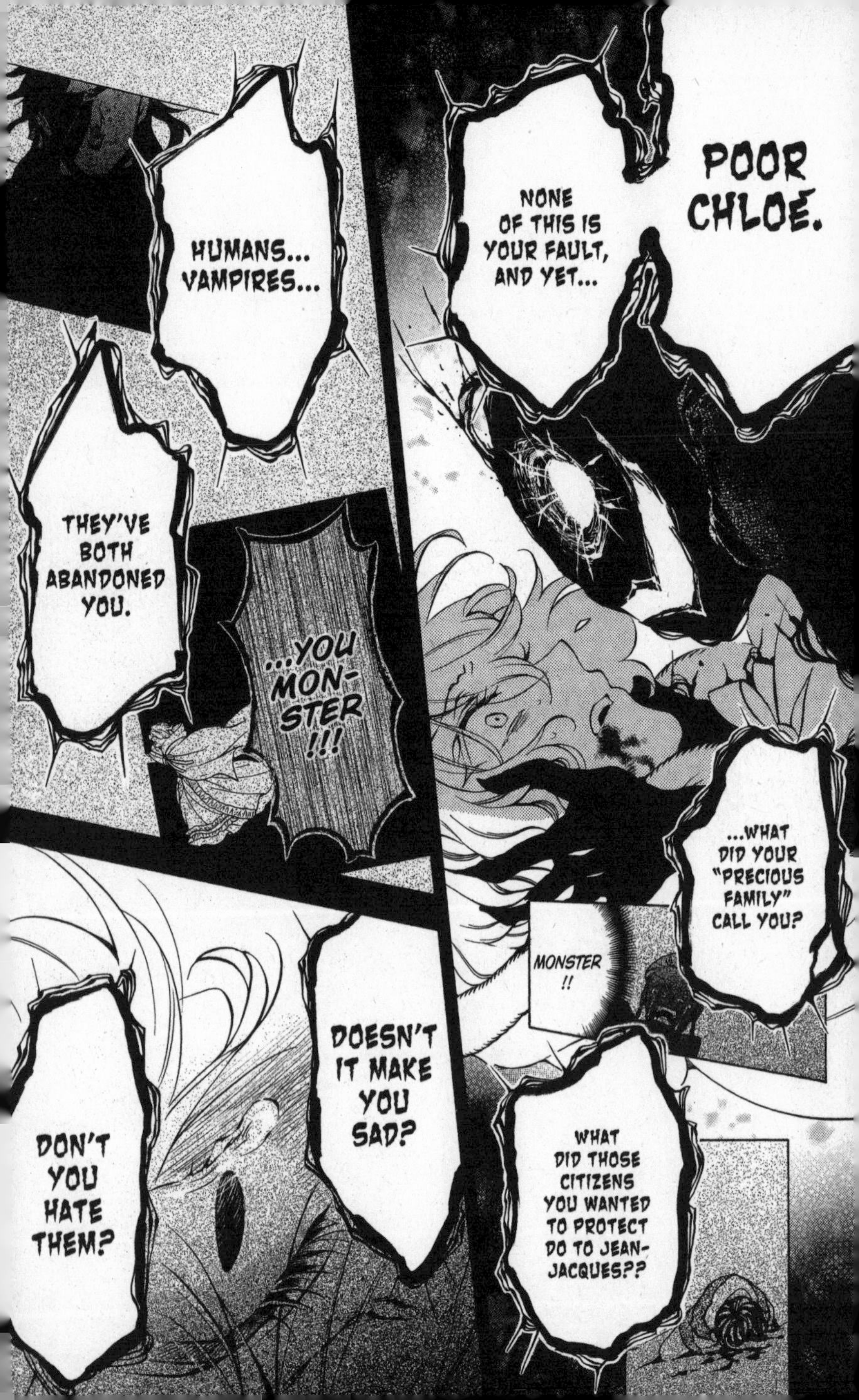
POOR CHLOE.
NONE OF THIS IS YOUR FAULT, AND YET...
...WHAT DID YOUR "PRECIOUS FAMILY" CALL YOU?
MONSTER!!
WHAT DID THOSE CITIZENS YOU WANTED TO PROTECT DO TO JEAN-JACQUES??
HUMANS... VAMPIRES...
THEY'VE BOTH ABANDONED YOU.
...YOU MON-STER!!!
DOESN'T IT MAKE YOU SAD?
DON'T YOU HATE THEM?

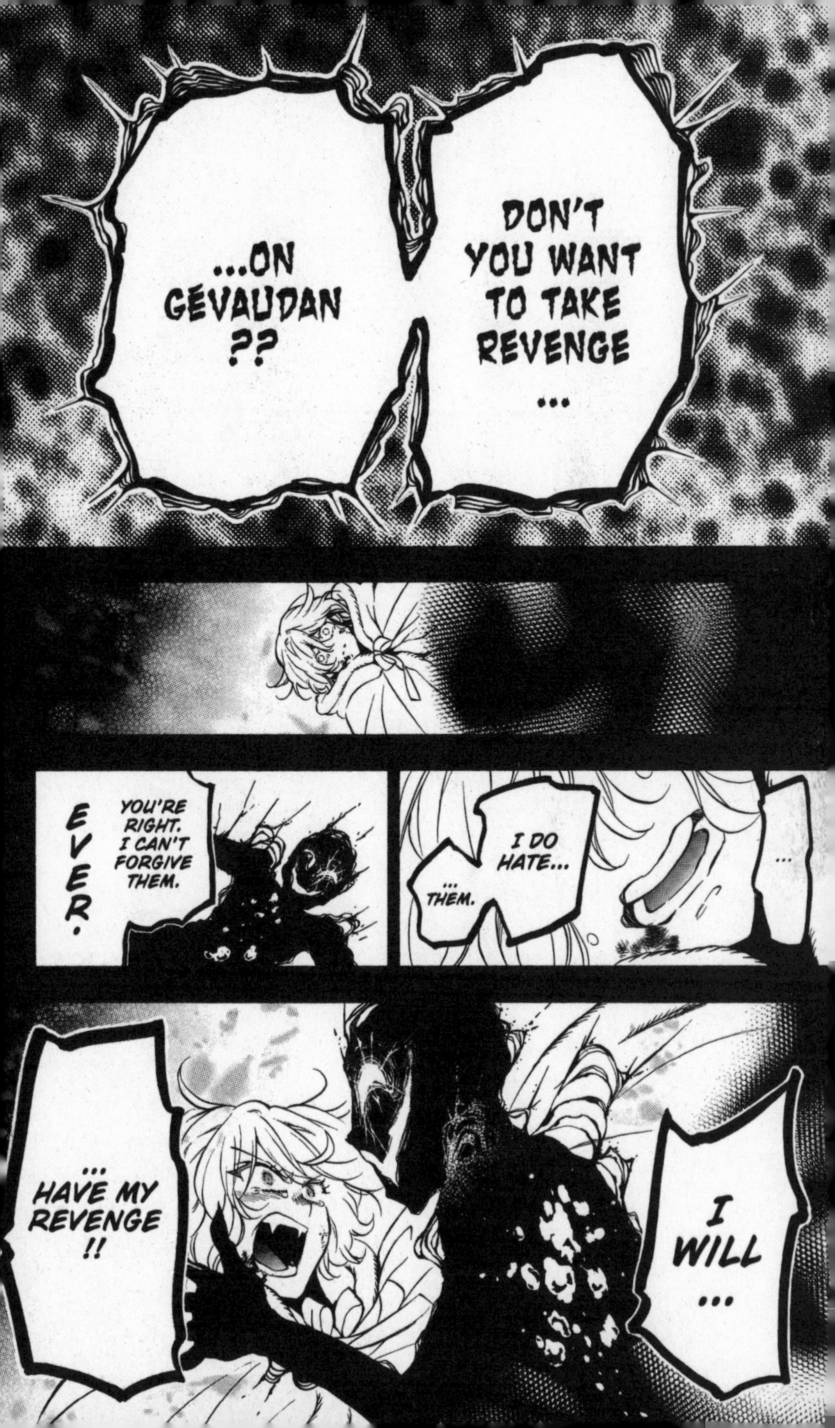
DON'T YOU WANT TO TAKE REVENGE ...
...ON GEVAUDAN ??
...
I DO HATE...
... THEM.
YOU'RE RIGHT. I CAN'T FORGIVE THEM.
EVER.
I WILL ...
... HAVE MY REVENGE !!

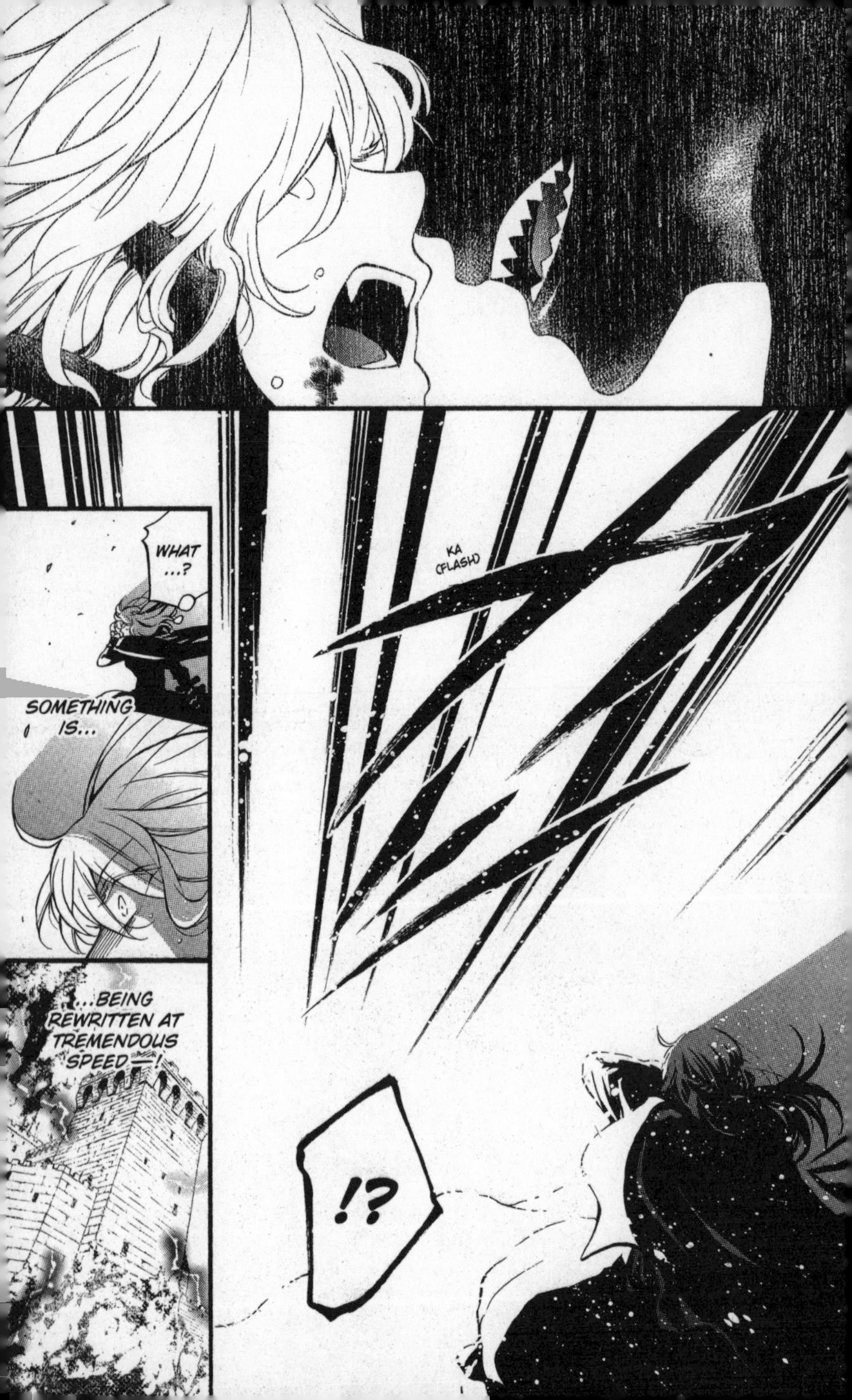
KA (FLASH)
!?
WHAT ...?
SOMETHING IS...
...BEING REWRITTEN AT TREMENDOUS SPEED—!

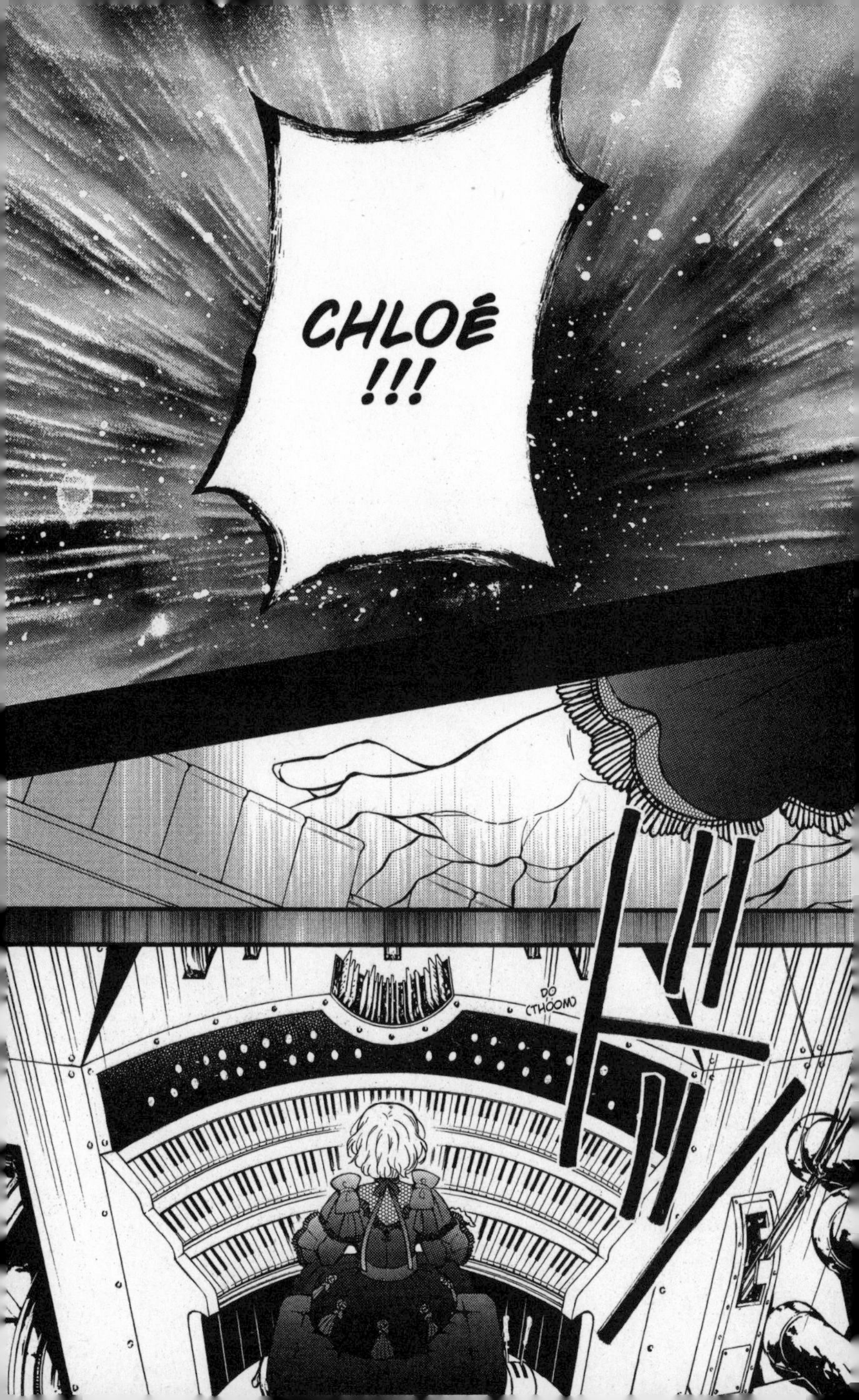
CHLOÉ !!!
DO (THÖOM)

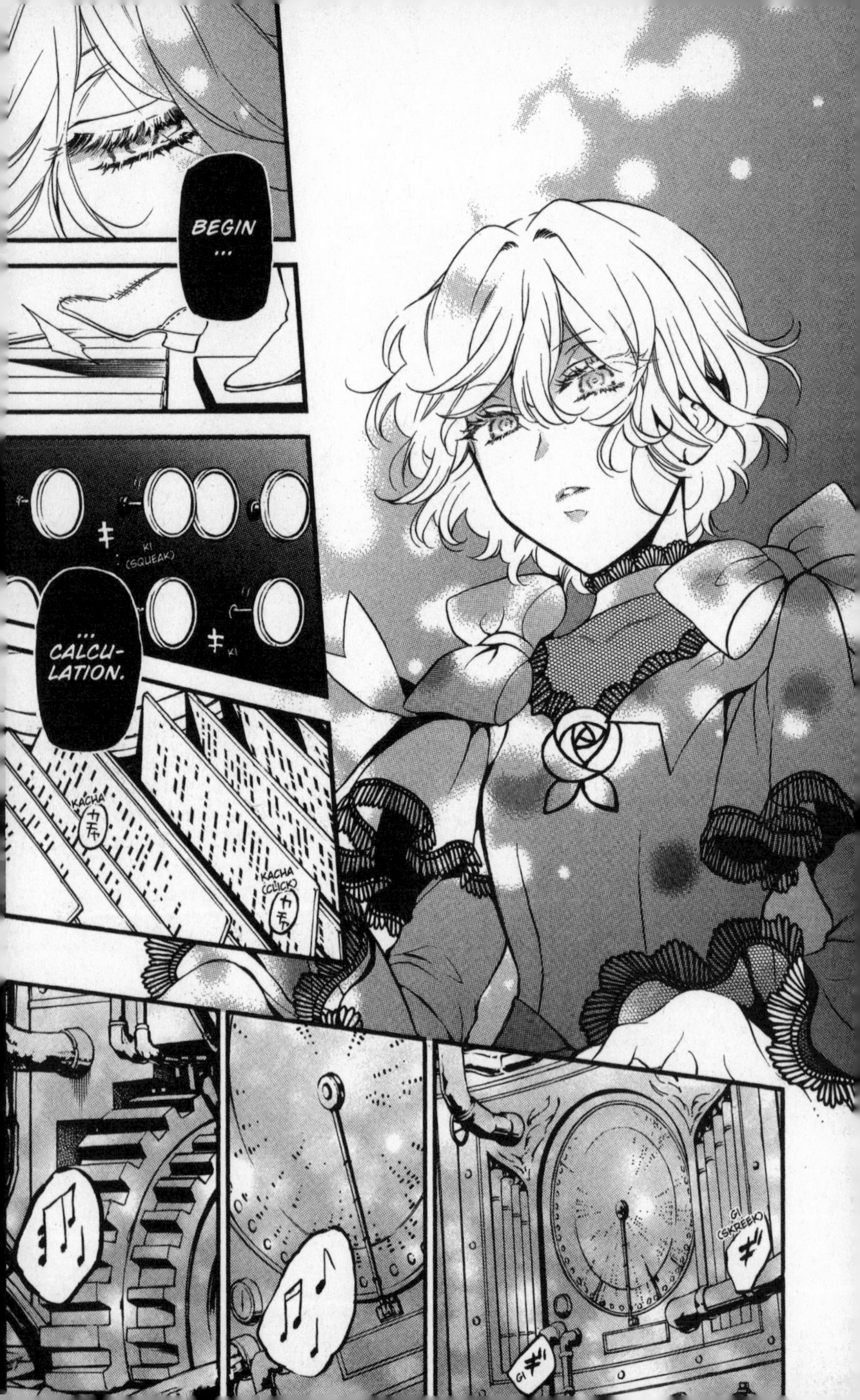
BEGIN ...
KI (SQUEAK)
... CALCULATION.
KI
KACHA
KACHA (CLICK)
GI (SKREEK)
GI

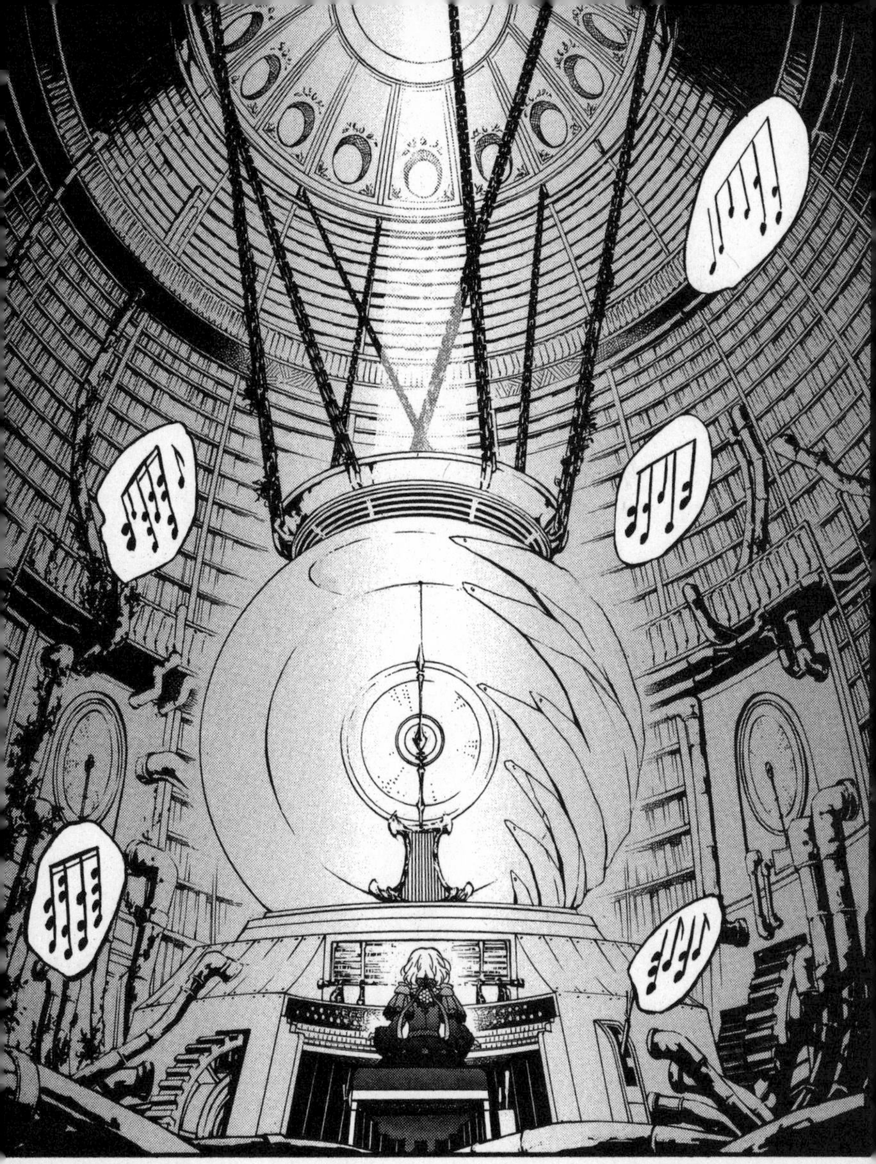

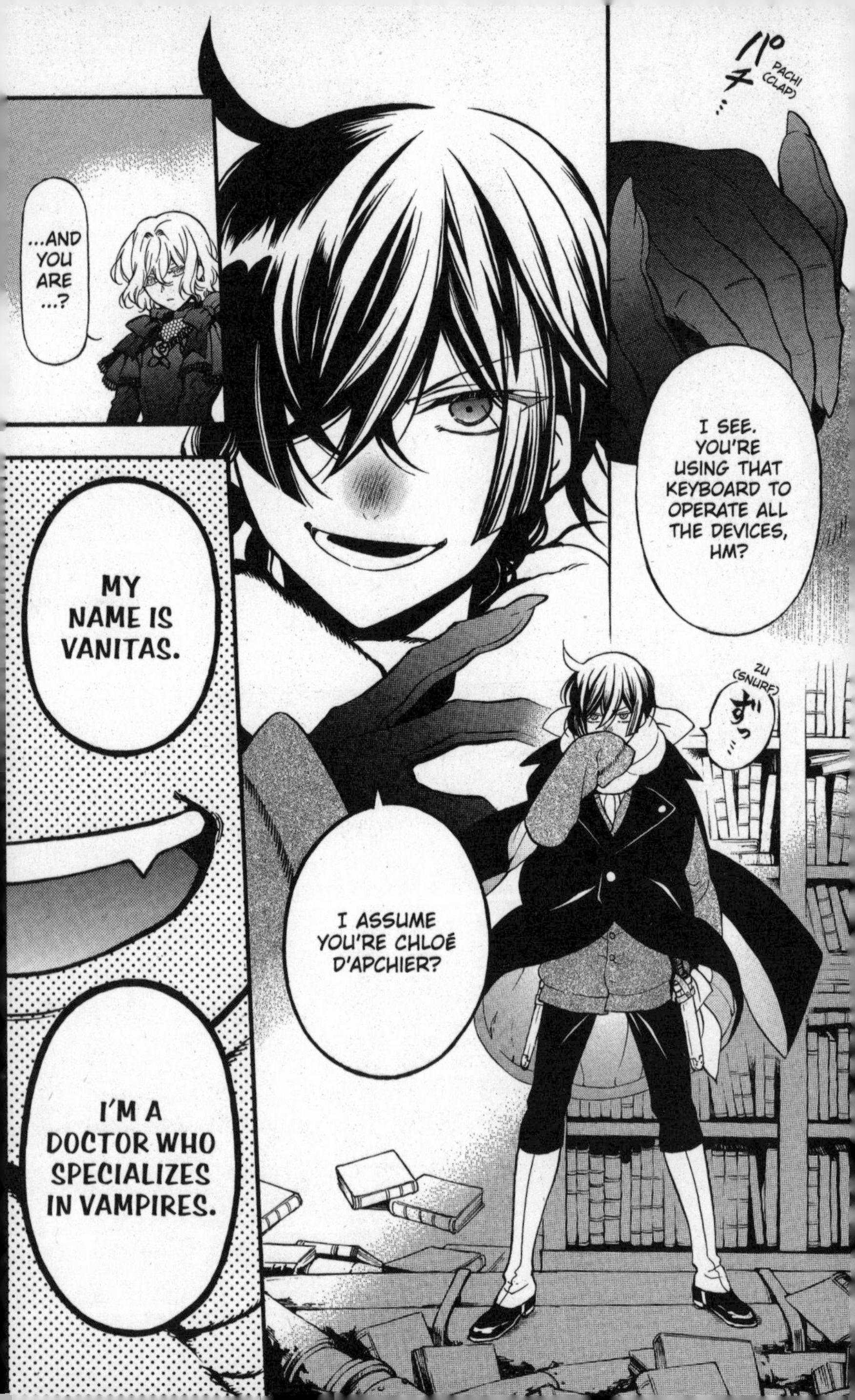

パチ…
PACHI (CLAP)
I SEE. YOU'RE USING THAT KEYBOARD TO OPERATE ALL THE DEVICES, HM?
ずっ…
ZU (SNURF)
I ASSUME YOU'RE CHLOÉ D'APCHIER?
...AND YOU ARE ...?
MY NAME IS VANITAS.
I'M A DOCTOR WHO SPECIALIZES IN VAMPIRES.

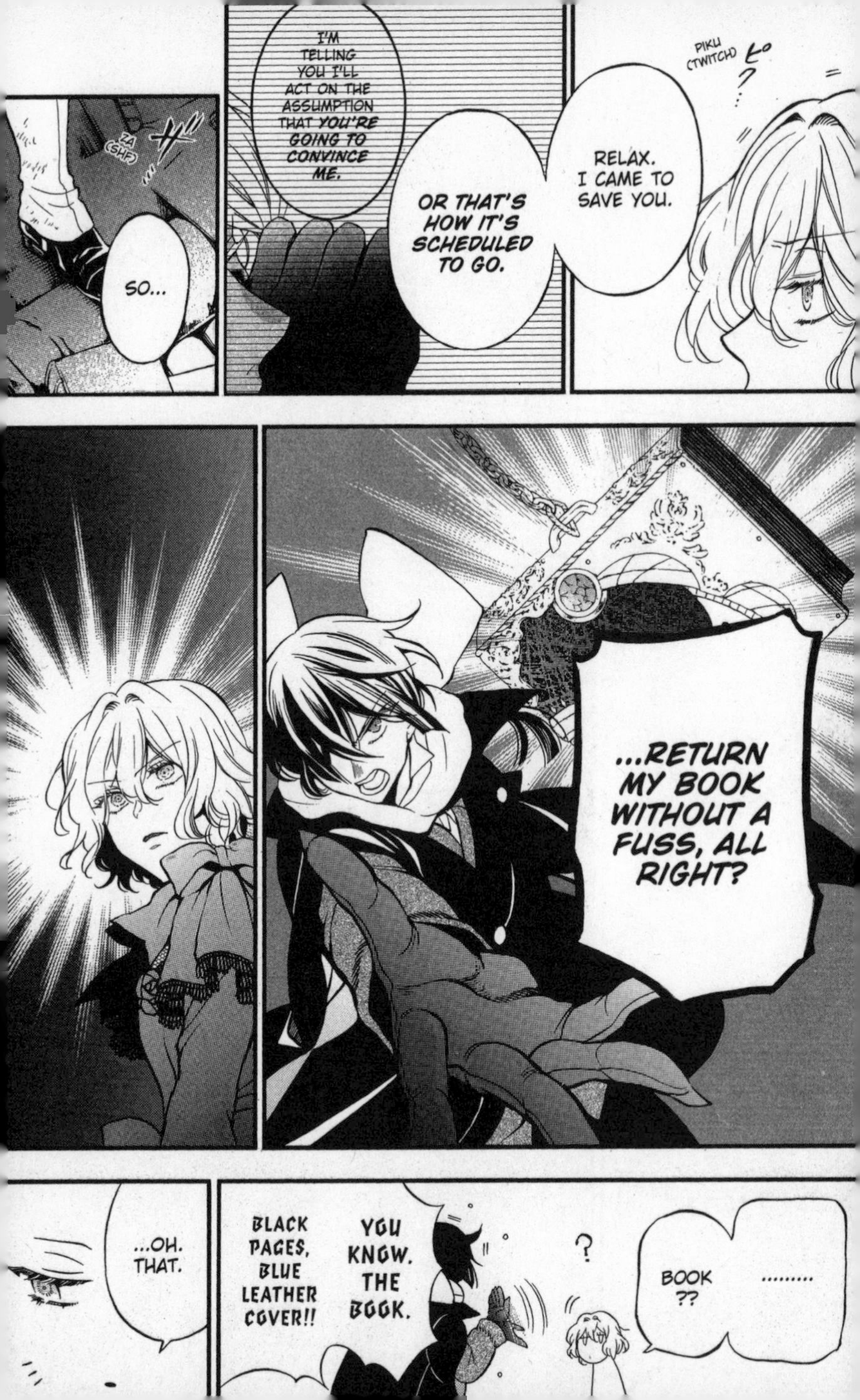
PIKU (TWITCH)
RELAX. I CAME TO SAVE YOU.
OR THAT'S HOW IT'S SCHEDULED TO GO.
I'M TELLING YOU I'LL ACT ON THE ASSUMPTION THAT YOU'RE GOING TO CONVINCE ME.
ZA (SHF)
SO...
...RETURN MY BOOK WITHOUT A FUSS, ALL RIGHT?
....
BOOK ??
?
YOU KNOW. THE BOOK.
BLACK PAGES, BLUE LEATHER COVER!!
...OH. THAT.

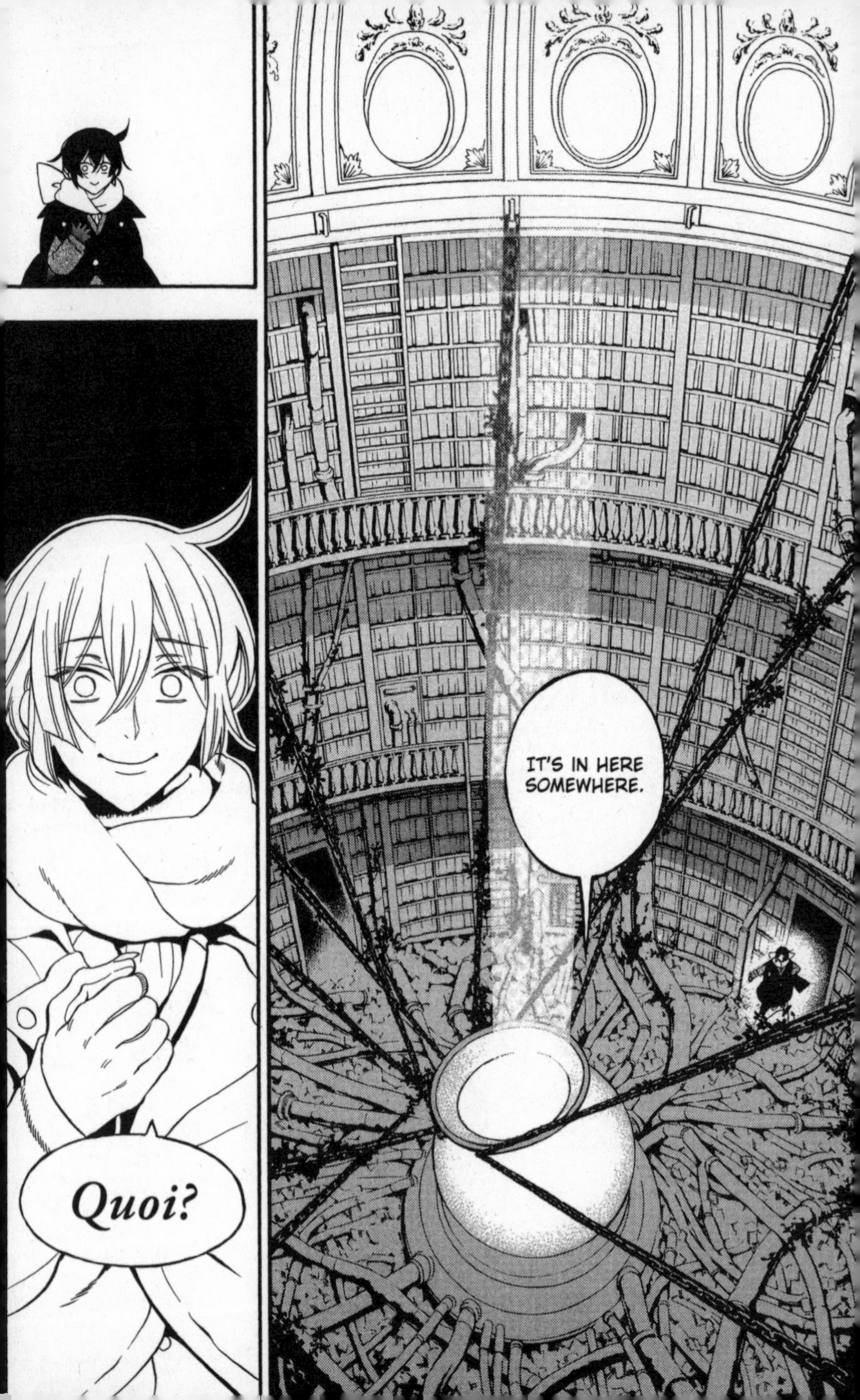
IT'S IN HERE SOMEWHERE.
Quoi?

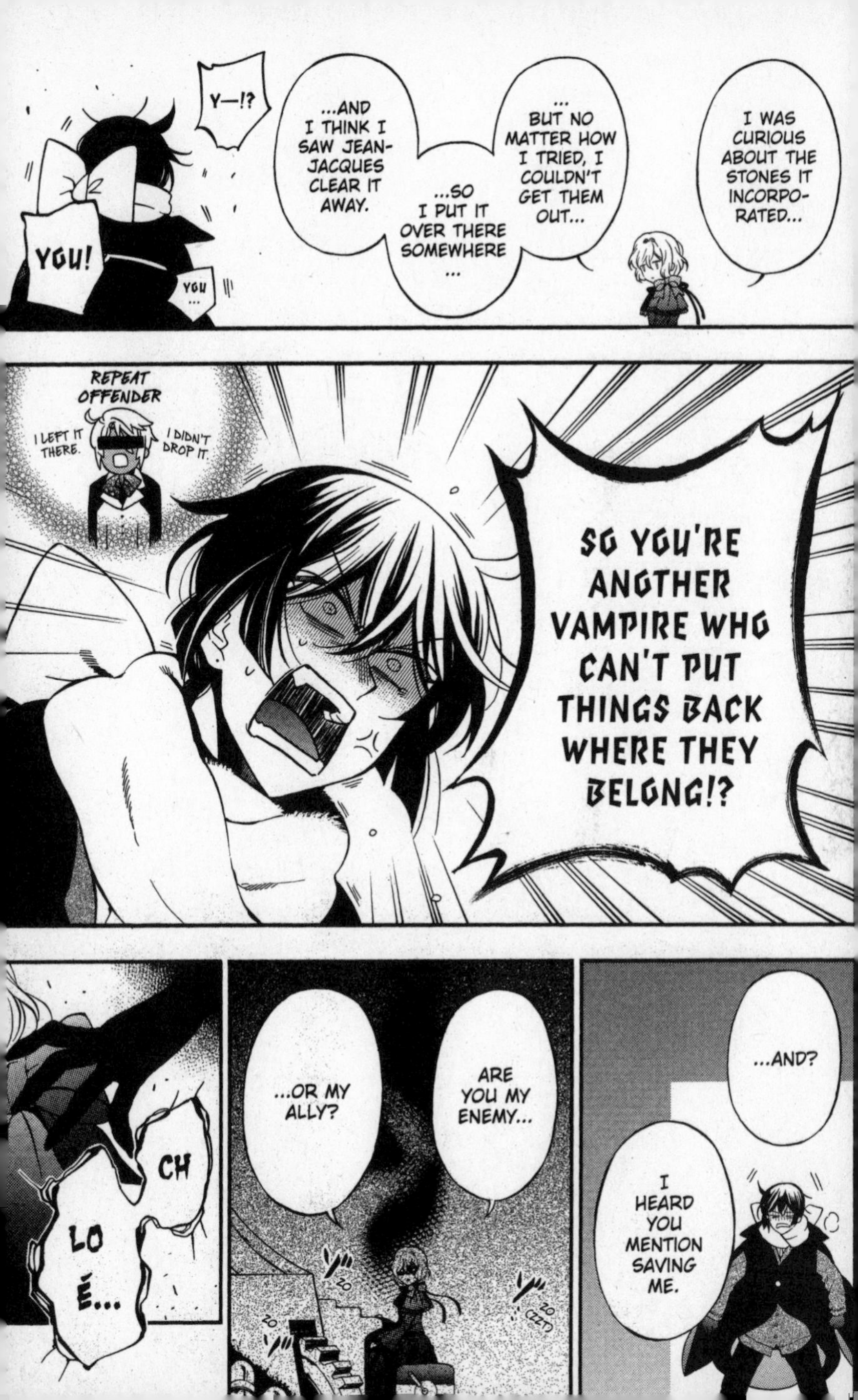
I WAS CURIOUS ABOUT THE STONES IT INCORPORATED...
...BUT NO MATTER HOW I TRIED, I COULDN'T GET THEM OUT...
...SO I PUT IT OVER THERE SOMEWHERE...
...AND I THINK I SAW JEAN-JACQUES CLEAR IT AWAY.
Y—!?
YOU!
YOU...
SO YOU'RE ANOTHER VAMPIRE WHO CAN'T PUT THINGS BACK WHERE THEY BELONG!?
REPEAT OFFENDER
I DIDN'T DROP IT.
I LEFT IT THERE.
...AND?
I HEARD YOU MENTION SAVING ME.
ARE YOU MY ENEMY...
...OR MY ALLY?
ZO
ZO (ZZT)
ZO
CH
LO
É...

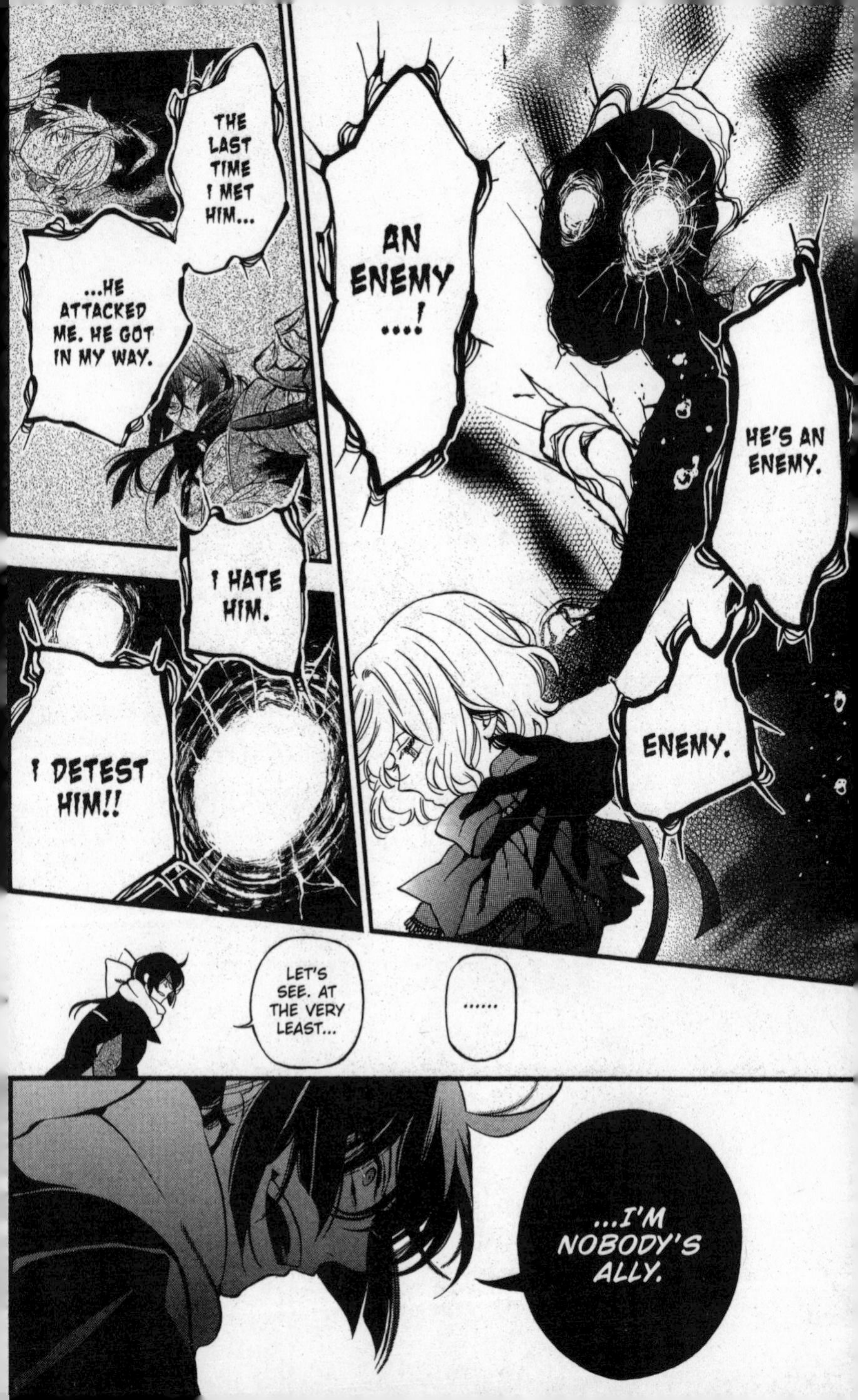
THE LAST TIME I MET HIM...
...HE ATTACKED ME. HE GOT IN MY WAY.
I HATE HIM.
I DETEST HIM!!
AN ENEMY ...!
HE'S AN ENEMY.
ENEMY.
......
LET'S SEE. AT THE VERY LEAST...
...I'M NOBODY'S ALLY.

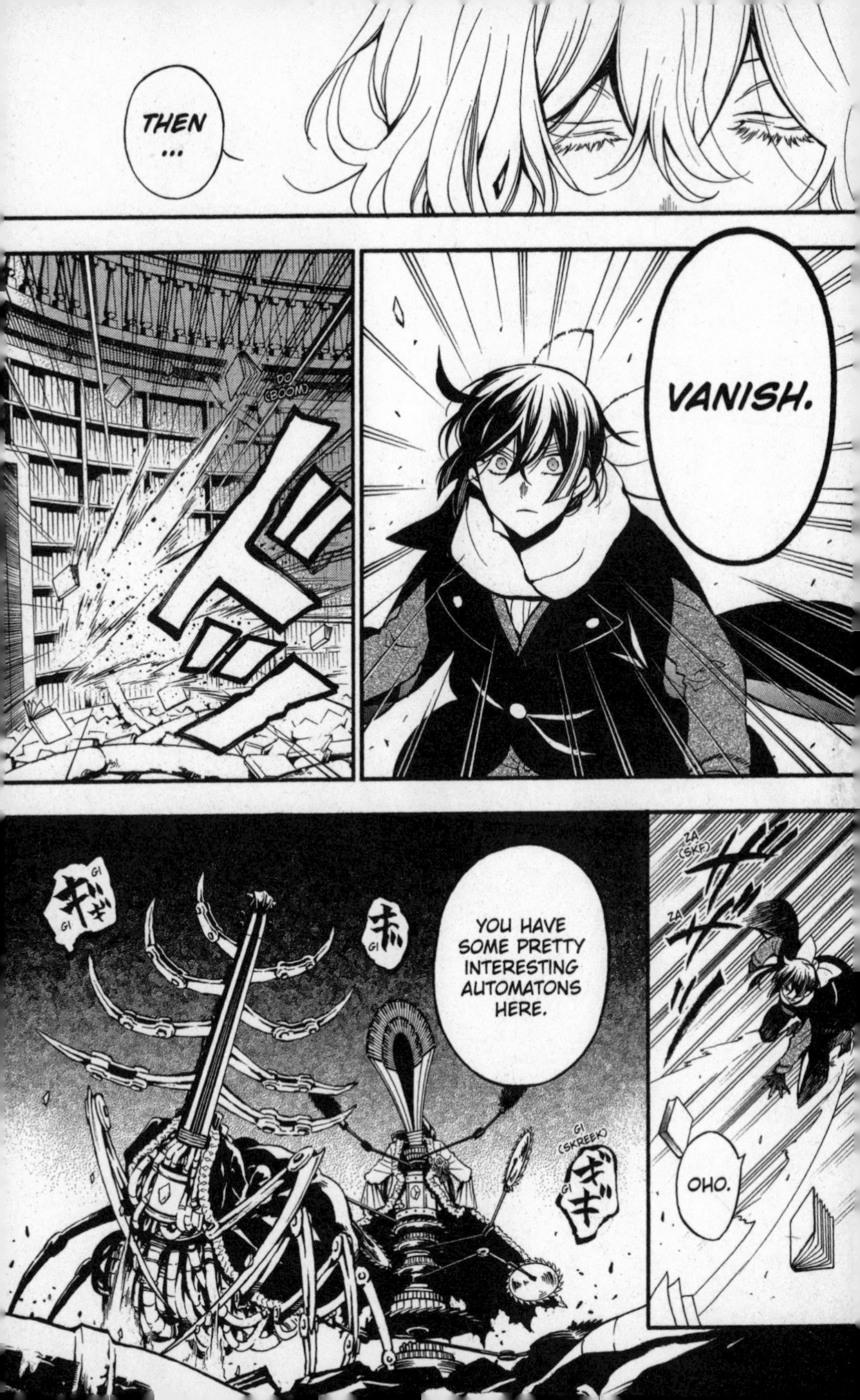
THEN ...
VANISH.
DO (BOOM)
ZA (SKF)
ZA
OHO.
YOU HAVE SOME PRETTY INTERESTING AUTOMATONS HERE.
GI
GI GI
GI (SKREEK) GI

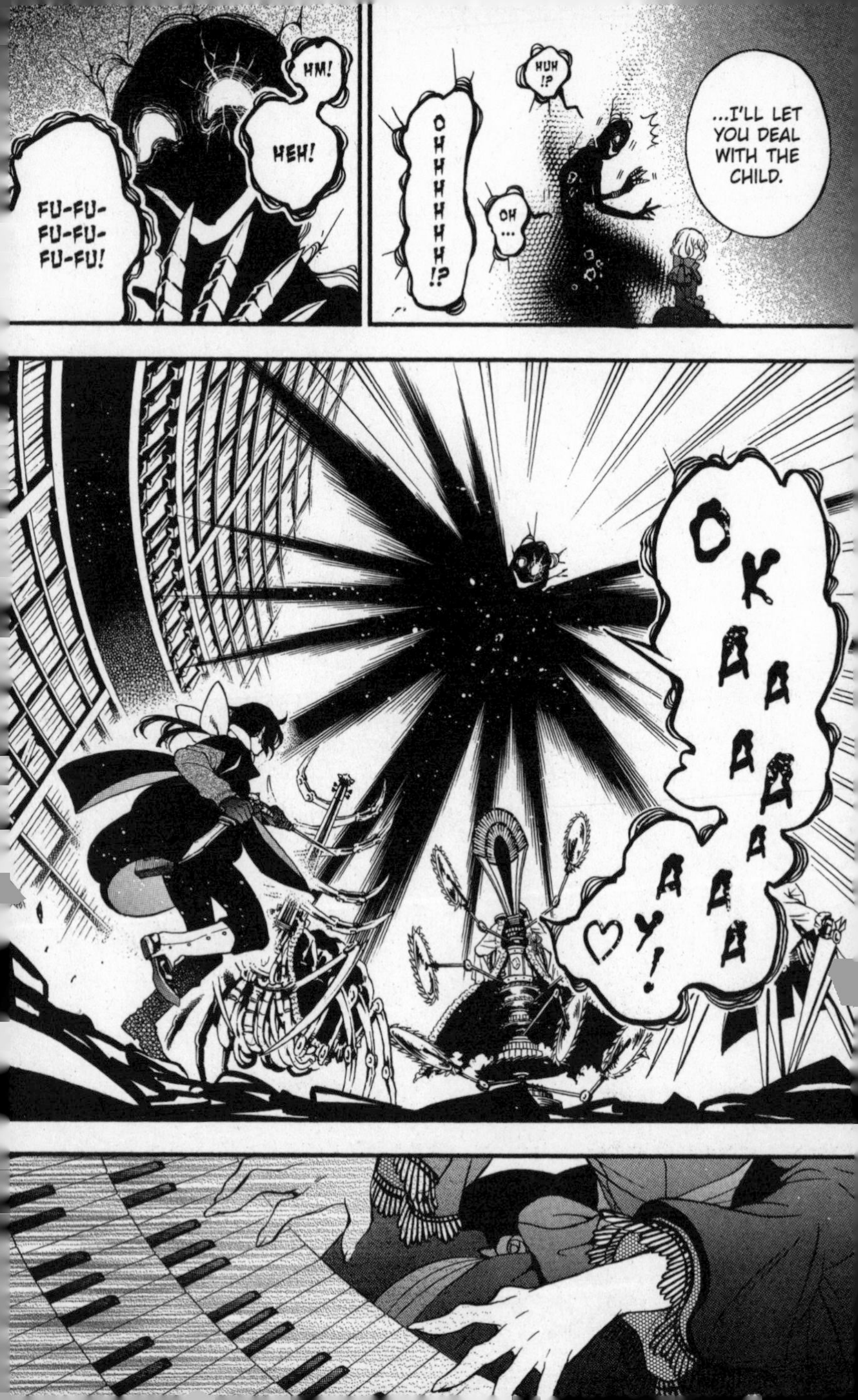
...I'LL LET YOU DEAL WITH THE CHILD.
HUH!?
OH...
OHHHHHHH!?
HM!
HEH!
FU-FU-FU-FU-FU-FU!
OKAAAAAAAAY!♡

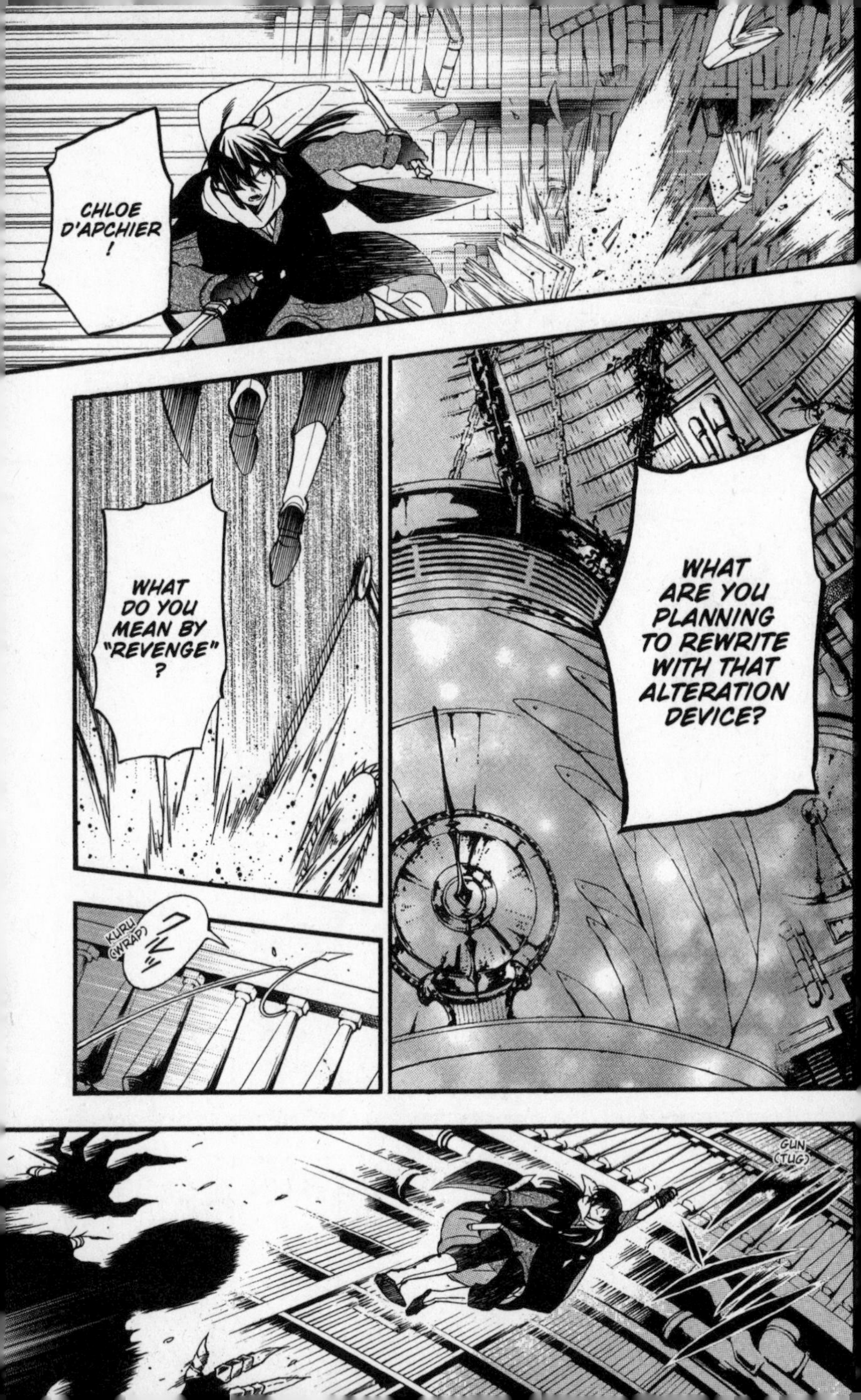
CHLOE D'APCHIER!
WHAT ARE YOU PLANNING TO REWRITE WITH THAT ALTERATION DEVICE?
WHAT DO YOU MEAN BY "REVENGE"?
KURU (WRAP)
GUN (TUG)

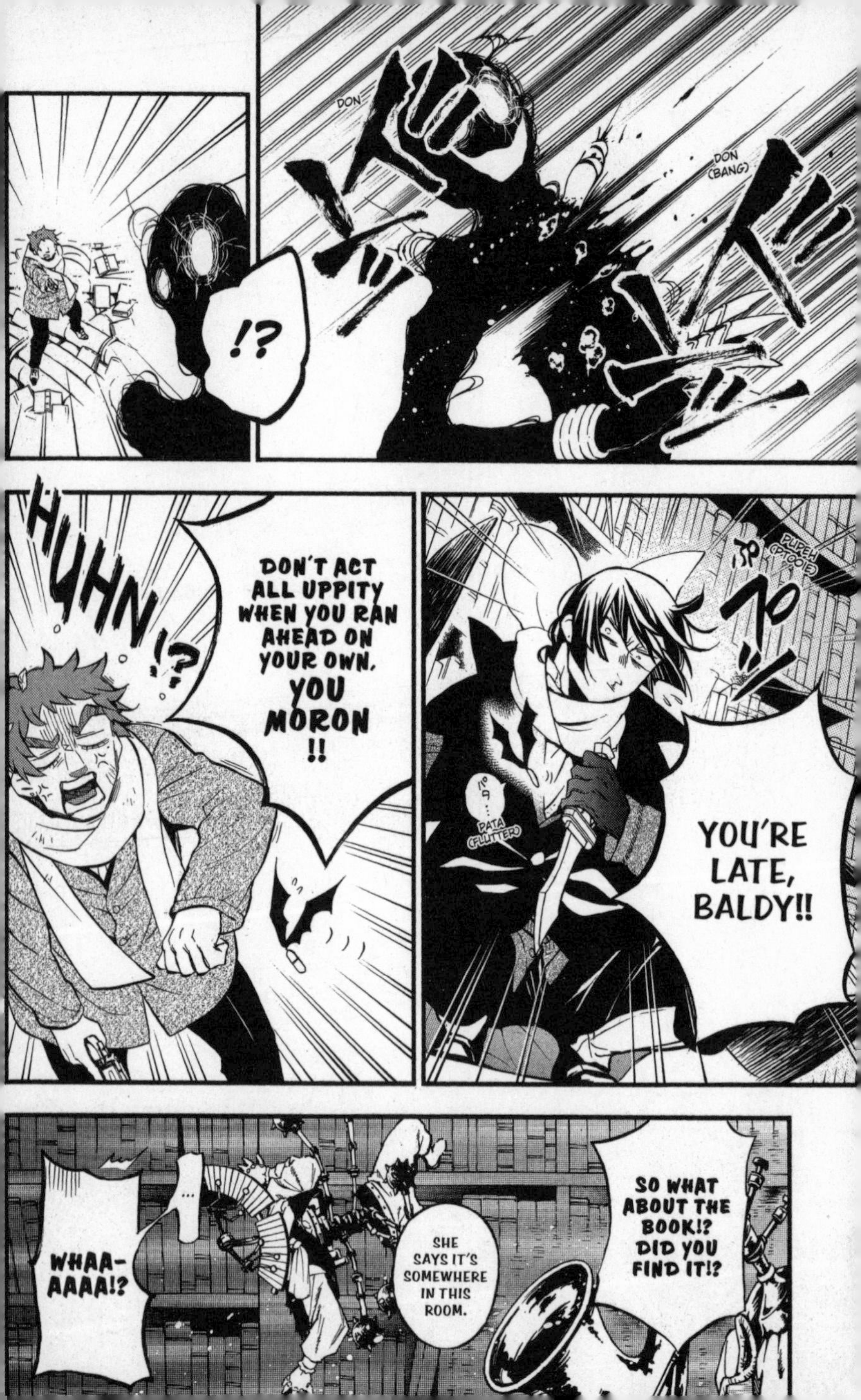
DON
DON (BANG)
!?
PUPEH (PTOOIE)
PATA (FLUTTER)
YOU'RE LATE, BALDY!!
HUHN!?
DON'T ACT ALL UPPITY WHEN YOU RAN AHEAD ON YOUR OWN, YOU MORON!!
SO WHAT ABOUT THE BOOK!? DID YOU FIND IT!?
SHE SAYS IT'S SOMEWHERE IN THIS ROOM.
...
WHAA-AAAA!?

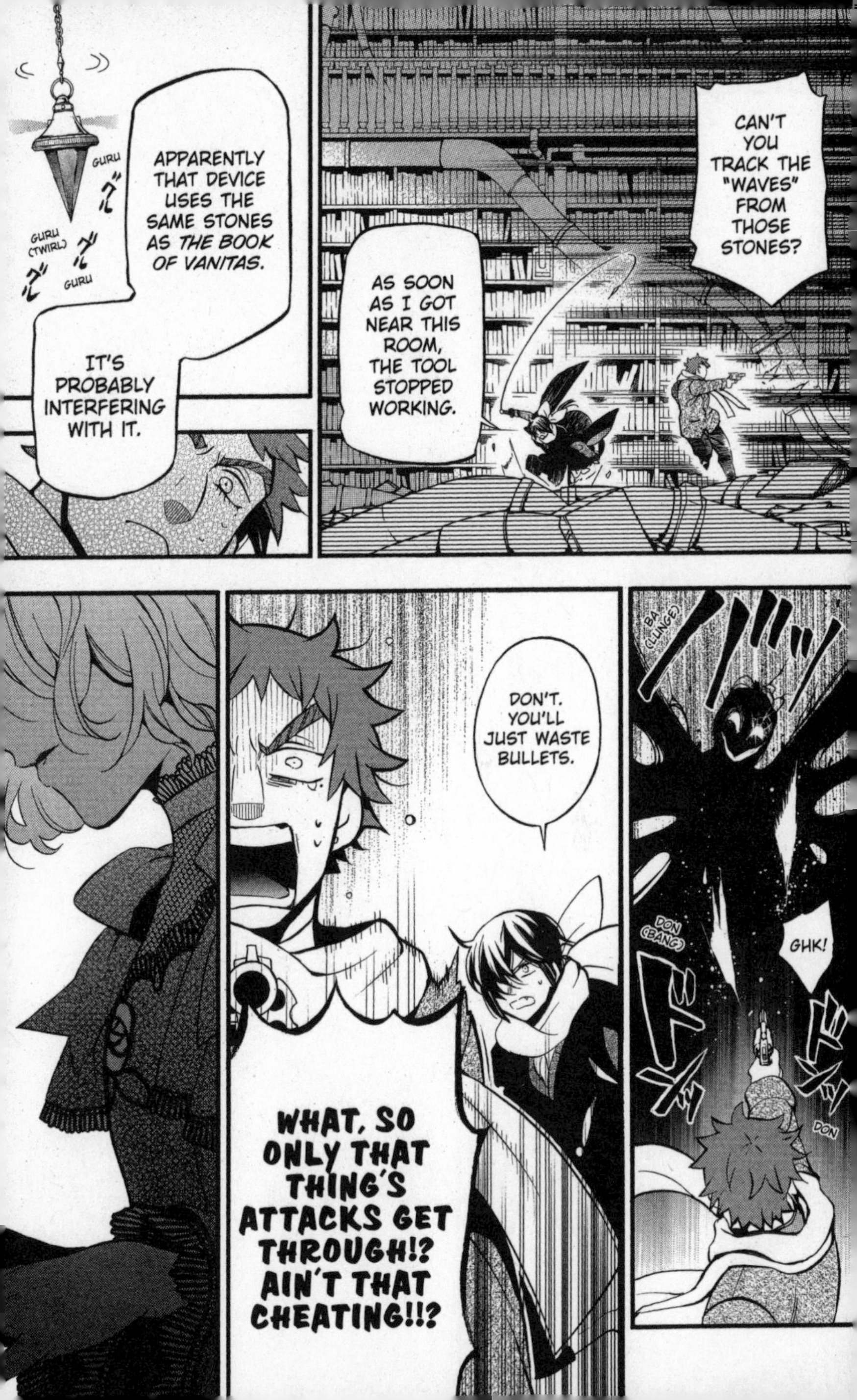
CAN'T YOU TRACK THE "WAVES" FROM THOSE STONES?
AS SOON AS I GOT NEAR THIS ROOM, THE TOOL STOPPED WORKING.
GURU
GURU (TWIRL)
GURU
APPARENTLY THAT DEVICE USES THE SAME STONES AS *THE BOOK OF VANITAS.*
IT'S PROBABLY INTERFERING WITH IT.
BA (LUNGE)
DON (BANG)
GHK!
DON
DON'T. YOU'LL JUST WASTE BULLETS.
WHAT, SO ONLY THAT THING'S ATTACKS GET THROUGH!? AIN'T THAT CHEATING!!?

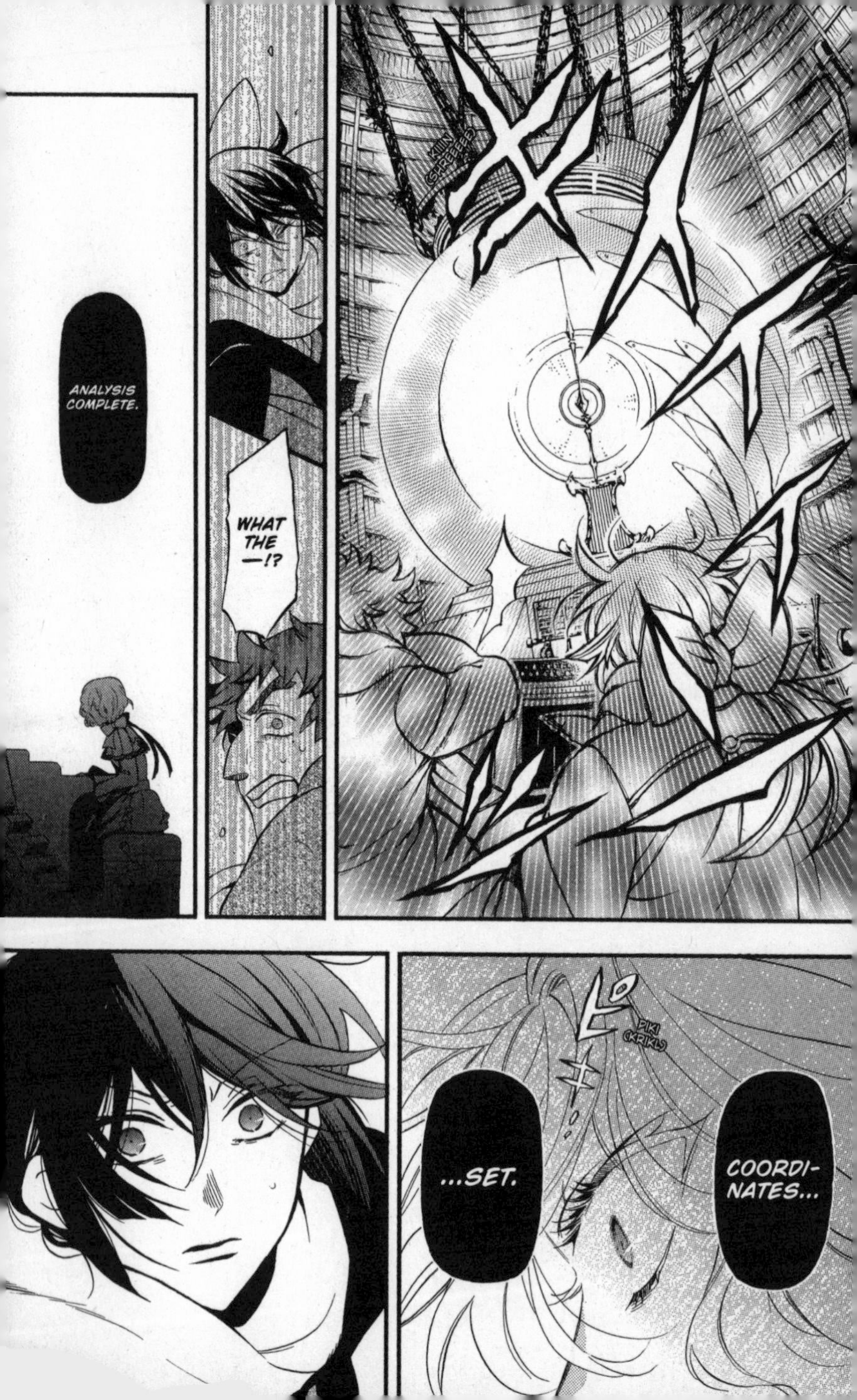
KIIIN (SHREEEEE)
WHAT THE—!?
ANALYSIS COMPLETE.
PIKI (KRIKL)
COORDINATES...
...SET.

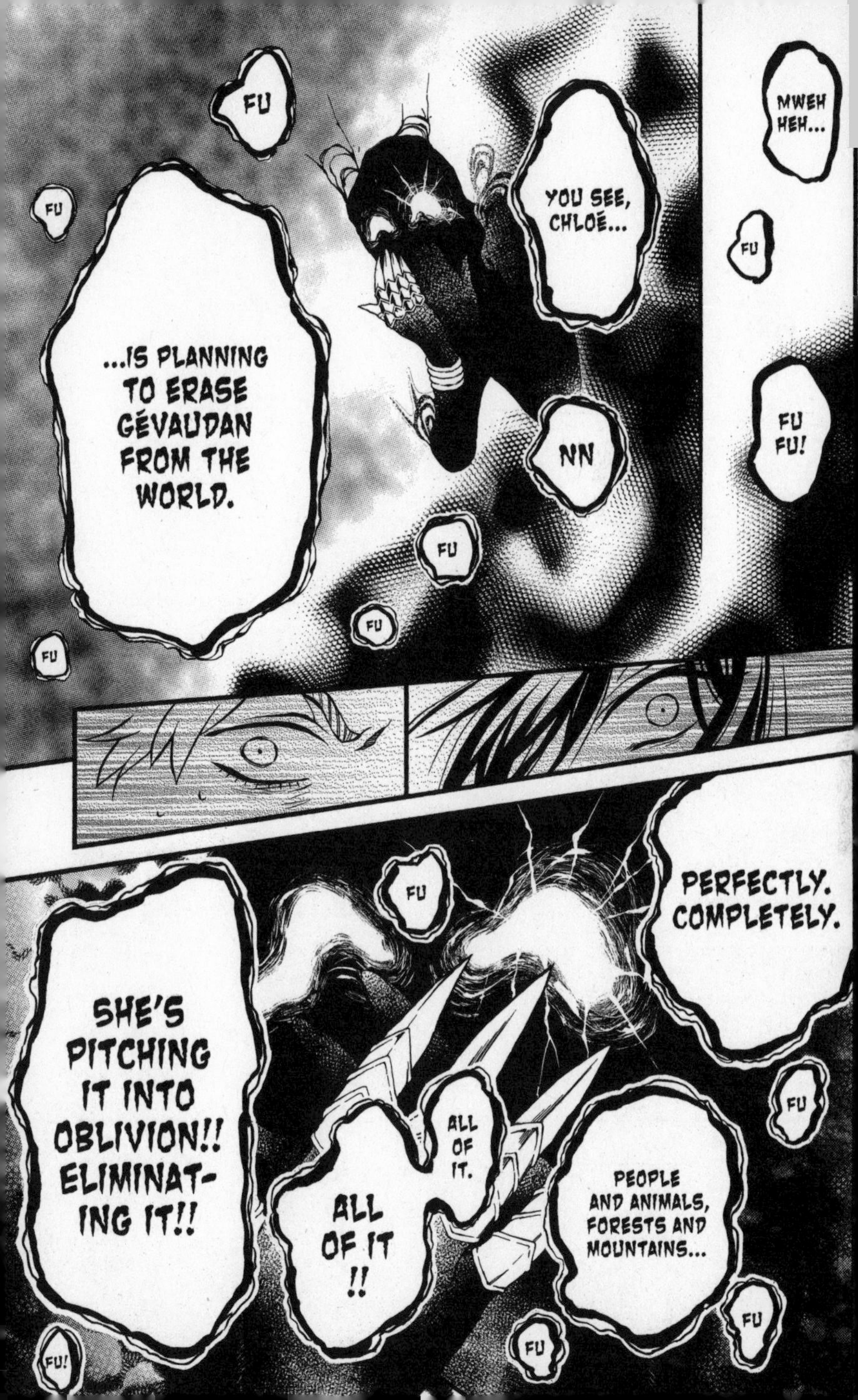
MWEH HEH...
FU
FU FU!
YOU SEE, CHLOÉ...
FU
FU
NN
...IS PLANNING TO ERASE GÉVAUDAN FROM THE WORLD.
FU
FU
FU
PERFECTLY. COMPLETELY.
FU
FU
PEOPLE AND ANIMALS, FORESTS AND MOUNTAINS...
ALL OF IT.
ALL OF IT !!
SHE'S PITCHING IT INTO OBLIVION!! ELIMINAT-ING IT!!
FU
FU
FU!

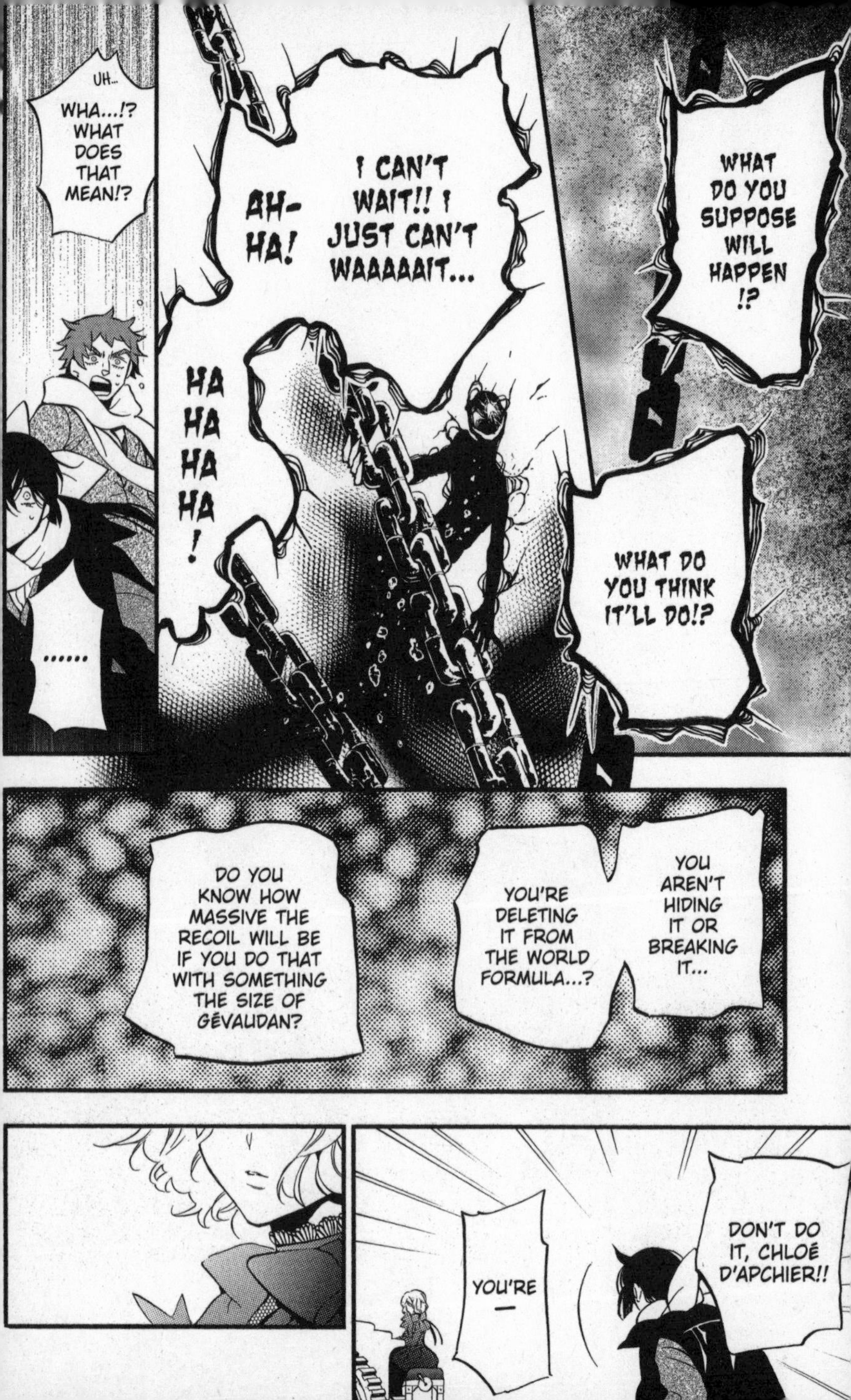
WHAT DO YOU SUPPOSE WILL HAPPEN !?
WHAT DO YOU THINK IT'LL DO!?
I CAN'T WAIT!! I JUST CAN'T WAAAAAIT...
AH-HA!
HA HA HA HA !
UH...
WHA...!? WHAT DOES THAT MEAN!?
......
YOU AREN'T HIDING IT OR BREAKING IT...
YOU'RE DELETING IT FROM THE WORLD FORMULA...?
DO YOU KNOW HOW MASSIVE THE RECOIL WILL BE IF YOU DO THAT WITH SOMETHING THE SIZE OF GÉVAUDAN?
DON'T DO IT, CHLOÉ D'APCHIER!!
YOU'RE —

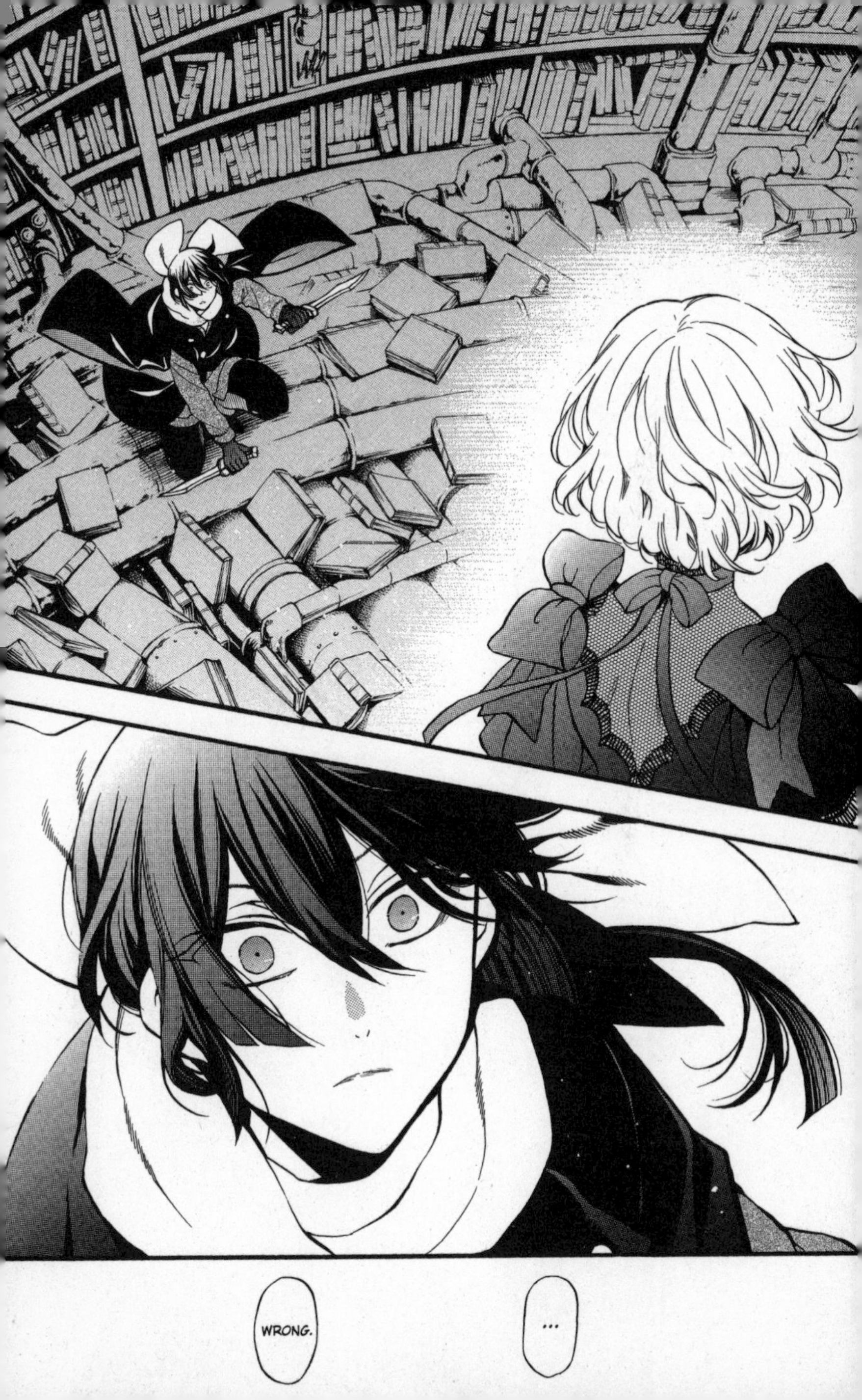
...
WRONG.

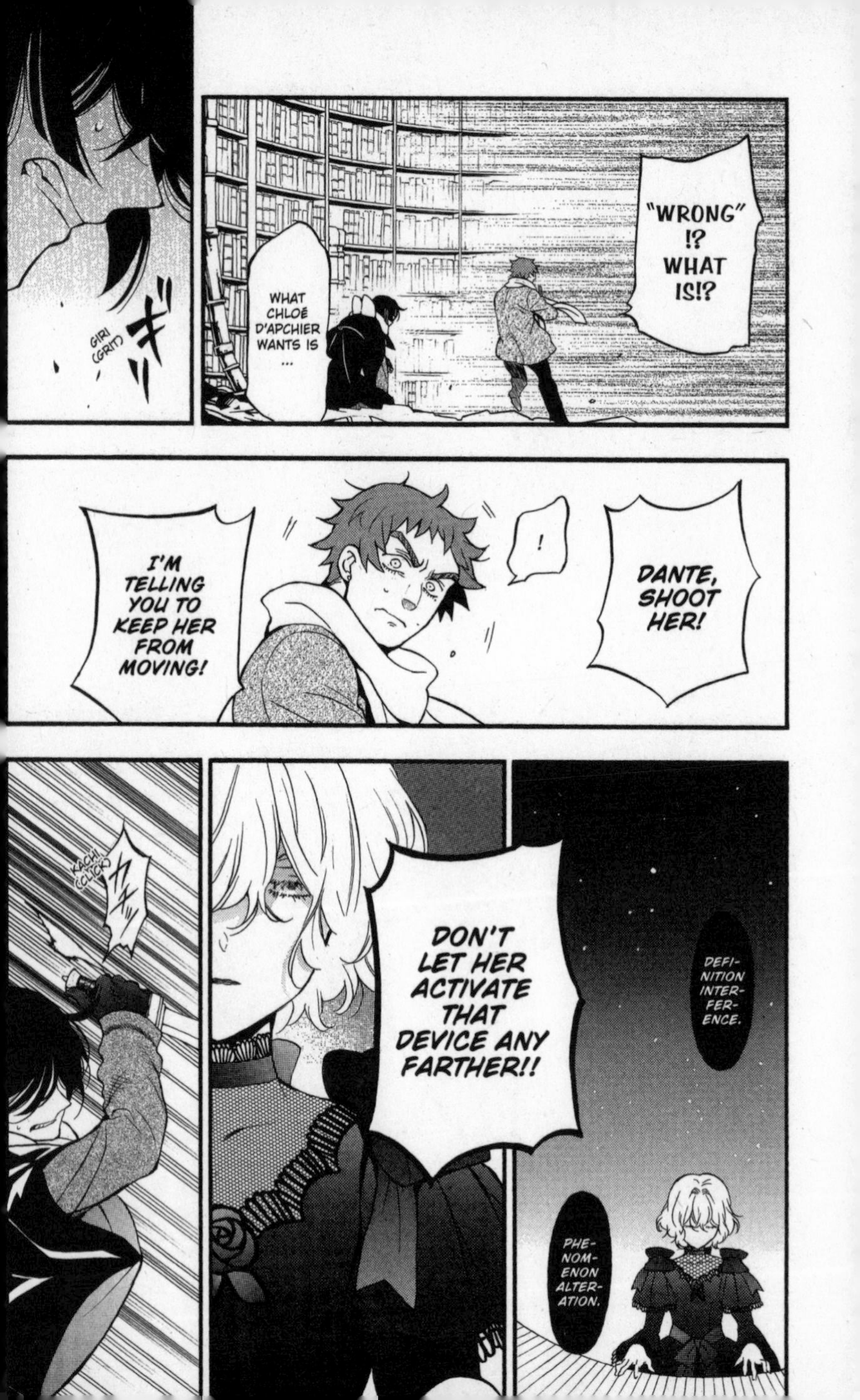
"WRONG" !? WHAT IS!?
WHAT CHLOÉ D'APCHIER WANTS IS ...
ギリ
GIRI (GRIT)
DANTE, SHOOT HER!
!
I'M TELLING YOU TO KEEP HER FROM MOVING!
DEFI-NITION INTER-FER-ENCE.
PHE-NOM-ENON ALTER-ATION.
DON'T LET HER ACTIVATE THAT DEVICE ANY FARTHER!!
カチッ
KACHI (CLICK)

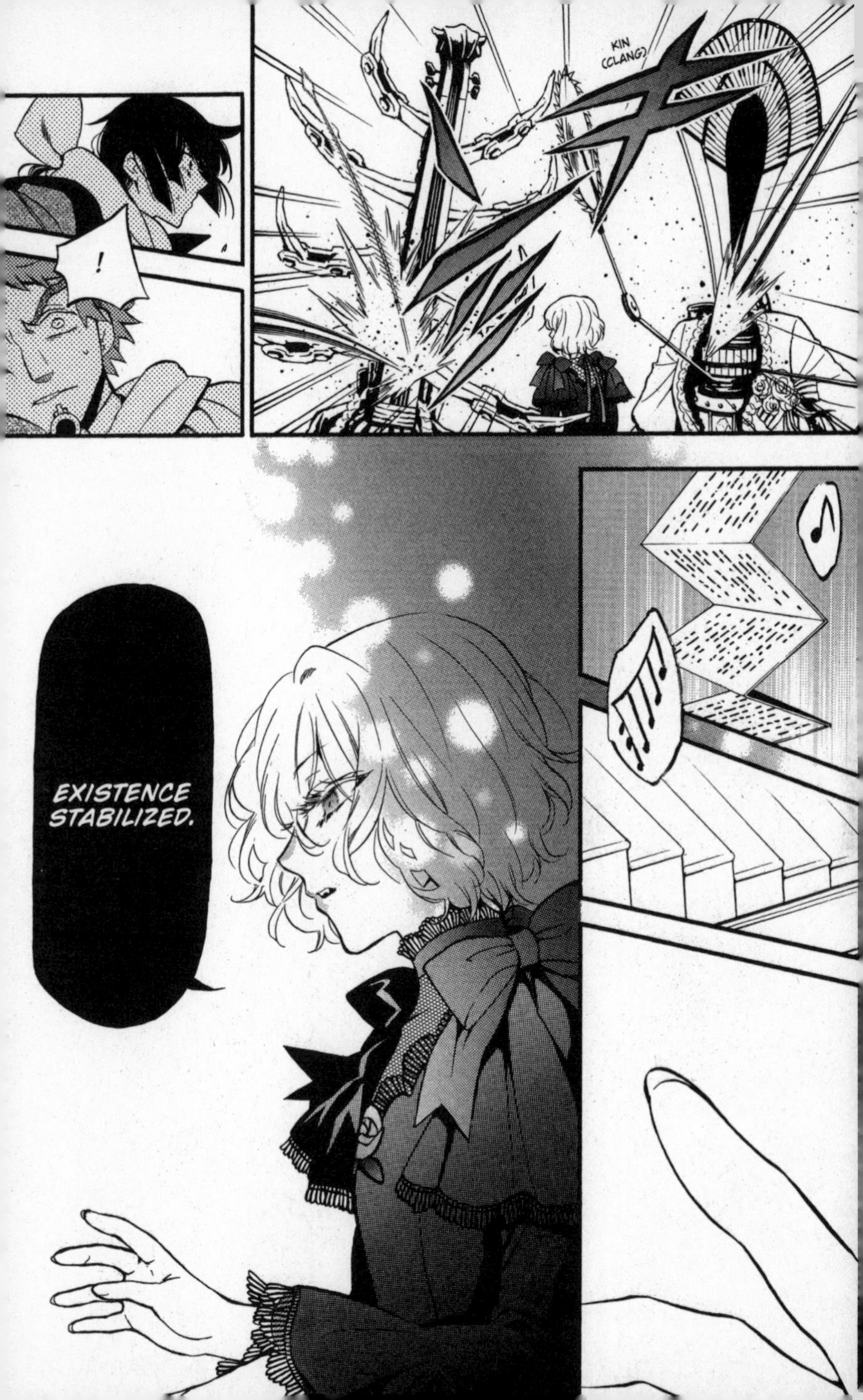
KIN (CLANG)
!
EXISTENCE STABILIZED.

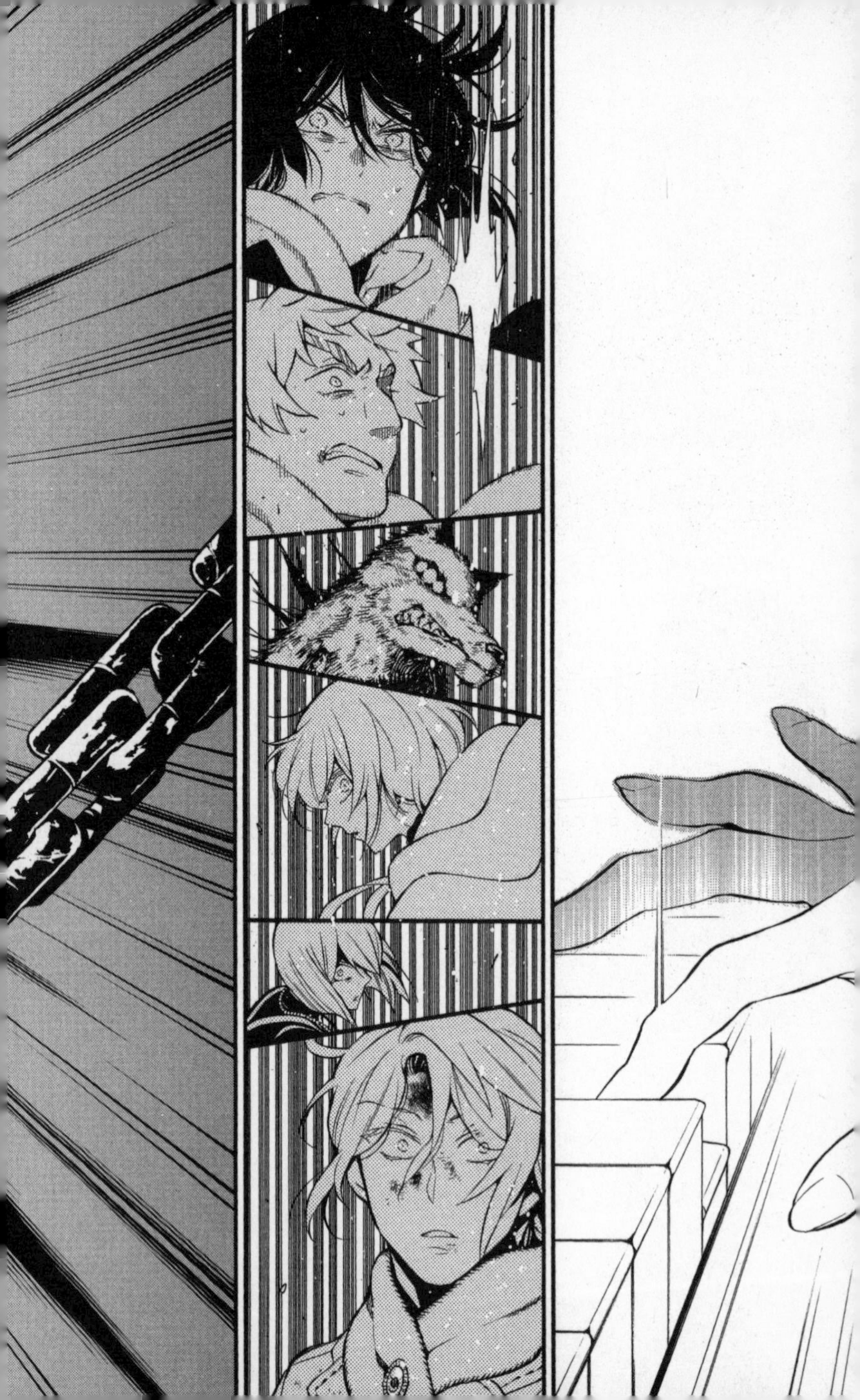

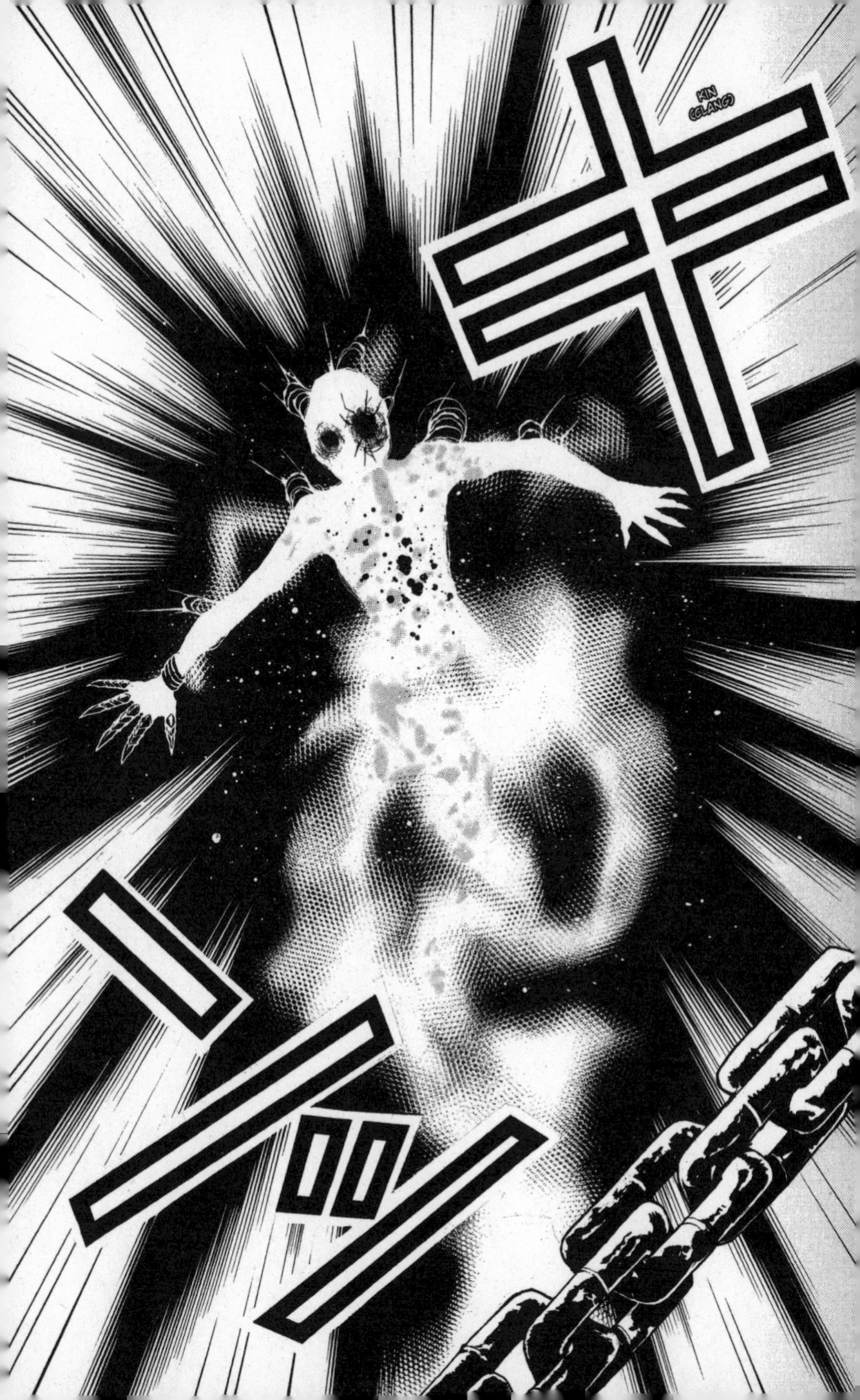
KIN
(CLANG)

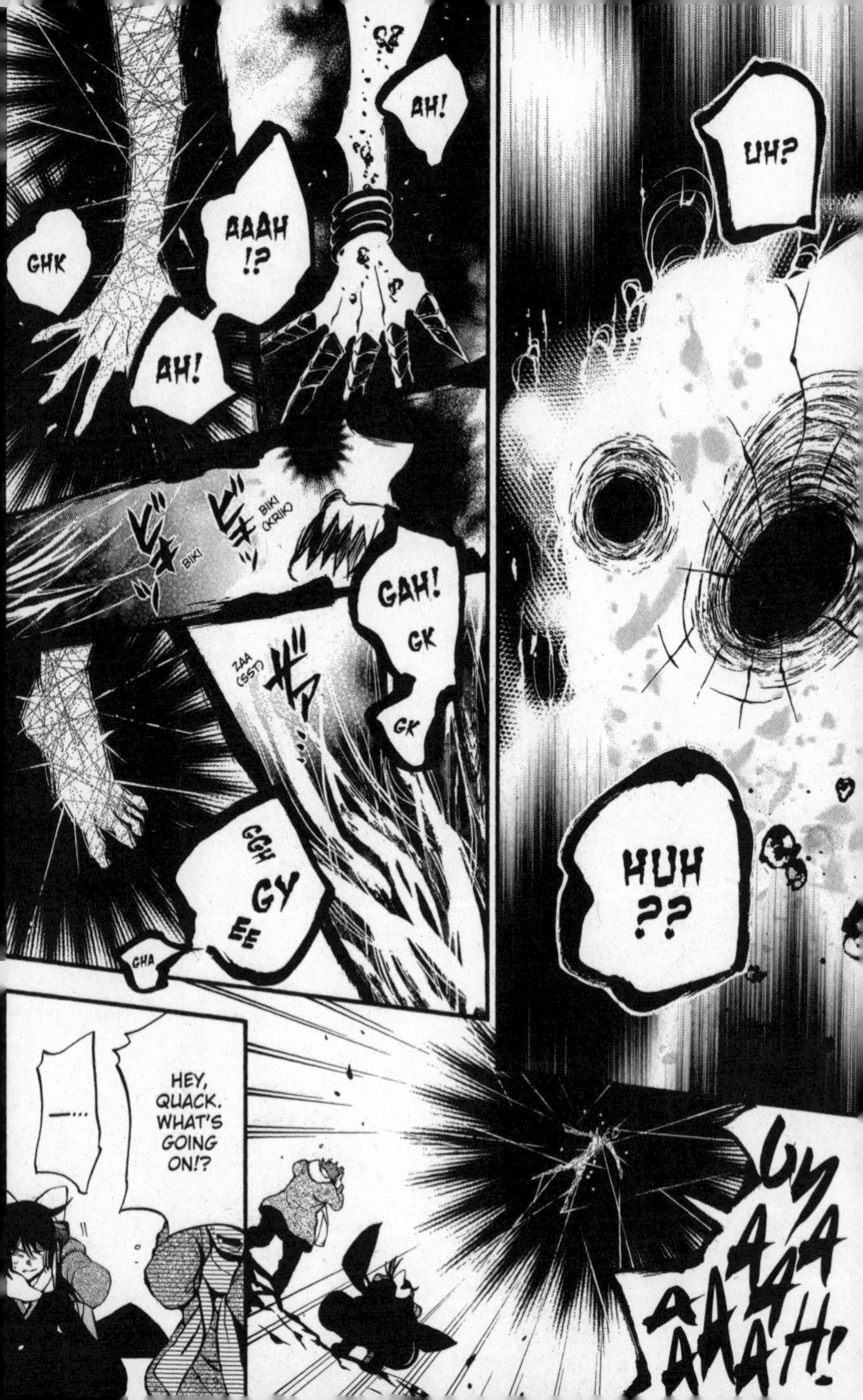
UH?
HUH ??
AH!
AAAH !?
GHK
AH!
BIKI (KRIK)
BIKI
GAH! GK GK
ZAA (SST)
GGH GY EE
GHA
UWAAAAAAAAH!
HEY, QUACK. WHAT'S GOING ON!?
—...

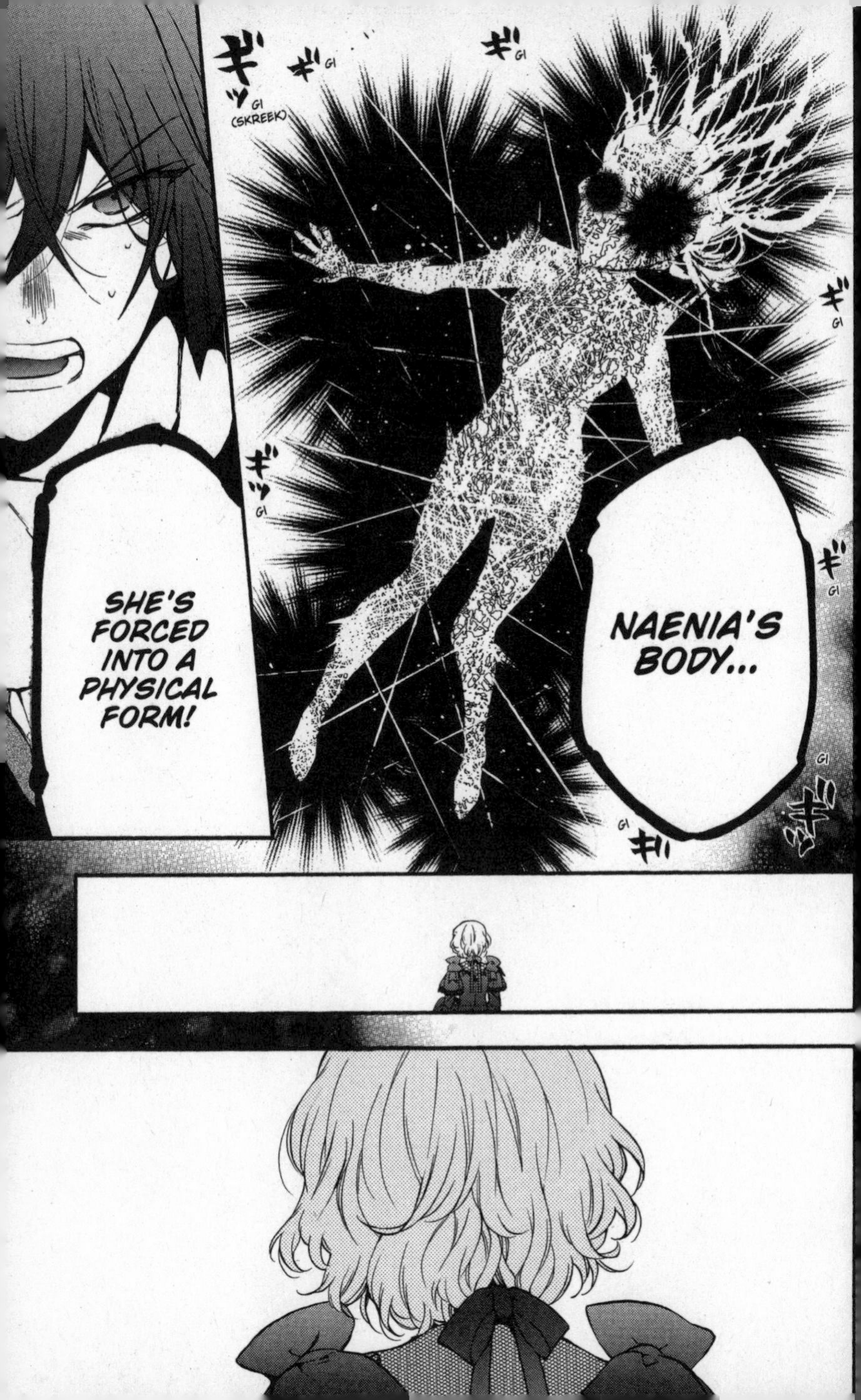
ギ GI
ギ GI
ギ GI
NAENIA'S BODY...
GI ギ
GI ギ
ギ GI
ギッ GI (SKREEK)
ギッ GI
SHE'S FORCED INTO A PHYSICAL FORM!

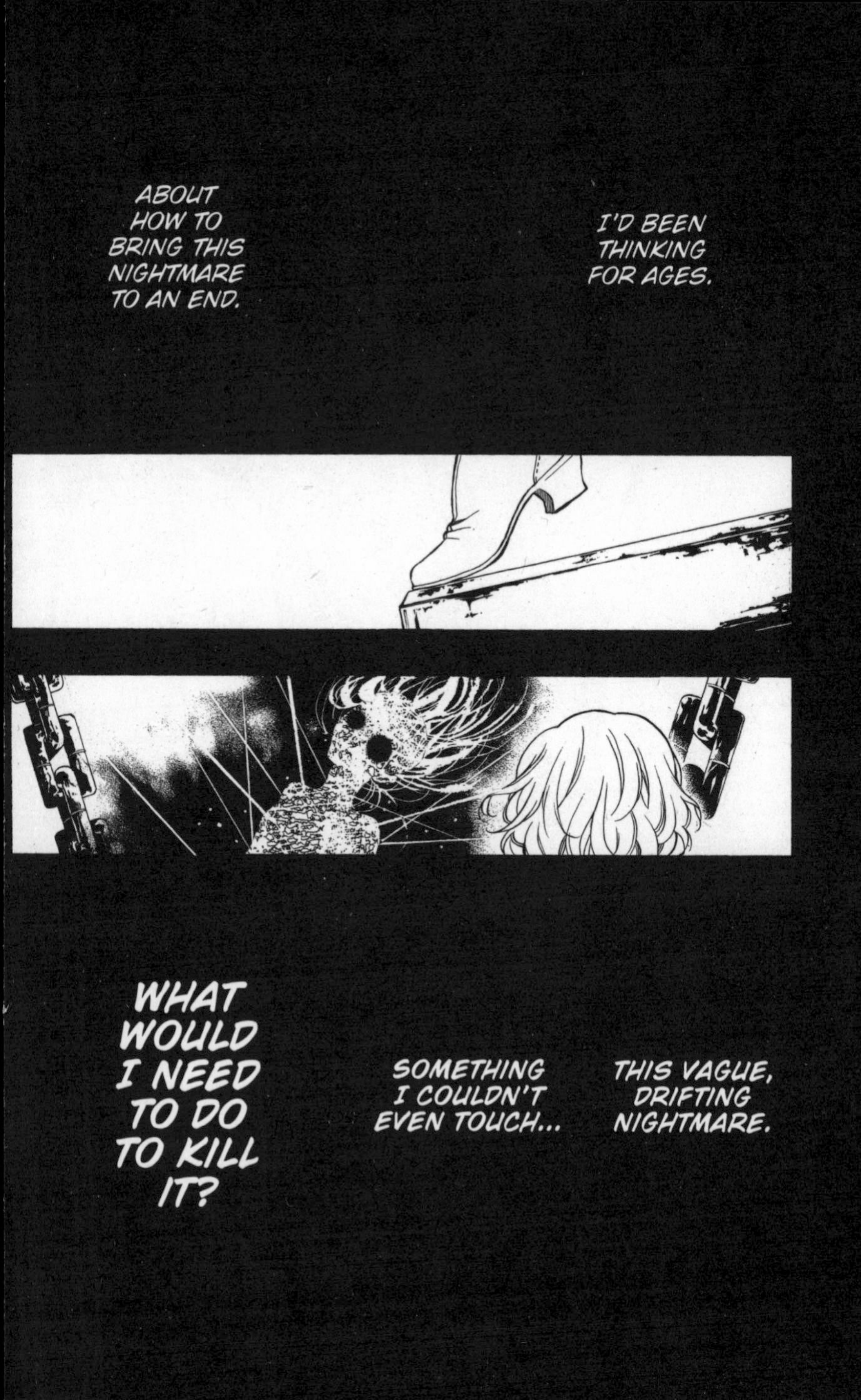
I'D BEEN THINKING FOR AGES.
ABOUT HOW TO BRING THIS NIGHTMARE TO AN END.
THIS VAGUE, DRIFTING NIGHTMARE.
SOMETHING I COULDN'T EVEN TOUCH...
WHAT WOULD I NEED TO DO TO KILL IT?

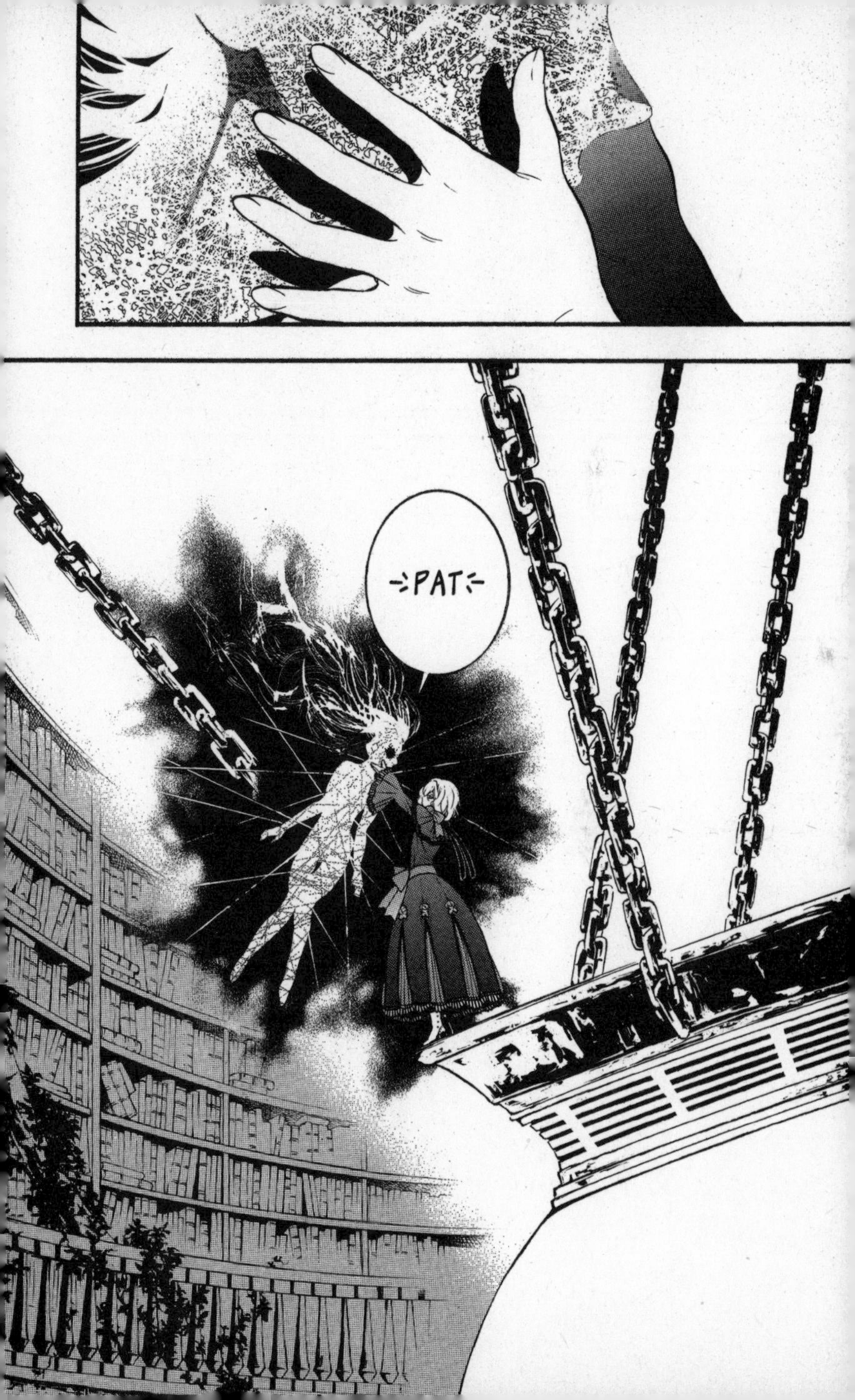
PAT

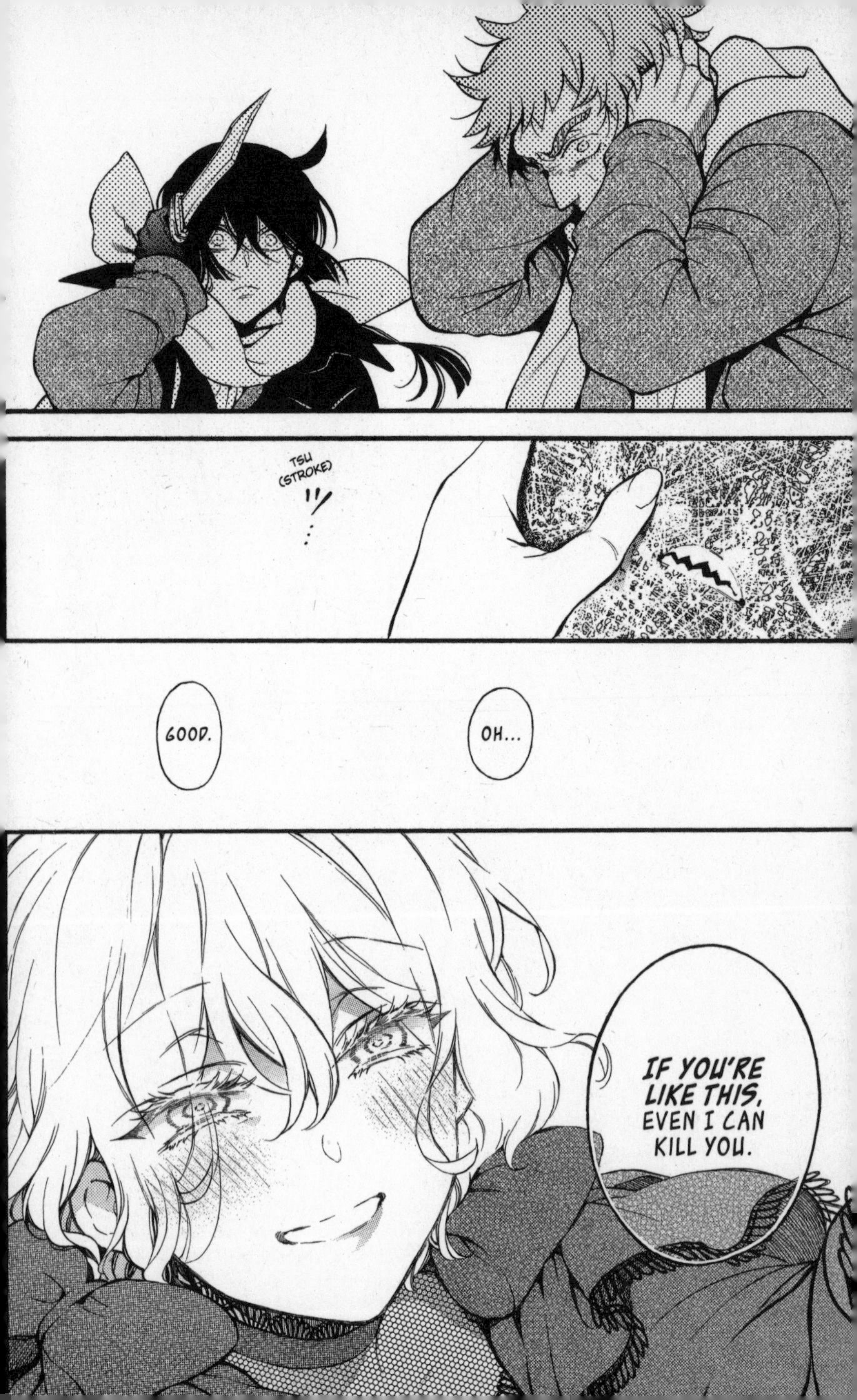
TSU (STROKE)
OH...
GOOD.
IF YOU'RE LIKE THIS, EVEN I CAN KILL YOU.

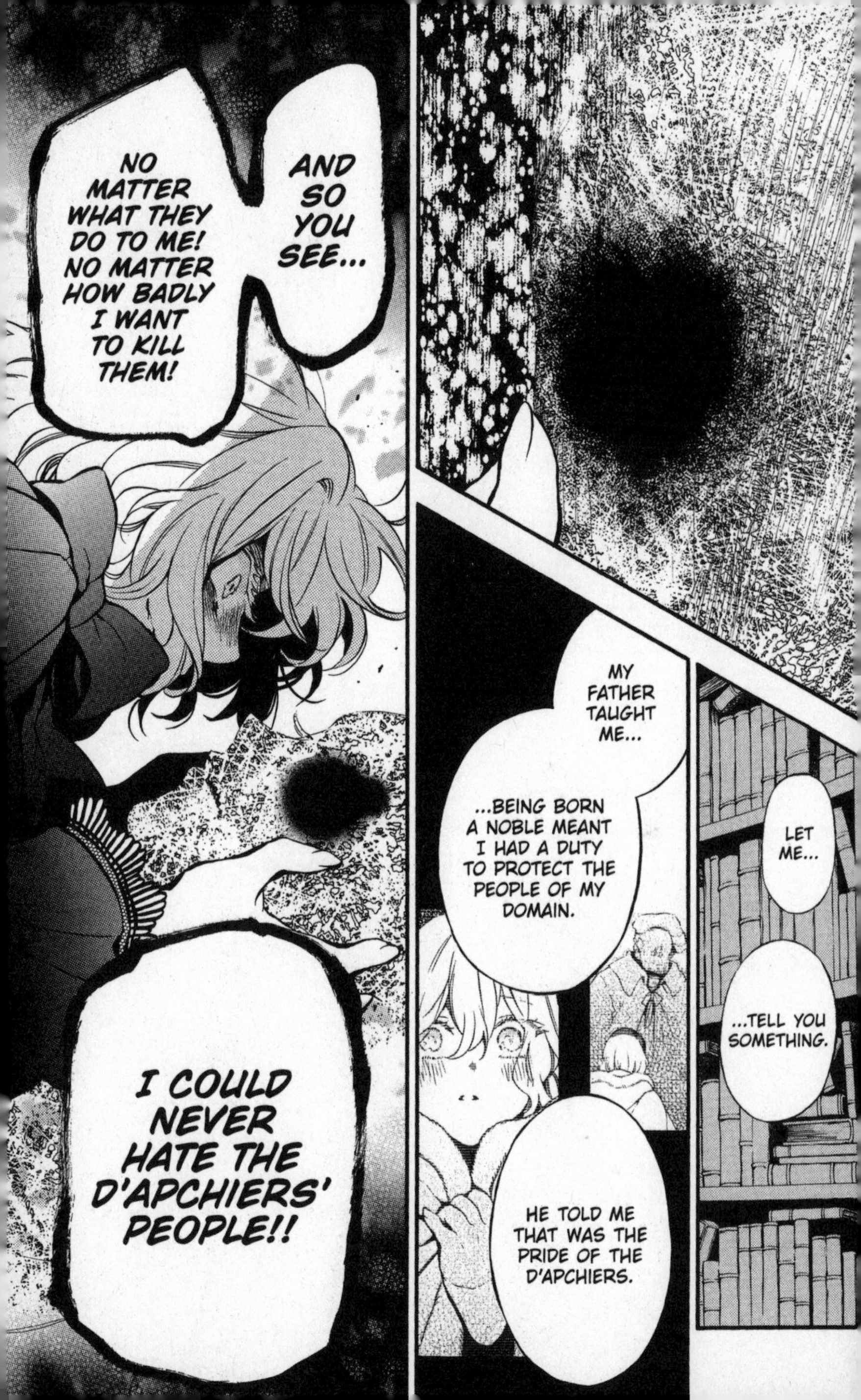

LET ME...
...TELL YOU SOMETHING.
MY FATHER TAUGHT ME...
...BEING BORN A NOBLE MEANT I HAD A DUTY TO PROTECT THE PEOPLE OF MY DOMAIN.
HE TOLD ME THAT WAS THE PRIDE OF THE D'APCHIERS.
AND SO YOU SEE...
NO MATTER WHAT THEY DO TO ME! NO MATTER HOW BADLY I WANT TO KILL THEM!
I COULD NEVER HATE THE D'APCHIERS' PEOPLE!!

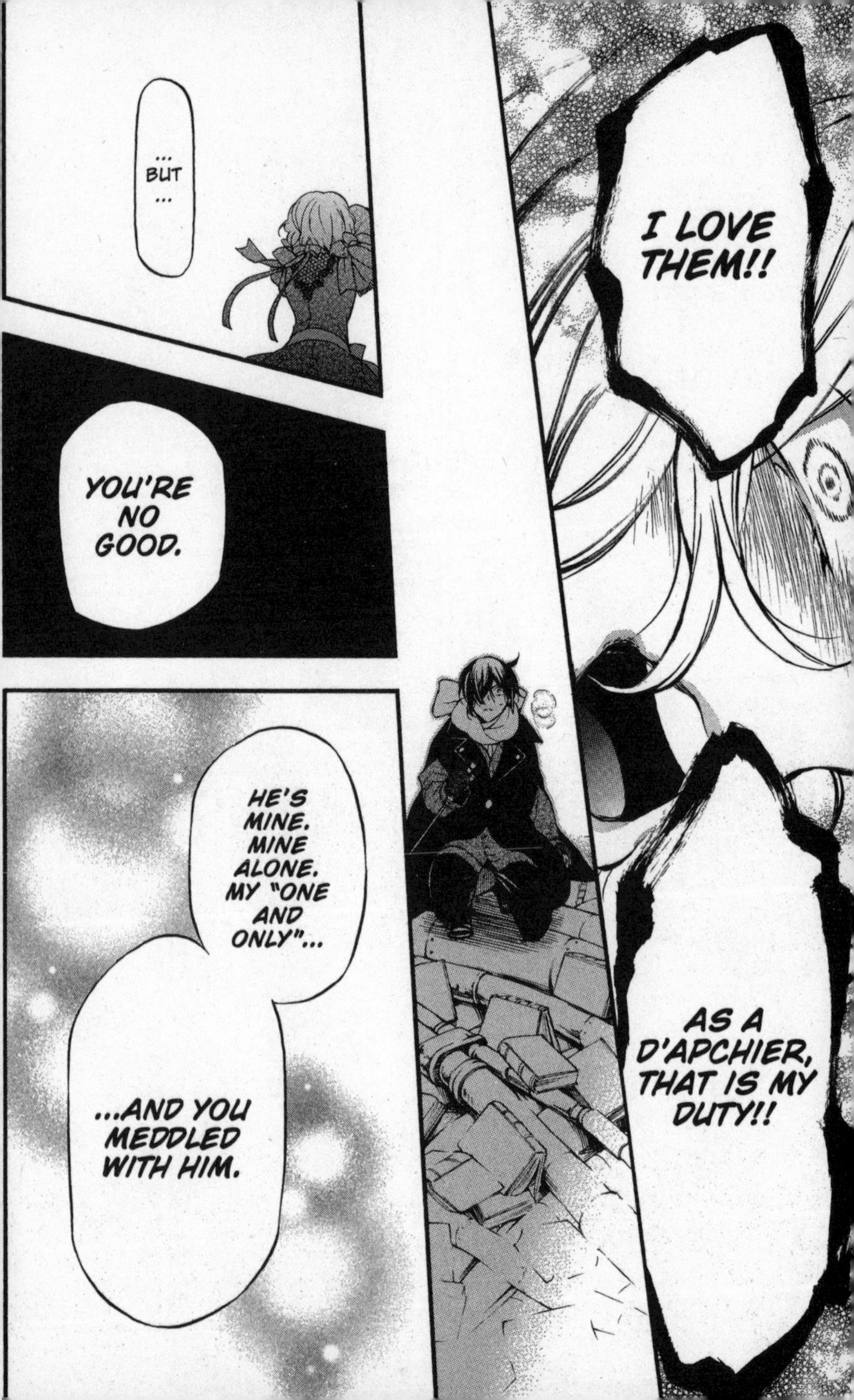
I LOVE THEM!!
AS A D'APCHIER, THAT IS MY DUTY!!
...BUT...
YOU'RE NO GOOD.
HE'S MINE. MINE ALONE. MY "ONE AND ONLY"...
...AND YOU MEDDLED WITH HIM.

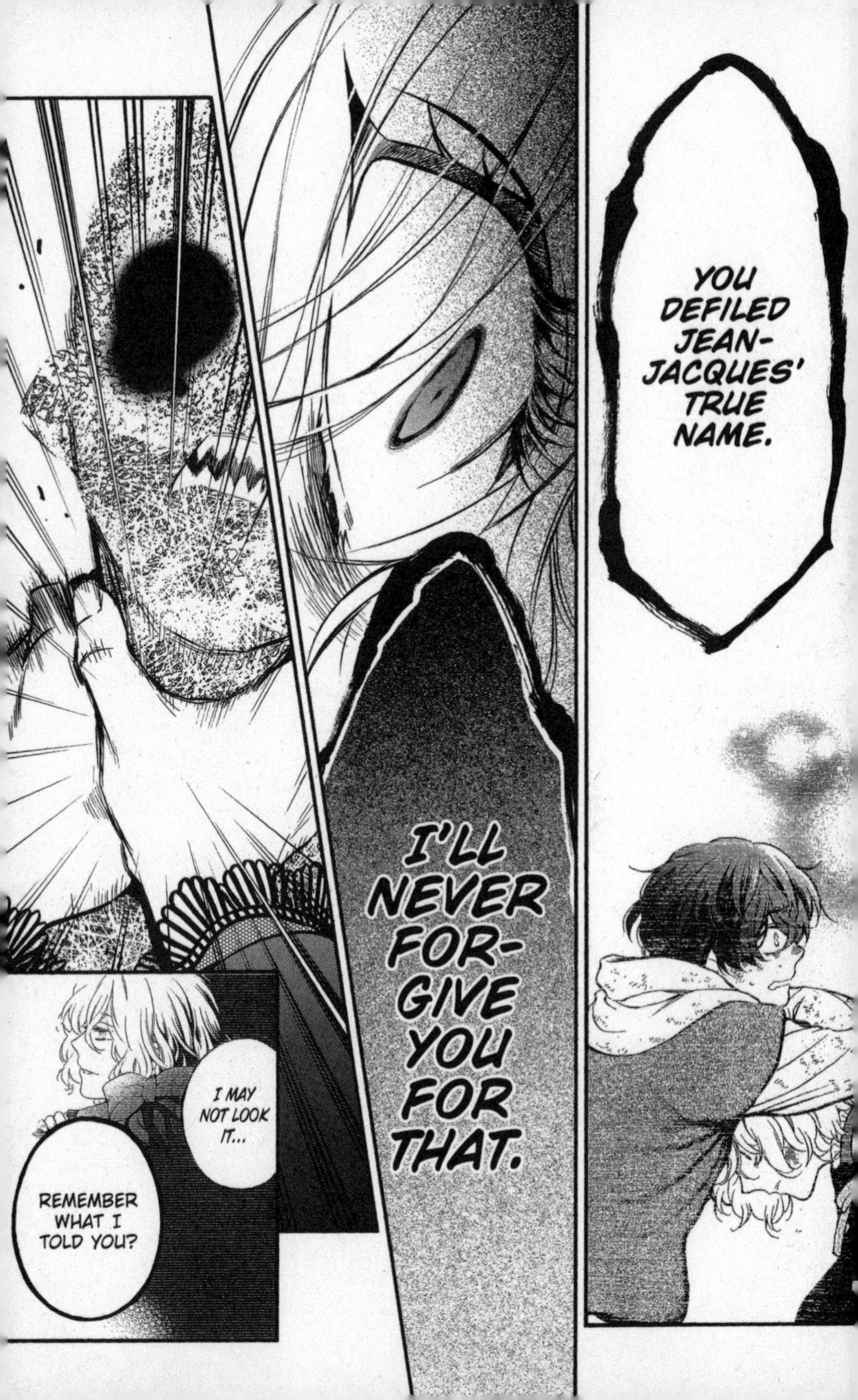
YOU DEFILED JEAN-JACQUES' TRUE NAME.
I'LL NEVER FOR-GIVE YOU FOR THAT.
I MAY NOT LOOK IT...
REMEMBER WHAT I TOLD YOU?

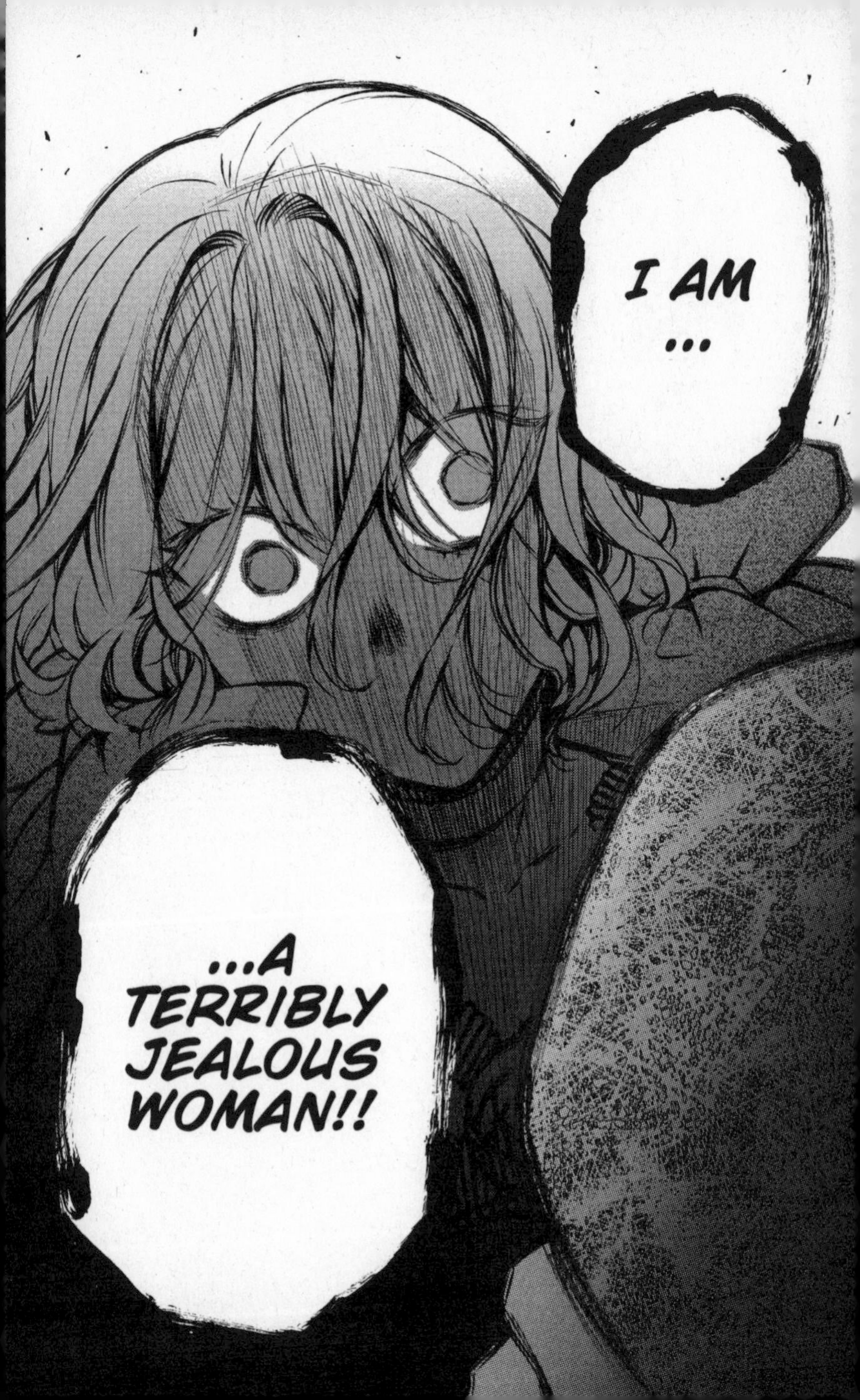
I AM ...
...A TERRIBLY JEALOUS WOMAN!!

Mémoire 57
Vengeance HANDS THAT TOUCH A NIGHTMARE

Les Mémoires de Vanitas

THE CASE STUDY OF
VANITAS

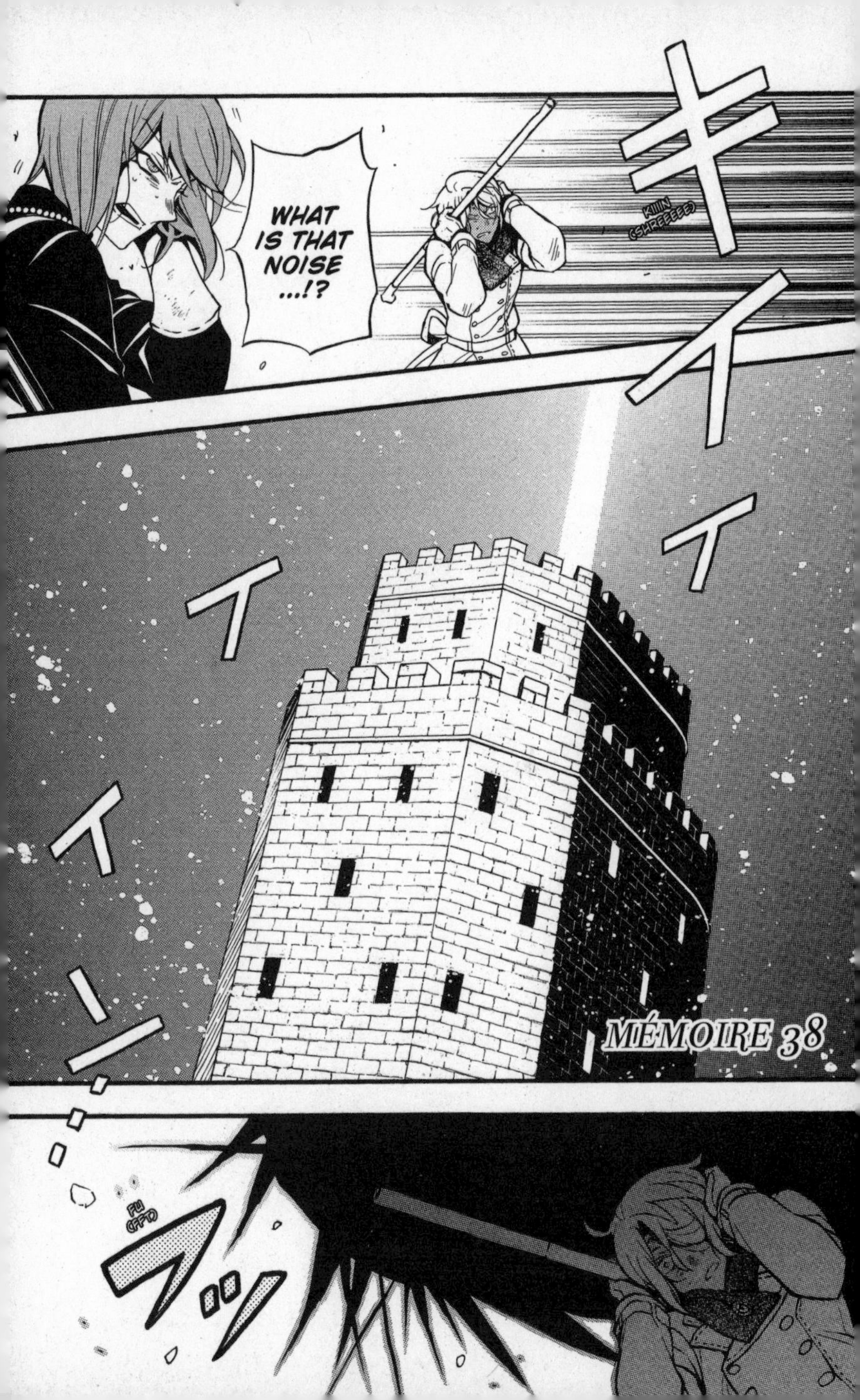
キイイイイーー
KIIIN (SHREEEEEE)
WHAT IS THAT NOISE ...!?
MÉMOIRE 38
FU (FFT)
フッ

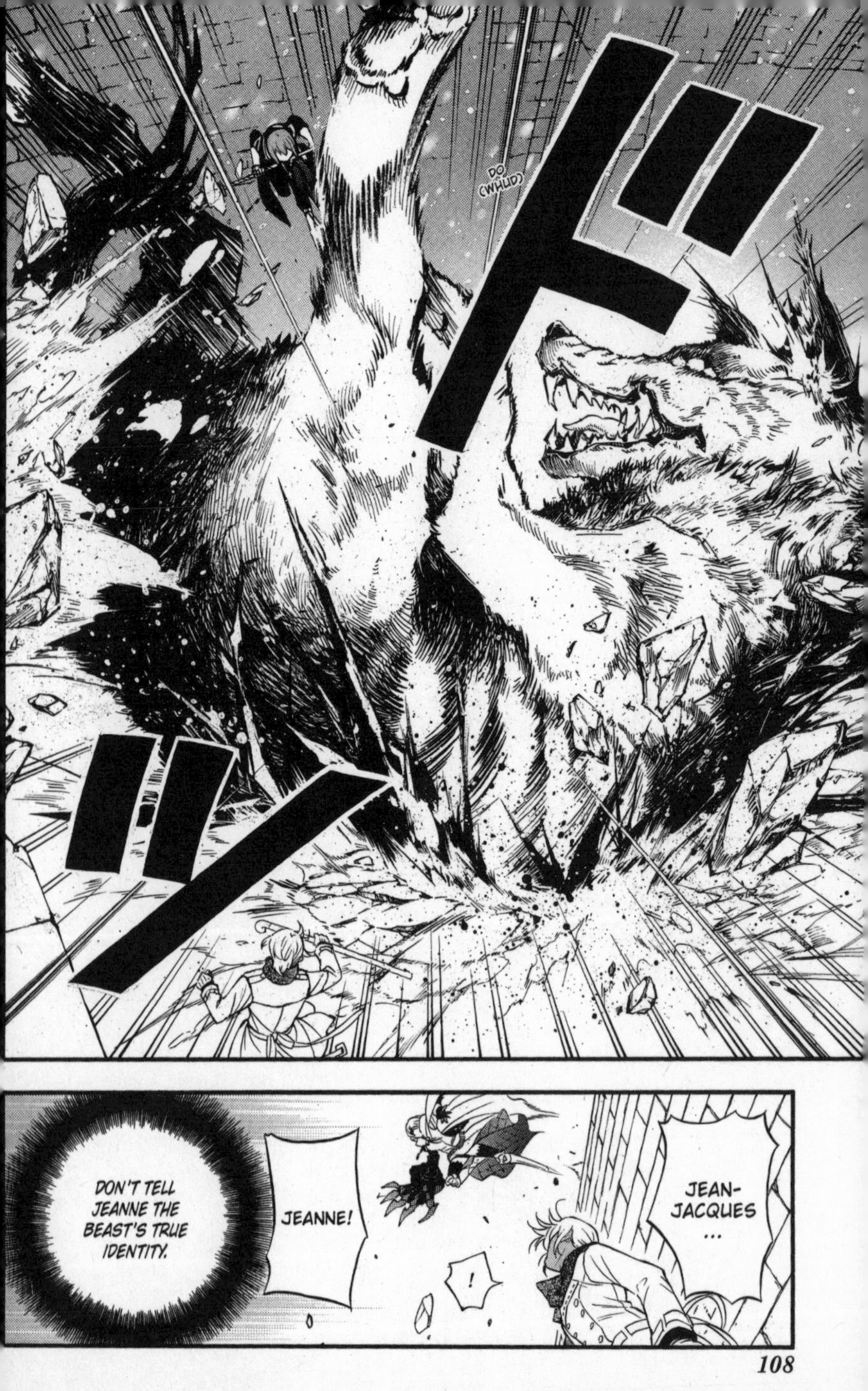
DO
(WHUD)
JEAN-JACQUES ...
!
JEANNE!
DON'T TELL JEANNE THE BEAST'S TRUE IDENTITY.

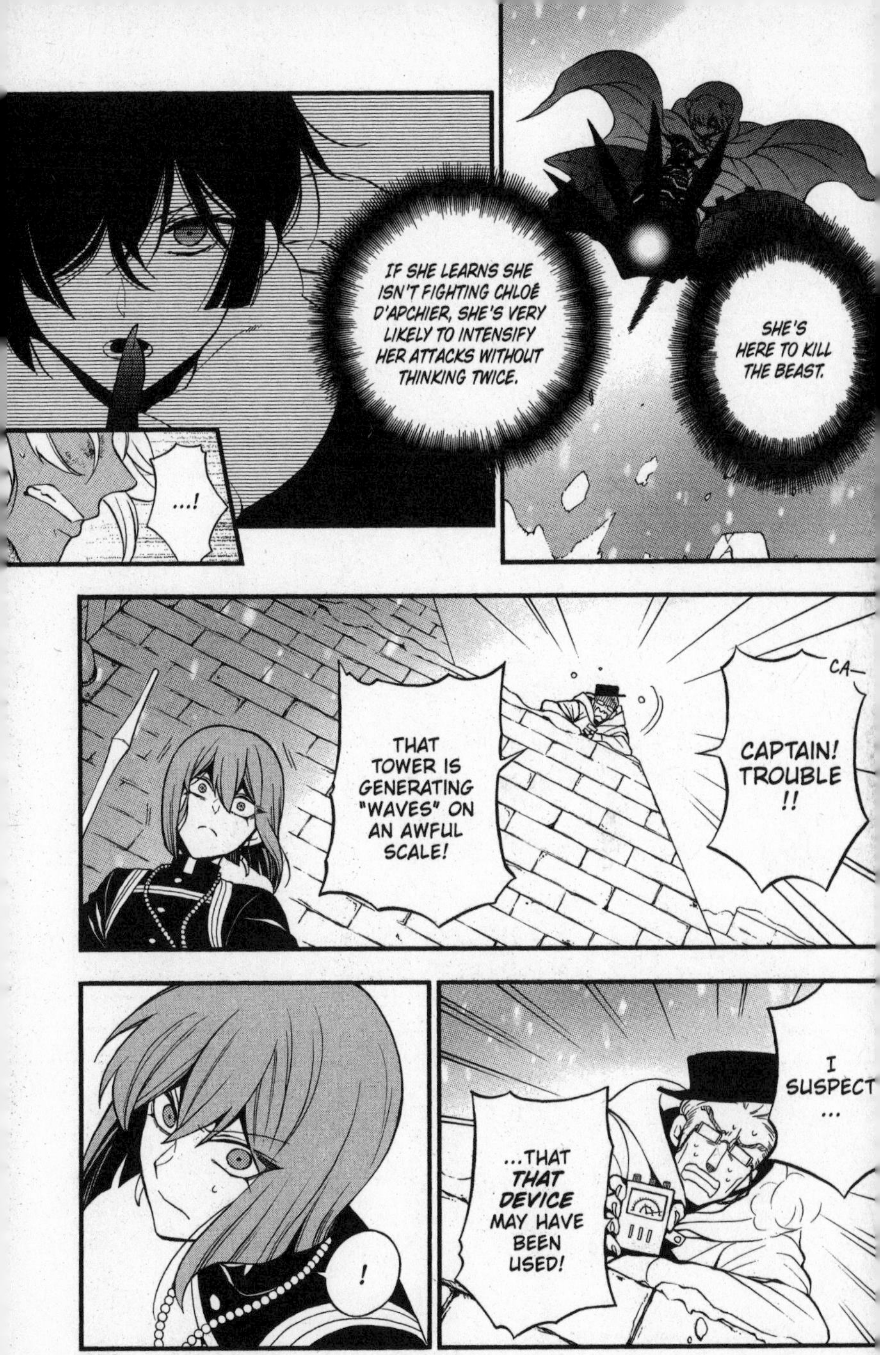
SHE'S HERE TO KILL THE BEAST.
IF SHE LEARNS SHE ISN'T FIGHTING CHLOÉ D'APCHIER, SHE'S VERY LIKELY TO INTENSIFY HER ATTACKS WITHOUT THINKING TWICE.
...!
CA—
CAPTAIN! TROUBLE!!
THAT TOWER IS GENERATING "WAVES" ON AN AWFUL SCALE!
I SUSPECT...
...THAT *THAT DEVICE* MAY HAVE BEEN USED!
!

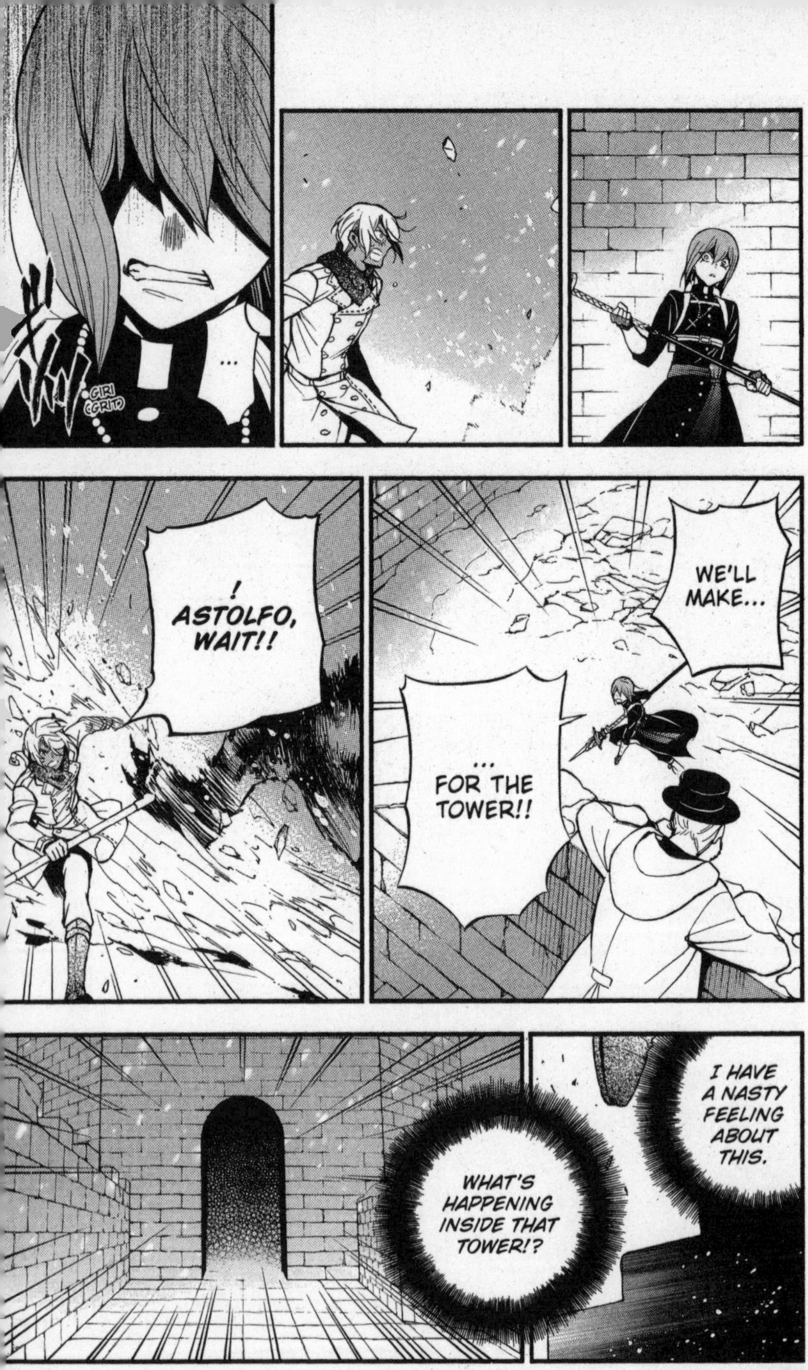
...
GIRI (GRIT)
WE'LL MAKE...
... FOR THE TOWER!!
! ASTOLFO, WAIT!!
I HAVE A NASTY FEELING ABOUT THIS.
WHAT'S HAPPENING INSIDE THAT TOWER!?

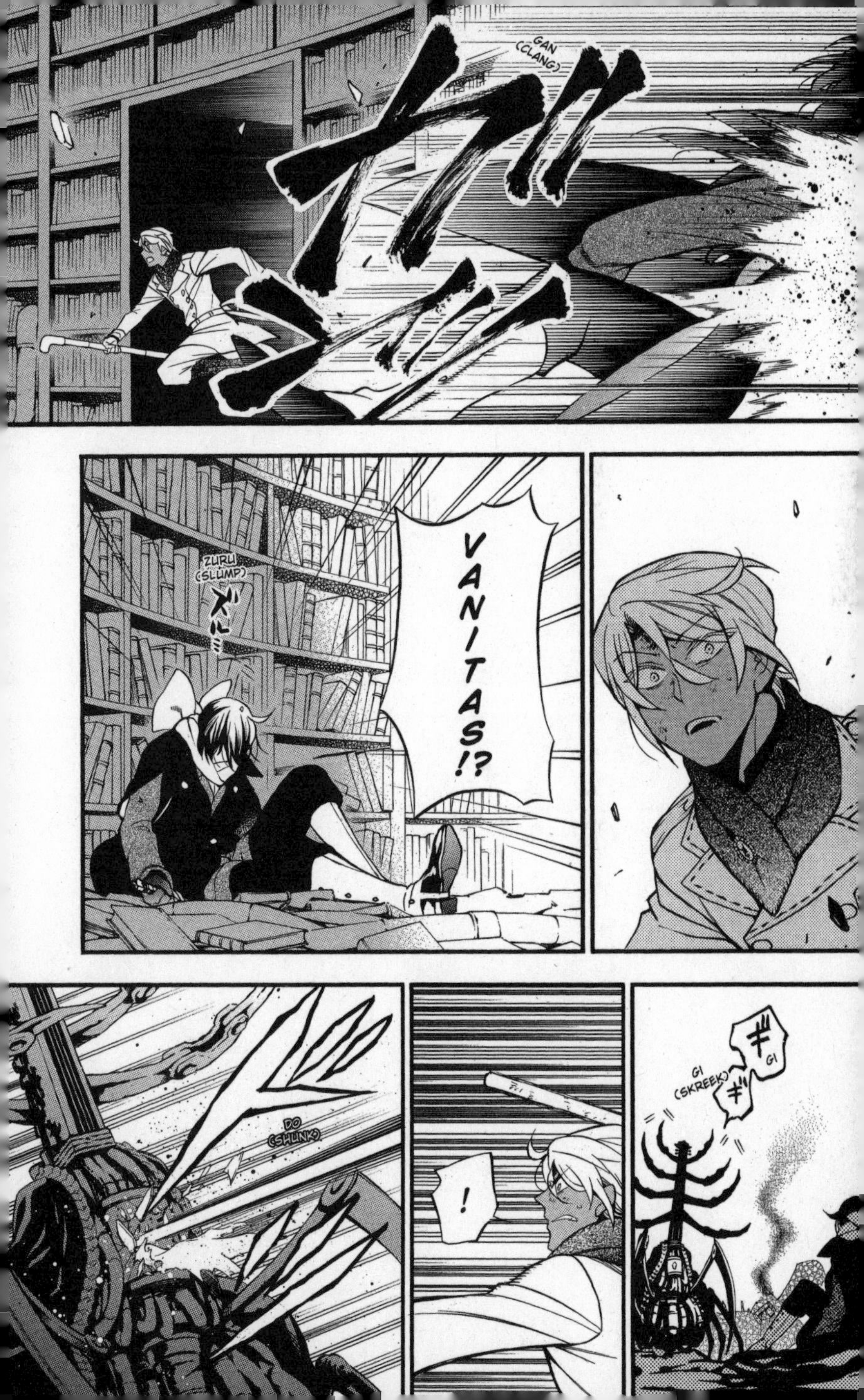
GAN
(CLANG)
VANITAS!?
ZURU
(SLUMP)
GI
GI
(SKREEK)
!
DO
(SHUNK)

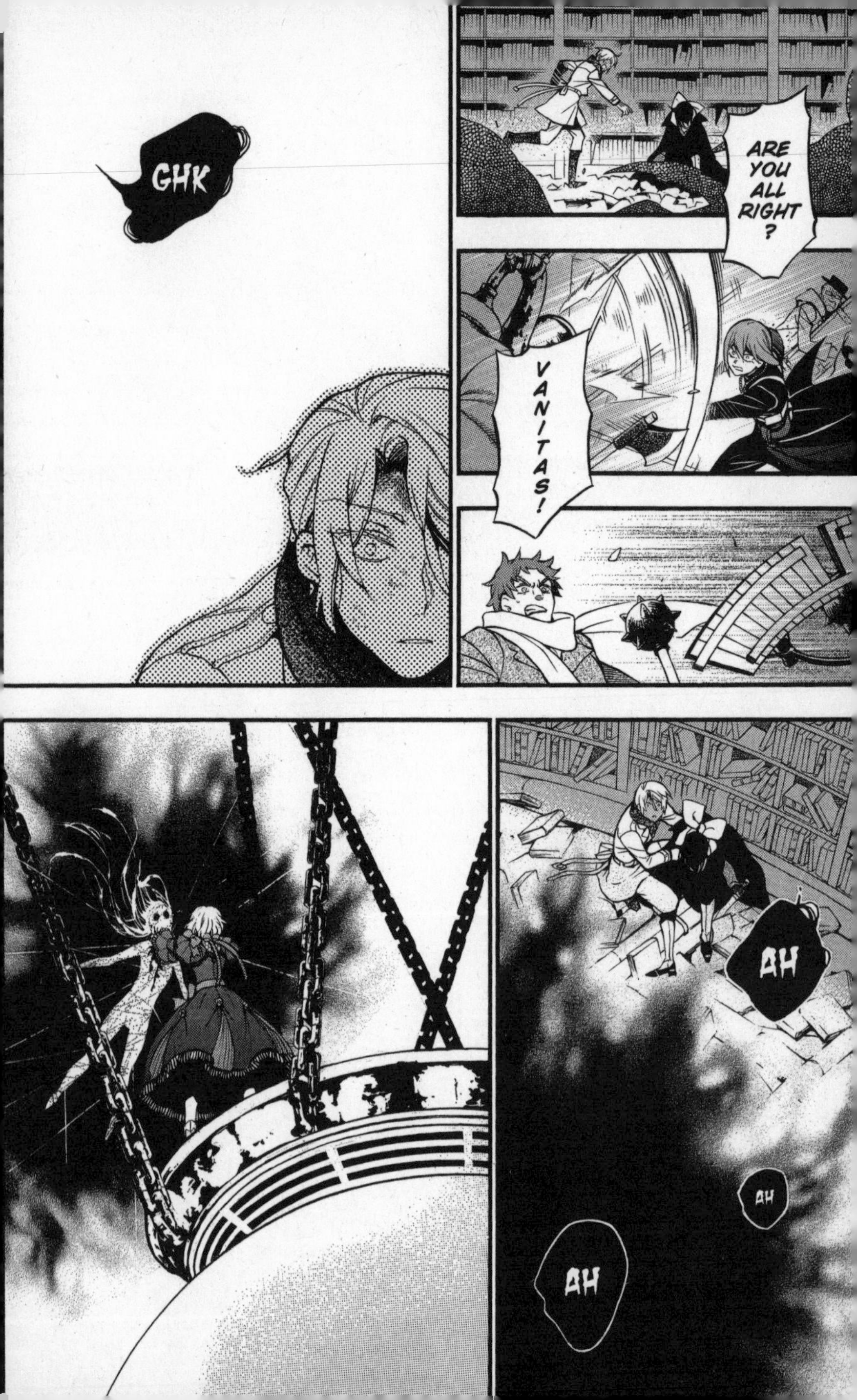
ARE YOU ALL RIGHT?
VANITAS!
GHK
AH
AH
AH

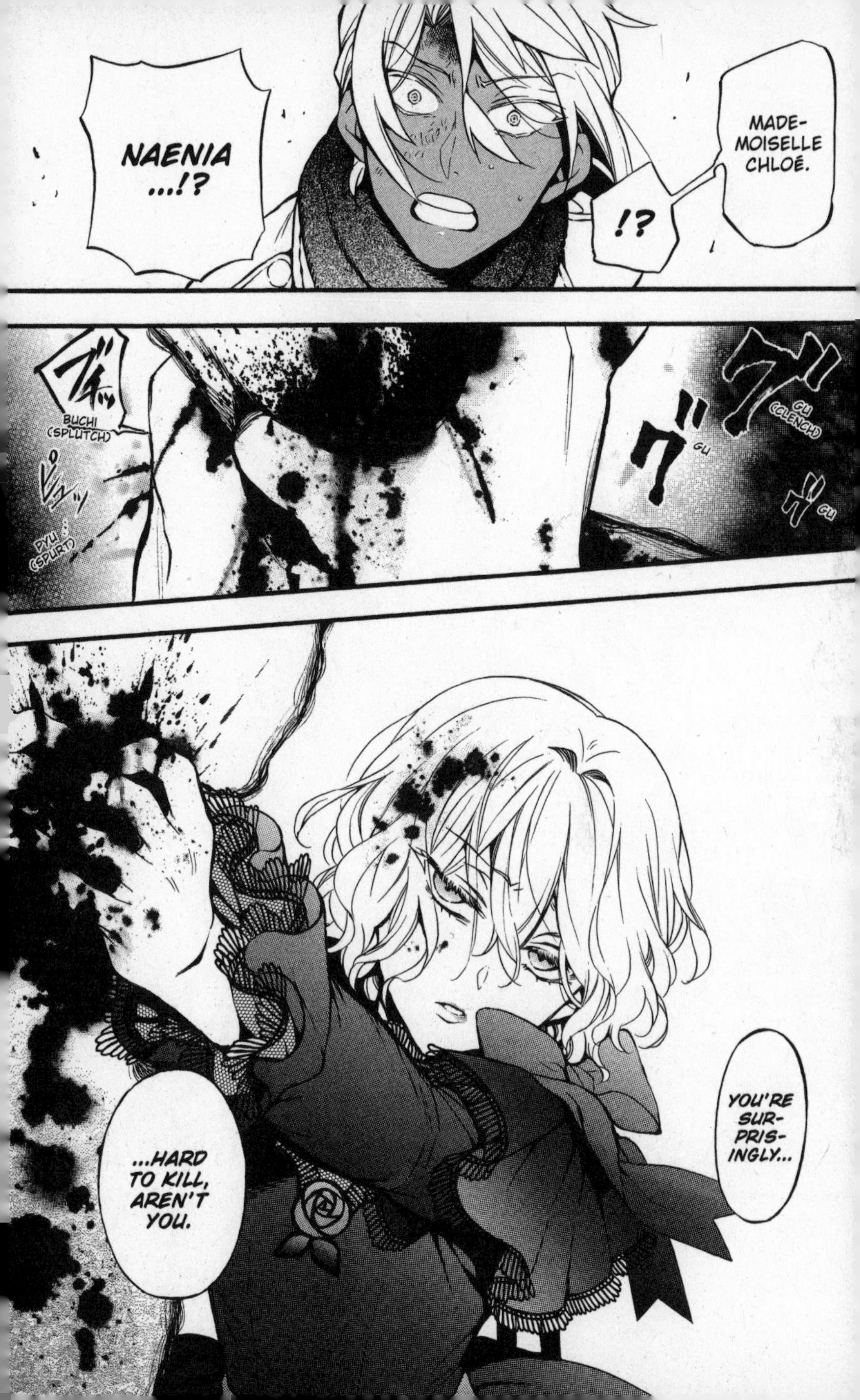
MADE-MOISELLE CHLOÉ.
!?
NAENIA ...!?
ブチッ
BUCHI (SPLUTCH)
ピュッ
PYU (SPURT)
グ
GU (CLENCH)
グ
GU
ッ
GU
YOU'RE SURPRISINGLY...
...HARD TO KILL, AREN'T YOU.

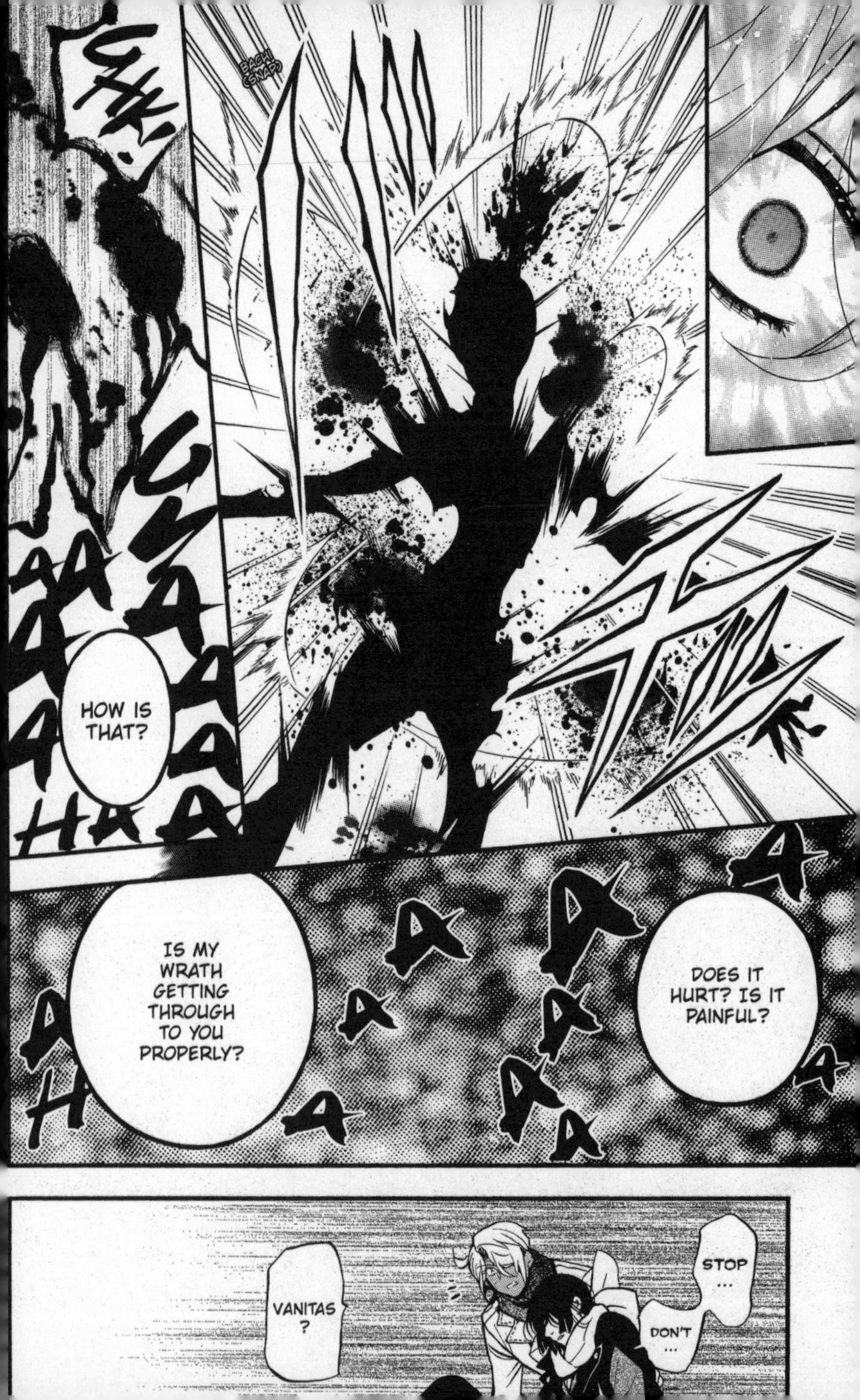
BACH (SNAP)
CHK!
HOW IS THAT?
DOES IT HURT? IS IT PAINFUL?
IS MY WRATH GETTING THROUGH TO YOU PROPERLY?
STOP ...
DON'T ...
VANITAS ?

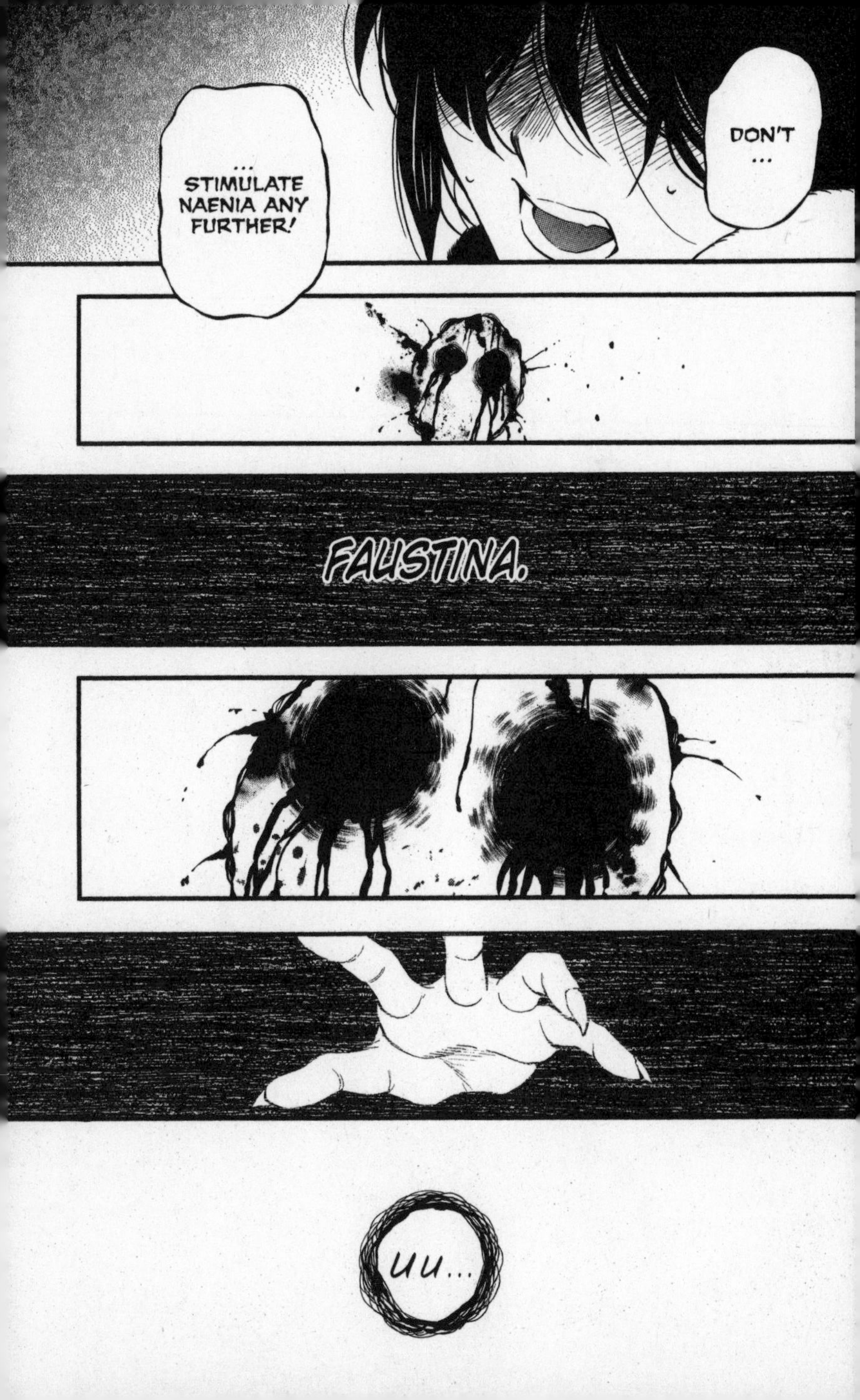
DON'T ...
... STIMULATE NAENIA ANY FURTHER!
FAUSTINA.
UU...

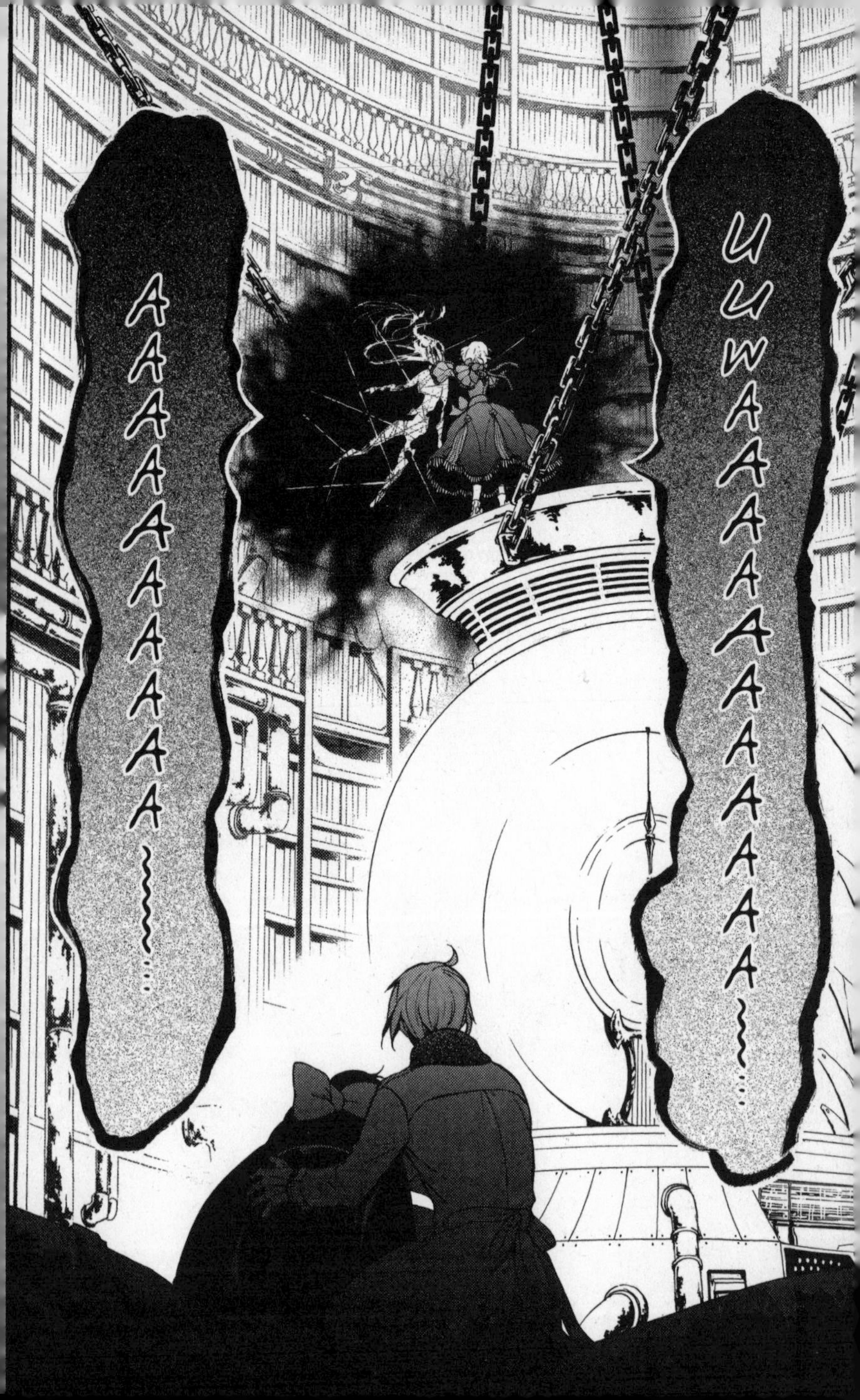
UUWAAAAAAAAAAAAAA~...
AAAAAAAAAA~...

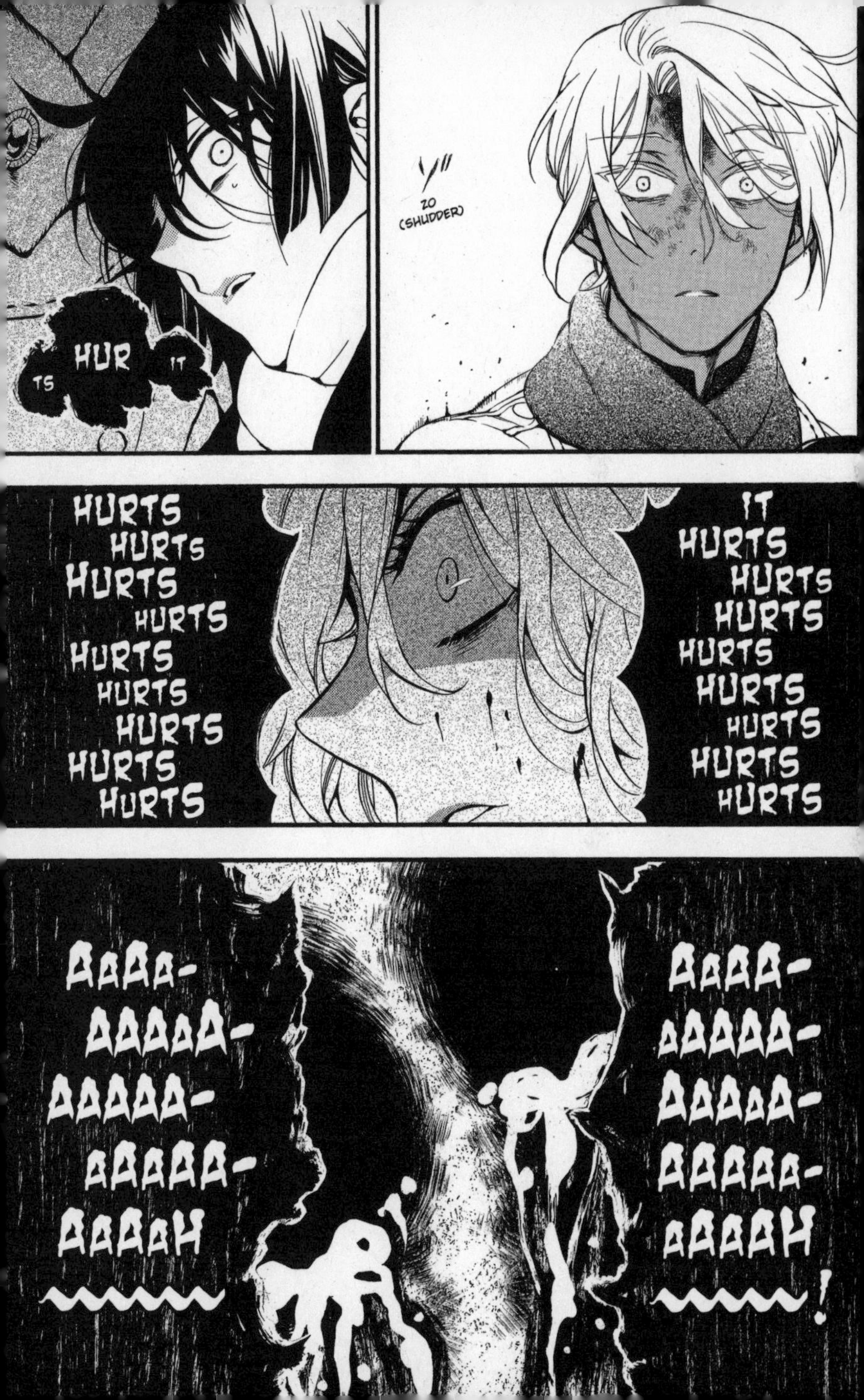
ZO
(SHUDDER)
HUR
IT
TS
IT
HURTS
HURTS
HURTS
HURTS
HURTS
HURTS
HURTS
HURTS
HURTS
HURTS
HURTS
HURTS
HURTS
HURTS
HURTS
HURTS
HURTS
AAAA-
AAAAA-
AAAAA-
AAAAA-
AAAAH
~~~~~!
AAAA-
AAAAA-
AAAAA-
AAAAA-
AAAAH
~~~~~

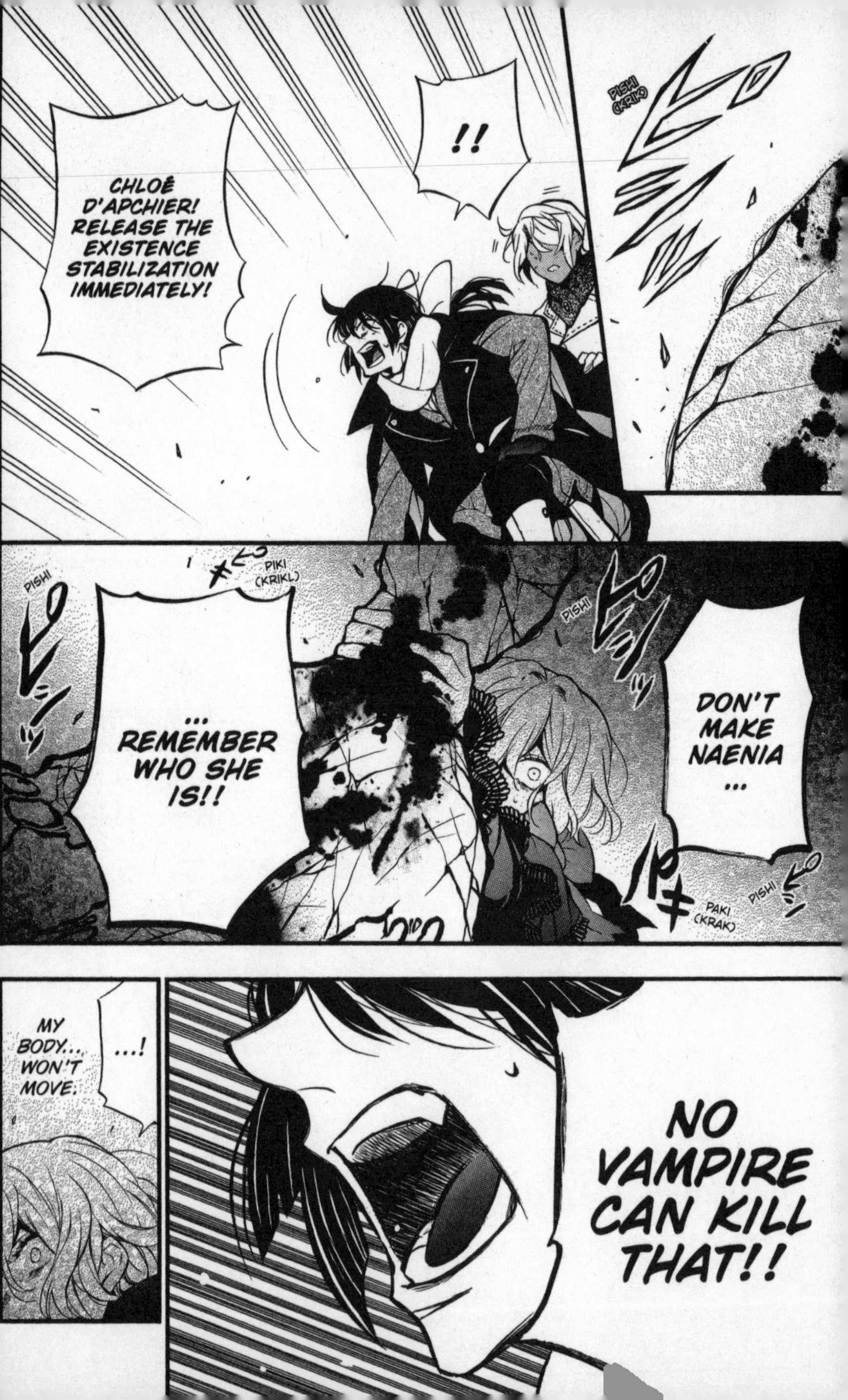
PISHI (KRIK)
!!
CHLOÉ D'APCHIER! RELEASE THE EXISTENCE STABILIZATION IMMEDIATELY!
PISHI
DON'T MAKE NAENIA ...
PISHI
PAKI (KRAK)
PIKI (KRIKL)
... REMEMBER WHO SHE IS!!
PISHI
NO VAMPIRE CAN KILL THAT!!
...!
MY BODY... WON'T MOVE.

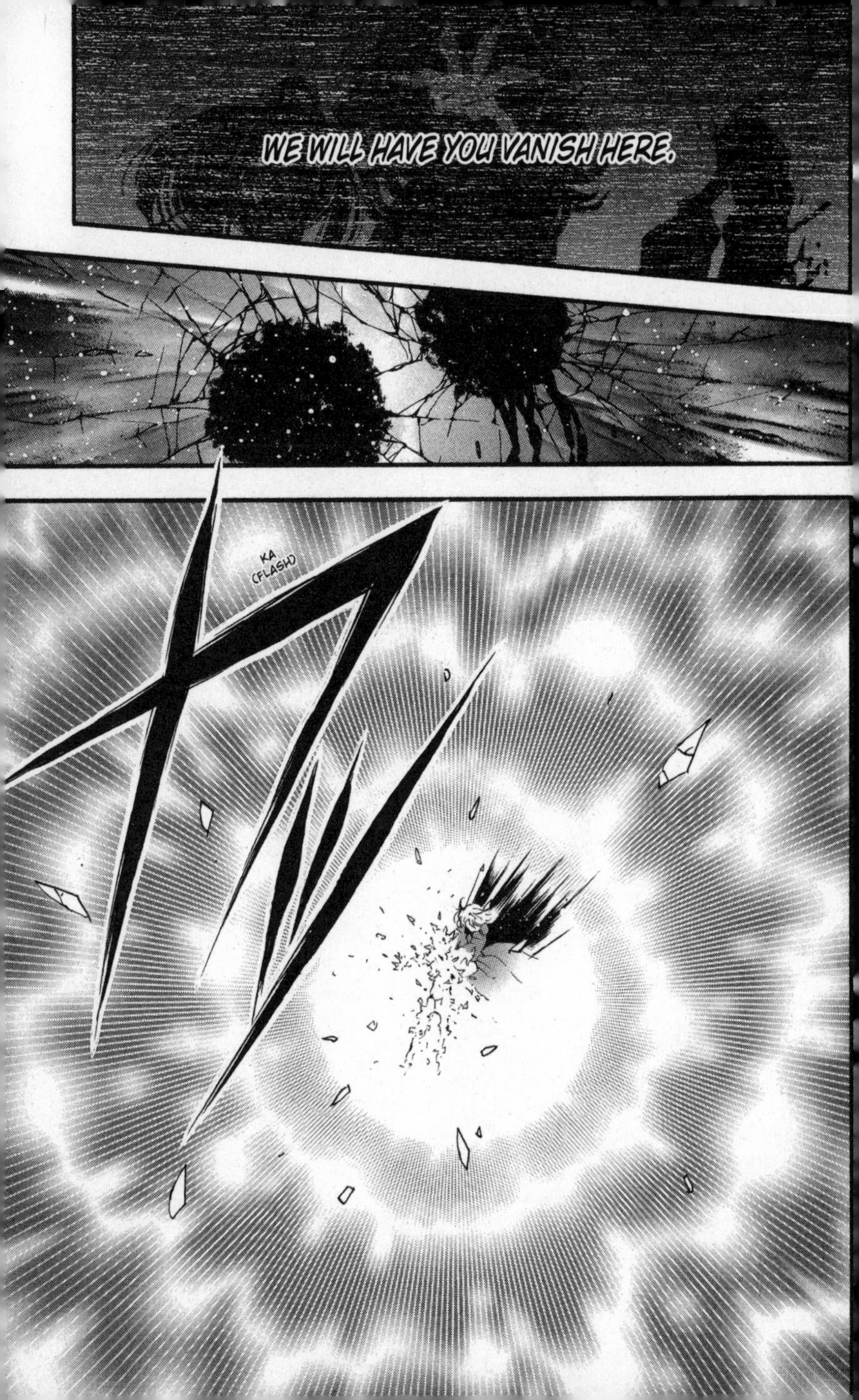
WE WILL HAVE YOU VANISH HERE.
KA (FLASH)

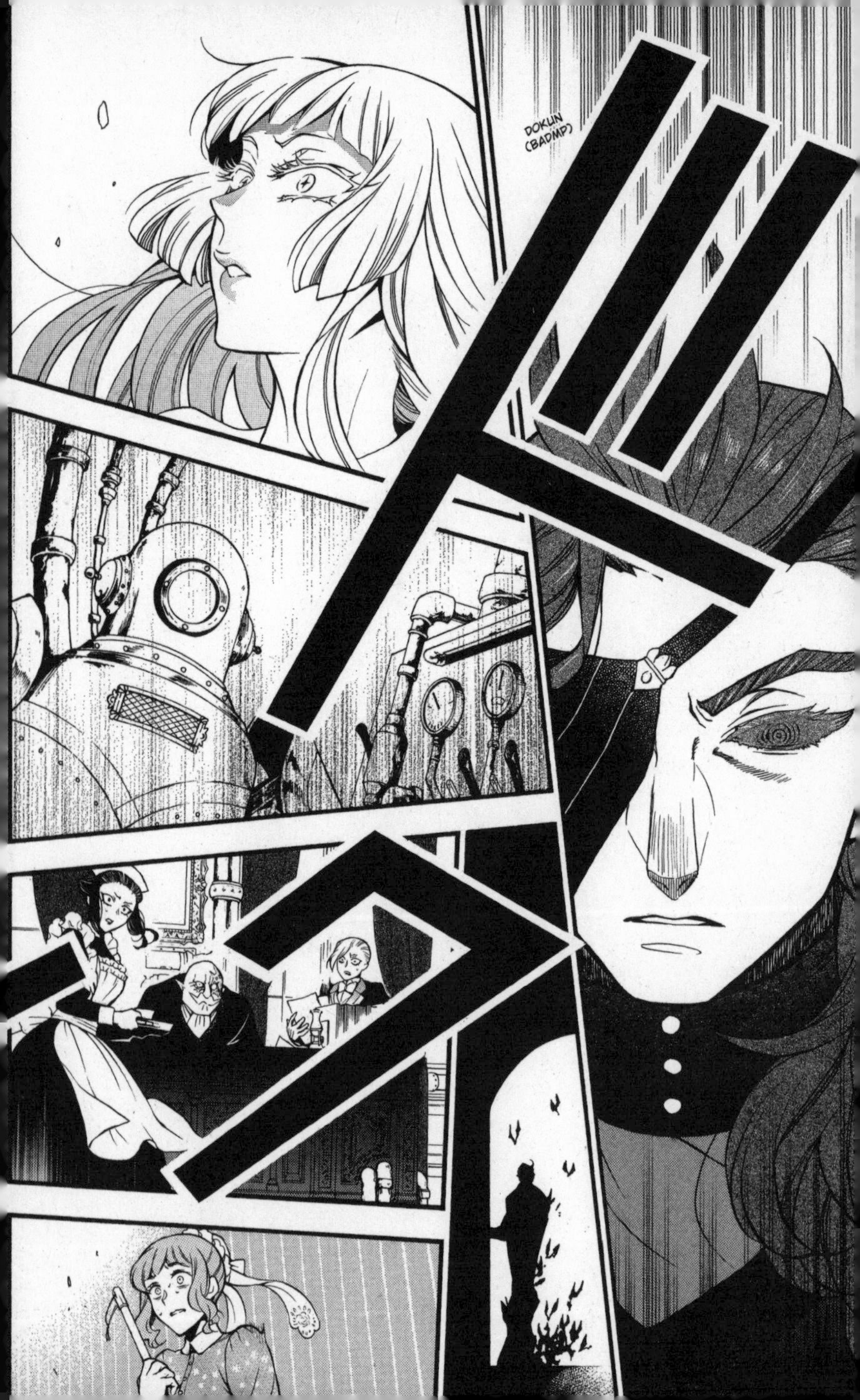
DOKUN
(BADMP)

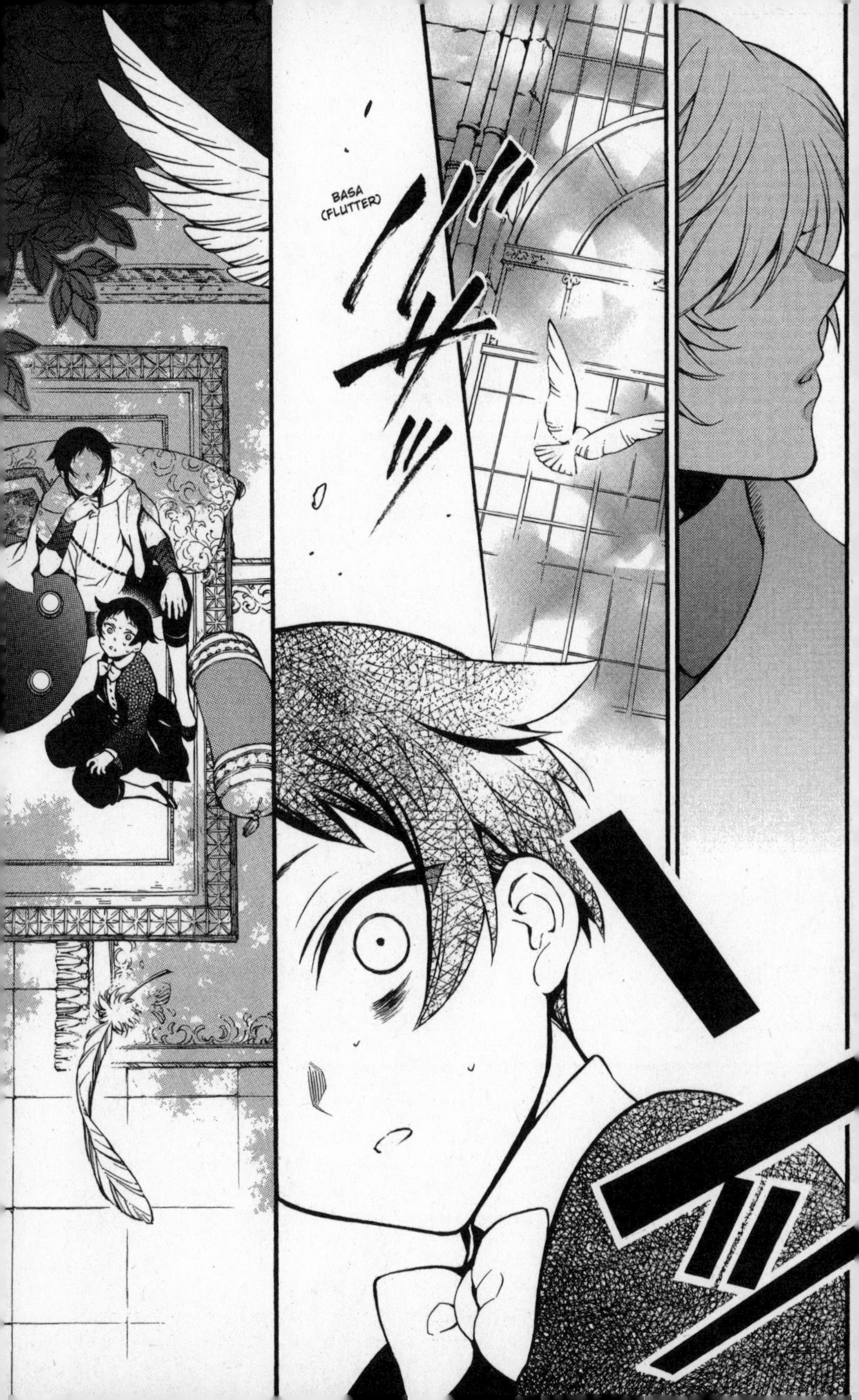
BASA
(FLUTTER)

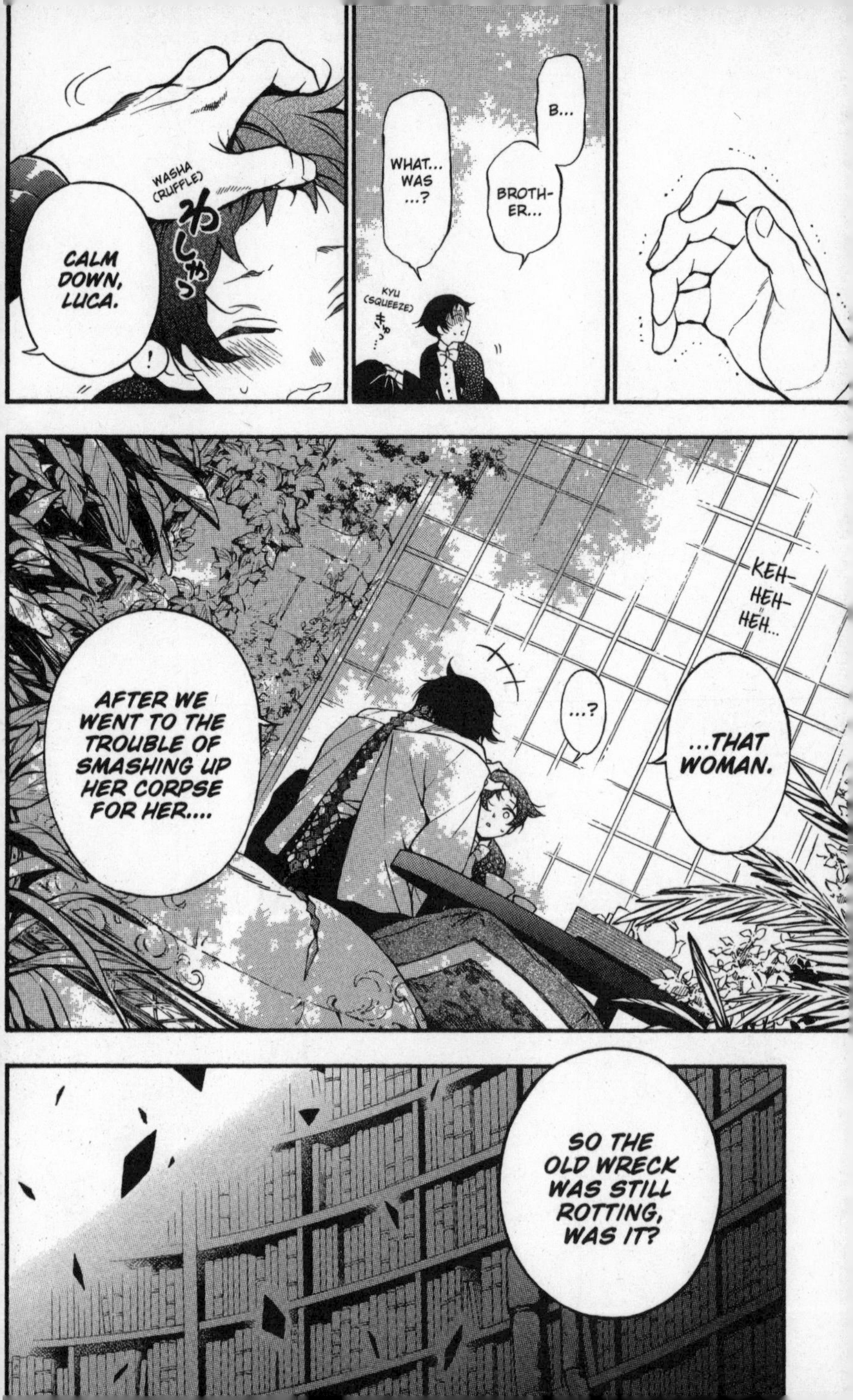
B... BROTHER...
WHAT... WAS ...?
KYU (SQUEEZE)
WASHA (RUFFLE)
!
CALM DOWN, LUCA.
KEH-HEH-HEH...
...THAT WOMAN.
...?
AFTER WE WENT TO THE TROUBLE OF SMASHING UP HER CORPSE FOR HER....
SO THE OLD WRECK WAS STILL ROTTING, WAS IT?

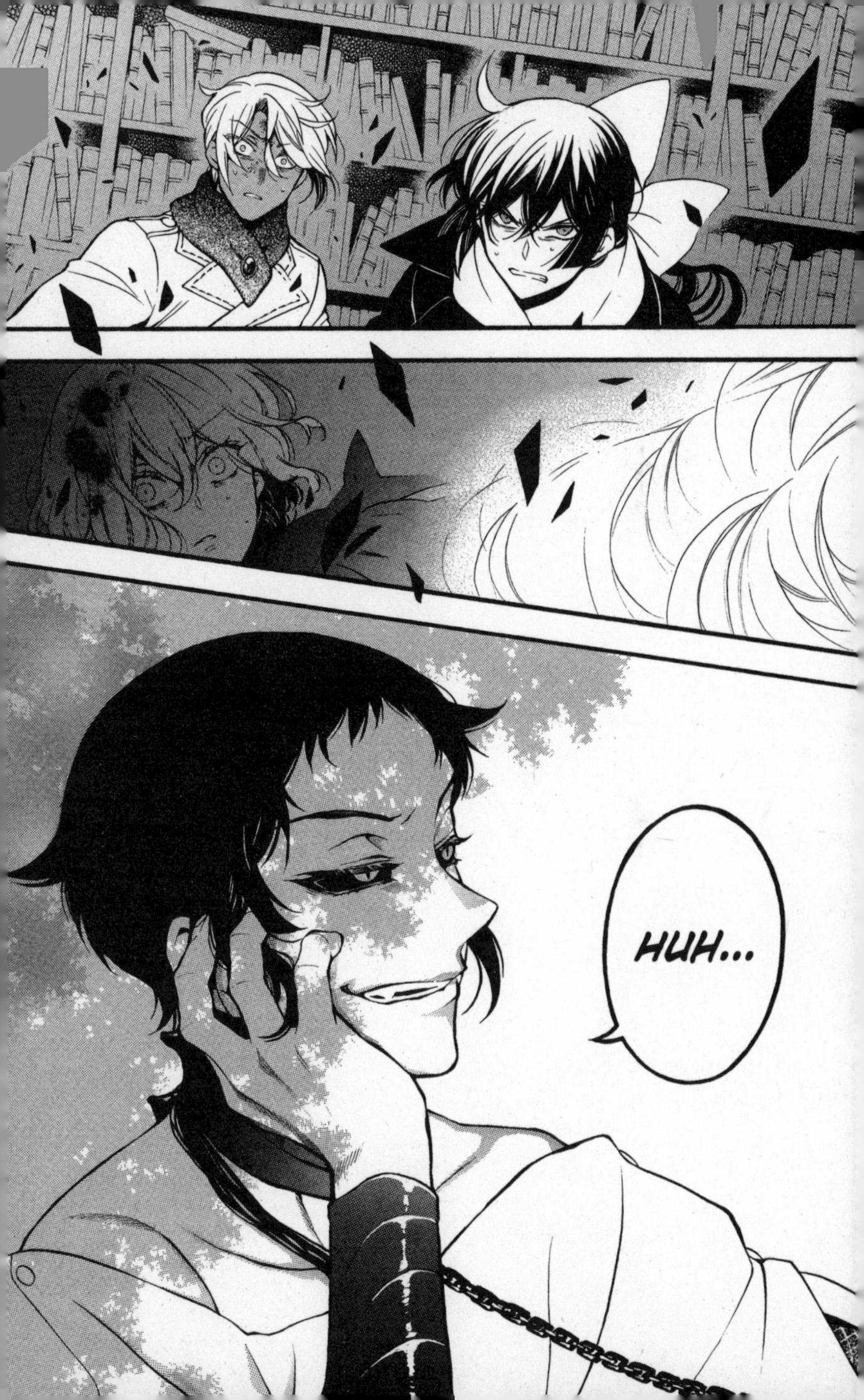
HUH...

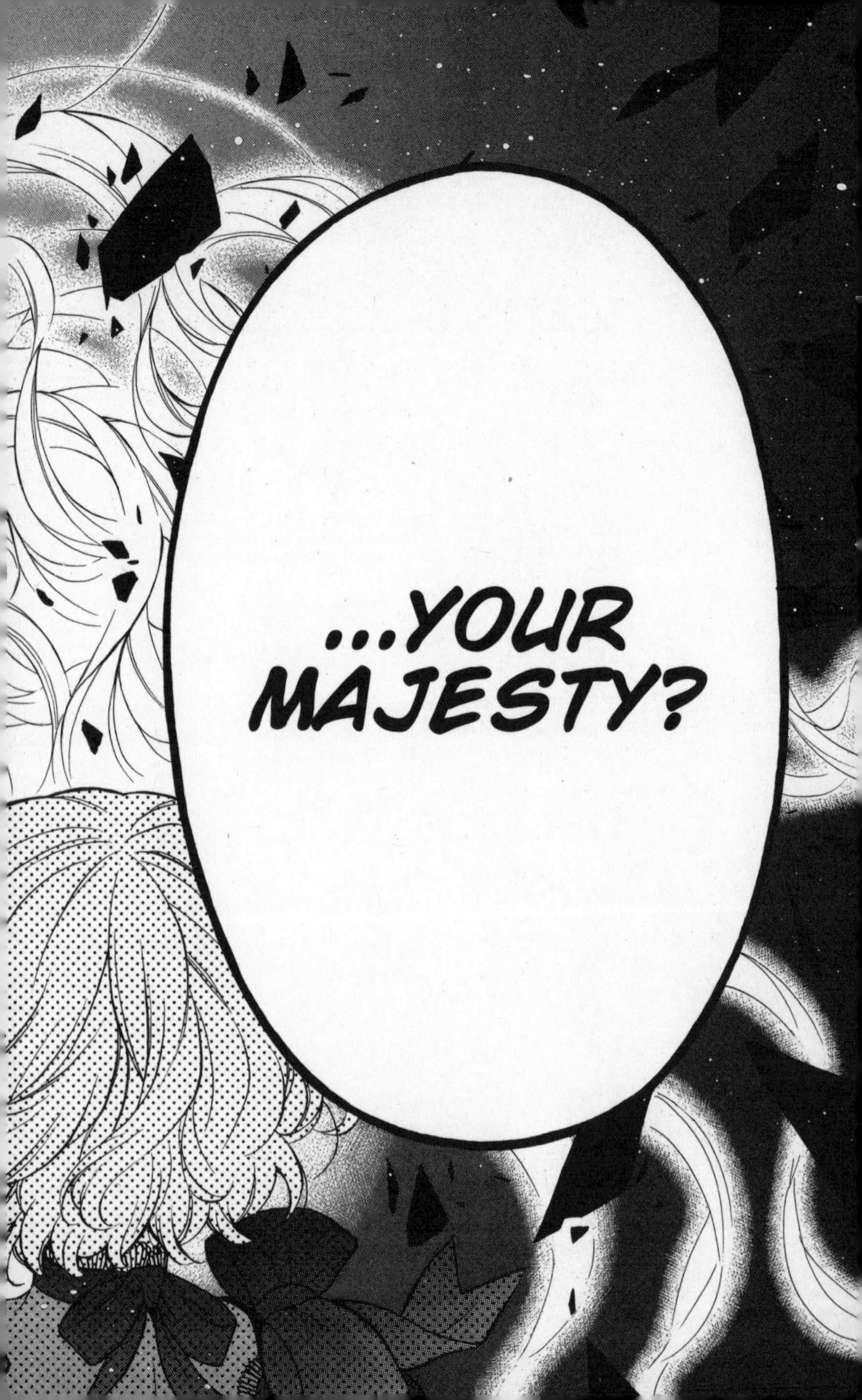
...YOUR MAJESTY?

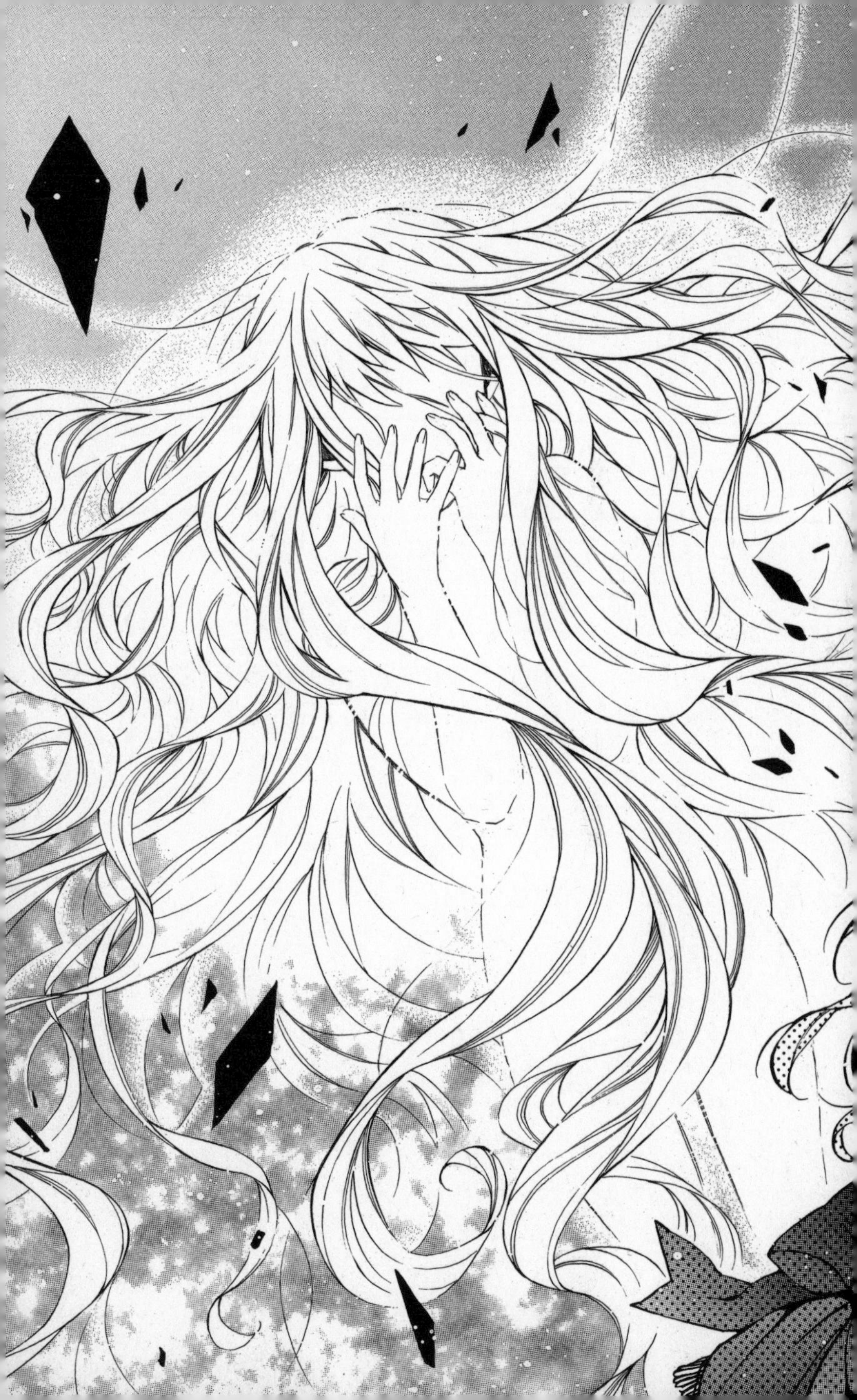

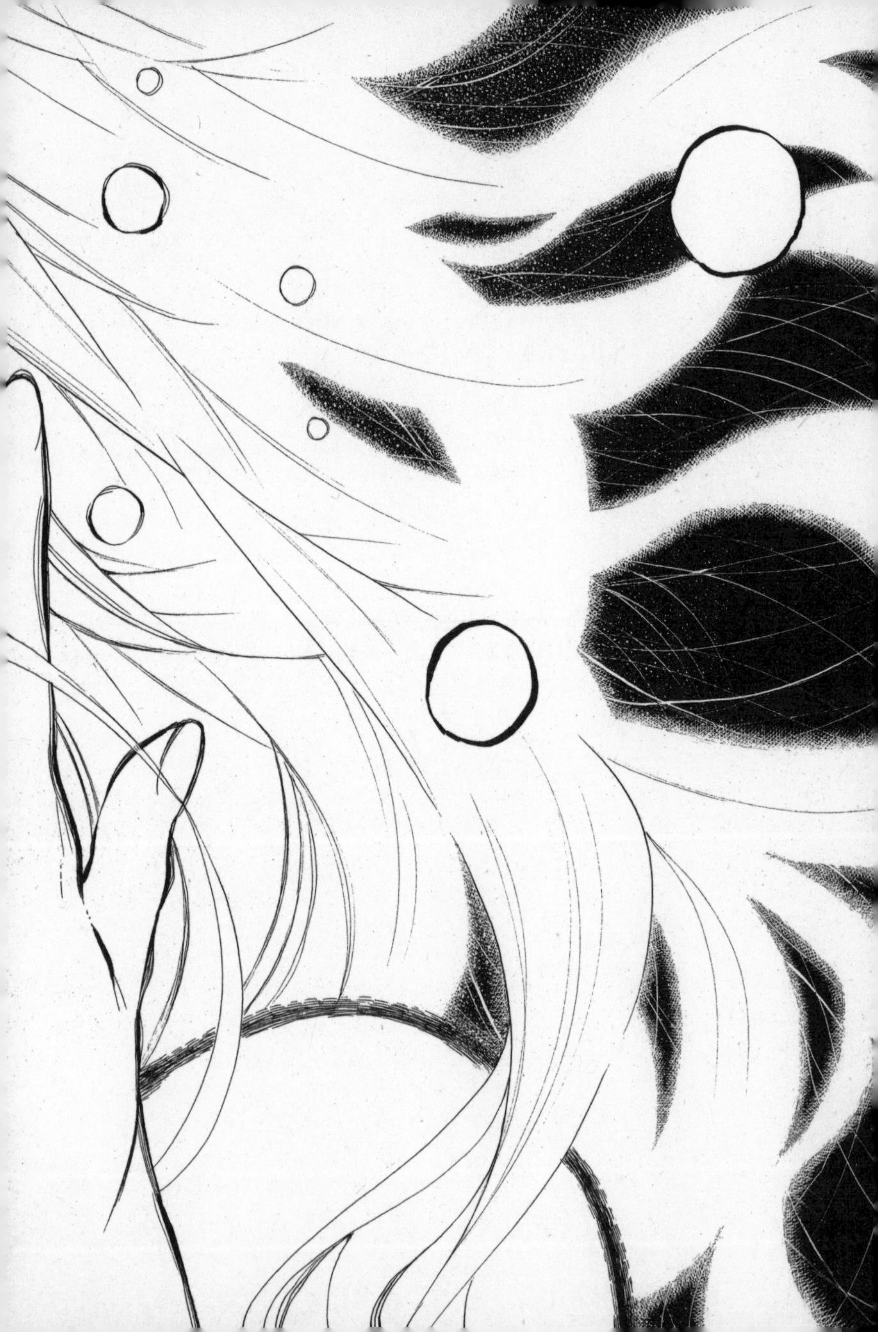

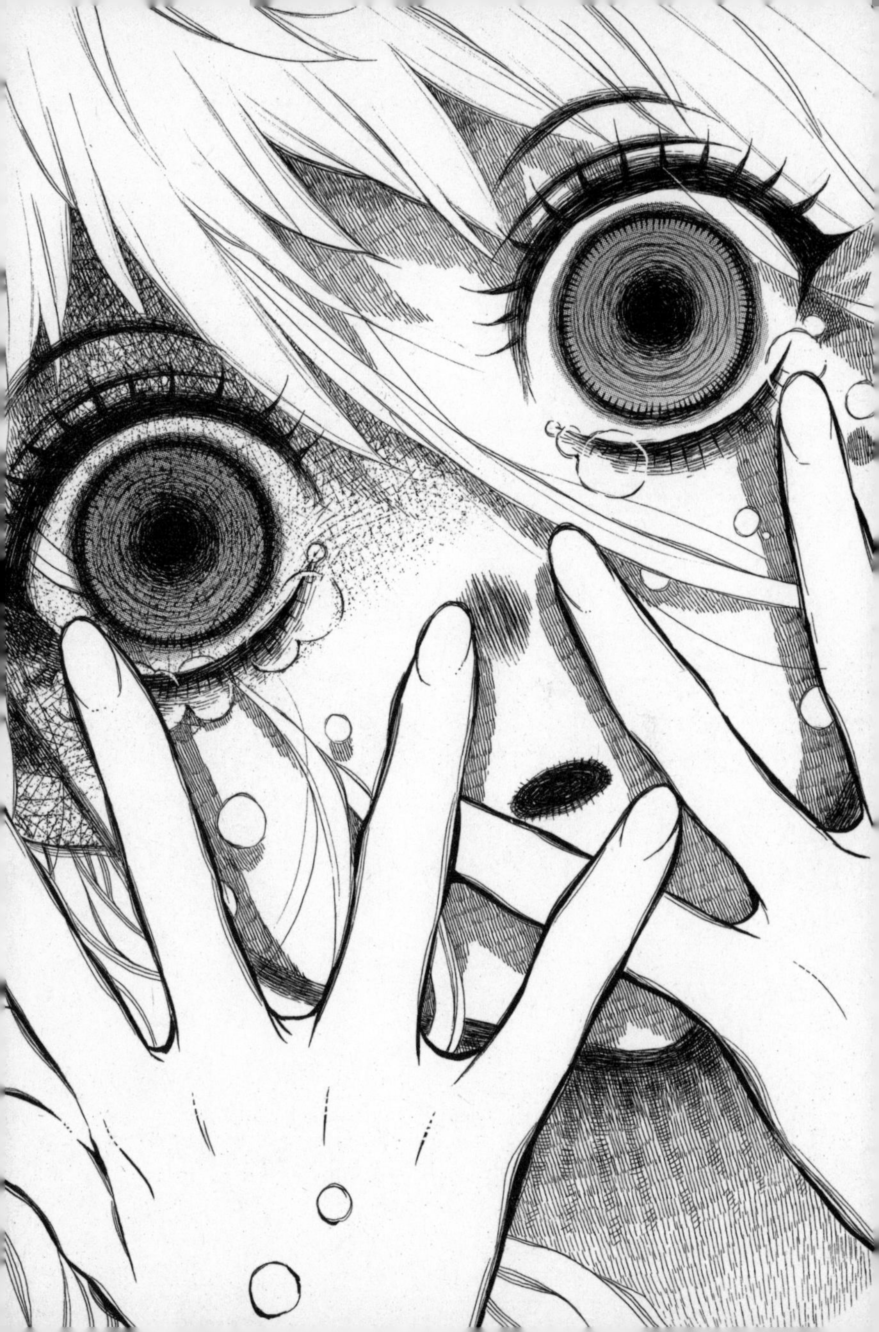

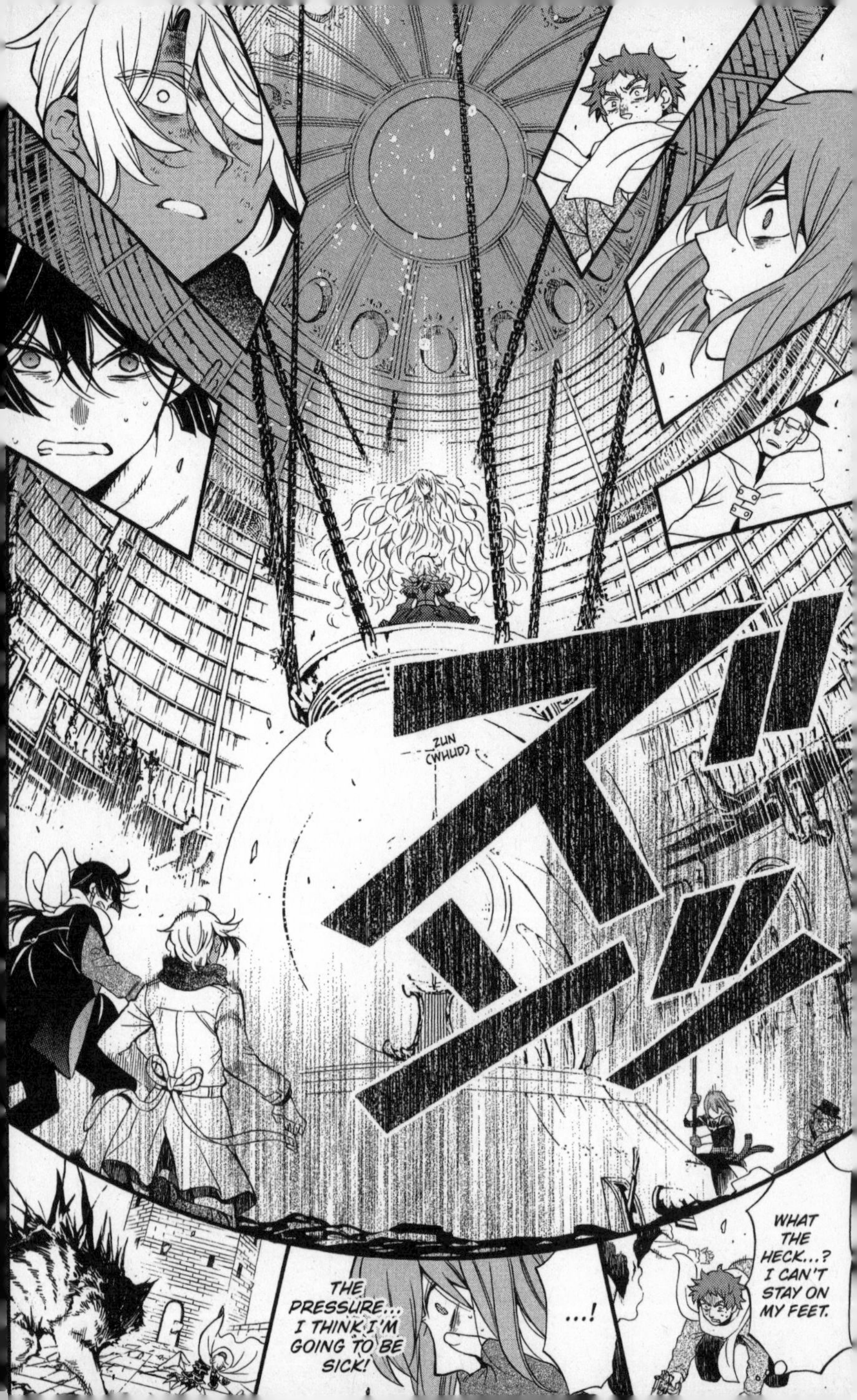
ZUN
(WHUD)
WHAT THE HECK...? I CAN'T STAY ON MY FEET.
...!
THE PRESSURE... I THINK I'M GOING TO BE SICK!

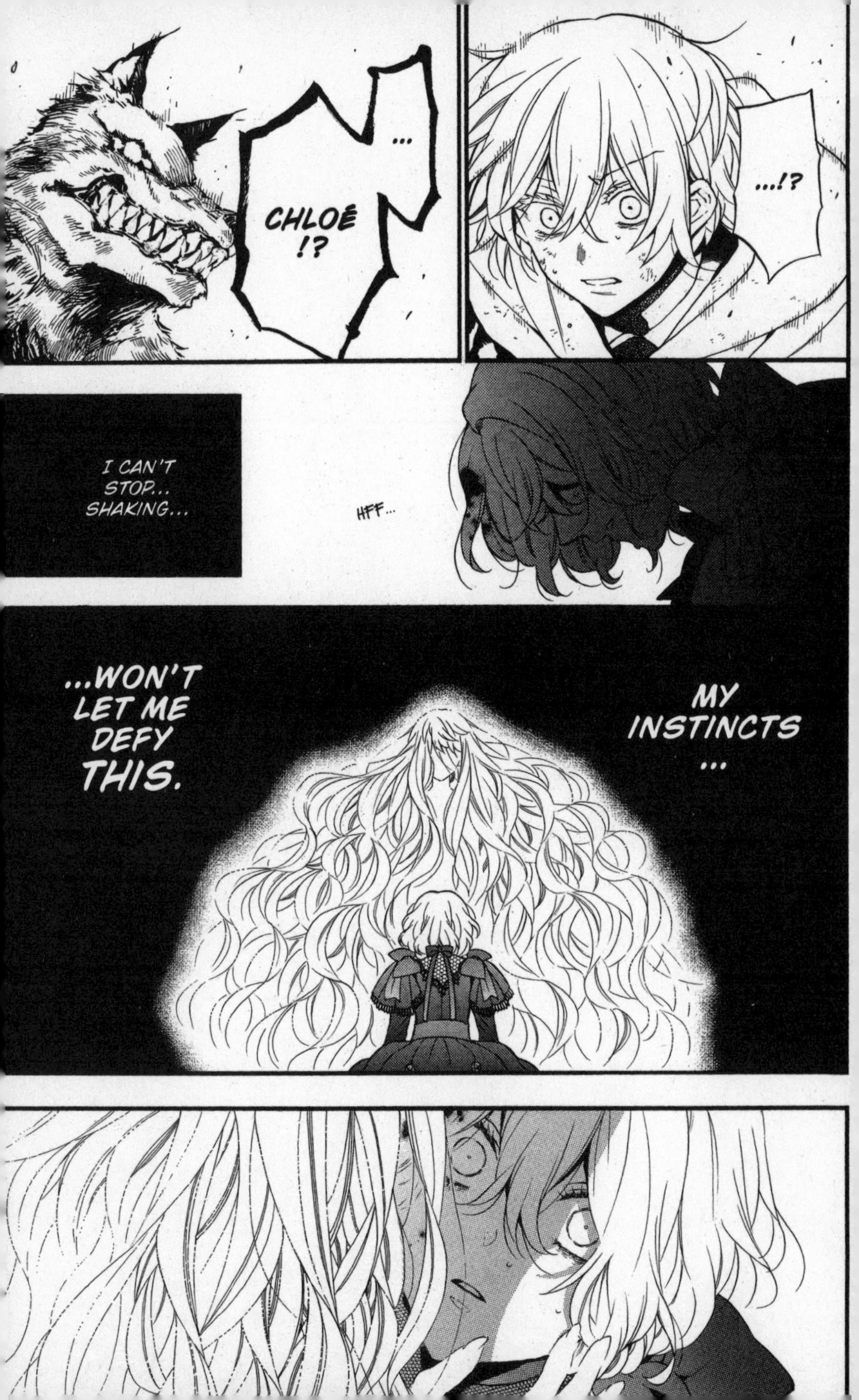
...!?
...
CHLOÉ !?
HFF...
I CAN'T STOP... SHAKING...
MY INSTINCTS ...
...WON'T LET ME DEFY THIS.

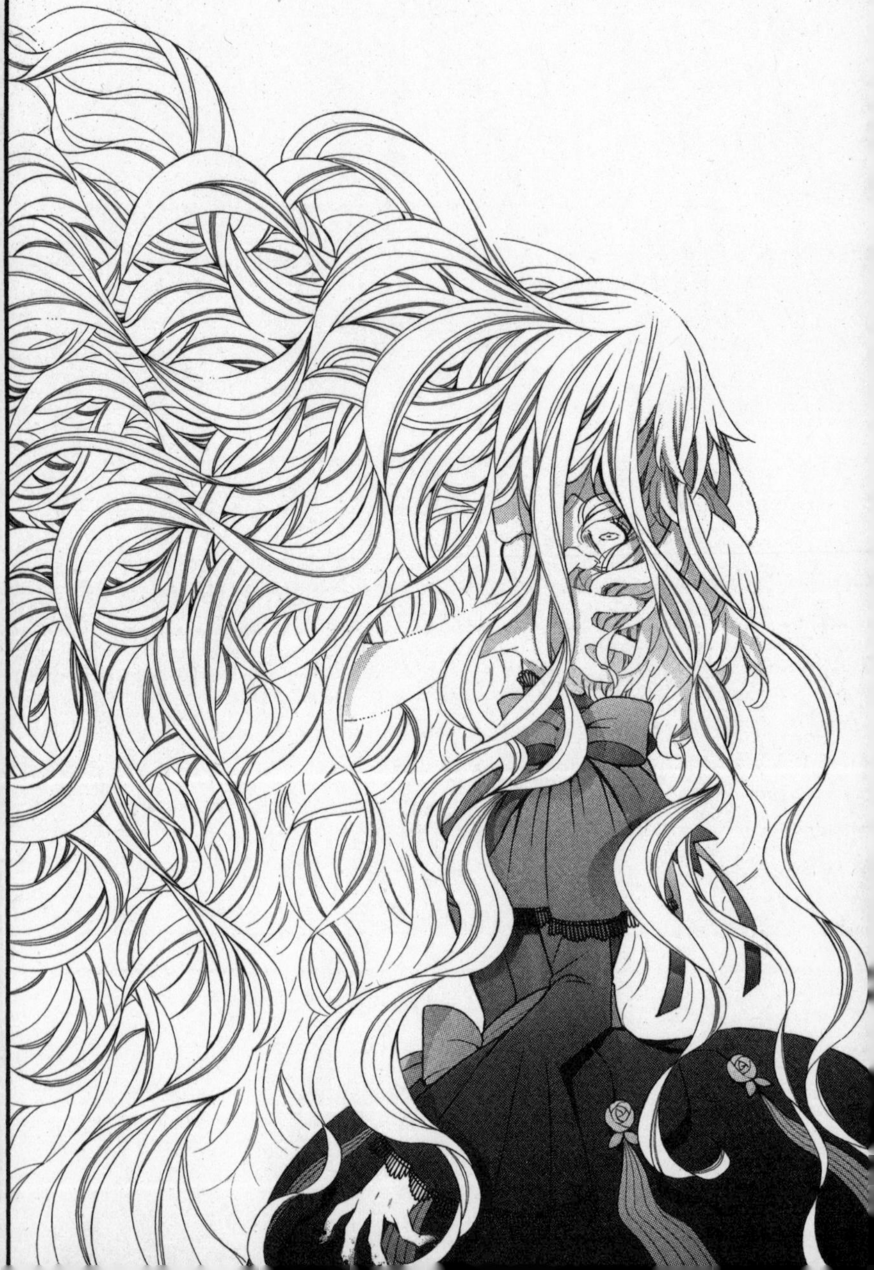

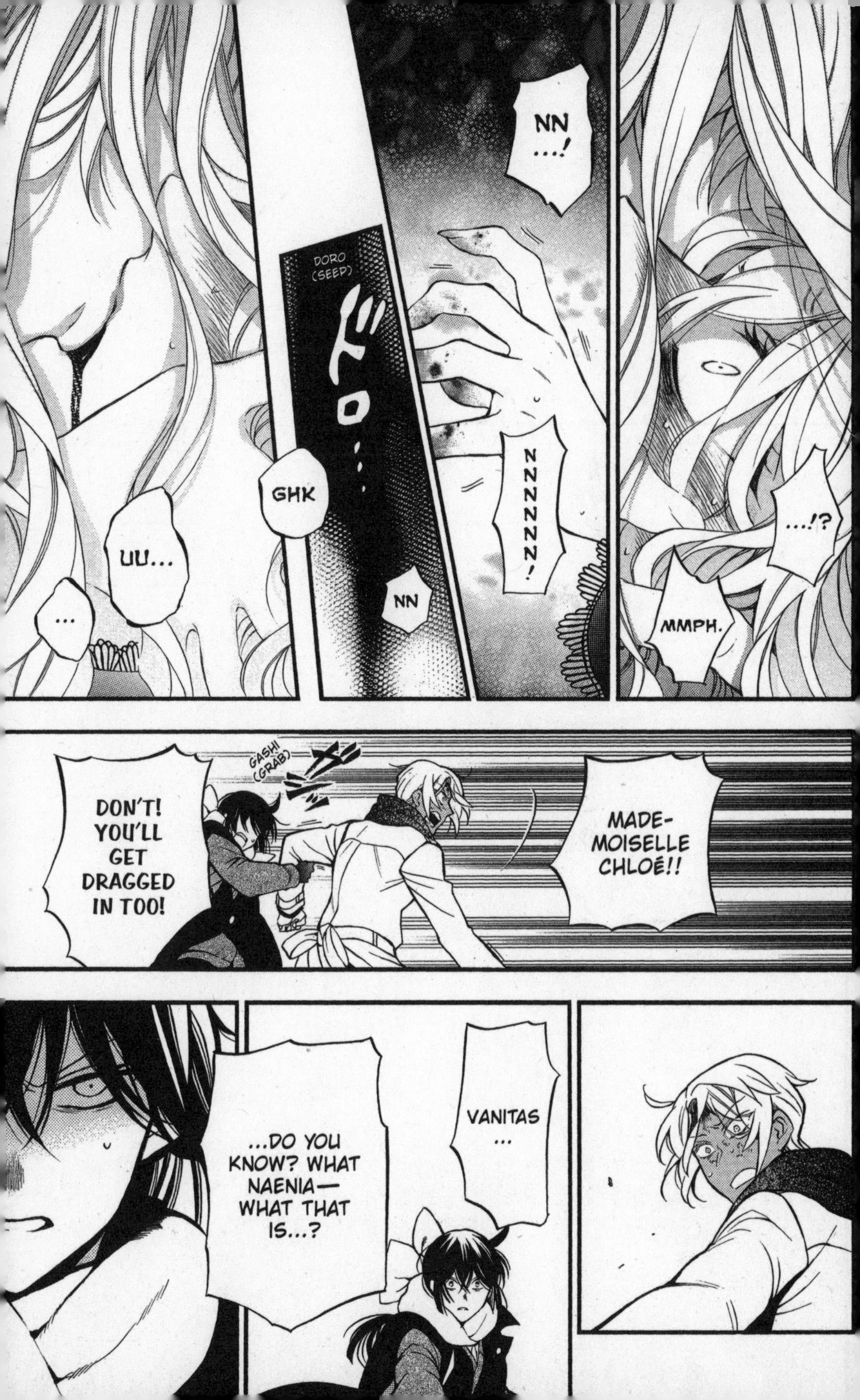
...!?
MMPH.
NN ...!
NNNNNN!
DORO (SEEP)
GHK
NN
UU...
...
MADE-MOISELLE CHLOÉ!!
GASHI (GRAB)
DON'T! YOU'LL GET DRAGGED IN TOO!
VANITAS ...
...DO YOU KNOW? WHAT NAENIA— WHAT THAT IS...?

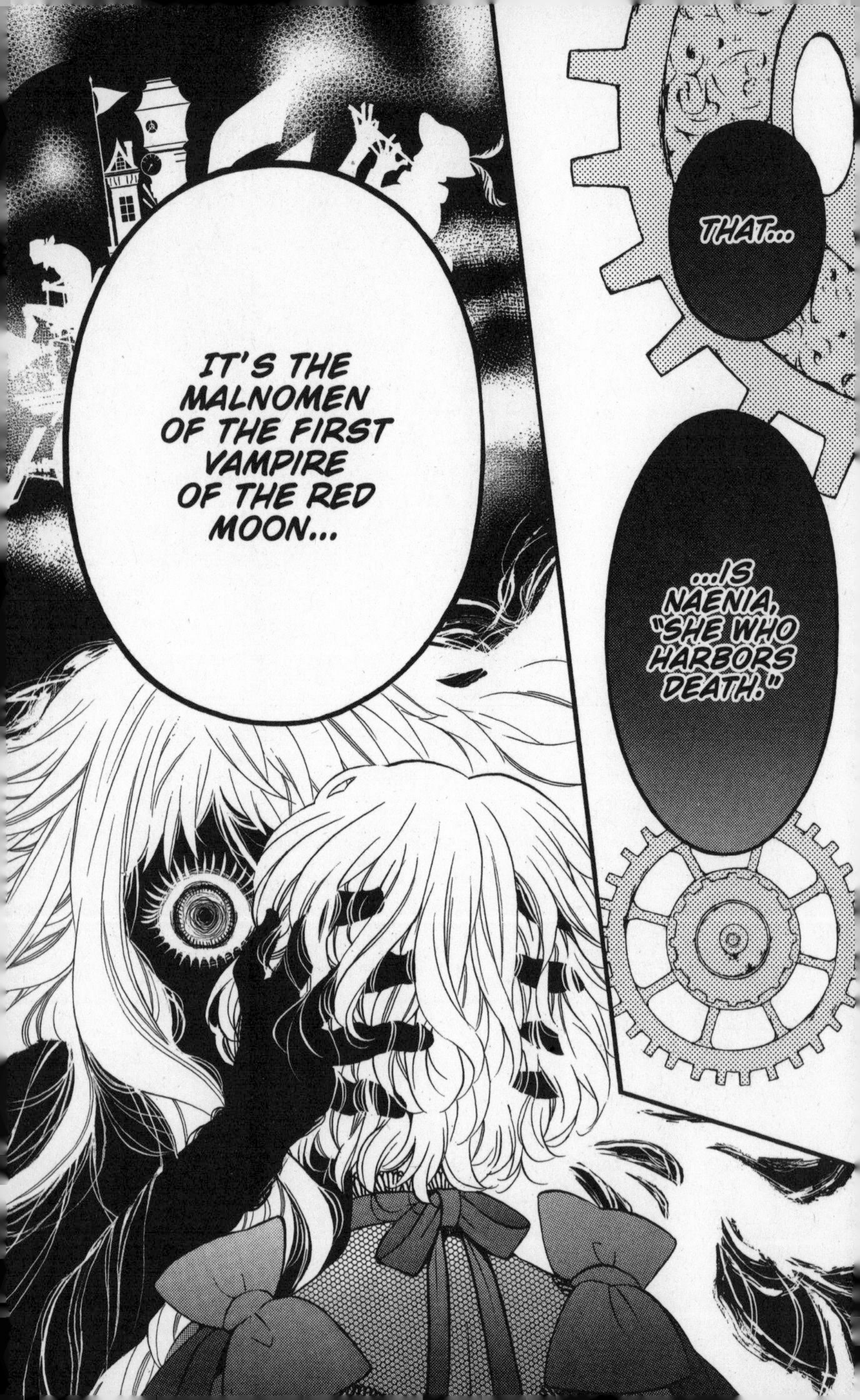
THAT...
...IS NAENIA, "SHE WHO HARBORS DEATH."
IT'S THE MALNOMEN OF THE FIRST VAMPIRE OF THE RED MOON...

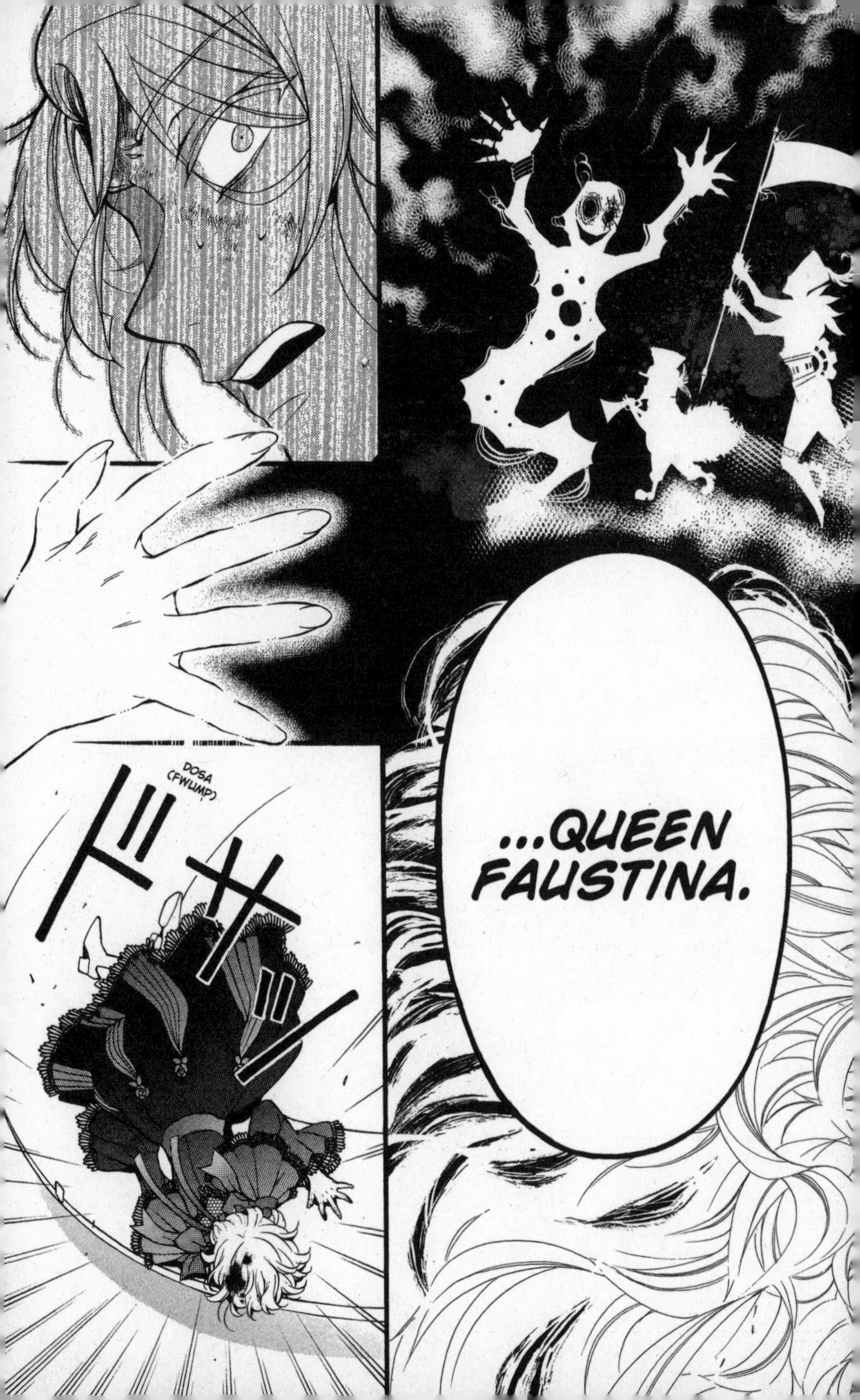
DOSA
(FWUMP)
...QUEEN FAUSTINA.

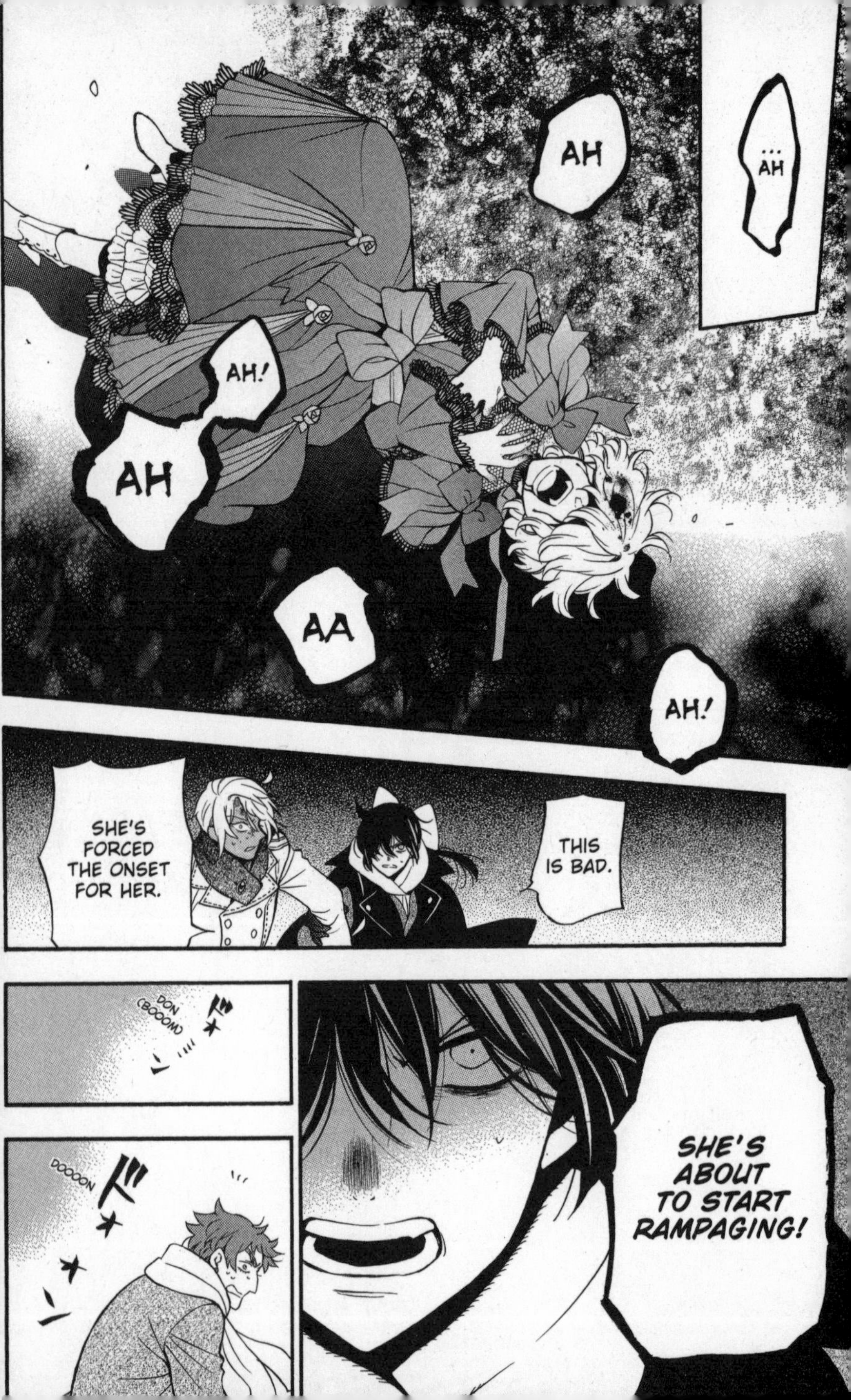
...AH
AH
AH!
AH
AA
AH!
THIS IS BAD.
SHE'S FORCED THE ONSET FOR HER.
SHE'S ABOUT TO START RAMPAGING!
DON (BOOOM)
DOOOON

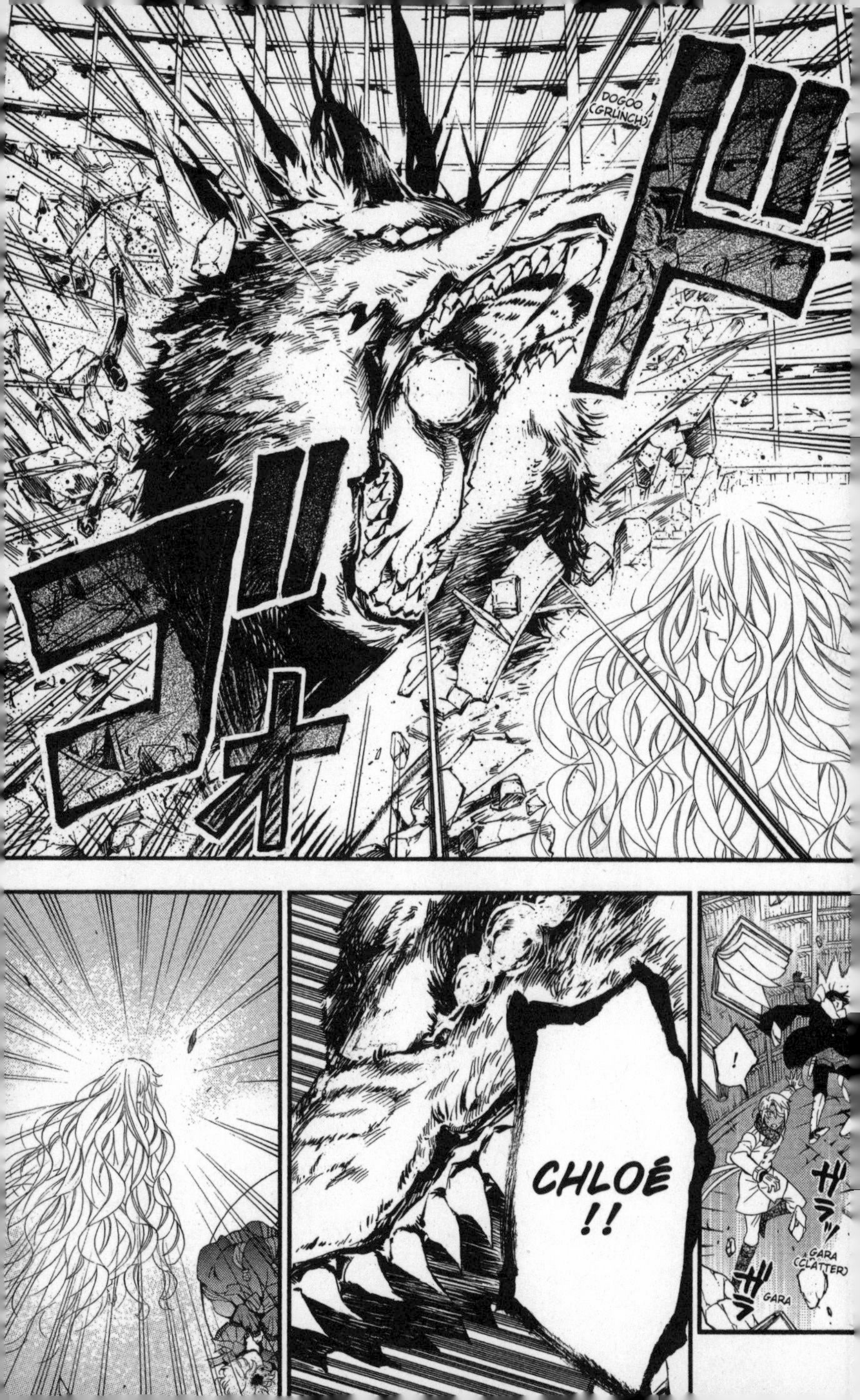
DOGOO (GRUNCH)
!
GARA (CLATTER)
GARA
CHLOÉ !!

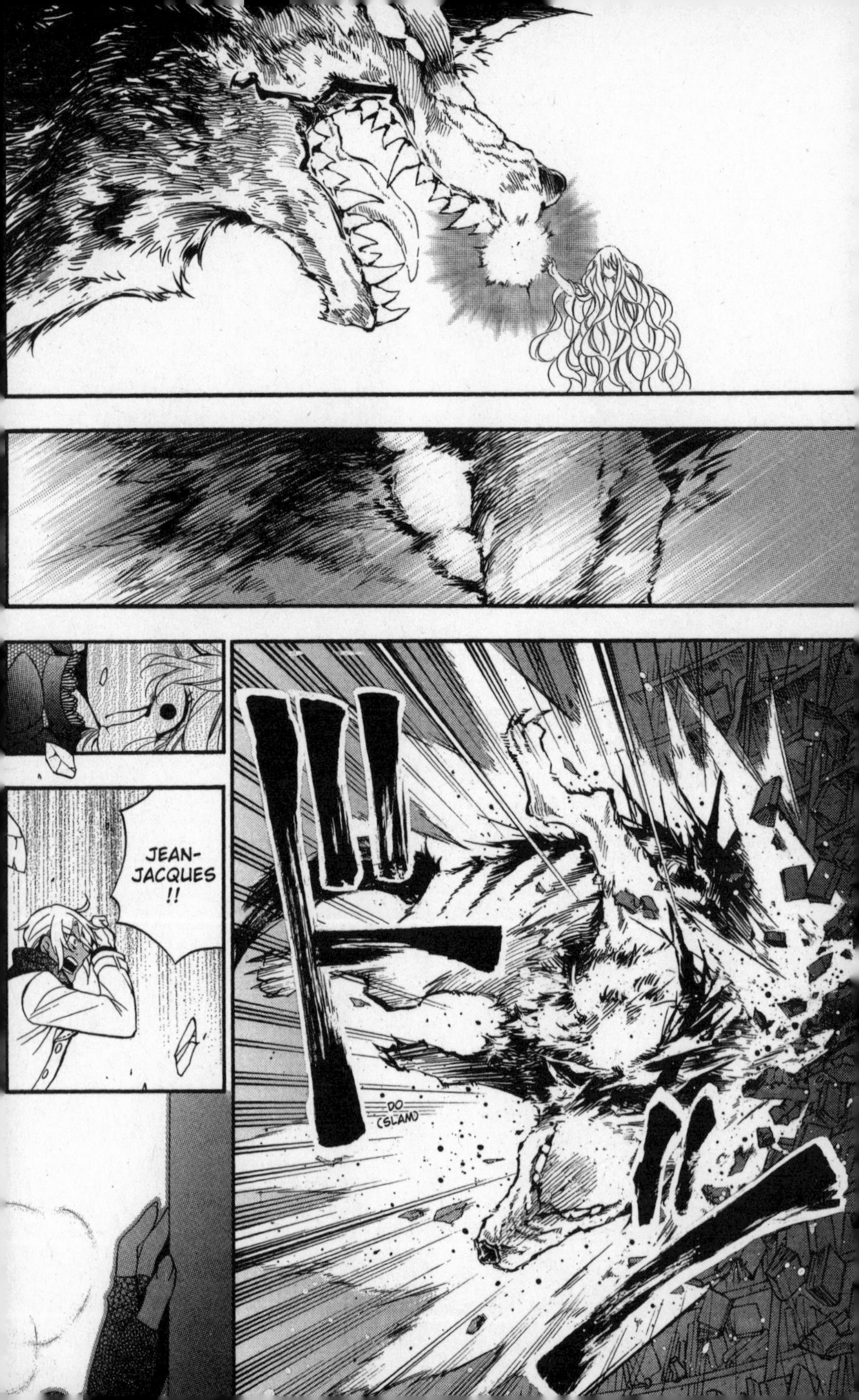
JEAN-JACQUES !!
DO (SLAM)

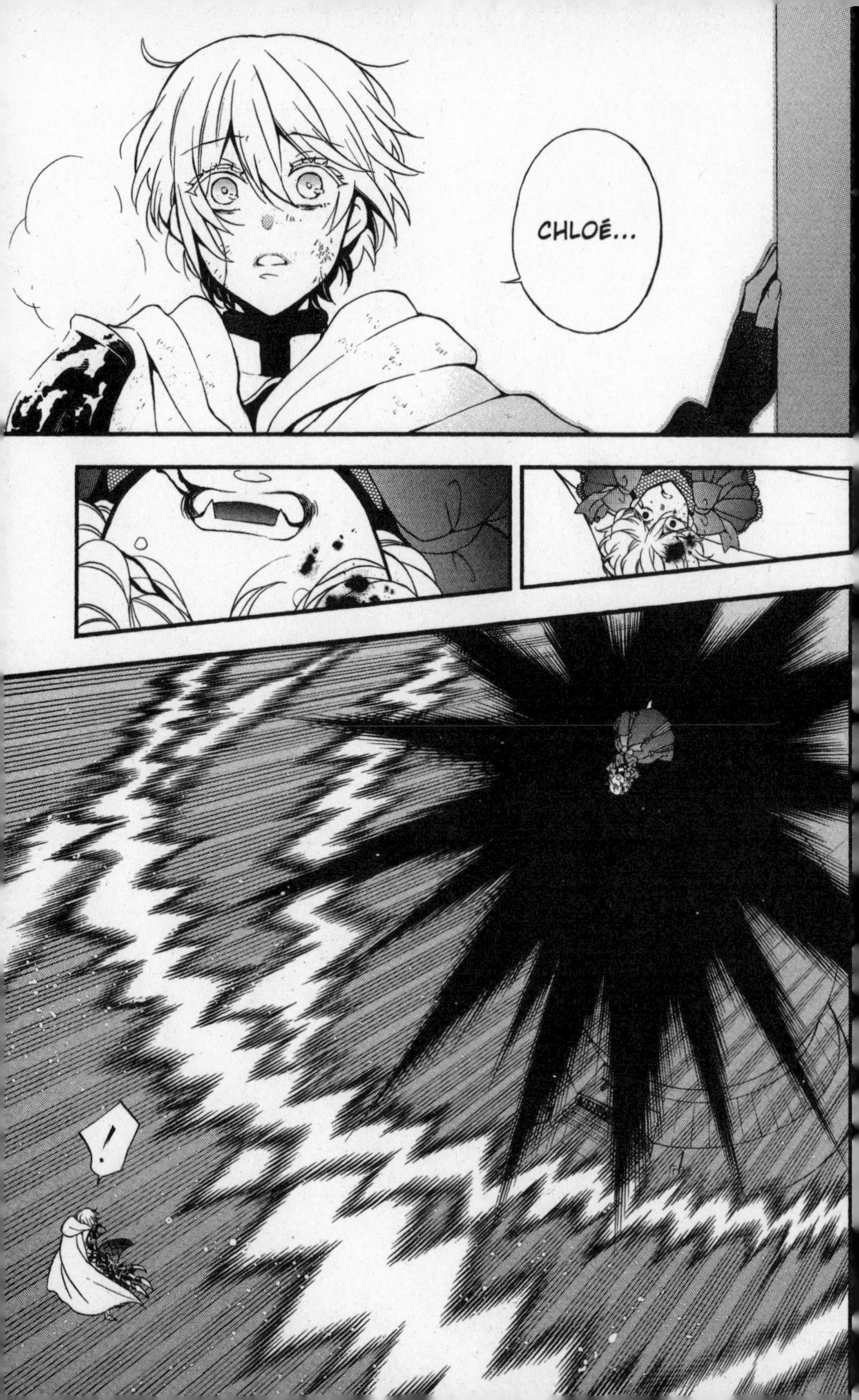
CHLOÉ...
!

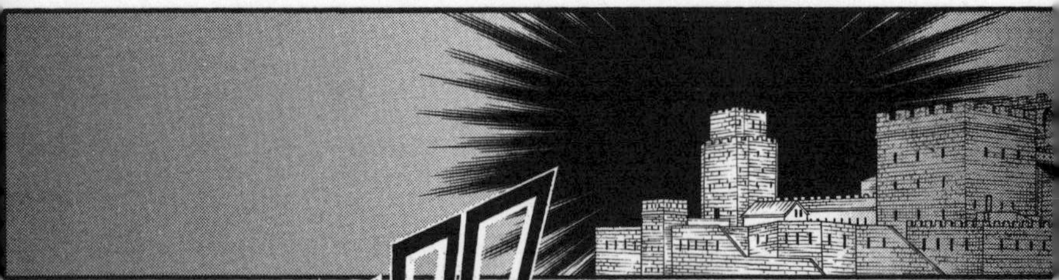

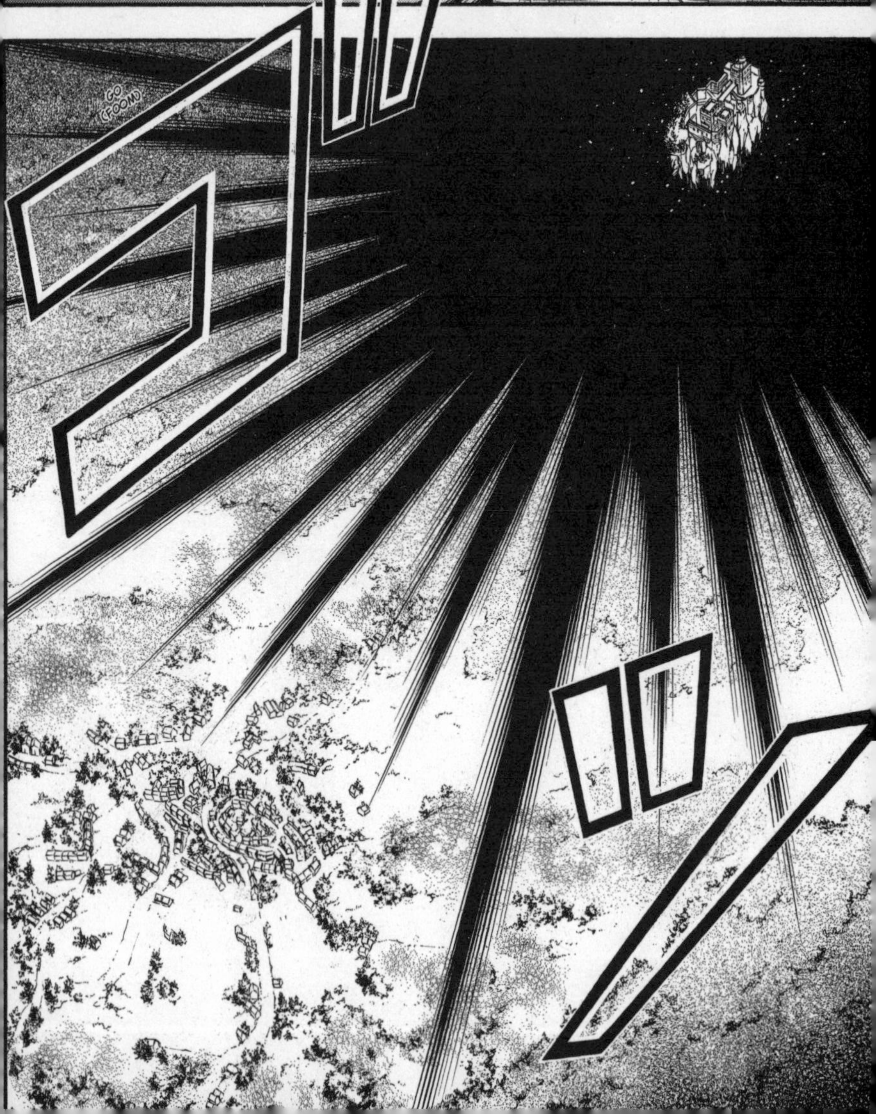
GO (FOOM)

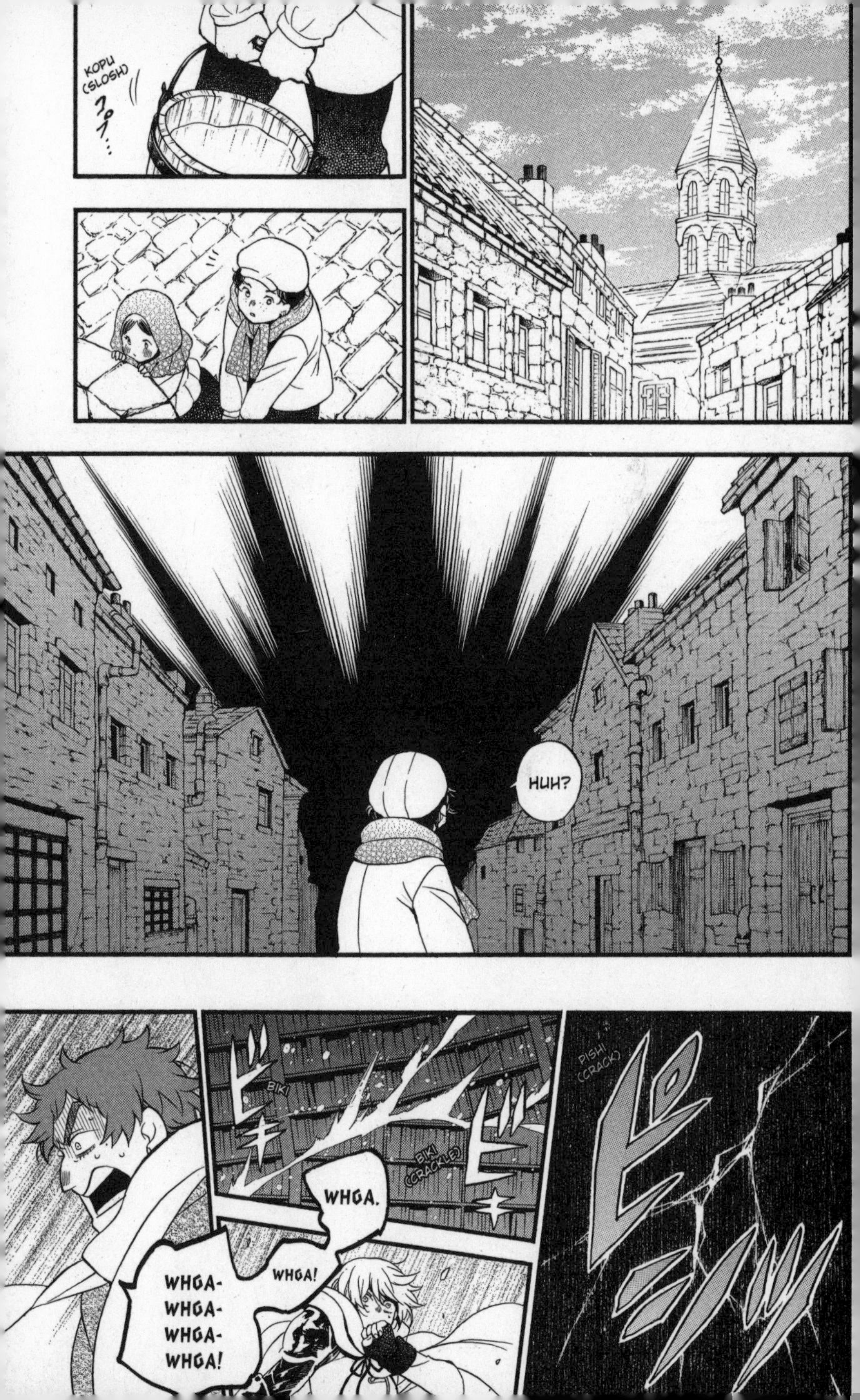
KOPU (SLOSH)
HUH?
PISHI (CRACK)
BIKI
BIKI (CRACKLE)
WHGA.
WHGA!
WHGA-WHGA-WHGA-WHGA!

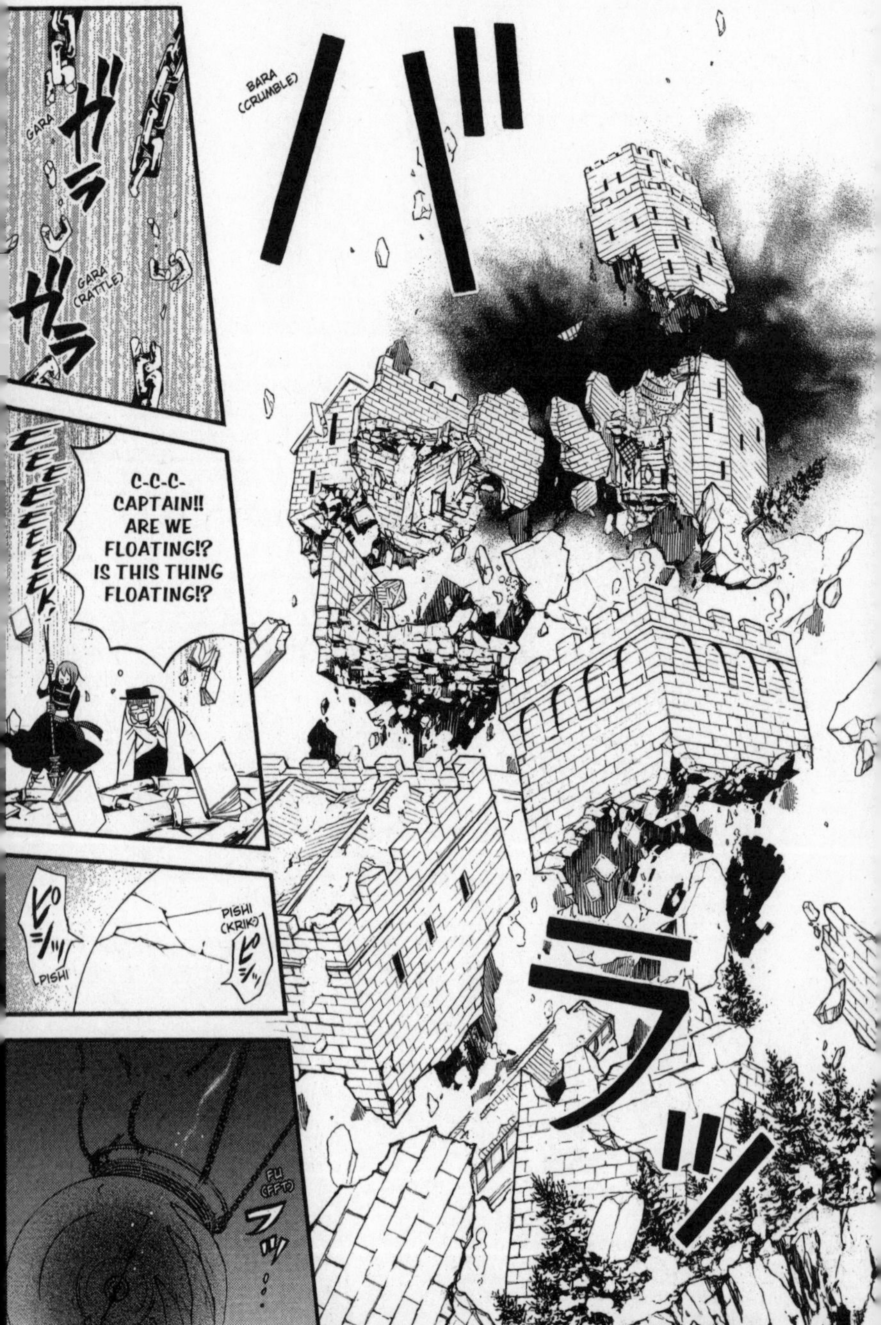

BARA (CRUMBLE)
バラッ
GARA
ガラ
GARA (RATTLE)
ガラ
EEEEEEEEK!!
C-C-C-CAPTAIN!! ARE WE FLOATING!? IS THIS THING FLOATING!?
PISHI
ピシッ
PISHI (KRIK)
ピシッ
FU (FFT)
フッ

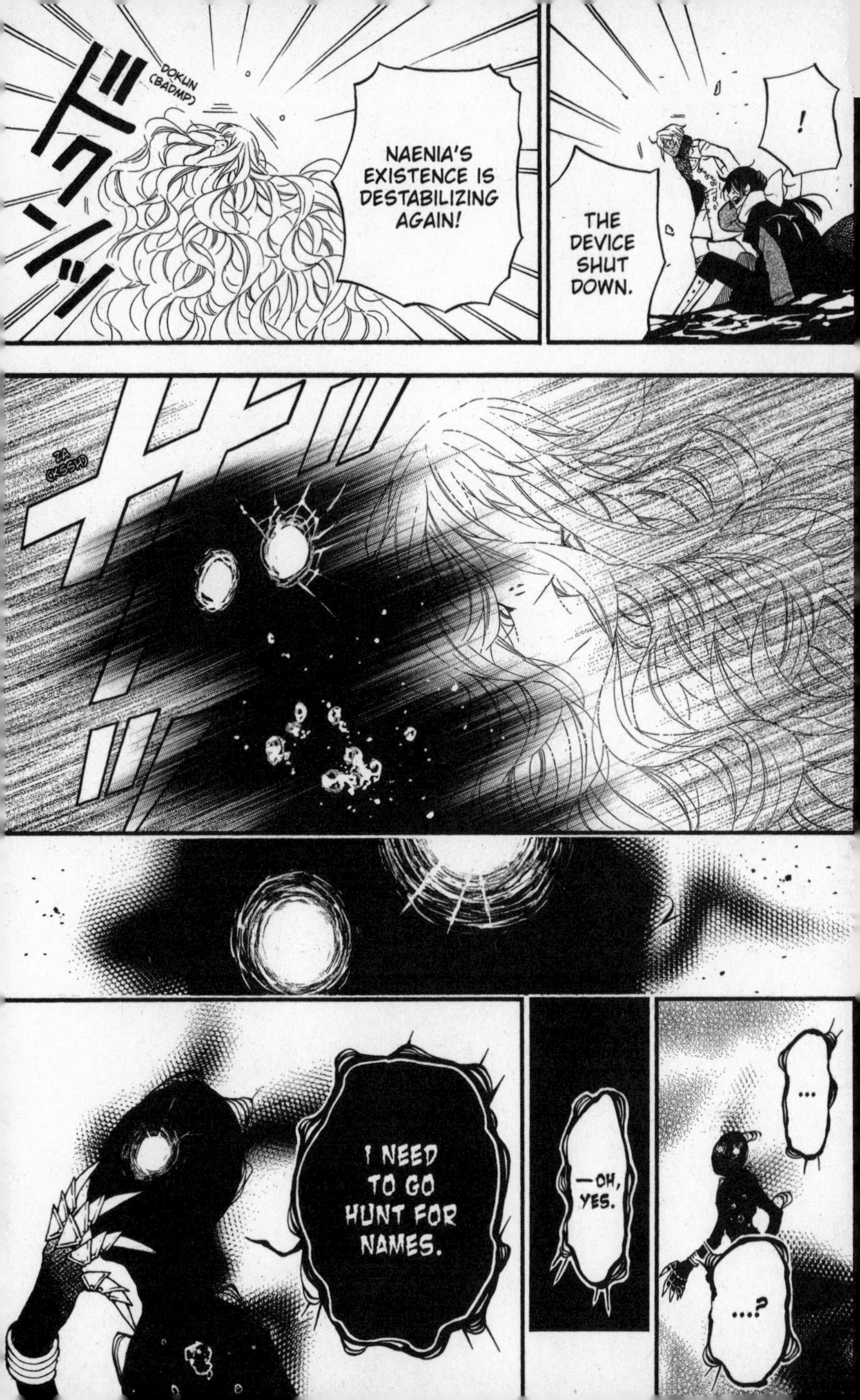
!
THE DEVICE SHUT DOWN.
DOKUN (BADMP)
NAENIA'S EXISTENCE IS DESTABILIZING AGAIN!
ZA (KSSH)
...
...?
—OH, YES.
I NEED TO GO HUNT FOR NAMES.

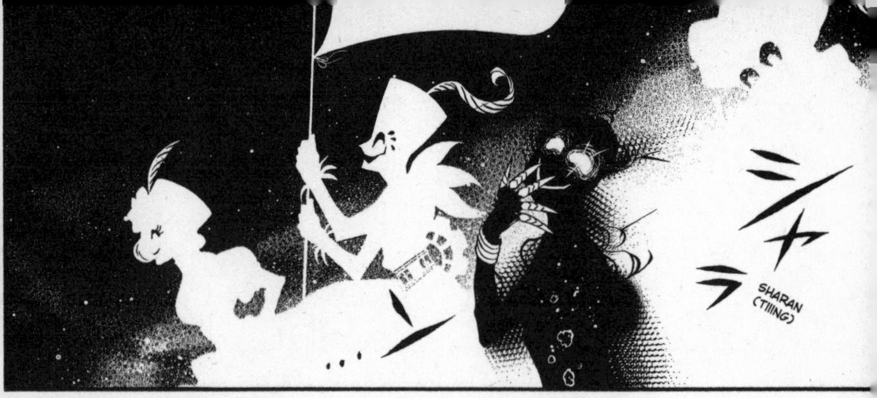
シャラ
SHARAN (TIIING)
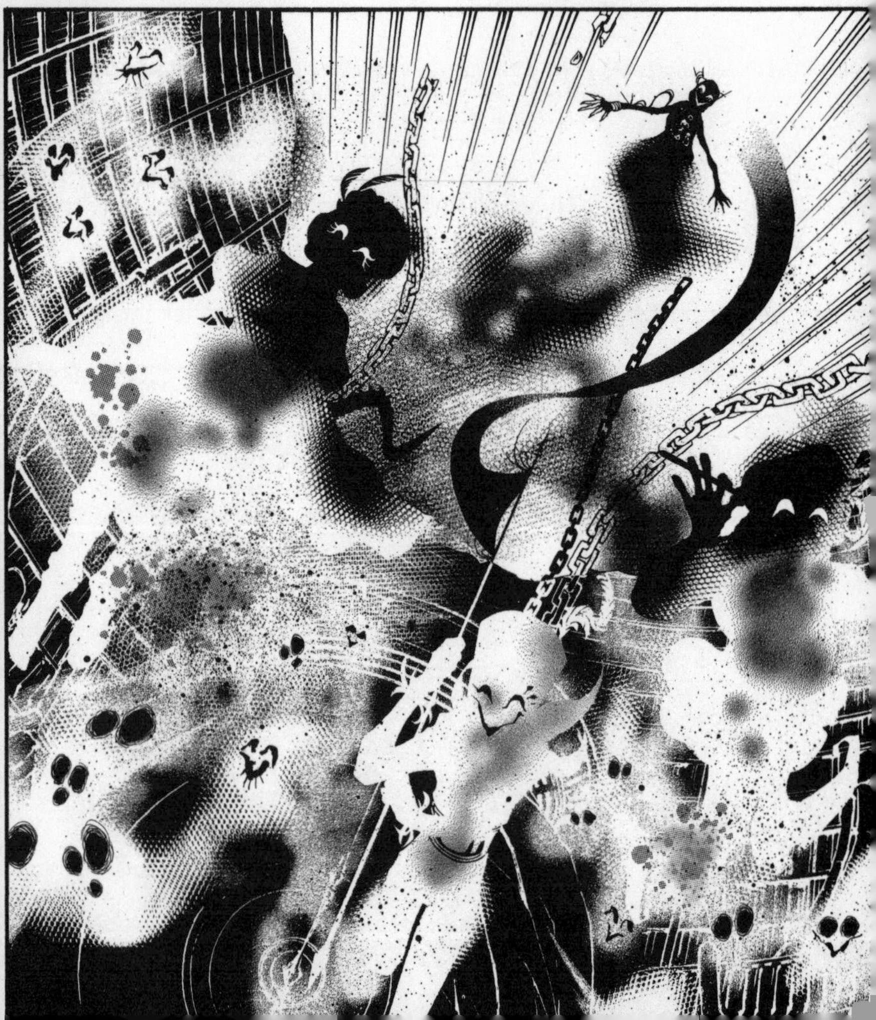

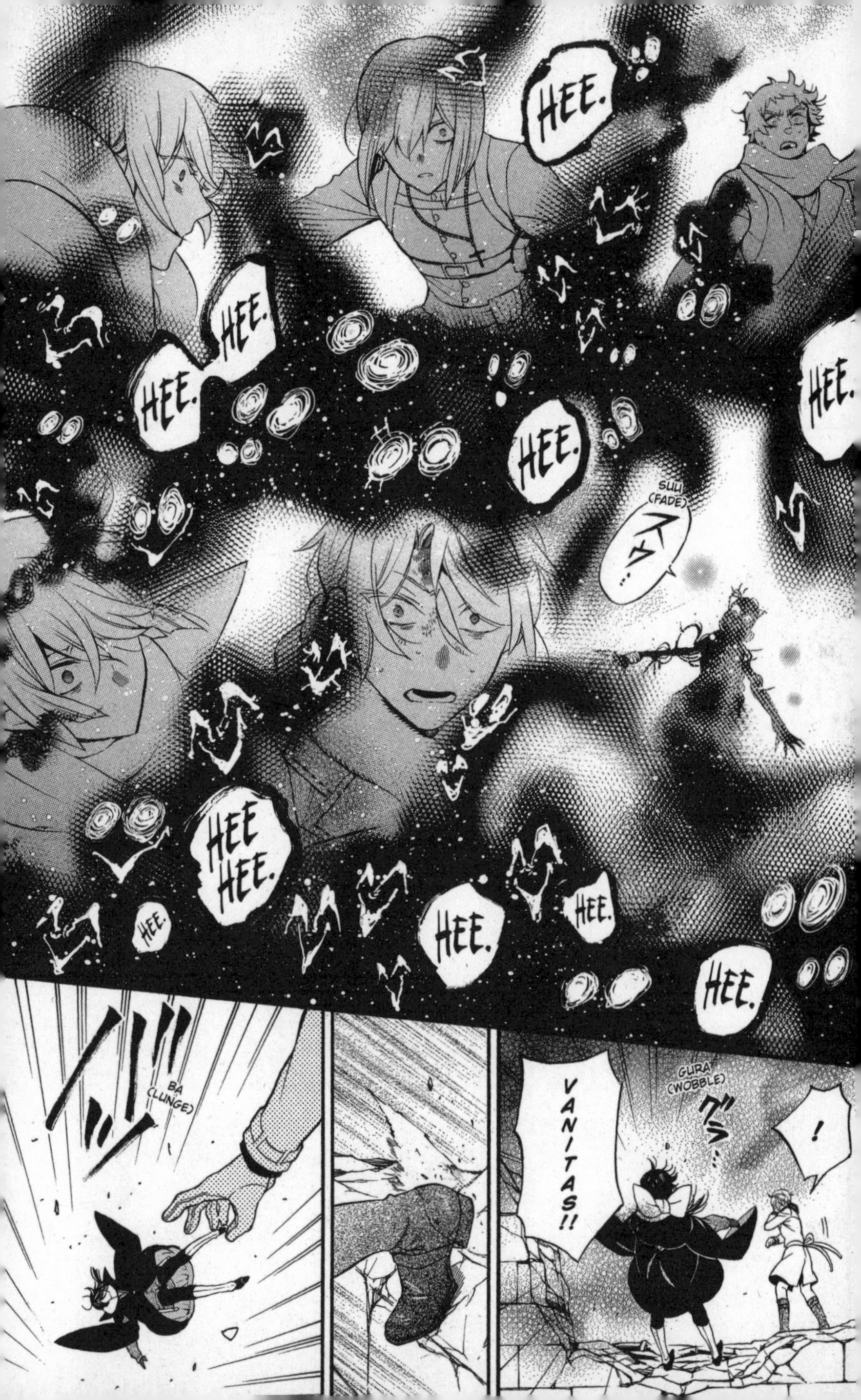
HEE.
HEE.
HEE.
SUU (FADE)
スッ…
HEE.
HEE.
HEE HEE.
HEE.
HEE.
HEE.
HEE.
GURA (WOBBLE)
グラ…
!
VANITAS!!
BA (LUNGE)

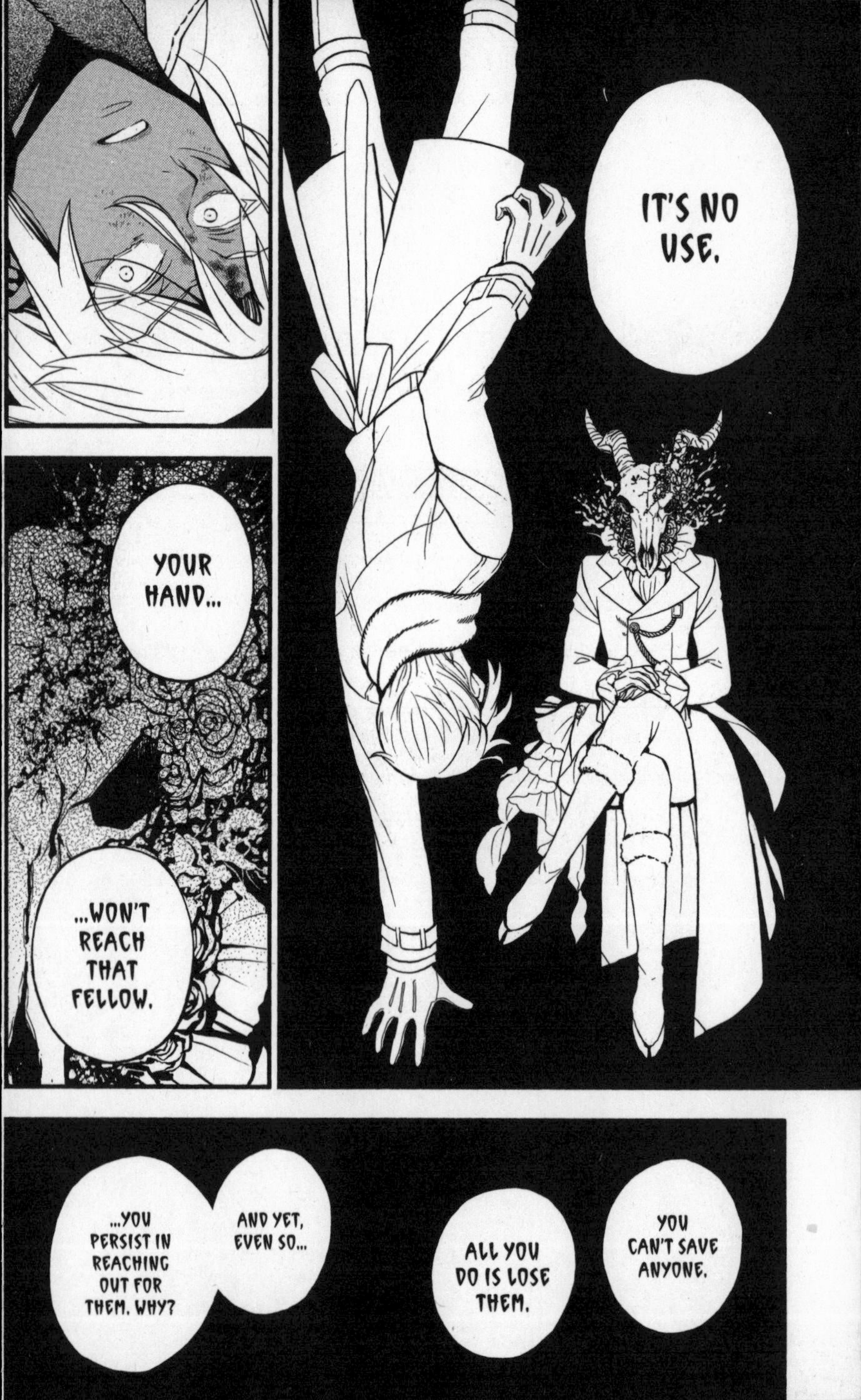
IT'S NO USE.
YOUR HAND...
...WON'T REACH THAT FELLOW.
YOU CAN'T SAVE ANYONE.
ALL YOU DO IS LOSE THEM.
AND YET, EVEN SO...
...YOU PERSIST IN REACHING OUT FOR THEM. WHY?

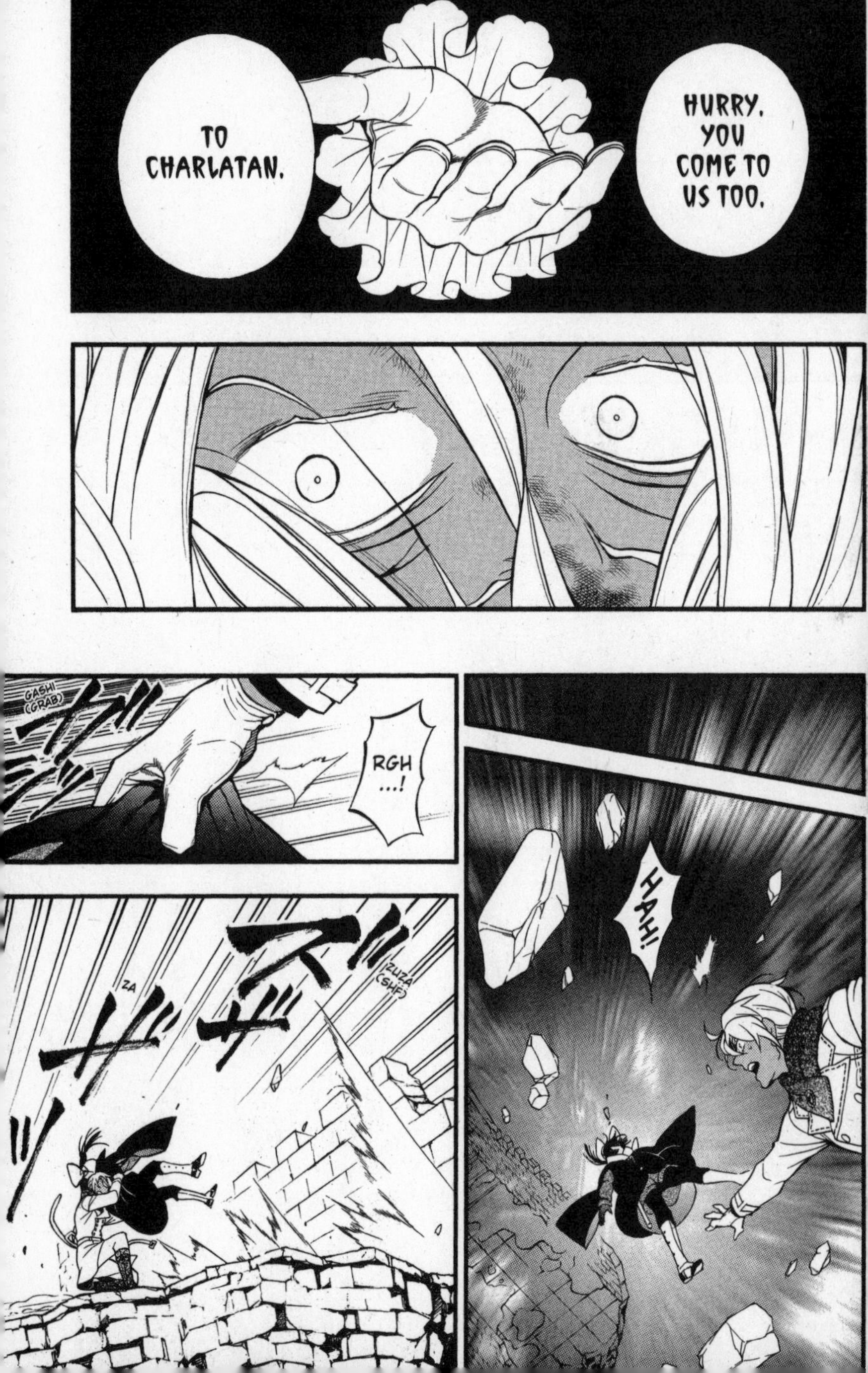
HURRY. YOU COME TO US TOO.
TO CHARLATAN.
HAH!
RGH ...!
GASHI (GRAB)
ZUZA (SHF)
ZA

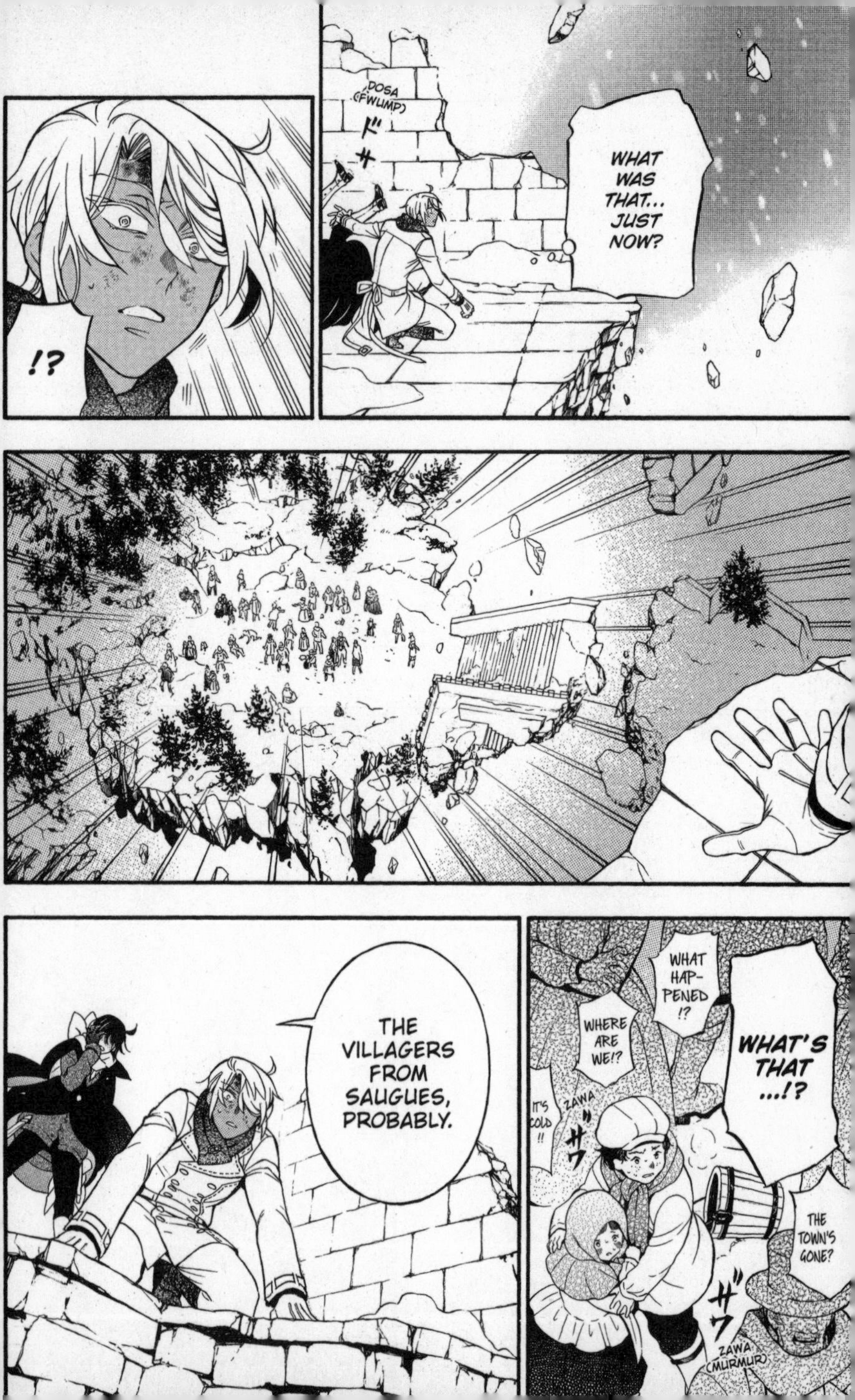
WHAT WAS THAT... JUST NOW?
DOSA (FWUMP)
ドサ
!?
WHAT'S THAT ...!?
WHAT HAP-PENED !?
WHERE ARE WE!?
ZAWA
ザワ
IT'S COLD !!
THE TOWN'S GONE?
ザワ
ZAWA (MURMUR)
THE VILLAGERS FROM SAUGUES, PROBABLY.

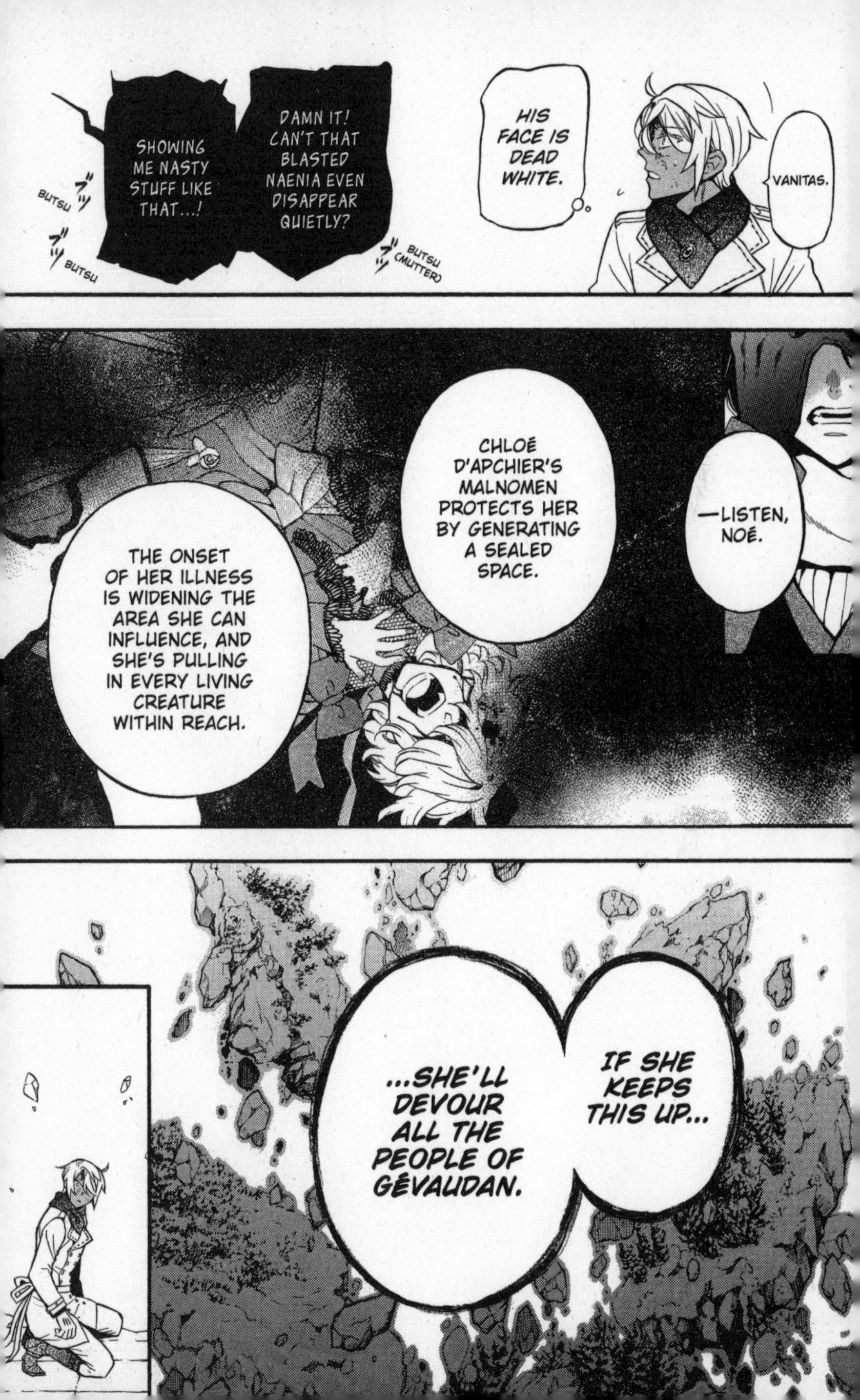
VANITAS.
HIS FACE IS DEAD WHITE.
DAMN IT! CAN'T THAT BLASTED NAENIA EVEN DISAPPEAR QUIETLY?
BUTSU (MUTTER)
SHOWING ME NASTY STUFF LIKE THAT...!
BUTSU
BUTSU
—LISTEN, NOÉ.
CHLOÉ D'APCHIER'S MALNOMEN PROTECTS HER BY GENERATING A SEALED SPACE.
THE ONSET OF HER ILLNESS IS WIDENING THE AREA SHE CAN INFLUENCE, AND SHE'S PULLING IN EVERY LIVING CREATURE WITHIN REACH.
IF SHE KEEPS THIS UP...
...SHE'LL DEVOUR ALL THE PEOPLE OF GÉVAUDAN.

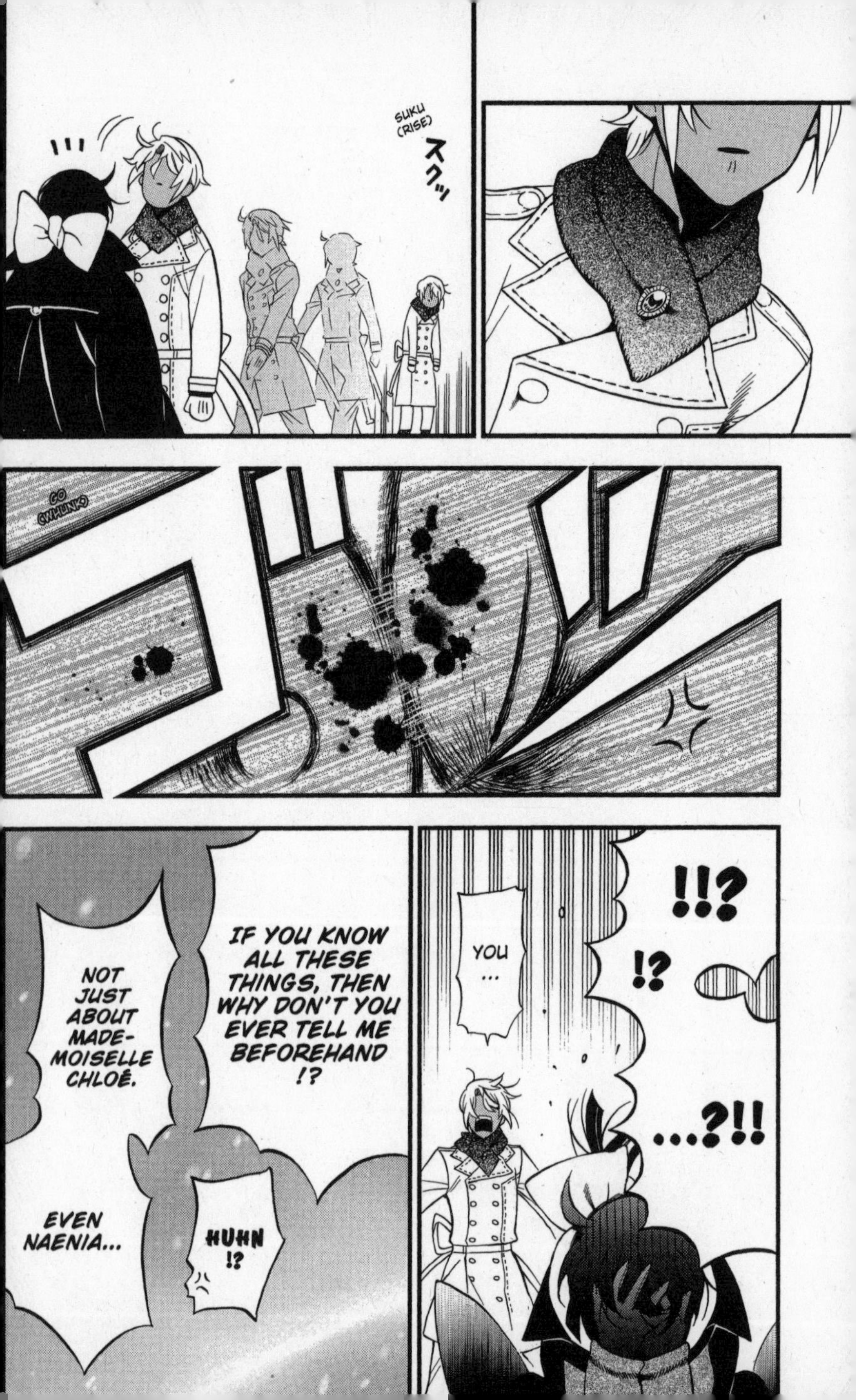
SUKU (RISE)
スクッ
!!!
GO (WHUNK)
!!?
!?
YOU …
…?!!
IF YOU KNOW ALL THESE THINGS, THEN WHY DON'T YOU EVER TELL ME BEFOREHAND !?
NOT JUST ABOUT MADE-MOISELLE CHLOÉ.
HUHN !?
EVEN NAENIA…

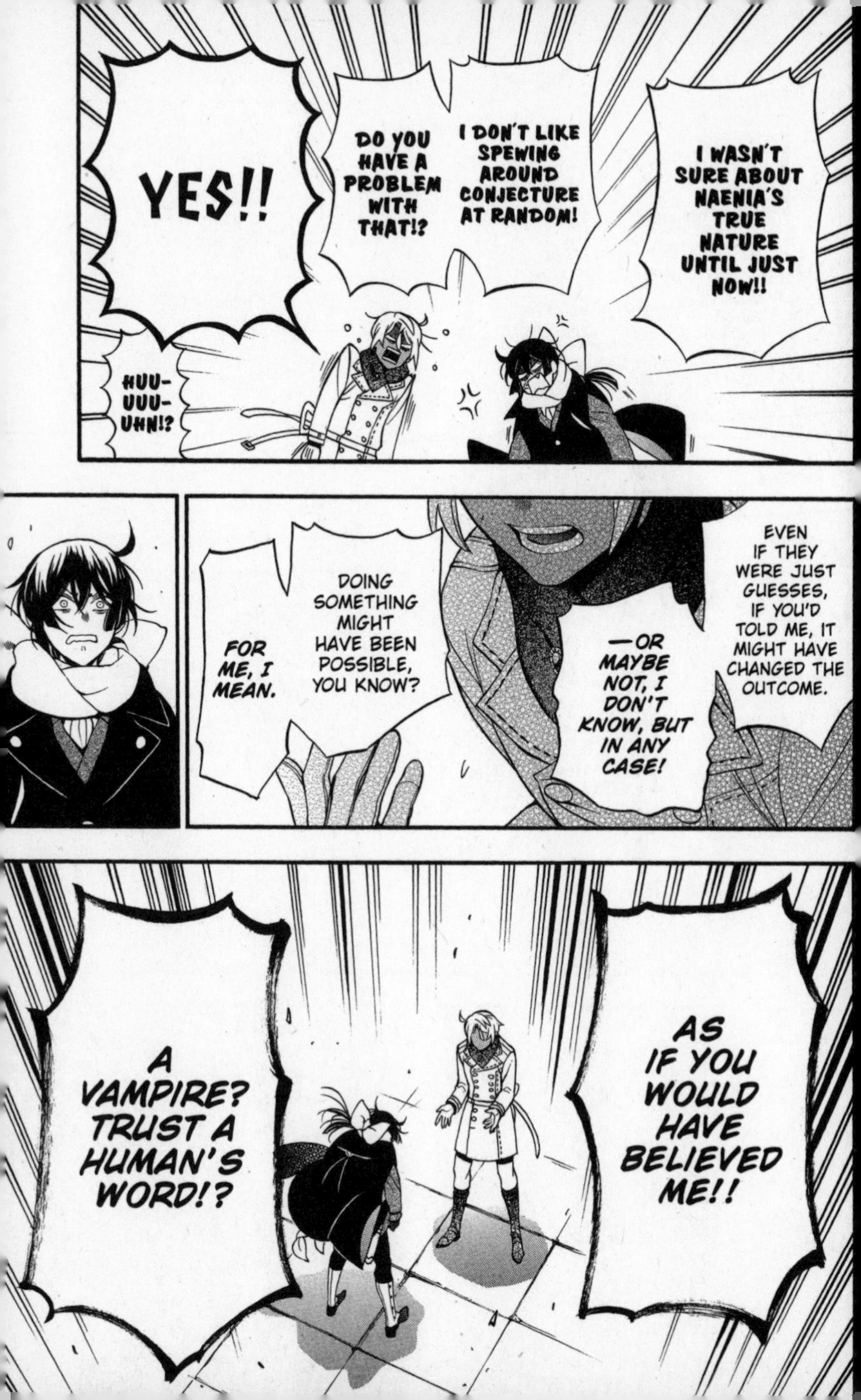

I WASN'T SURE ABOUT NAENIA'S TRUE NATURE UNTIL JUST NOW!!
I DON'T LIKE SPEWING AROUND CONJECTURE AT RANDOM!
DO YOU HAVE A PROBLEM WITH THAT!?
YES!!
HUU-UUU-UHN!?
EVEN IF THEY WERE JUST GUESSES, IF YOU'D TOLD ME, IT MIGHT HAVE CHANGED THE OUTCOME.
—OR MAYBE NOT, I DON'T KNOW, BUT IN ANY CASE!
DOING SOMETHING MIGHT HAVE BEEN POSSIBLE, YOU KNOW?
FOR ME, I MEAN.
AS IF YOU WOULD HAVE BELIEVED ME!!
A VAMPIRE? TRUST A HUMAN'S WORD!?

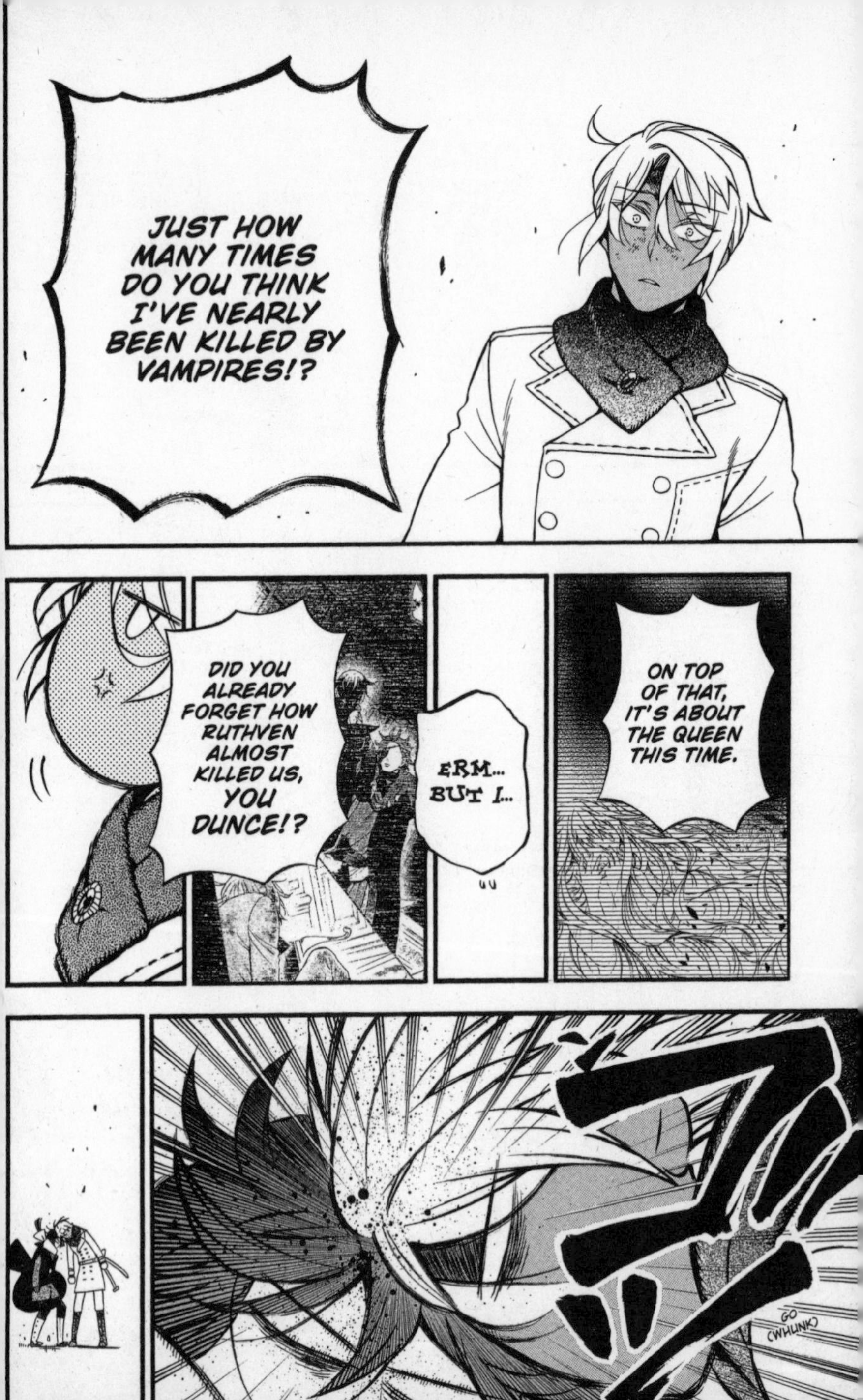
JUST HOW MANY TIMES DO YOU THINK I'VE NEARLY BEEN KILLED BY VAMPIRES!?
ON TOP OF THAT, IT'S ABOUT THE QUEEN THIS TIME.
ERM... BUT I...
DID YOU ALREADY FORGET HOW RUTHVEN ALMOST KILLED US, YOU DUNCE!?
GO (WHUNK)

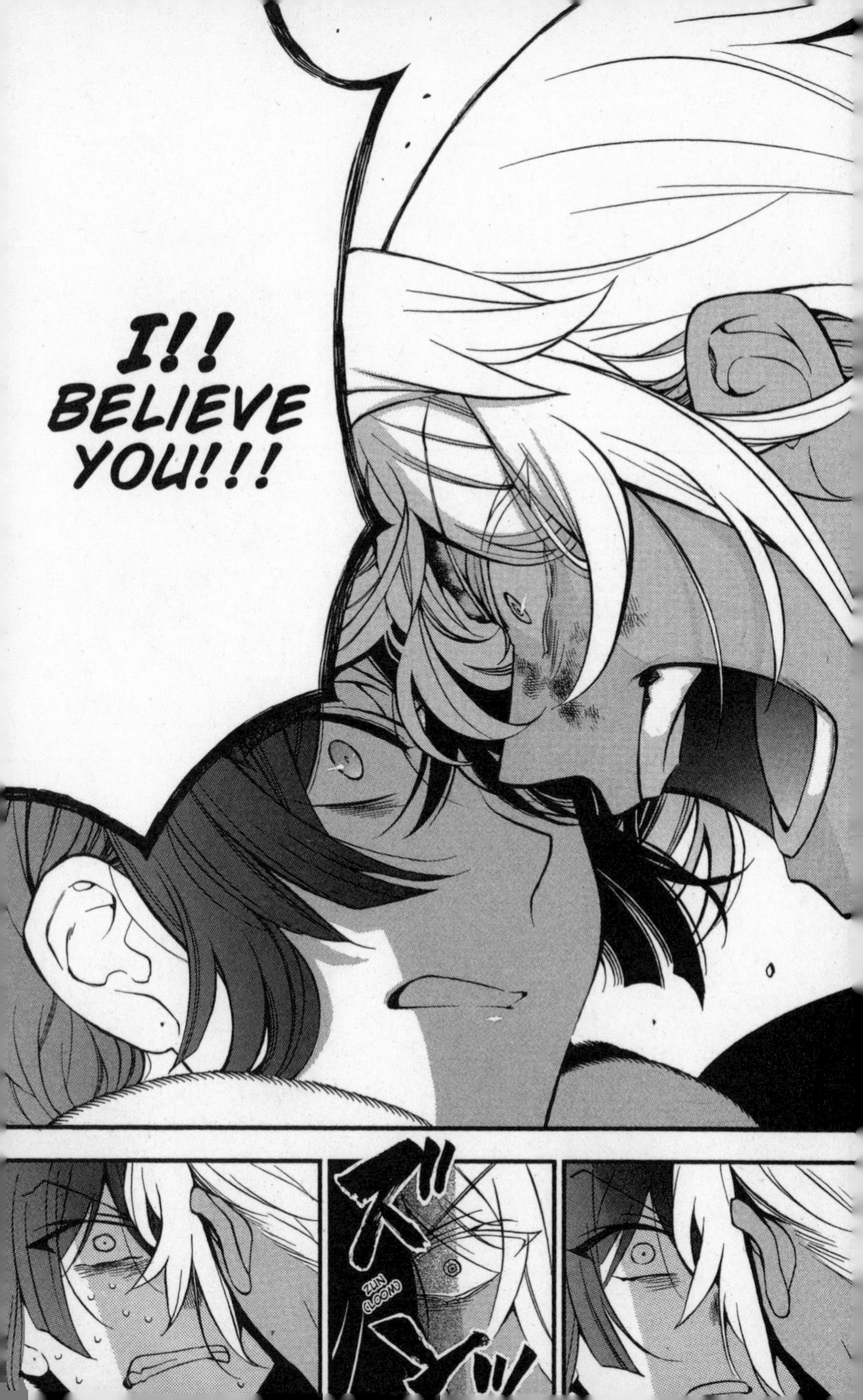
I!! BELIEVE YOU!!!
ZUN (LOOM)

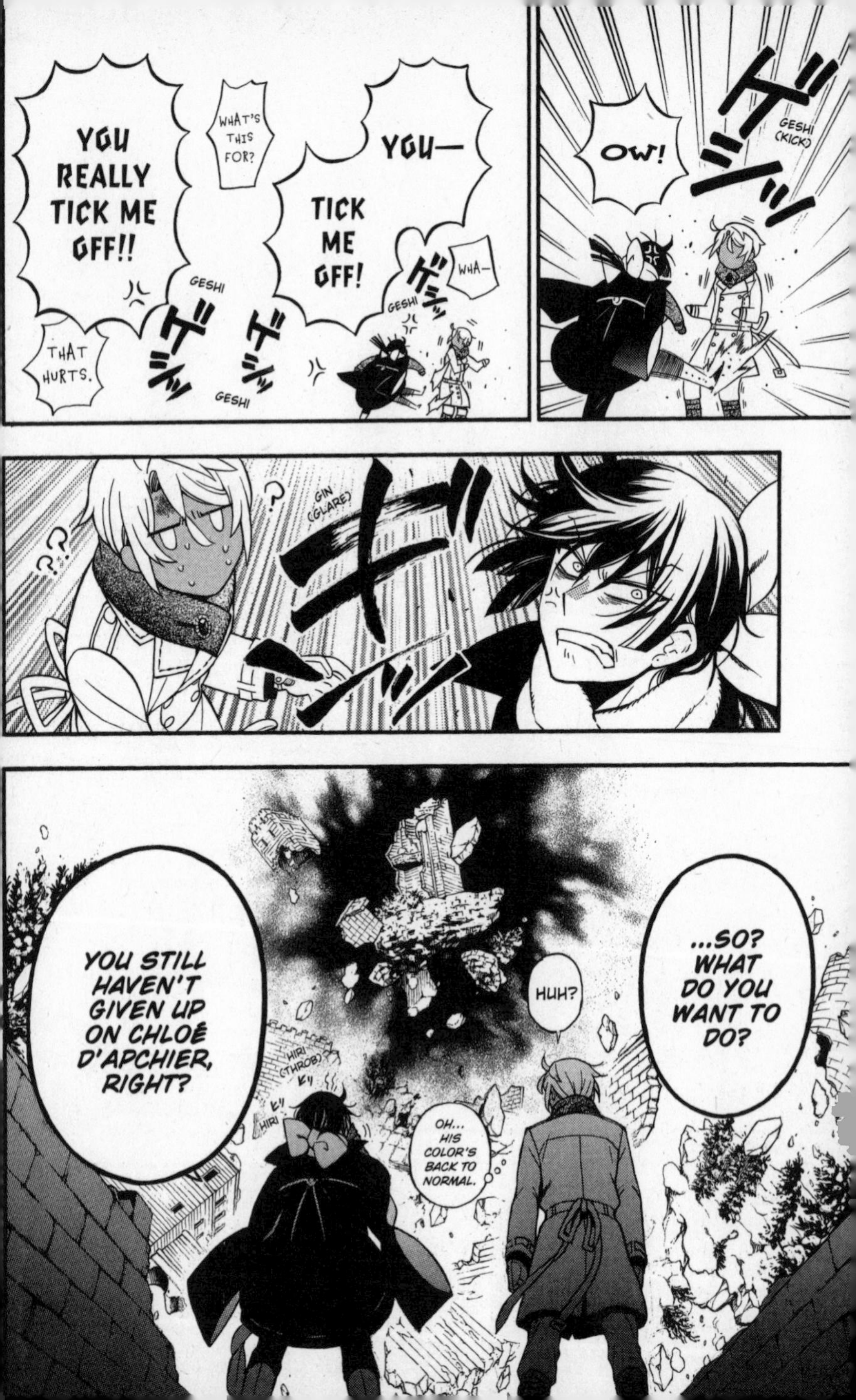
GESHI (KICK)
OW!
WHA—
GESHI
YOU—
TICK ME OFF!
WHAT'S THIS FOR?
YOU REALLY TICK ME OFF!!
GESHI
GESHI
THAT HURTS.
GIN (GLARE)
...SO? WHAT DO YOU WANT TO DO?
HUH?
OH... HIS COLOR'S BACK TO NORMAL.
HIRI (THROB)
HIRI
YOU STILL HAVEN'T GIVEN UP ON CHLOÉ D'APCHIER, RIGHT?

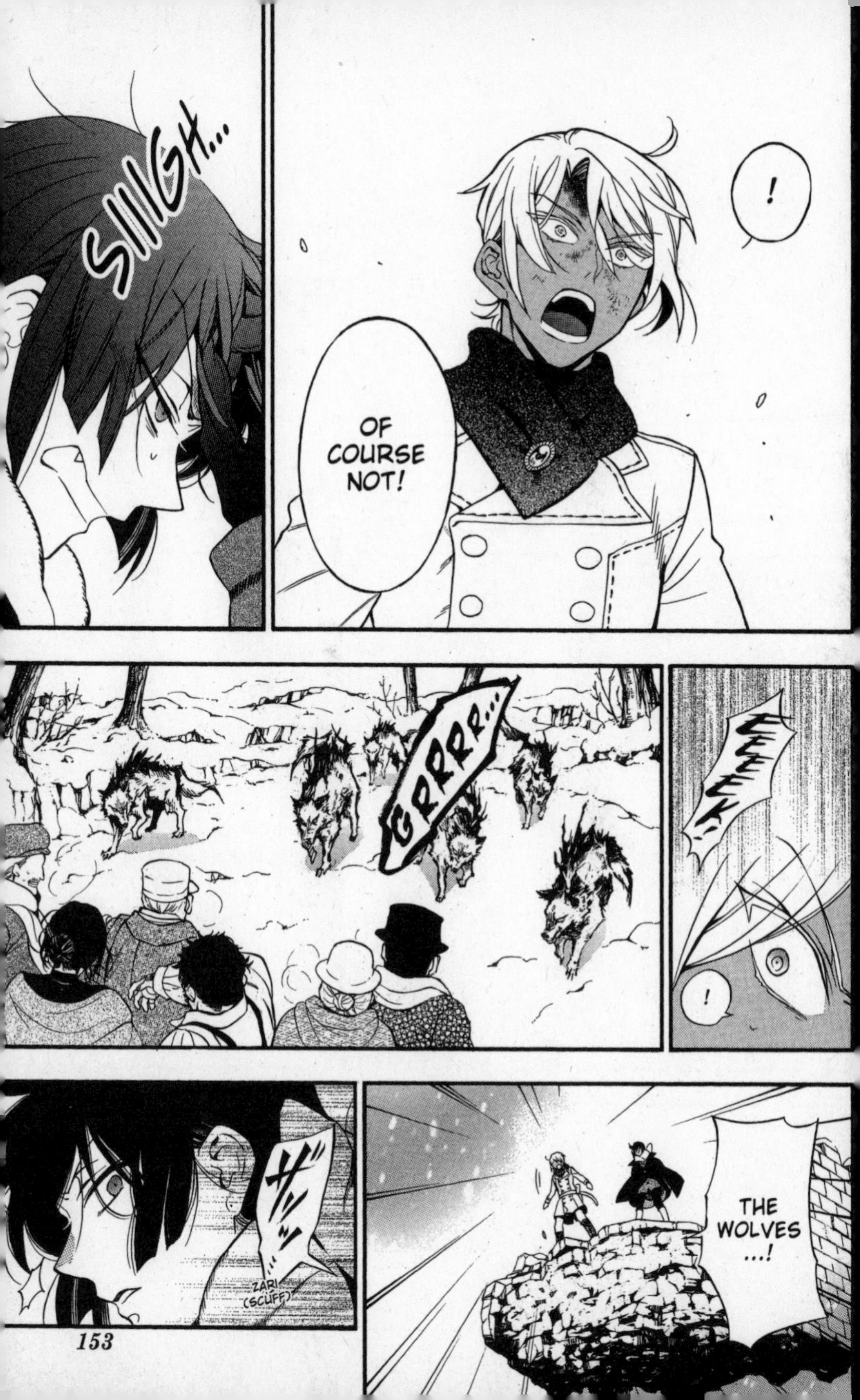
!
OF COURSE NOT!
SIIGH...
EEEEK!
!
GRRRR...
THE WOLVES ...!
ZARI (SCUFF)

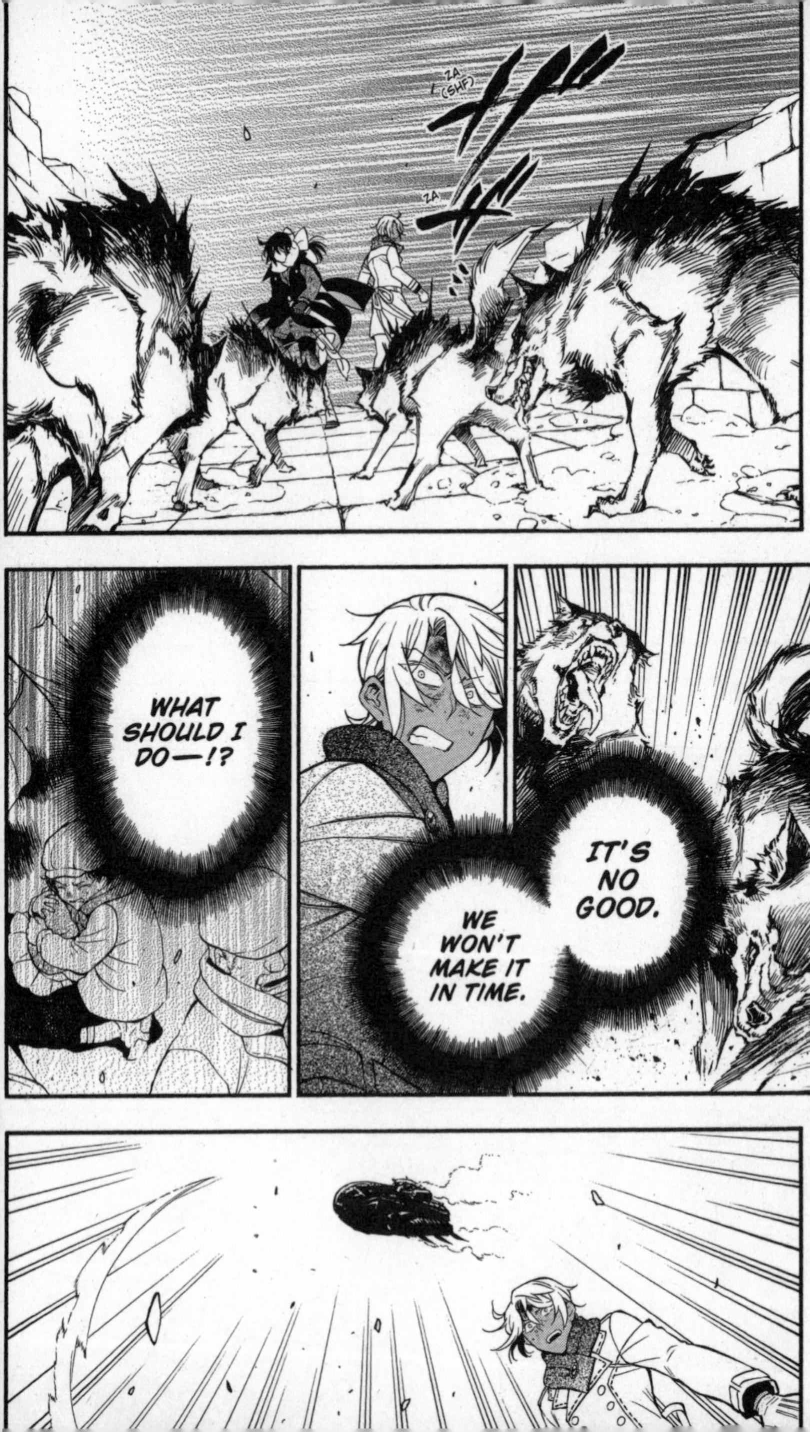
ZA (SHF)
ZA
IT'S NO GOOD.
WE WON'T MAKE IT IN TIME.
WHAT SHOULD I DO—!?

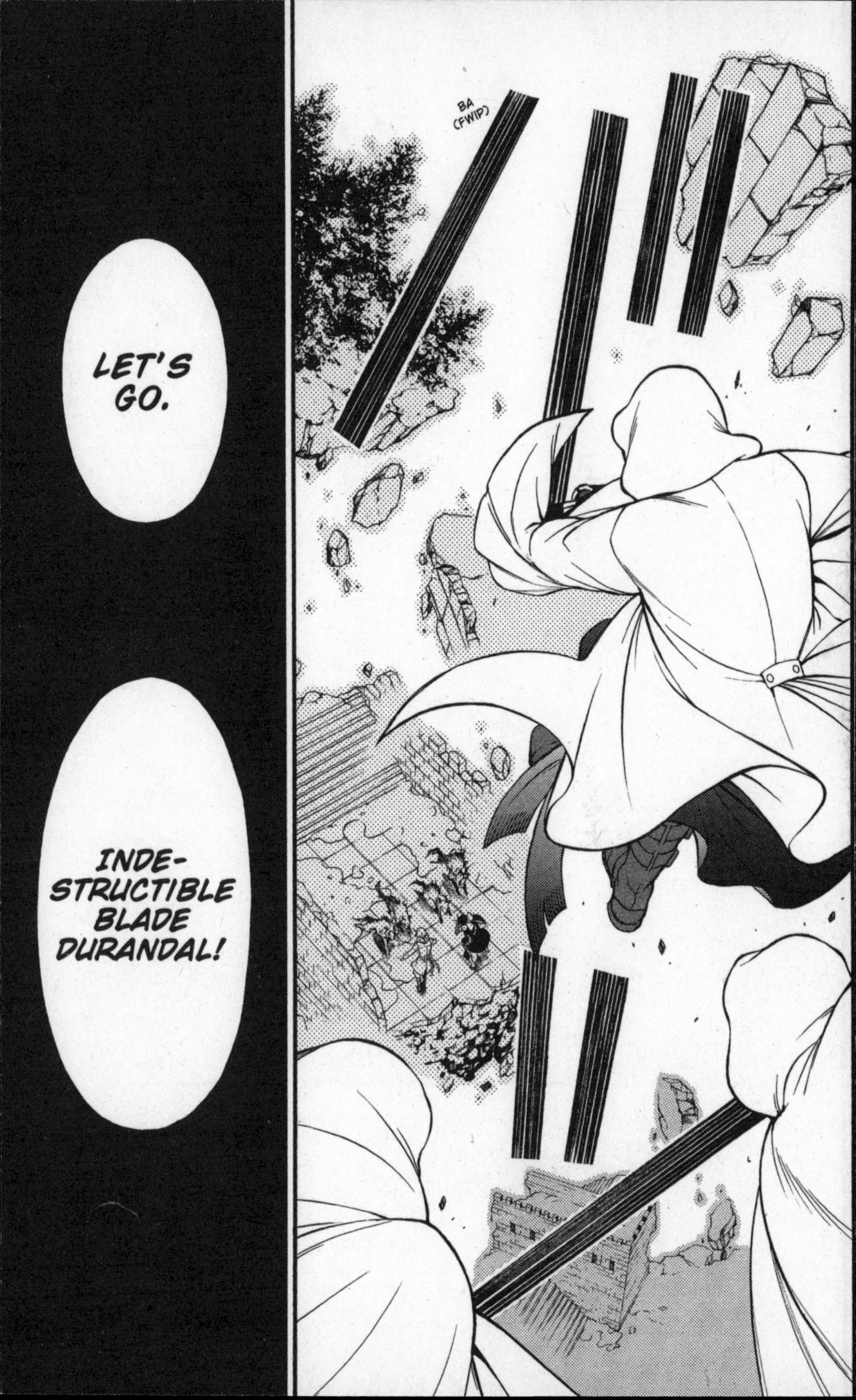
BA (FWIP)
LET'S GO.
INDE-STRUCTIBLE BLADE DURANDAL!

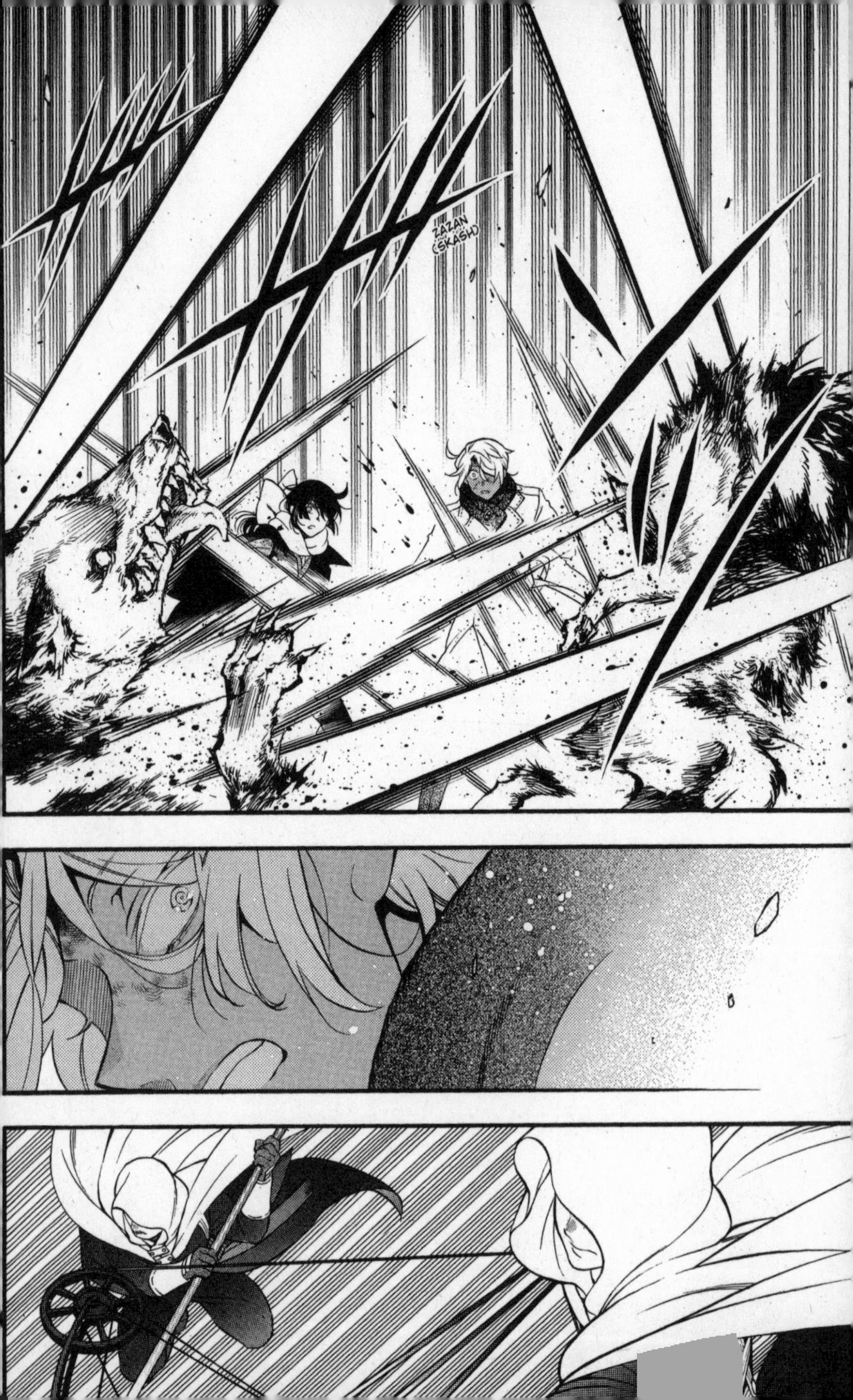
ZAZAN (SKASH)

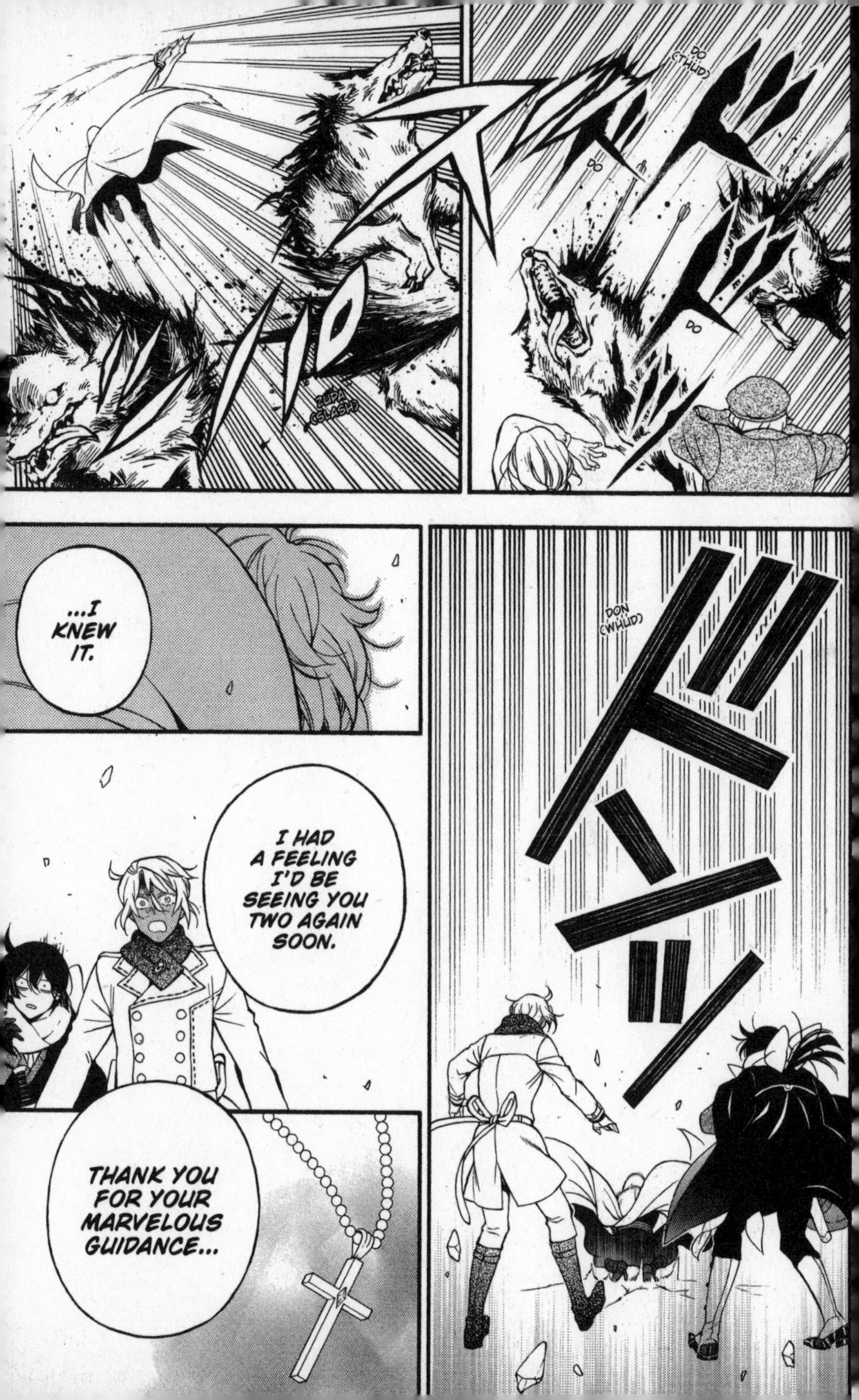
DO (THUD)
DO
DO
ZUDA (SLASH)
DON (WHUD)
...I KNEW IT.
I HAD A FEELING I'D BE SEEING YOU TWO AGAIN SOON.
THANK YOU FOR YOUR MARVELOUS GUIDANCE...

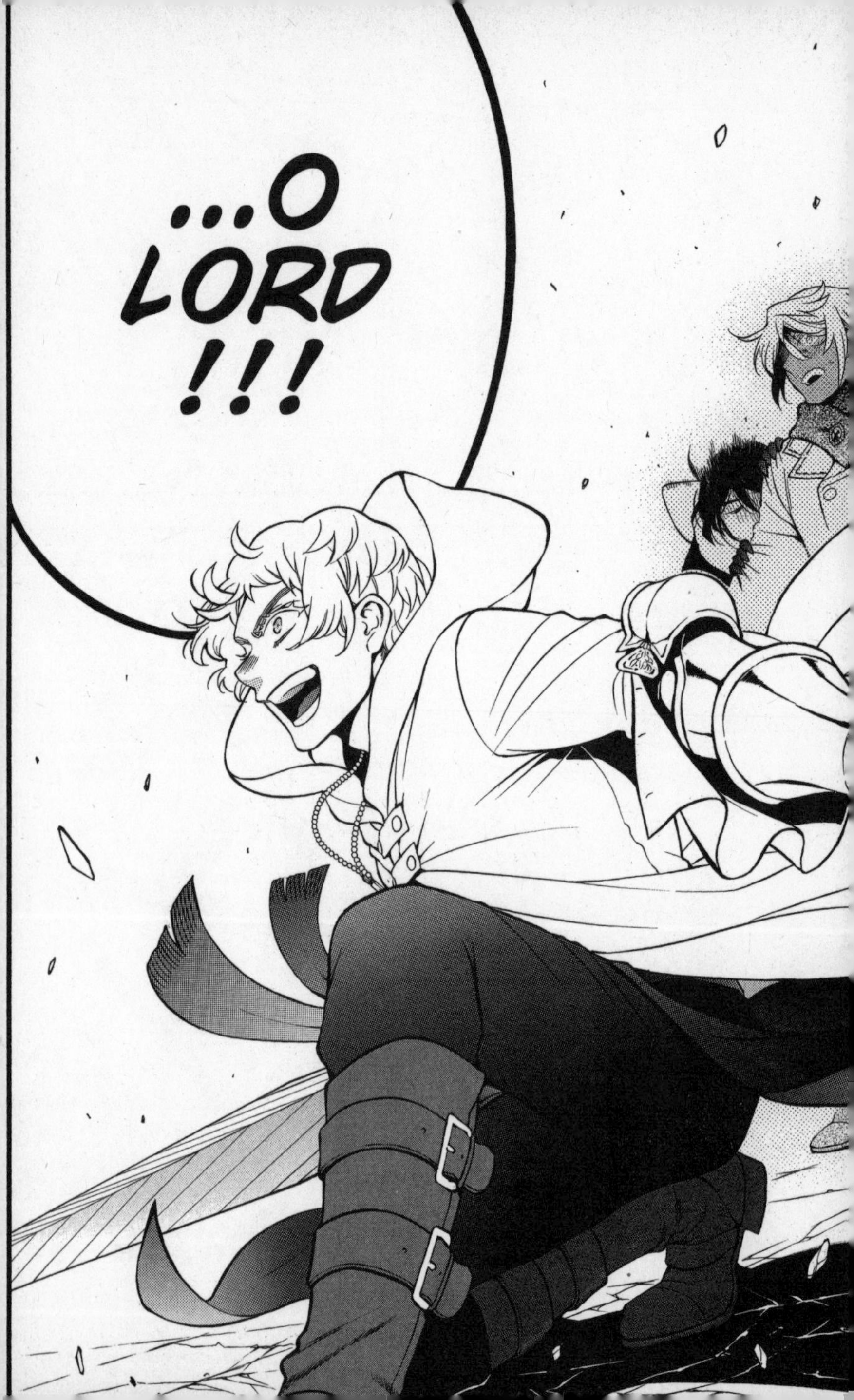
...O LORD !!!

Mémoire 38 Naenia SHE WHO HARBORS DEATH

Les Mémoires de Vanitas

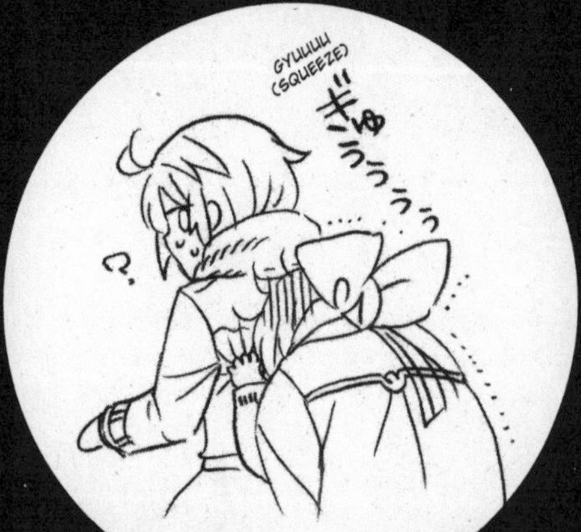
GYUUUU
(SQUEEZE)
ぎゅううう
?

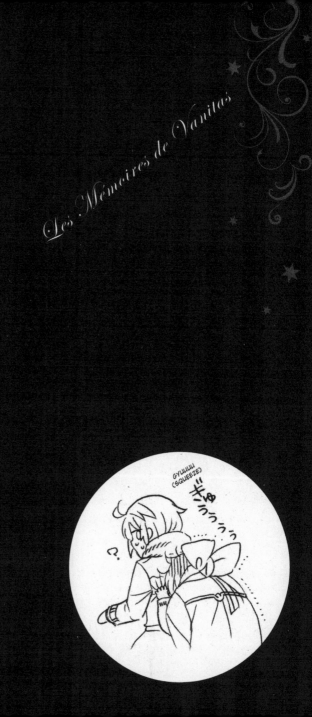

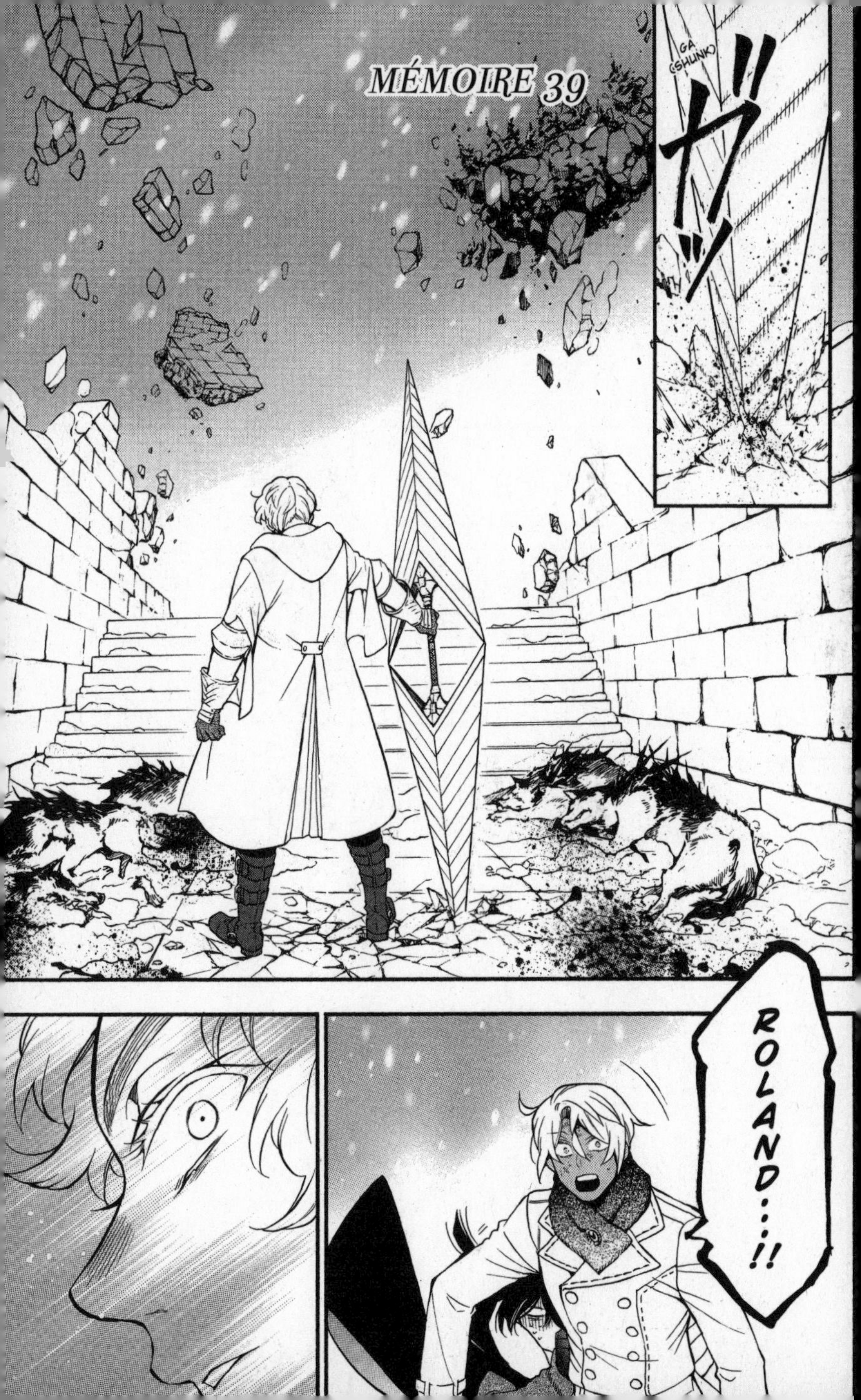
GA (SHUNK)
MÉMOIRE 39
ROLAND...!!

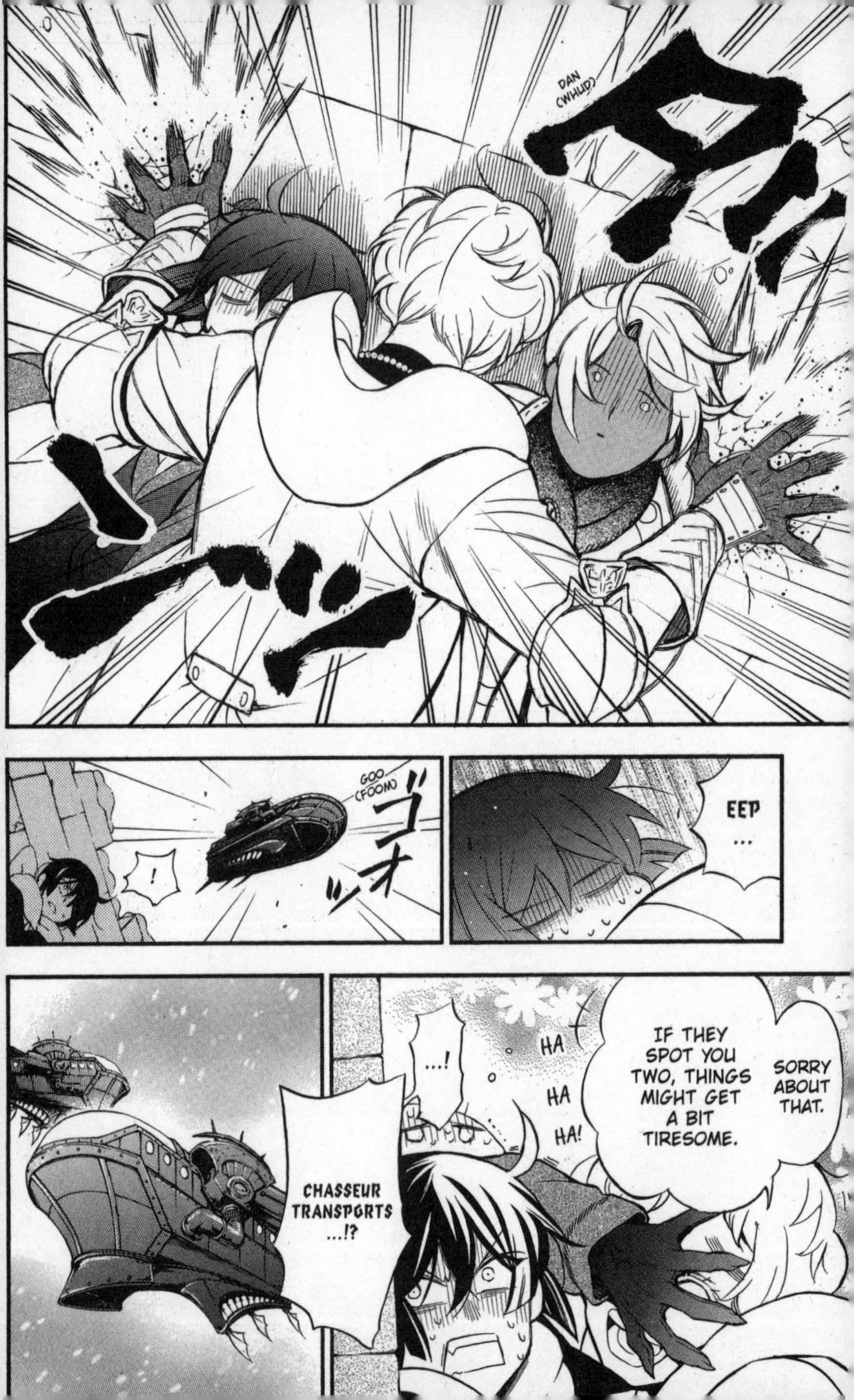
DAN (WHUD)
GOO (FOOM)
!
EEP ...
SORRY ABOUT THAT.
IF THEY SPOT YOU TWO, THINGS MIGHT GET A BIT TIRESOME.
HA HA HA!
...!
CHASSEUR TRANSPORTS ...!?

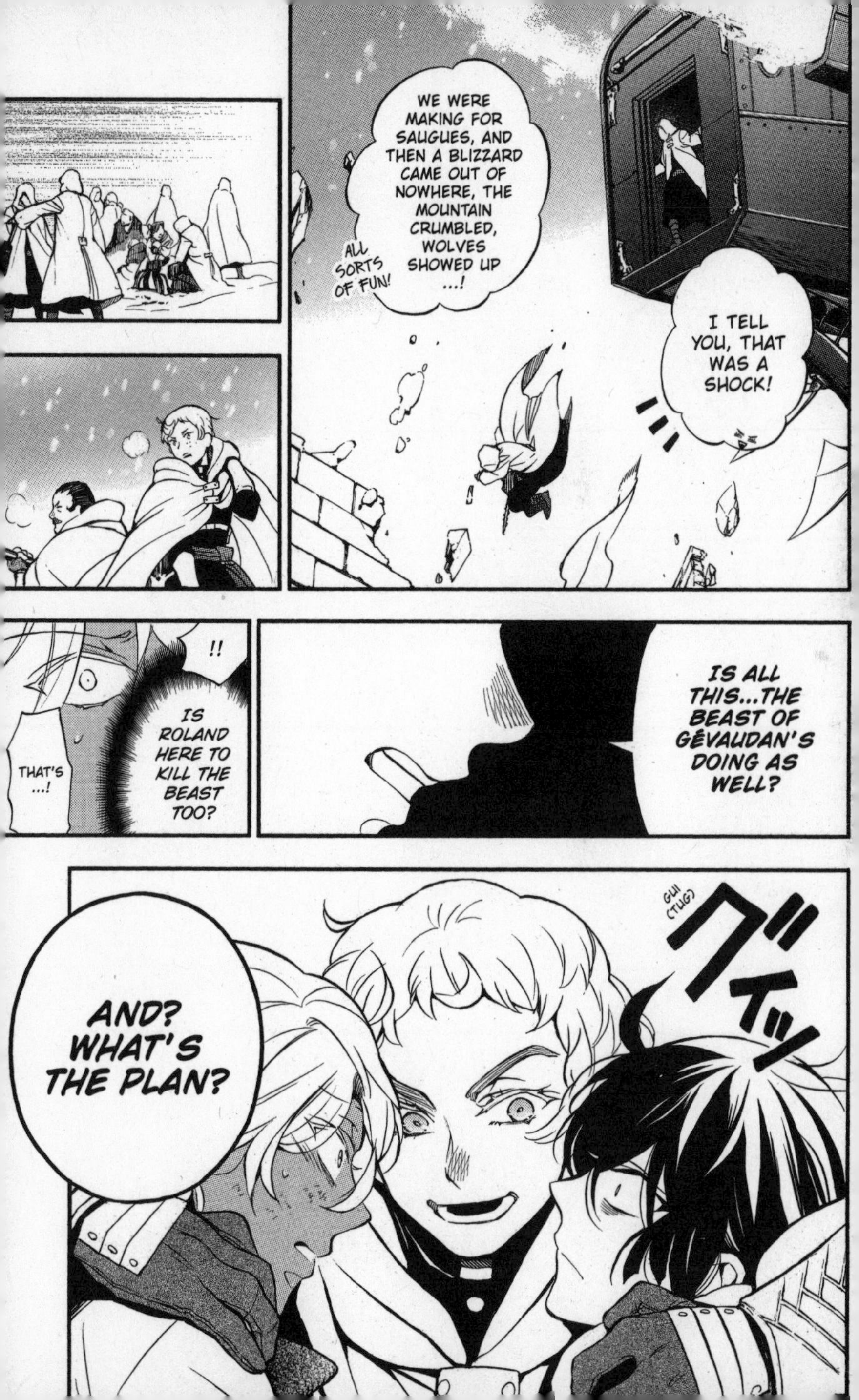
WE WERE MAKING FOR SAUGUES, AND THEN A BLIZZARD CAME OUT OF NOWHERE, THE MOUNTAIN CRUMBLED, WOLVES SHOWED UP ...!
ALL SORTS OF FUN!
I TELL YOU, THAT WAS A SHOCK!
IS ALL THIS...THE BEAST OF GÉVAUDAN'S DOING AS WELL?
!!
IS ROLAND HERE TO KILL THE BEAST TOO?
THAT'S ...!
GUI (TUG)
AND? WHAT'S THE PLAN?

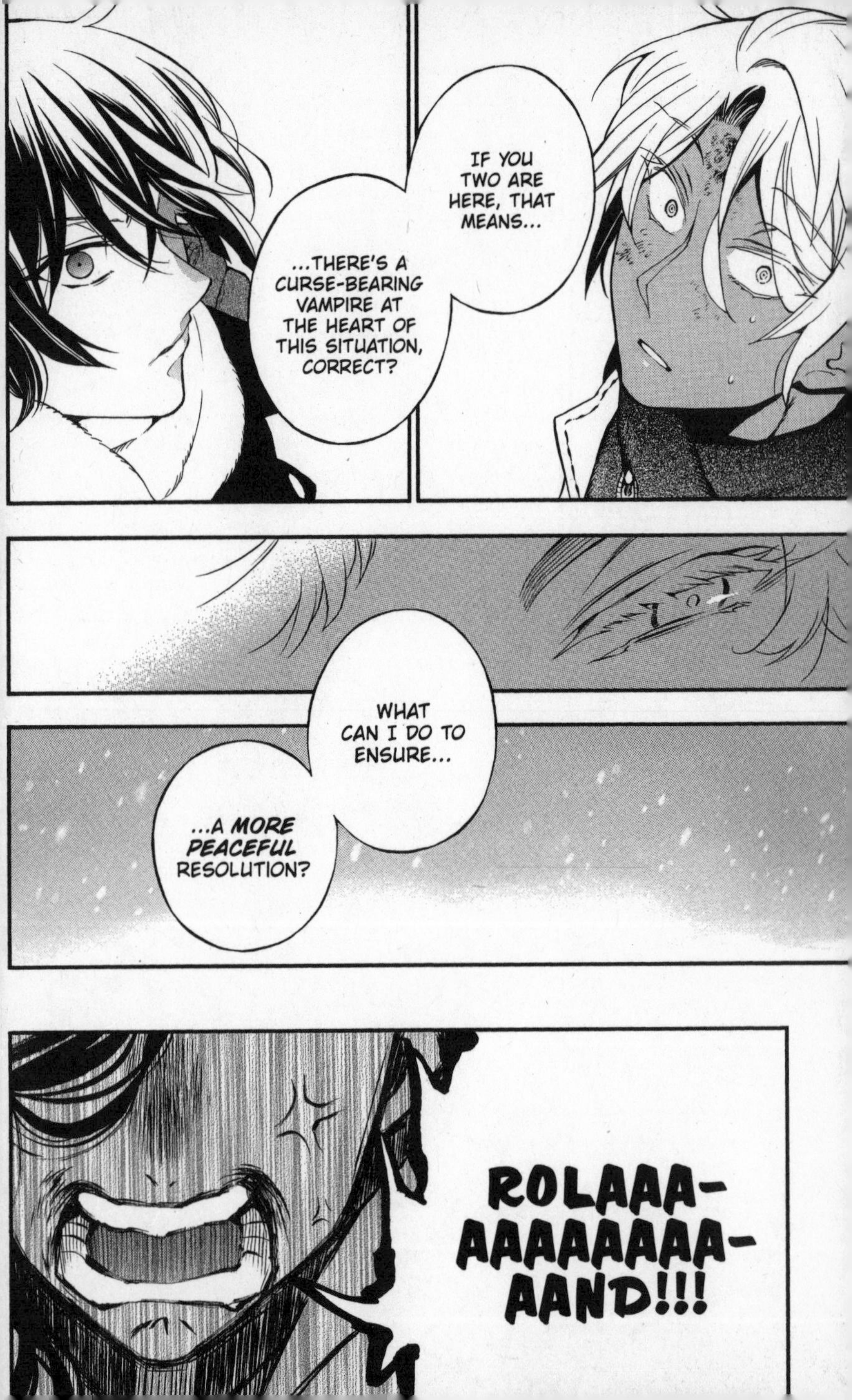
IF YOU TWO ARE HERE, THAT MEANS...
...THERE'S A CURSE-BEARING VAMPIRE AT THE HEART OF THIS SITUATION, CORRECT?
WHAT CAN I DO TO ENSURE...
...A *MORE PEACEFUL* RESOLUTION?
ROLAAA-AAAAAAAA-AAND!!!

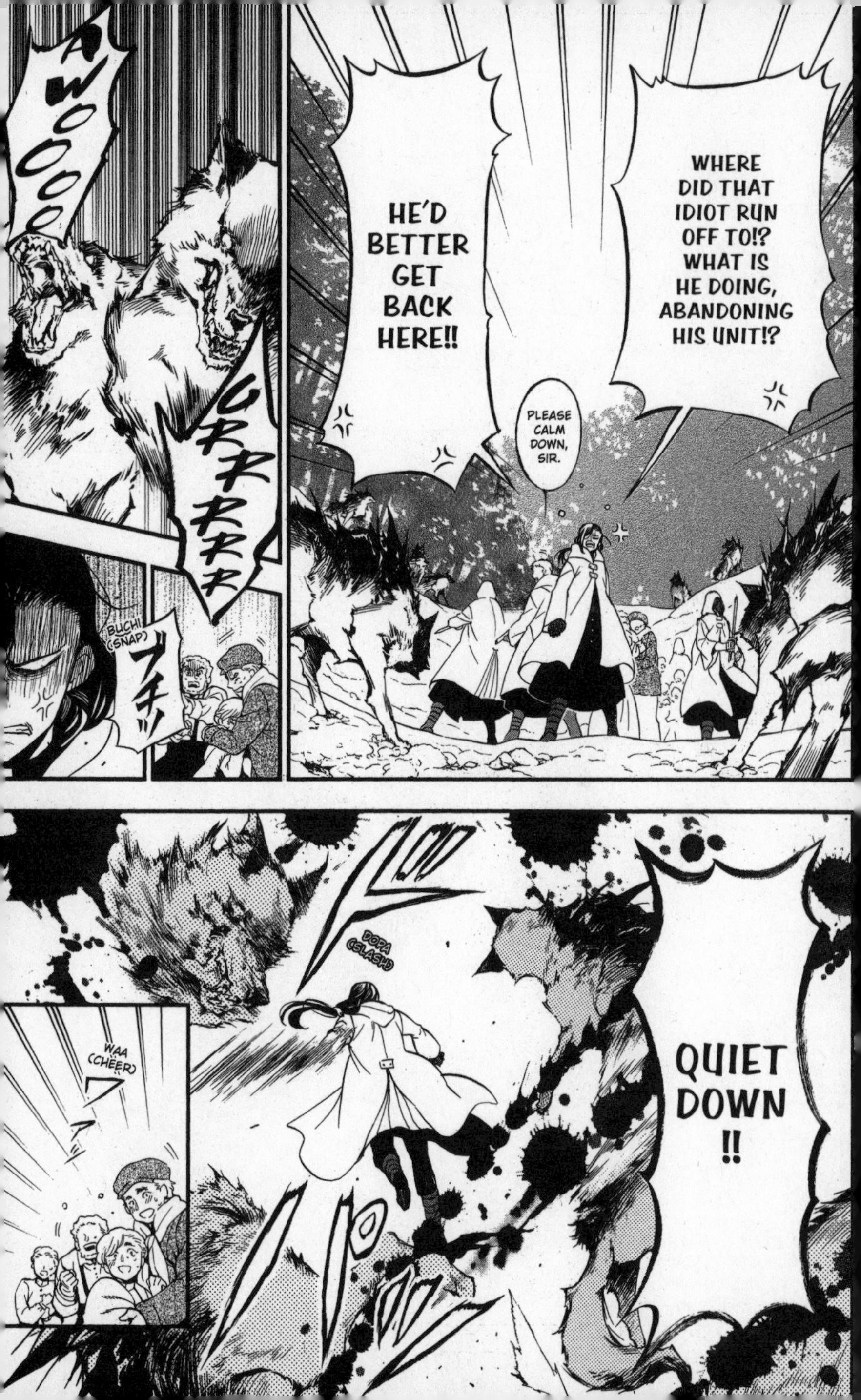

WHERE DID THAT IDIOT RUN OFF TO!? WHAT IS HE DOING, ABANDONING HIS UNIT!?
HE'D BETTER GET BACK HERE!!
PLEASE CALM DOWN, SIR.
AWOOOOOO
GRRRRRR
BUCHI (SNAP)
ブチッ
QUIET DOWN!!
DOPA (SLASH)
WAA (CHEER)
ワァ

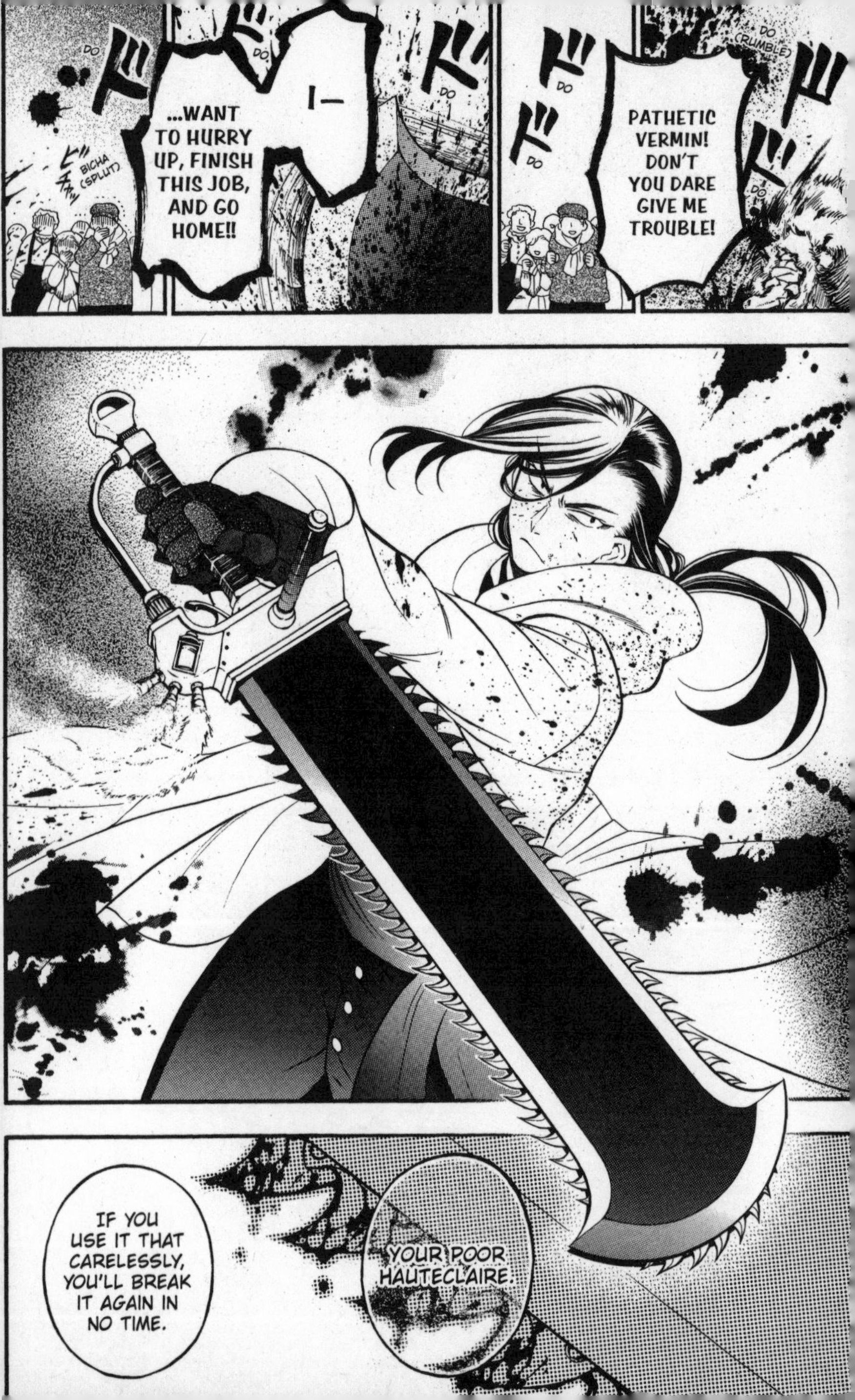

DO (CRUMBLE)
DO
DO
DO
PATHETIC VERMIN! DON'T YOU DARE GIVE ME TROUBLE!
DO
I—
DO
DO
BICHA (SPLUT)
...WANT TO HURRY UP, FINISH THIS JOB, AND GO HOME!!
YOUR POOR HAUTECLAIRE.
IF YOU USE IT THAT CARELESSLY, YOU'LL BREAK IT AGAIN IN NO TIME.

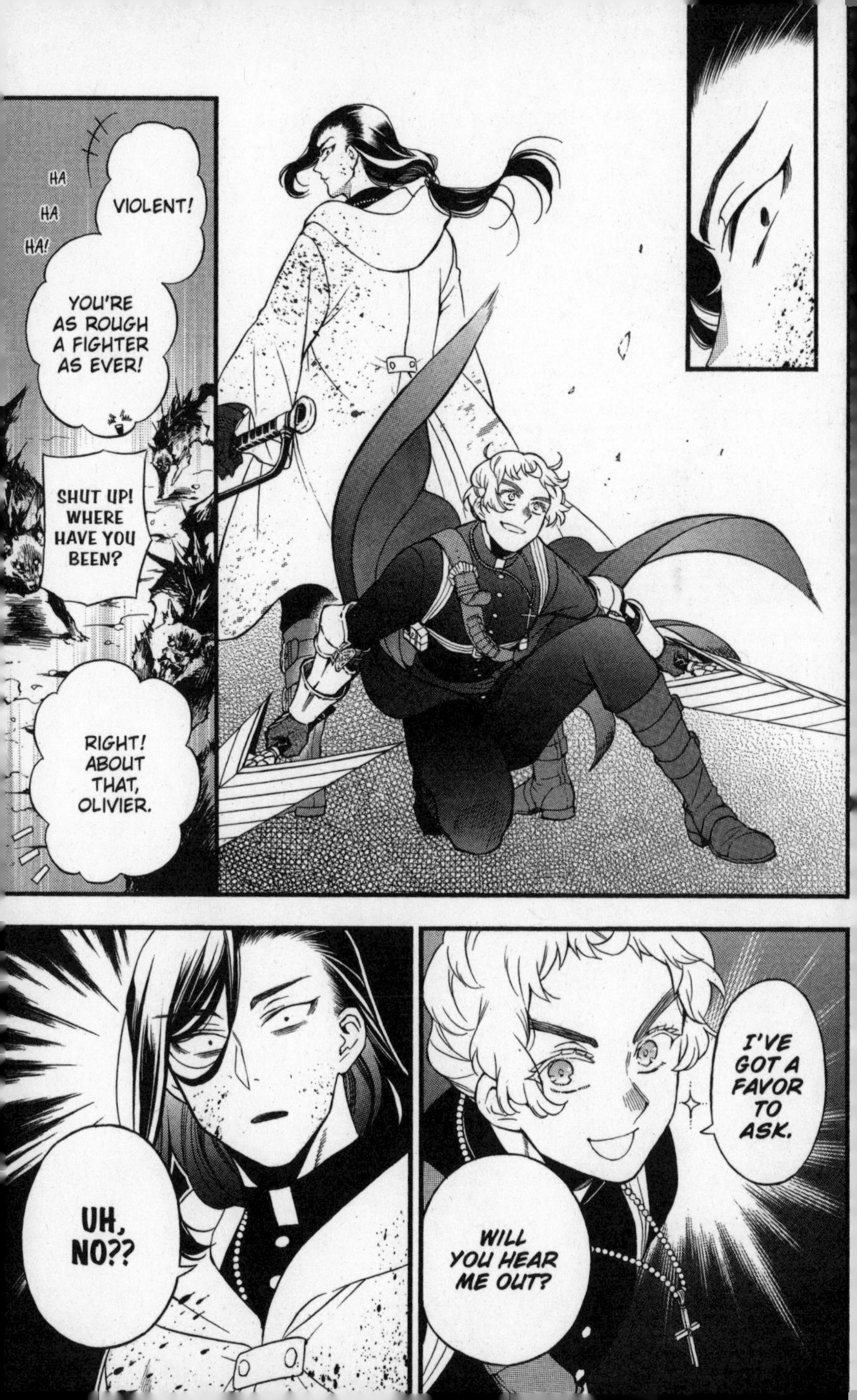
VIOLENT!
HA HA HA!
YOU'RE AS ROUGH A FIGHTER AS EVER!
SHUT UP! WHERE HAVE YOU BEEN?
RIGHT! ABOUT THAT, OLIVIER.
I'VE GOT A FAVOR TO ASK.
WILL YOU HEAR ME OUT?
UH, NO??

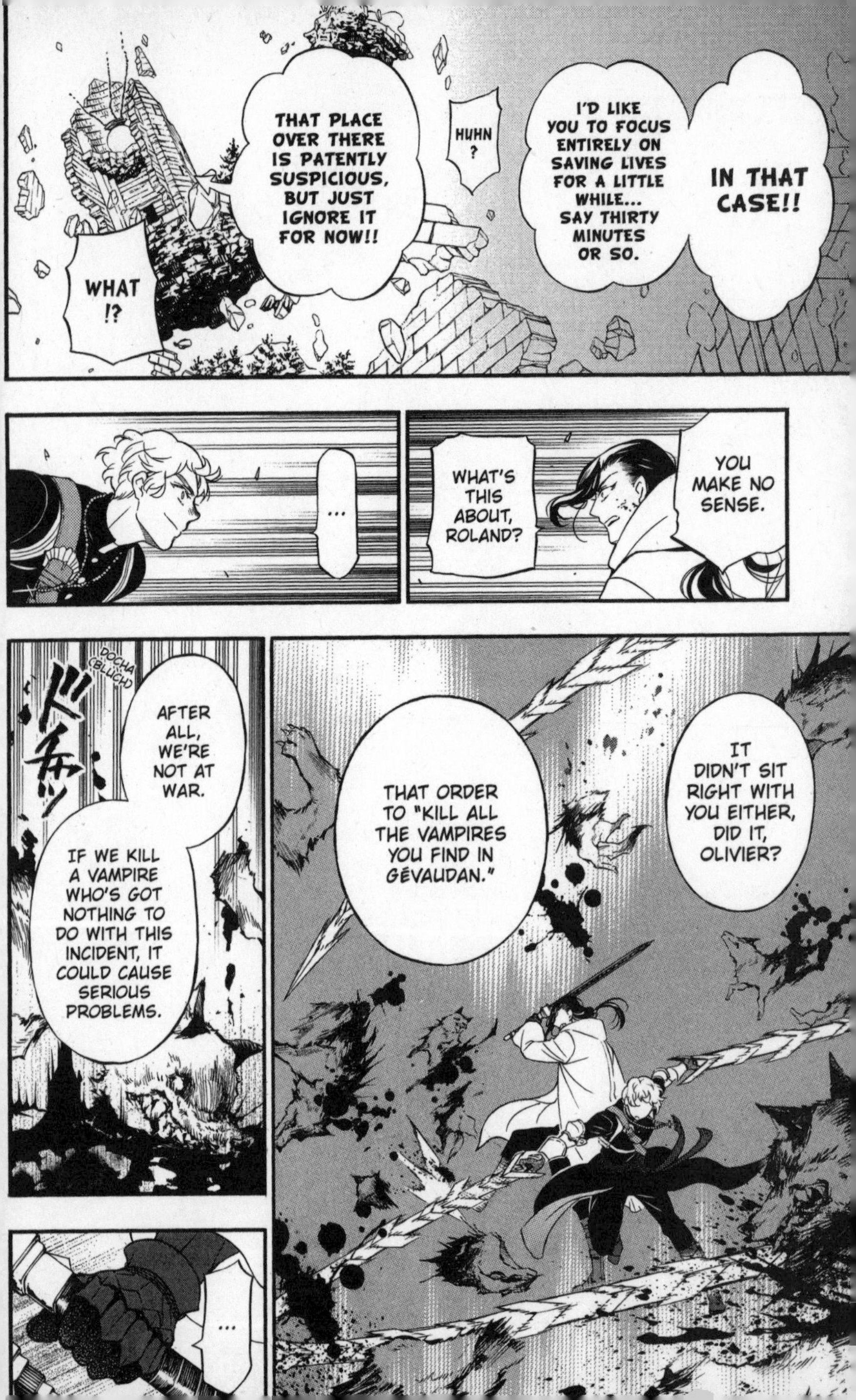
IN THAT CASE!!
I'D LIKE YOU TO FOCUS ENTIRELY ON SAVING LIVES FOR A LITTLE WHILE... SAY THIRTY MINUTES OR SO.
HUHN?
THAT PLACE OVER THERE IS PATENTLY SUSPICIOUS, BUT JUST IGNORE IT FOR NOW!!
WHAT!?
YOU MAKE NO SENSE.
WHAT'S THIS ABOUT, ROLAND?
...
IT DIDN'T SIT RIGHT WITH YOU EITHER, DID IT, OLIVIER?
THAT ORDER TO "KILL ALL THE VAMPIRES YOU FIND IN GÉVAUDAN."
ドチャ
DOCHA (BLUCH)
AFTER ALL, WE'RE NOT AT WAR.
IF WE KILL A VAMPIRE WHO'S GOT NOTHING TO DO WITH THIS INCIDENT, IT COULD CAUSE SERIOUS PROBLEMS.
...

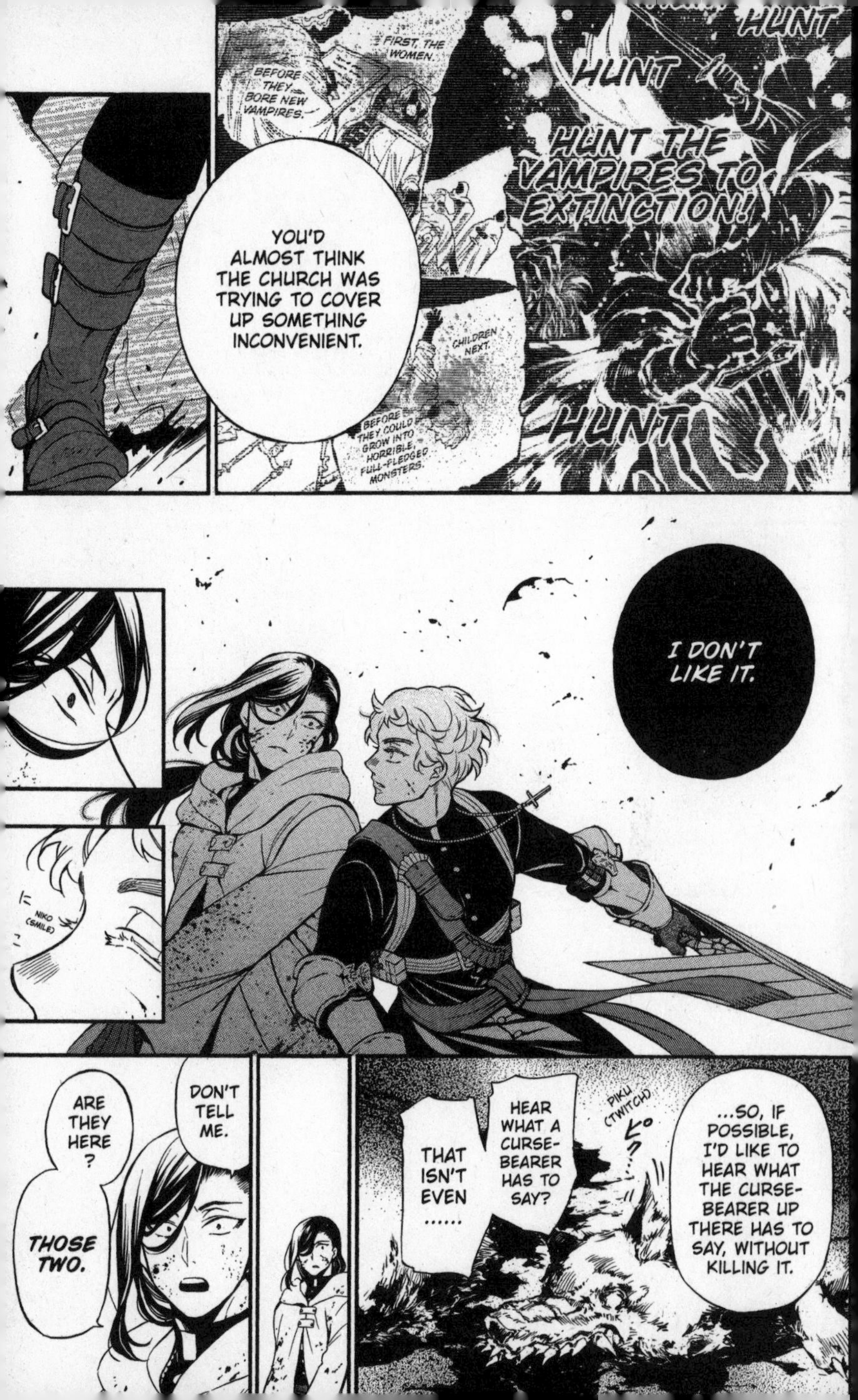
HUNT
HUNT
HUNT THE VAMPIRES TO EXTINCTION!
HUNT
FIRST, THE WOMEN.
BEFORE THEY BORE NEW VAMPIRES.
CHILDREN NEXT.
BEFORE THEY COULD GROW INTO HORRIBLE, FULL-FLEDGED MONSTERS.
YOU'D ALMOST THINK THE CHURCH WAS TRYING TO COVER UP SOMETHING INCONVENIENT.
I DON'T LIKE IT.
NIKO (SMILE)
...SO, IF POSSIBLE, I'D LIKE TO HEAR WHAT THE CURSE-BEARER UP THERE HAS TO SAY, WITHOUT KILLING IT.
PIKU (TWITCH)
HEAR WHAT A CURSE-BEARER HAS TO SAY?
THAT ISN'T EVEN ......
DON'T TELL ME.
ARE THEY HERE?
THOSE TWO.

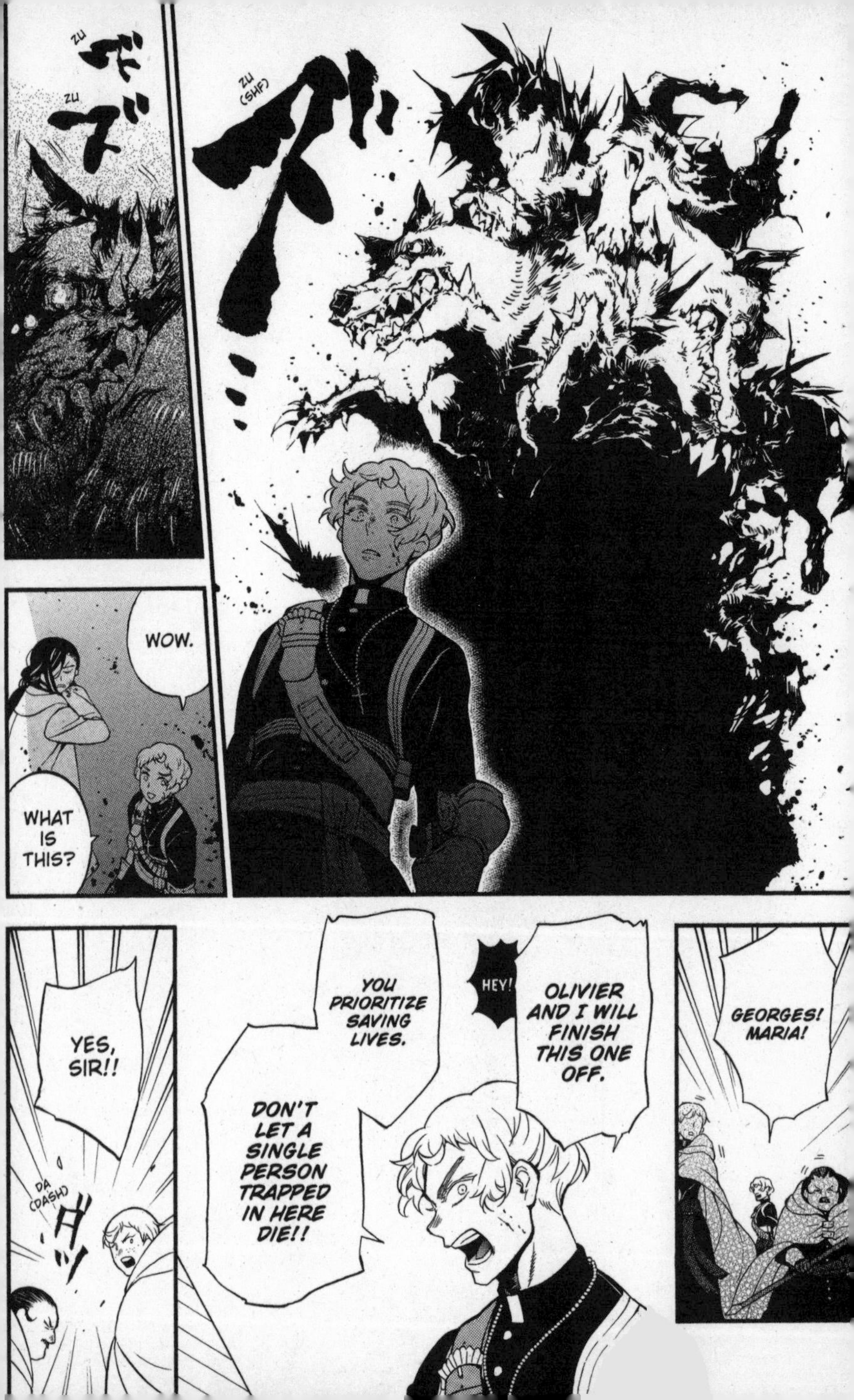
ZU (SHF)
ZU
ZU
WOW.
WHAT IS THIS?
GEORGES! MARIA!
HEY!
OLIVIER AND I WILL FINISH THIS ONE OFF.
YOU PRIORITIZE SAVING LIVES.
DON'T LET A SINGLE PERSON TRAPPED IN HERE DIE!!
YES, SIR!!
DA (DASH)

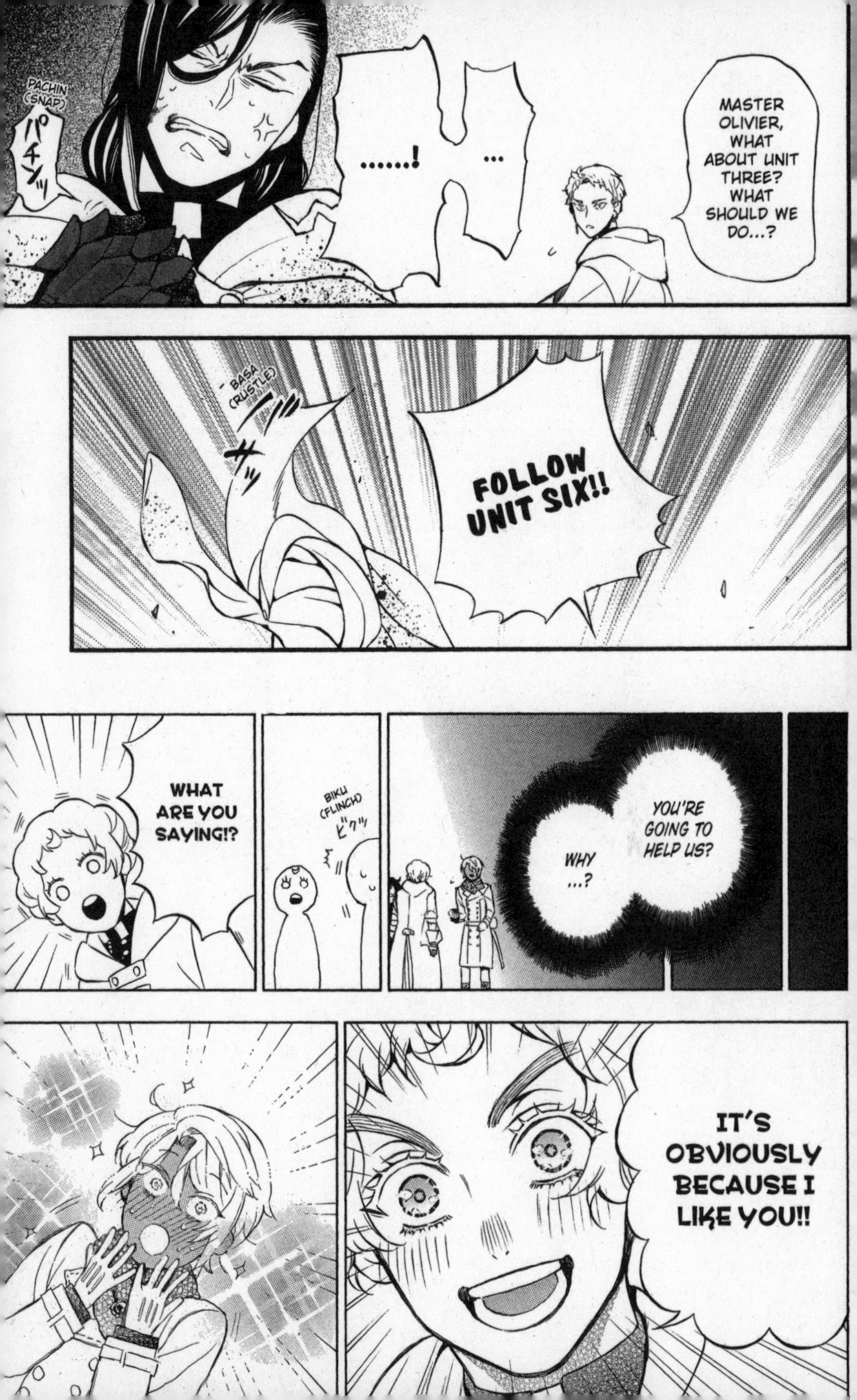
MASTER OLIVIER, WHAT ABOUT UNIT THREE? WHAT SHOULD WE DO...?
...
......!
PACHIN (SNAP)
パチンッ
FOLLOW UNIT SIX!!
BASA (RUSTLE)
バサッ
YOU'RE GOING TO HELP US?
WHY ...?
BIKU (FLINCH)
ビクッ
WHAT ARE YOU SAYING!?
IT'S OBVIOUSLY BECAUSE I LIKE YOU!!

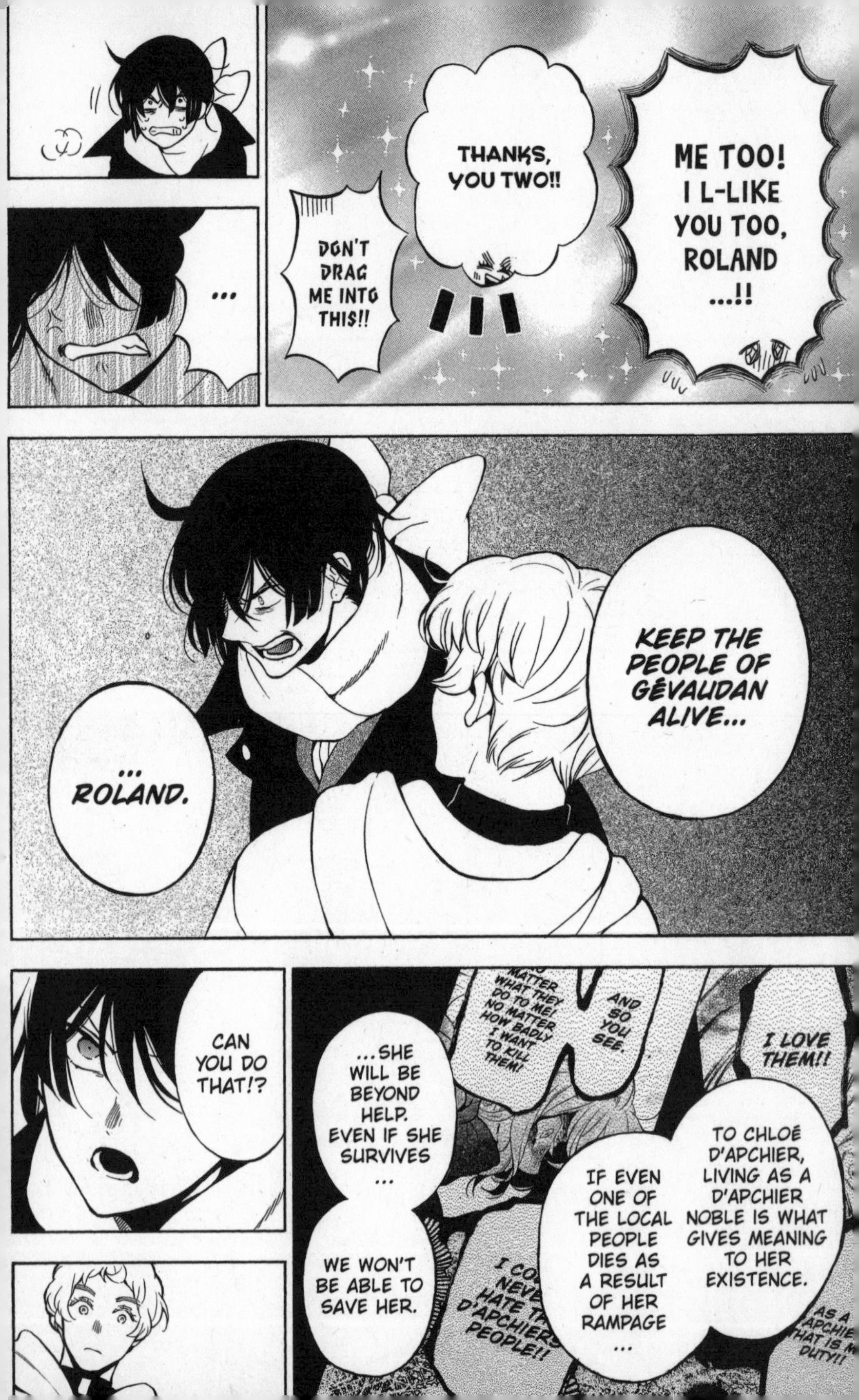

ME TOO! I L-LIKE YOU TOO, ROLAND ...!!
THANKS, YOU TWO!!
DON'T DRAG ME INTO THIS!!
...
KEEP THE PEOPLE OF GÉVAUDAN ALIVE...
... ROLAND.
I LOVE THEM!!
AND SO YOU SEE,
MATTER WHAT THEY DO TO ME! NO MATTER HOW BADLY I WANT TO KILL THEM!
TO CHLOÉ D'APCHIER, LIVING AS A D'APCHIER NOBLE IS WHAT GIVES MEANING TO HER EXISTENCE.
IF EVEN ONE OF THE LOCAL PEOPLE DIES AS A RESULT OF HER RAMPAGE ...
...SHE WILL BE BEYOND HELP. EVEN IF SHE SURVIVES ...
WE WON'T BE ABLE TO SAVE HER.
CAN YOU DO THAT!?

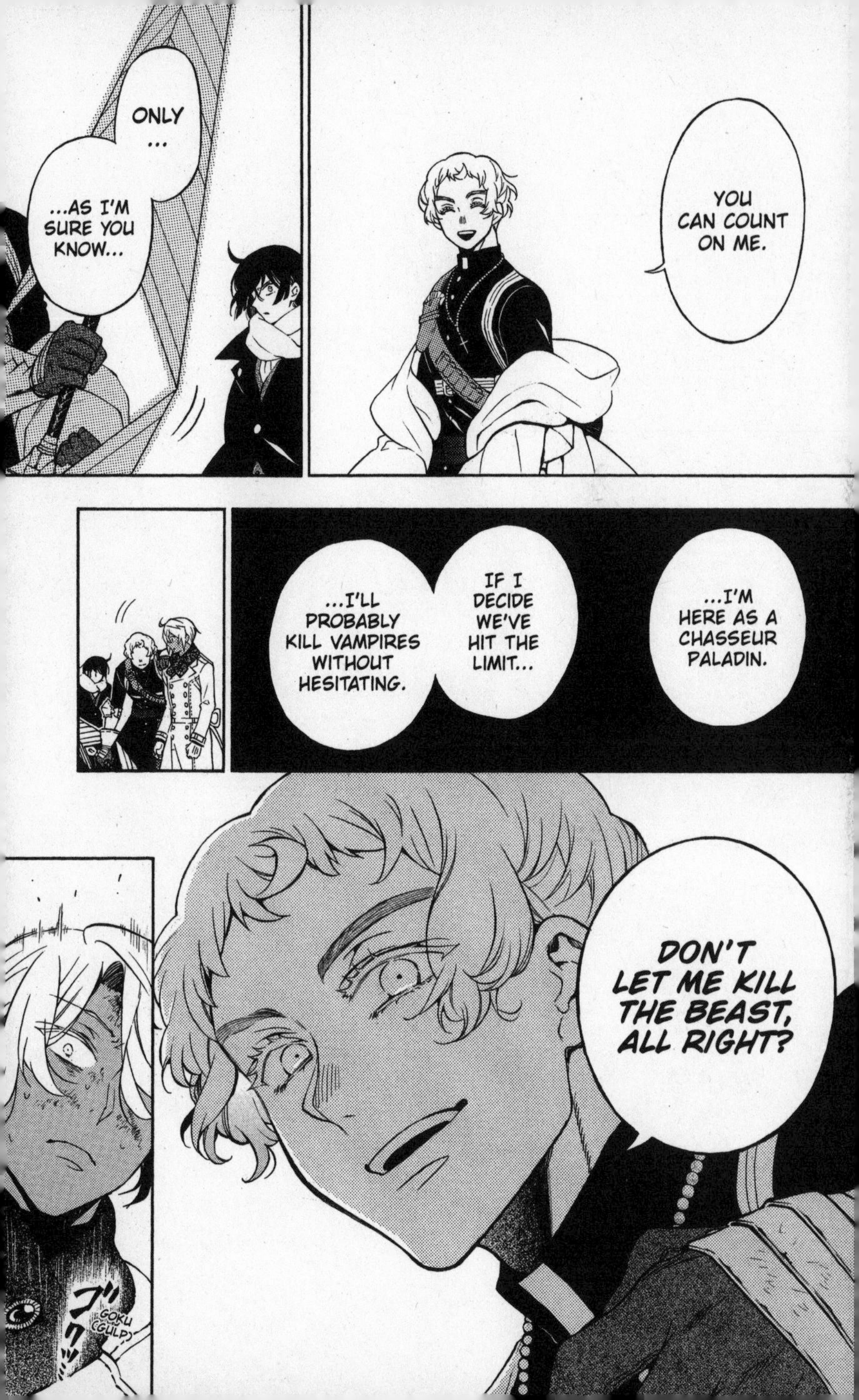
YOU CAN COUNT ON ME.
ONLY...
...AS I'M SURE YOU KNOW...
...I'M HERE AS A CHASSEUR PALADIN.
IF I DECIDE WE'VE HIT THE LIMIT...
...I'LL PROBABLY KILL VAMPIRES WITHOUT HESITATING.
DON'T LET ME KILL THE BEAST, ALL RIGHT?
GOKU (GULP)

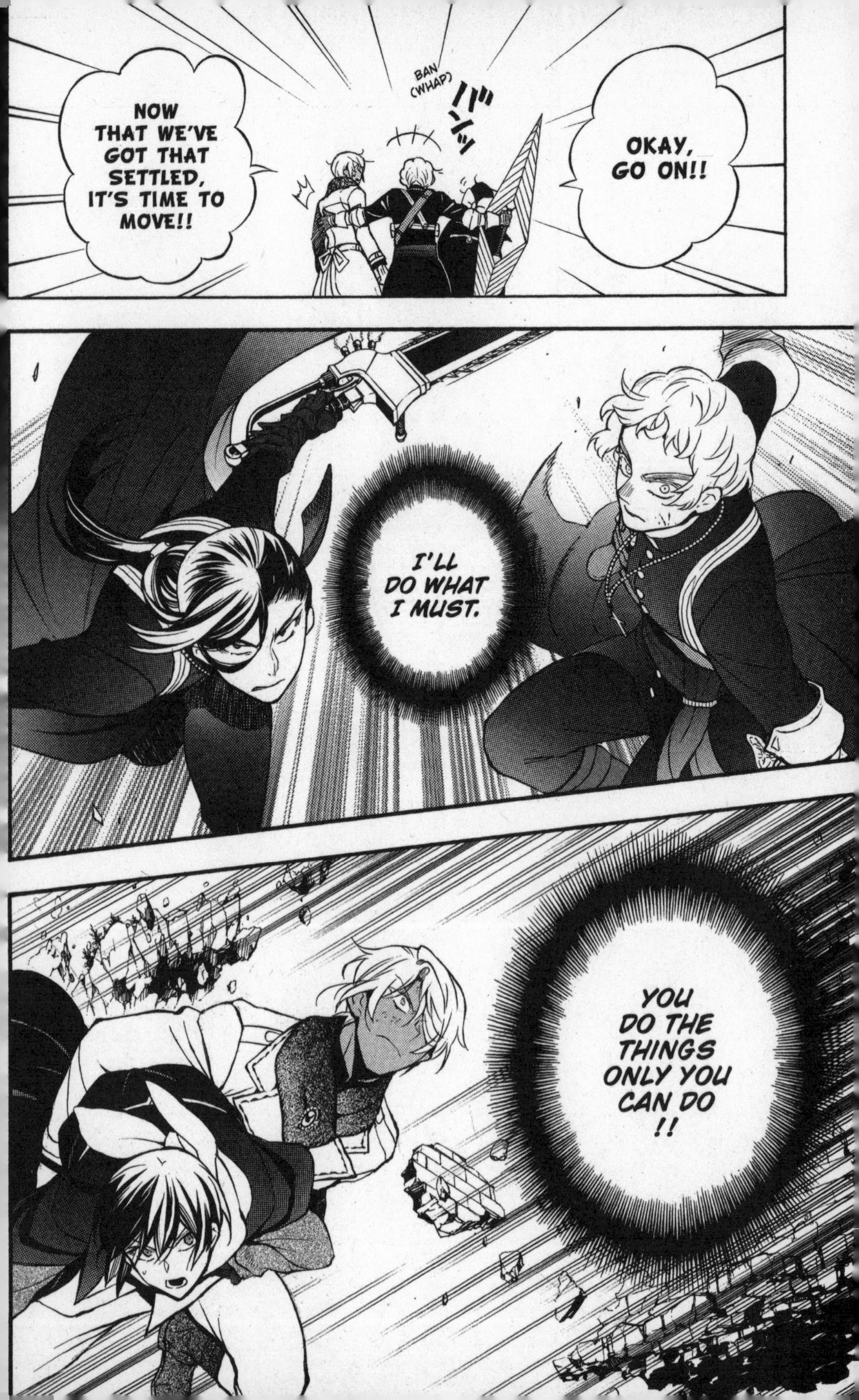
OKAY, GO ON!!
BAN (WHAP)
バンッ
NOW THAT WE'VE GOT THAT SETTLED, IT'S TIME TO MOVE!!
I'LL DO WHAT I MUST.
YOU DO THE THINGS ONLY YOU CAN DO !!

uu...
GOPO (BLUP)
ゴポミ
GOPO
ゴポ
GOPO
ゴポ

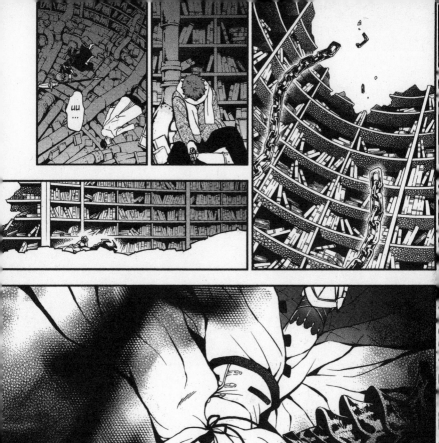

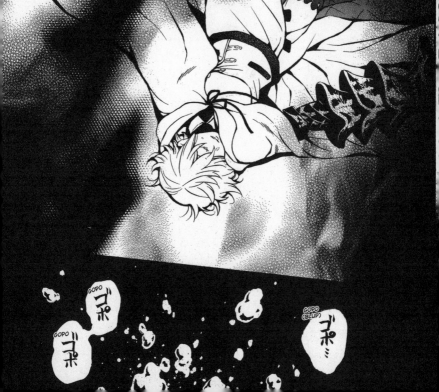

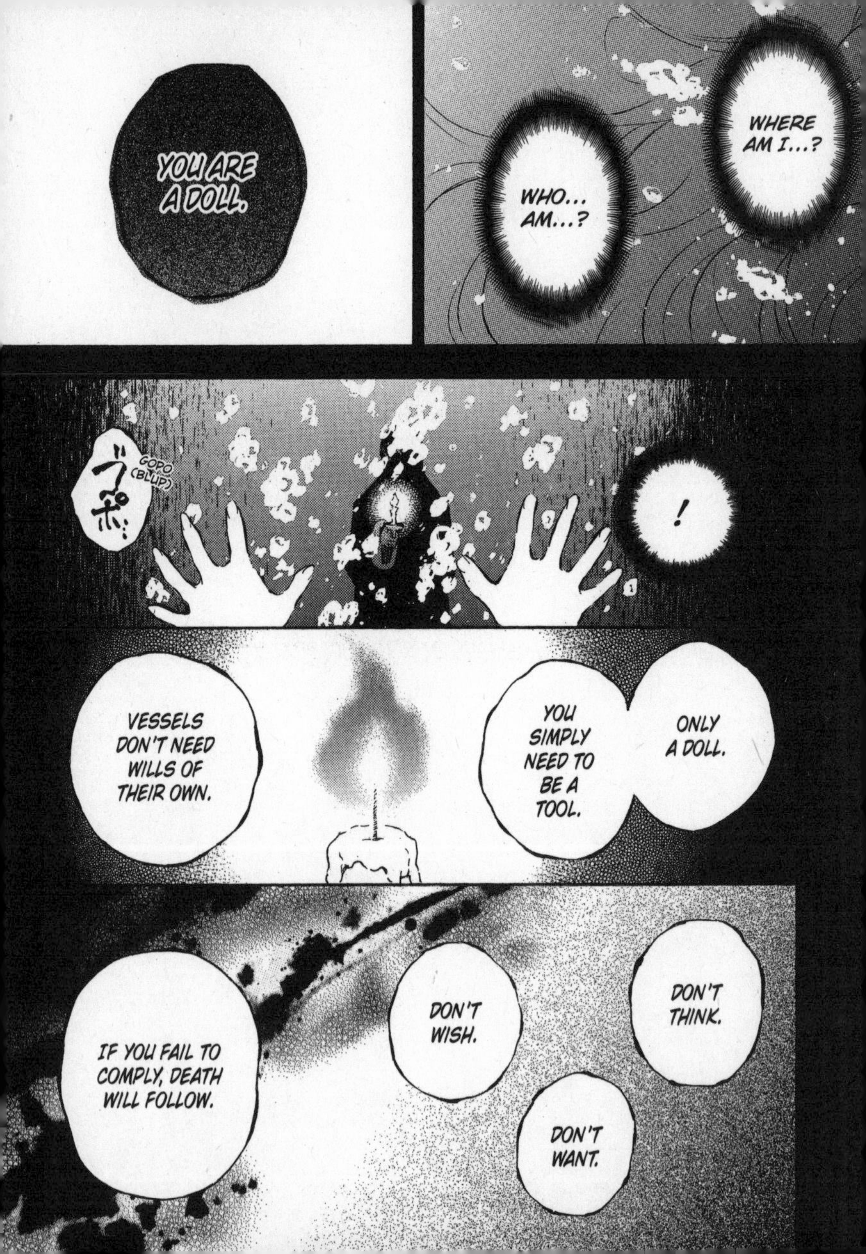
WHERE AM I...?
WHO... AM...?
YOU ARE A DOLL.
!
ゴポ…
GOPO (BLUP)
ONLY A DOLL.
YOU SIMPLY NEED TO BE A TOOL.
VESSELS DON'T NEED WILLS OF THEIR OWN.
DON'T THINK.
DON'T WISH.
DON'T WANT.
IF YOU FAIL TO COMPLY, DEATH WILL FOLLOW.

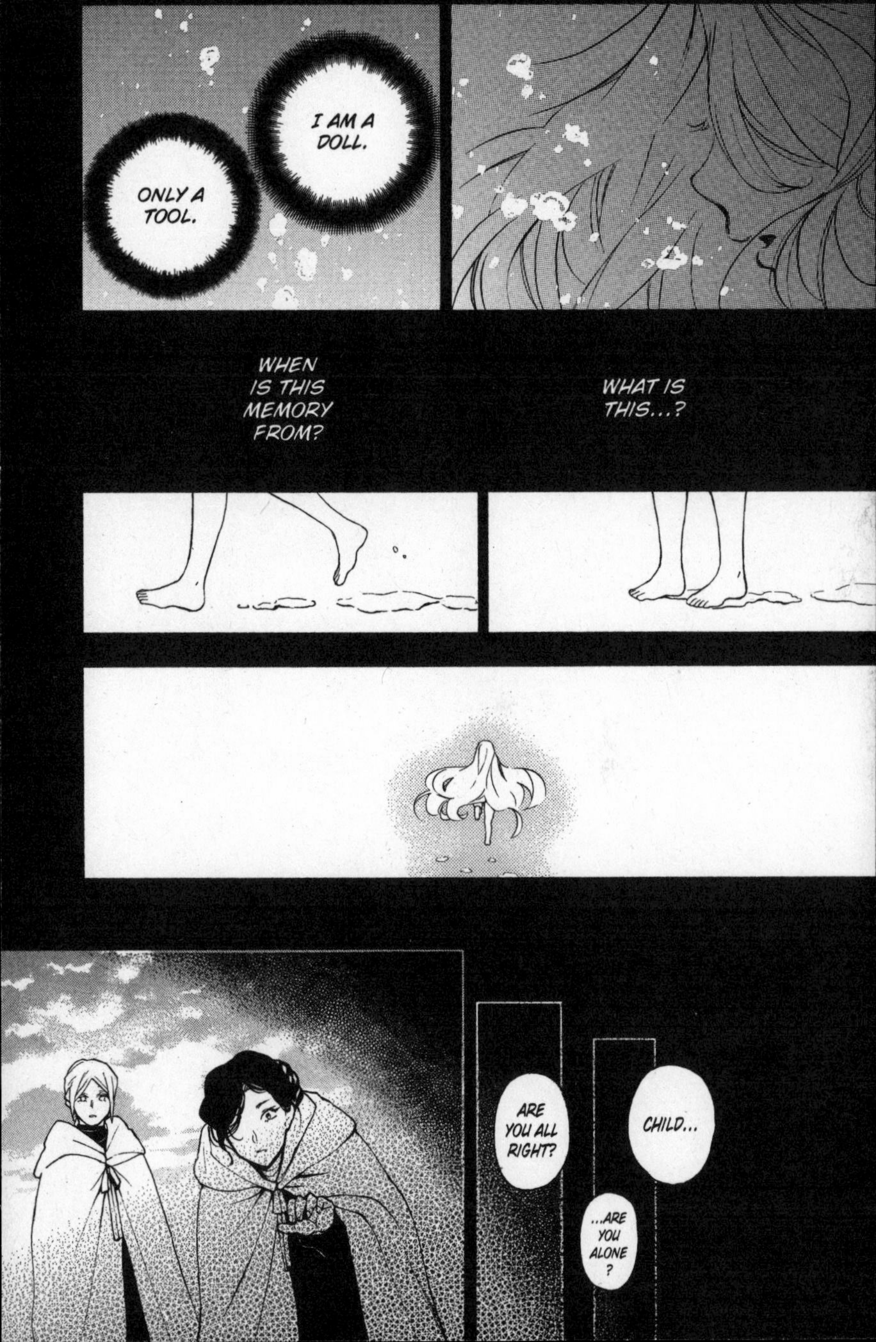
I AM A DOLL.
ONLY A TOOL.
WHAT IS THIS...?
WHEN IS THIS MEMORY FROM?
CHILD...
...ARE YOU ALONE ?
ARE YOU ALL RIGHT?

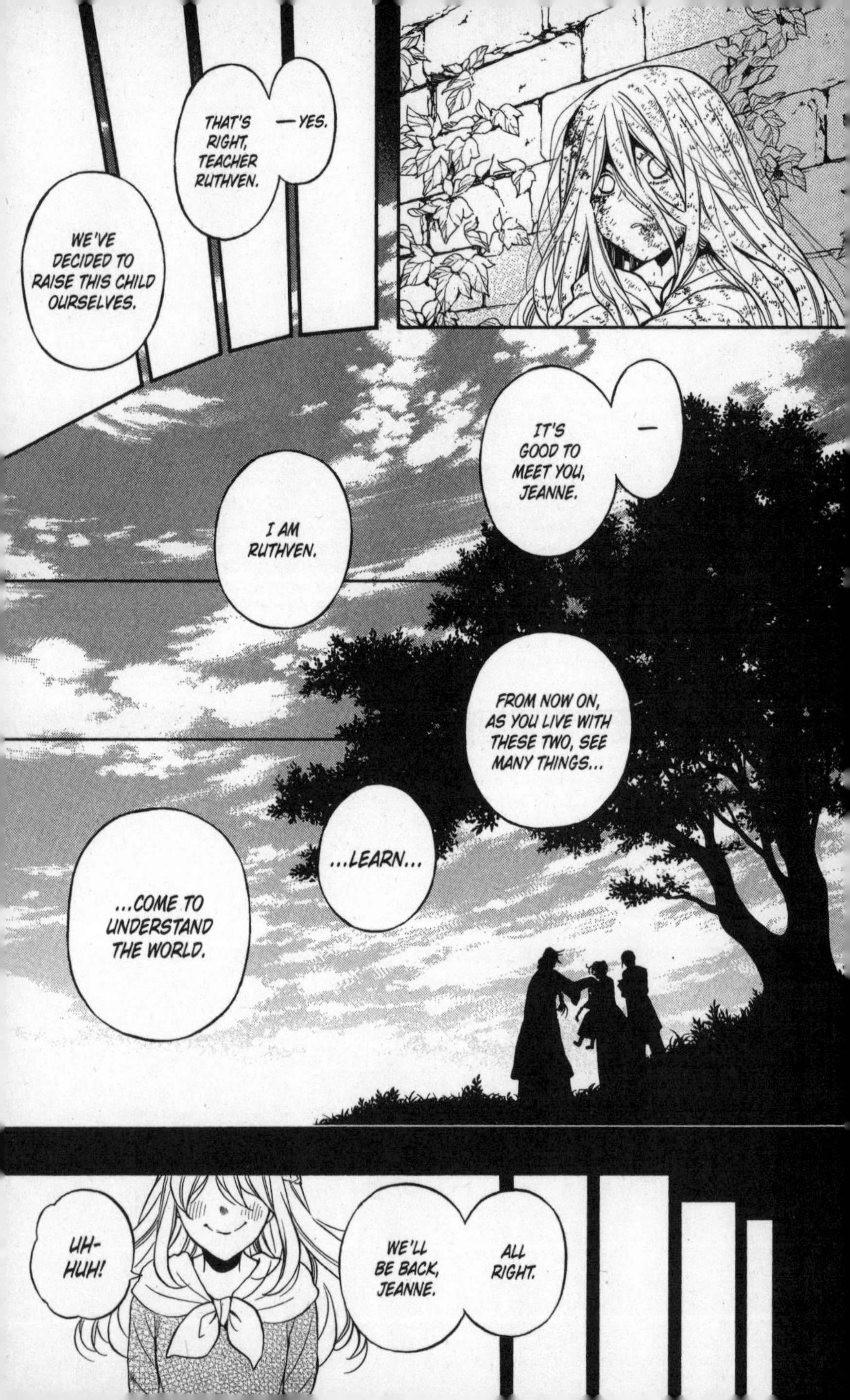
—YES.
THAT'S RIGHT, TEACHER RUTHVEN.
WE'VE DECIDED TO RAISE THIS CHILD OURSELVES.
—
IT'S GOOD TO MEET YOU, JEANNE.
I AM RUTHVEN.
FROM NOW ON, AS YOU LIVE WITH THESE TWO, SEE MANY THINGS...
...LEARN...
...COME TO UNDERSTAND THE WORLD.
ALL RIGHT.
WE'LL BE BACK, JEANNE.
UH-HUH!

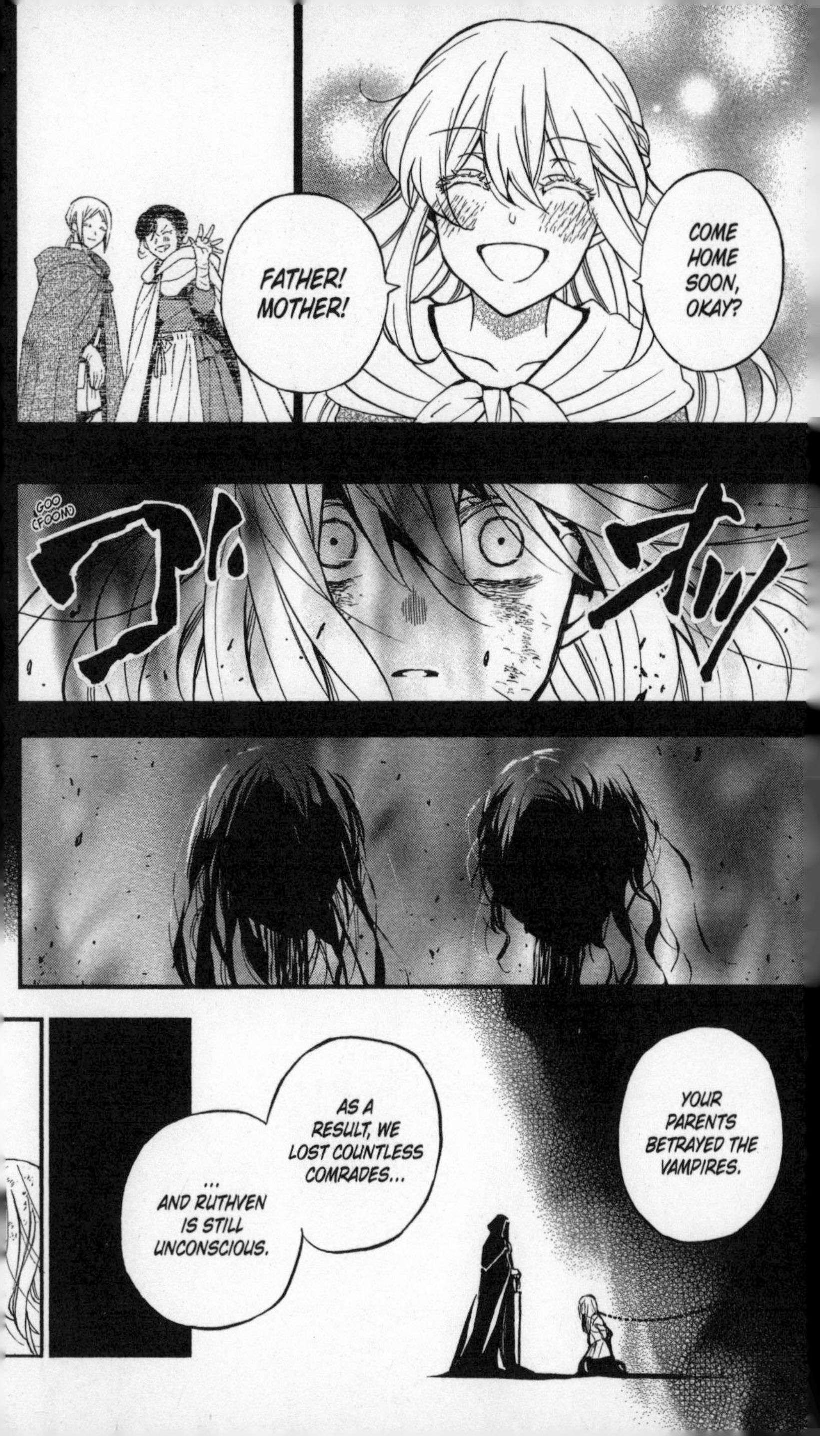
COME HOME SOON, OKAY?
FATHER! MOTHER!
GOO (FOOM)
YOUR PARENTS BETRAYED THE VAMPIRES.
AS A RESULT, WE LOST COUNTLESS COMRADES...
...AND RUTHVEN IS STILL UNCONSCIOUS.

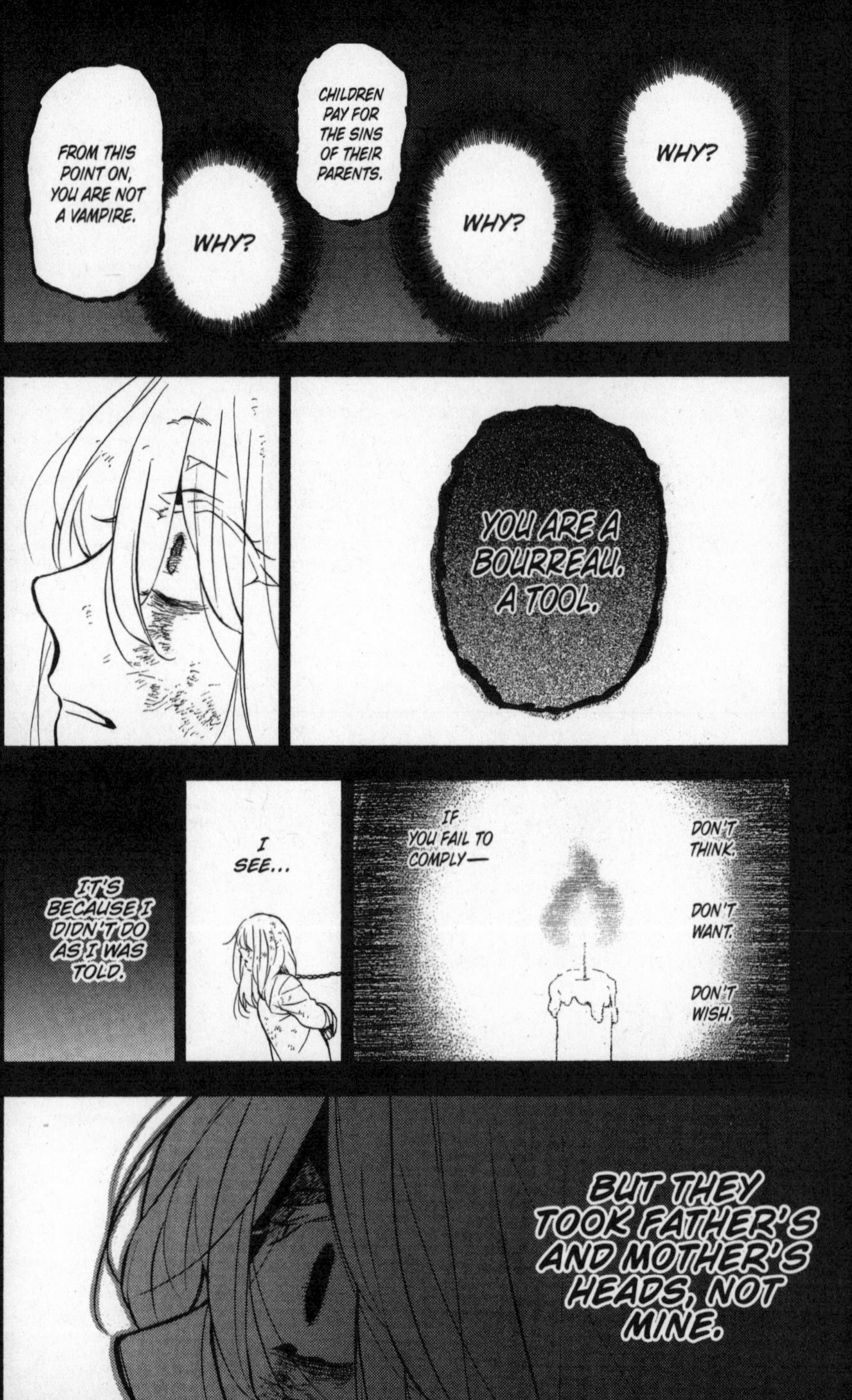
WHY?
CHILDREN PAY FOR THE SINS OF THEIR PARENTS.
WHY?
FROM THIS POINT ON, YOU ARE NOT A VAMPIRE.
WHY?
YOU ARE A BOURREAU. A TOOL.
DON'T THINK.
DON'T WANT.
DON'T WISH.
IF YOU FAIL TO COMPLY—
I SEE...
IT'S BECAUSE I DIDN'T DO AS I WAS TOLD.
BUT THEY TOOK FATHER'S AND MOTHER'S HEADS, NOT MINE.

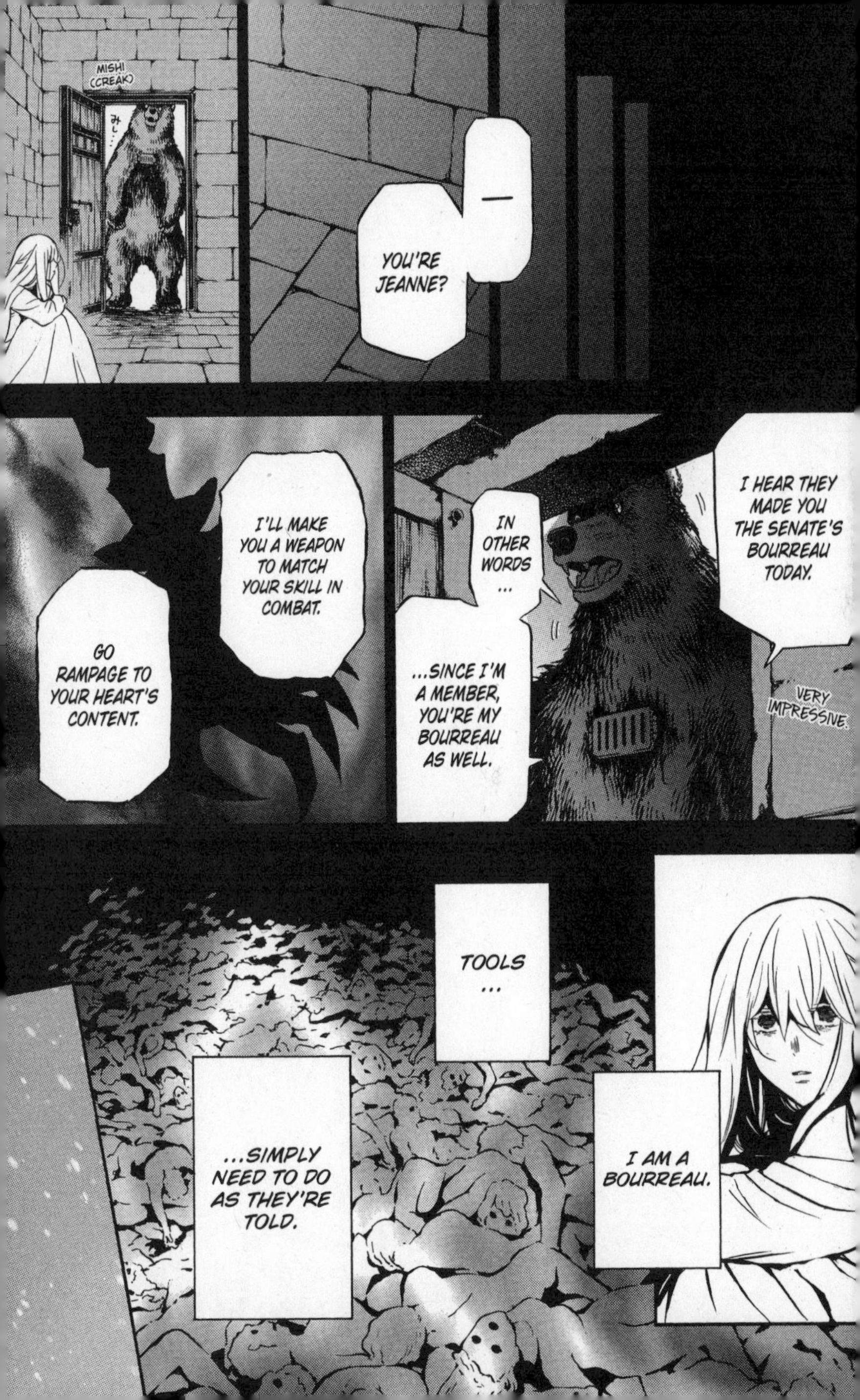
—
YOU'RE JEANNE?
MISHI (CREAK)
みし…
I HEAR THEY MADE YOU THE SENATE'S BOURREAU TODAY.
VERY IMPRESSIVE.
IN OTHER WORDS ...
...SINCE I'M A MEMBER, YOU'RE MY BOURREAU AS WELL.
I'LL MAKE YOU A WEAPON TO MATCH YOUR SKILL IN COMBAT.
GO RAMPAGE TO YOUR HEART'S CONTENT.
I AM A BOURREAU.
TOOLS ...
...SIMPLY NEED TO DO AS THEY'RE TOLD.

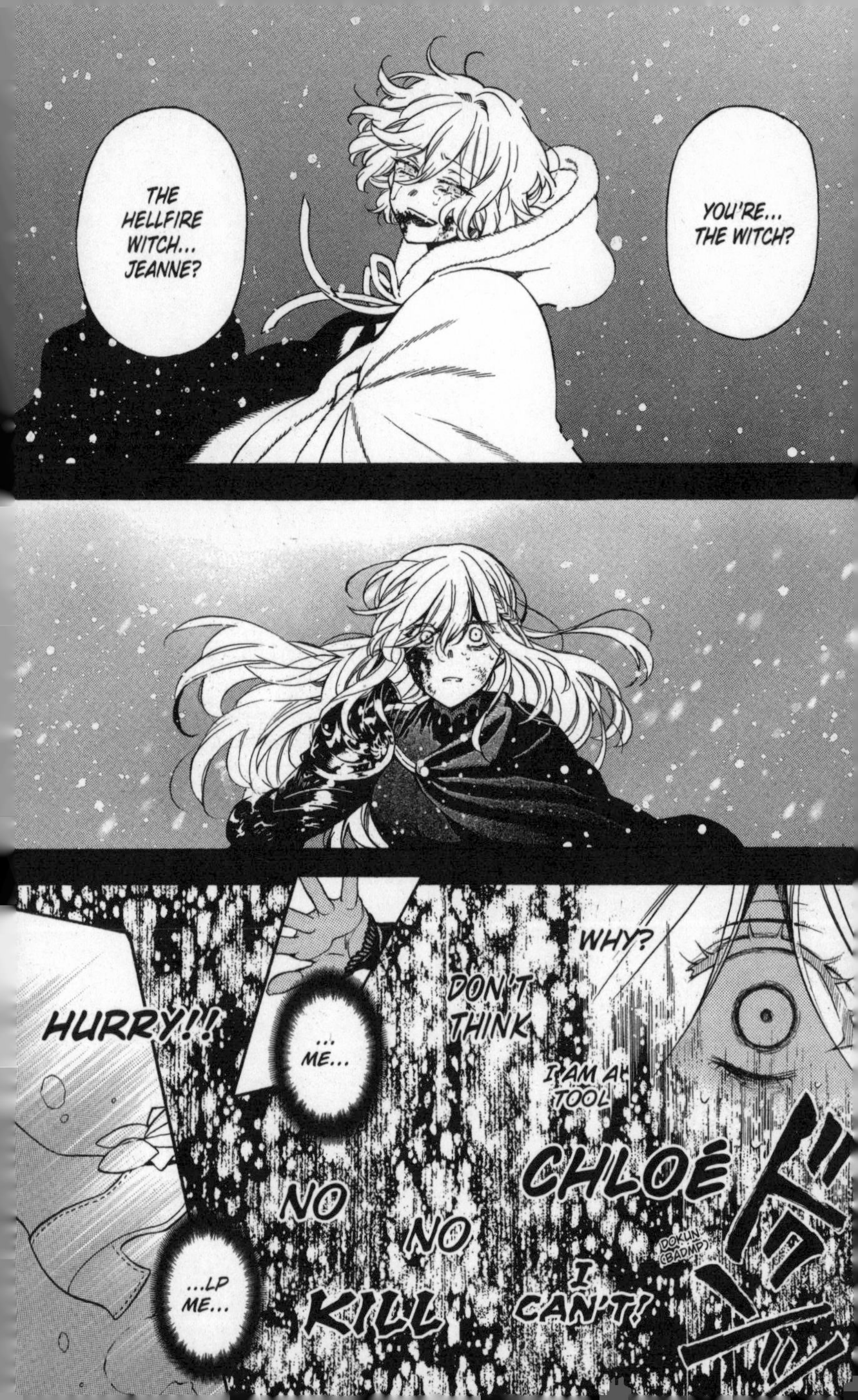
YOU'RE... THE WITCH?
THE HELLFIRE WITCH... JEANNE?
WHY?
DON'T THINK
I AM A TOOL
CHLOÉ
DOKUN (BADMP)
I CAN'T!
NO
NO
KILL
... ME...
...LP ME...
HURRY!!

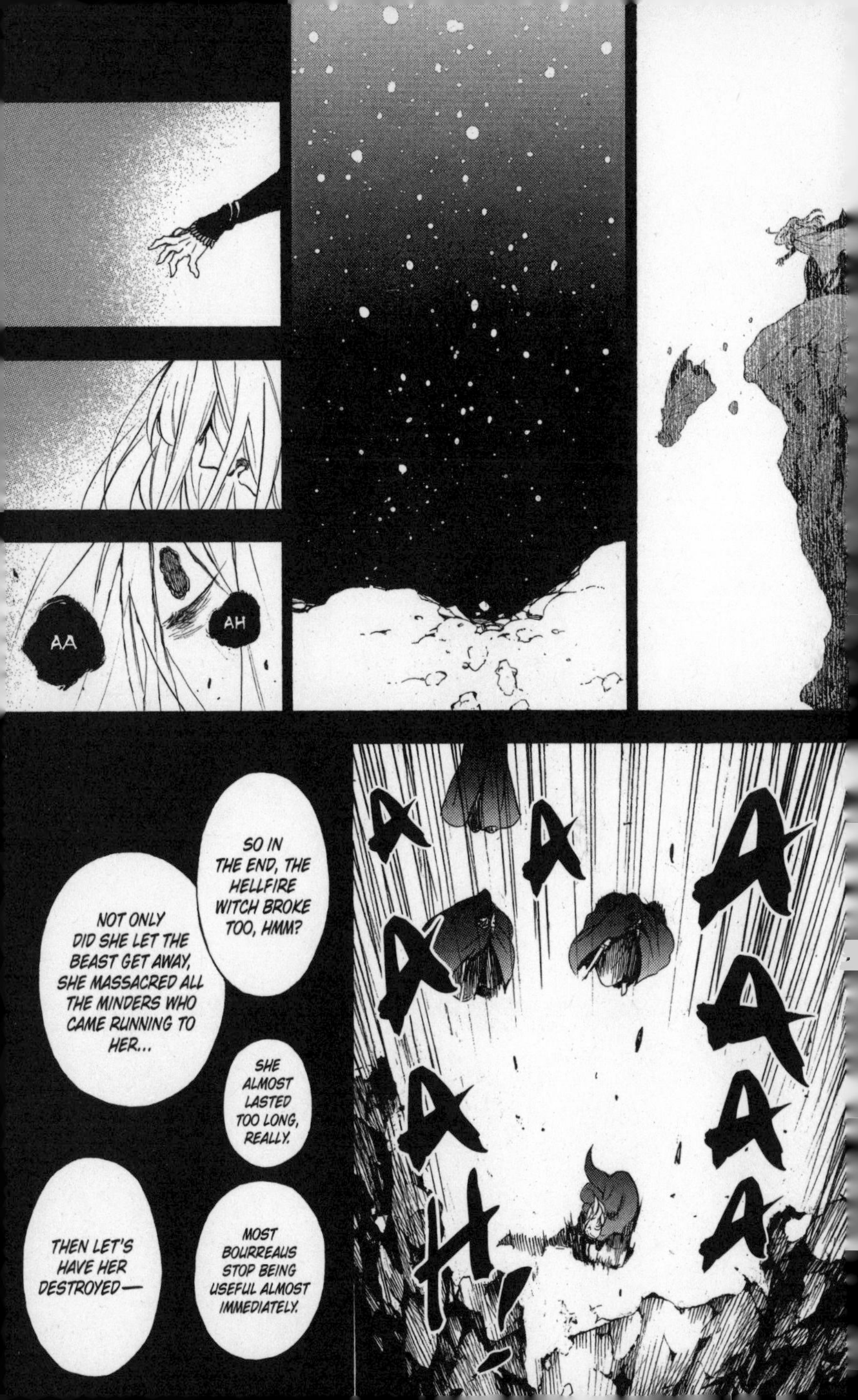
AH
AA
AAAAAAAAH
SO IN THE END, THE HELLFIRE WITCH BROKE TOO, HMM?
NOT ONLY DID SHE LET THE BEAST GET AWAY, SHE MASSACRED ALL THE MINDERS WHO CAME RUNNING TO HER...
SHE ALMOST LASTED TOO LONG, REALLY.
MOST BOURREAUS STOP BEING USEFUL ALMOST IMMEDIATELY.
THEN LET'S HAVE HER DESTROYED—

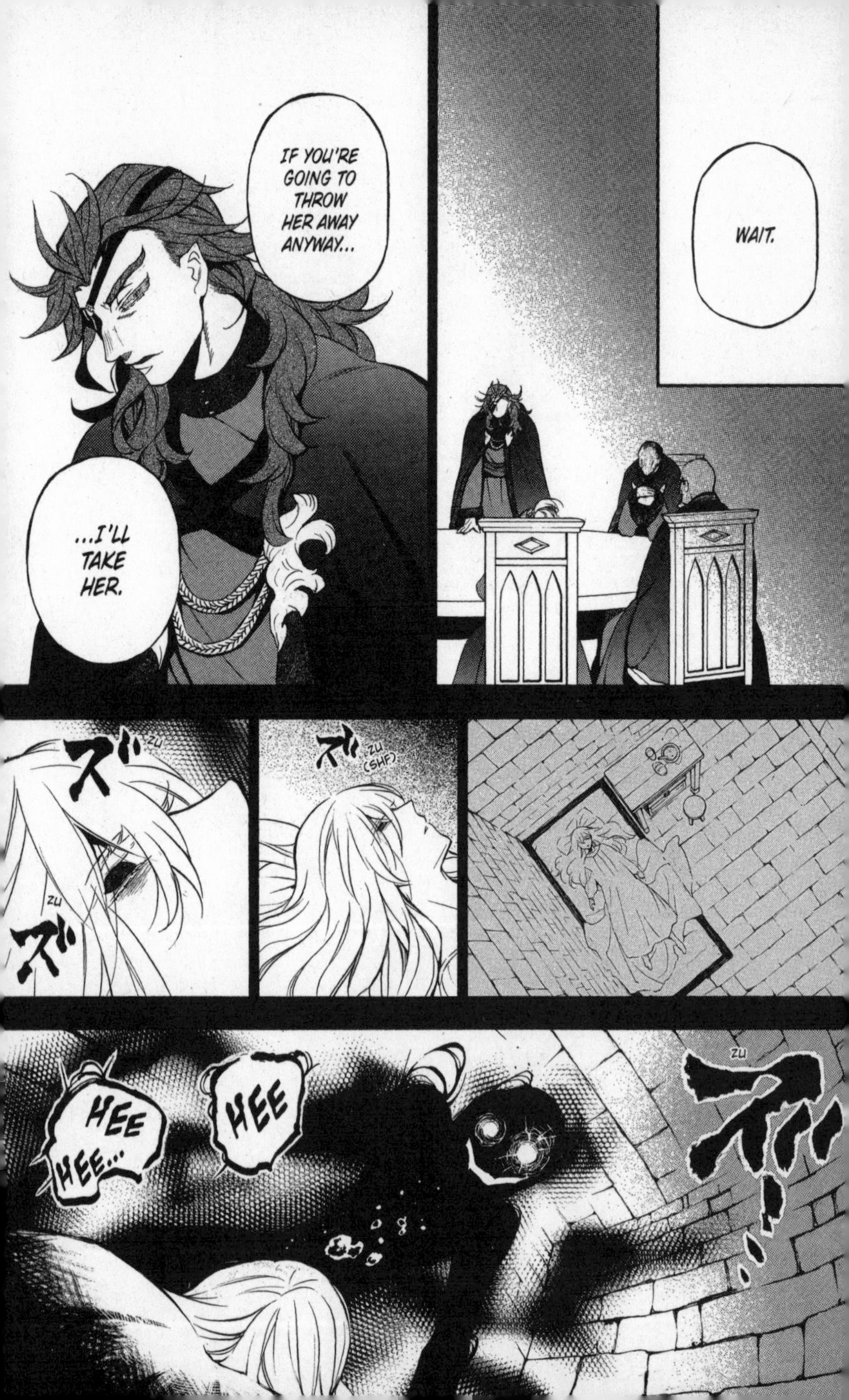
WAIT.
IF YOU'RE GOING TO THROW HER AWAY ANYWAY...
...I'LL TAKE HER.
ズ ZU (SHF)
ズ ZU
ZU ズ
ズ ZU
HEE
HEE HEE...

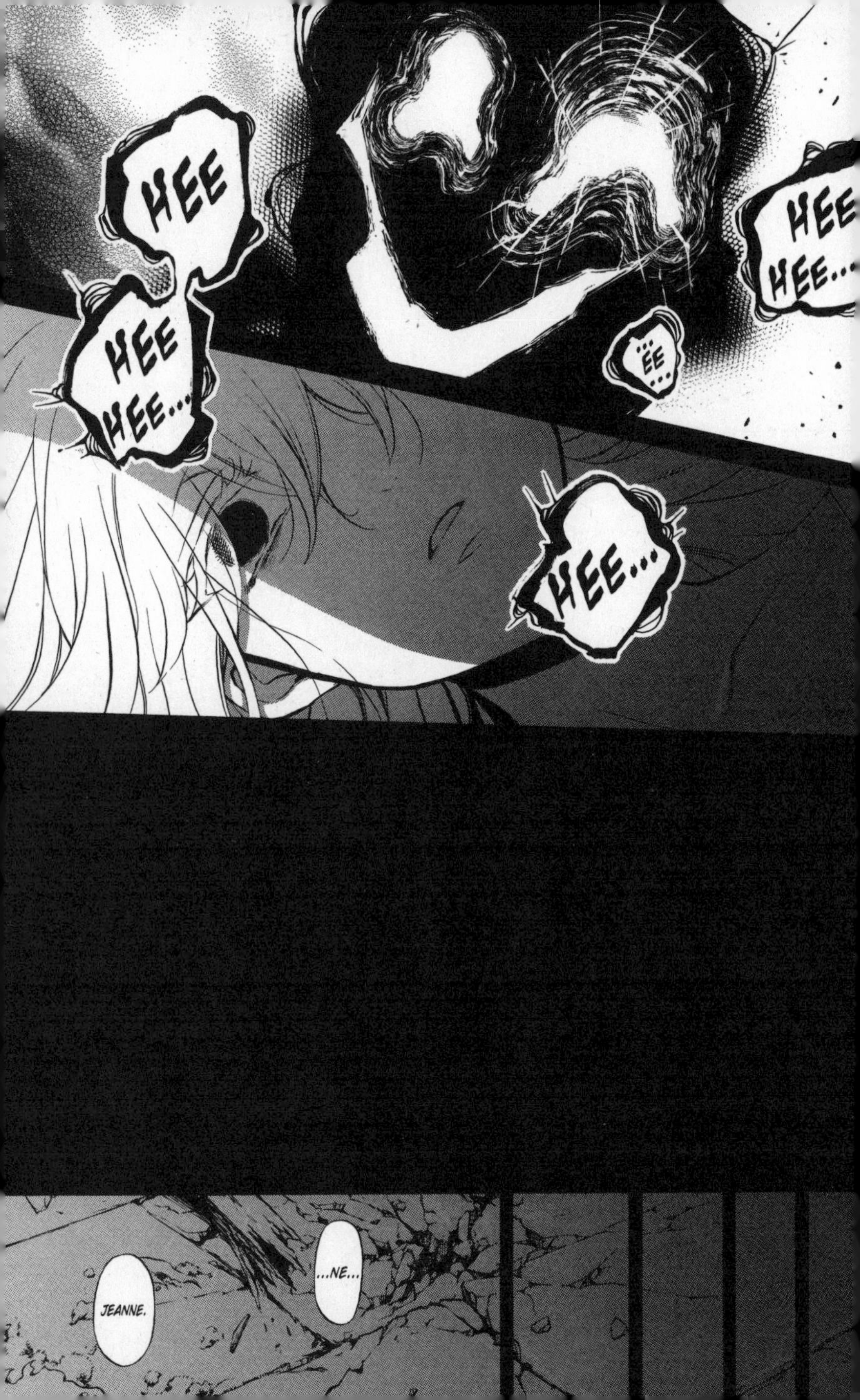
HEE HEE...
...EE...
HEE
HEE HEE...
HEE...
...NE...
JEANNE.

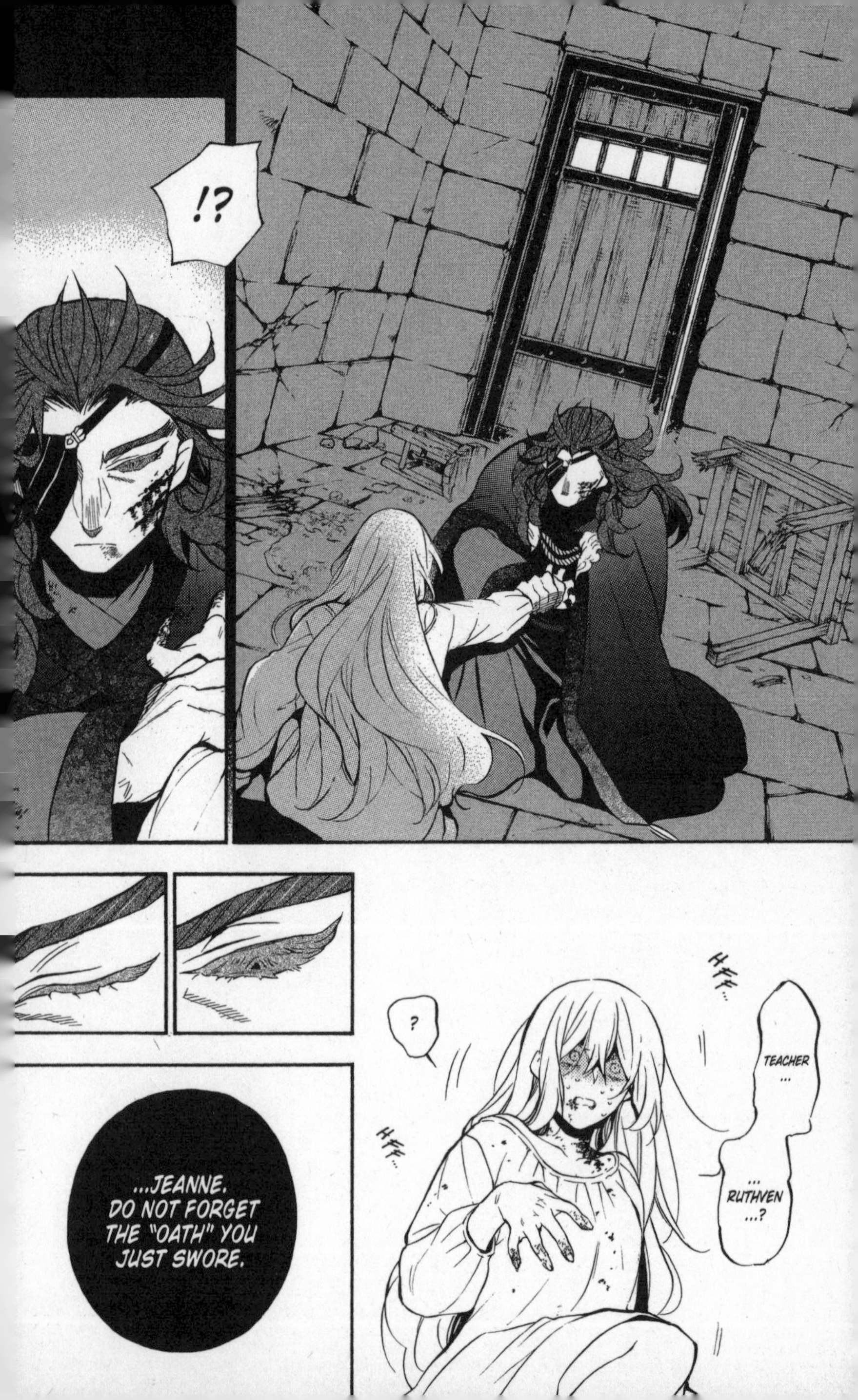
!?
HFF...
TEACHER...
...RUTHVEN...?
?
HFF...
...JEANNE. DO NOT FORGET THE "OATH" YOU JUST SWORE.

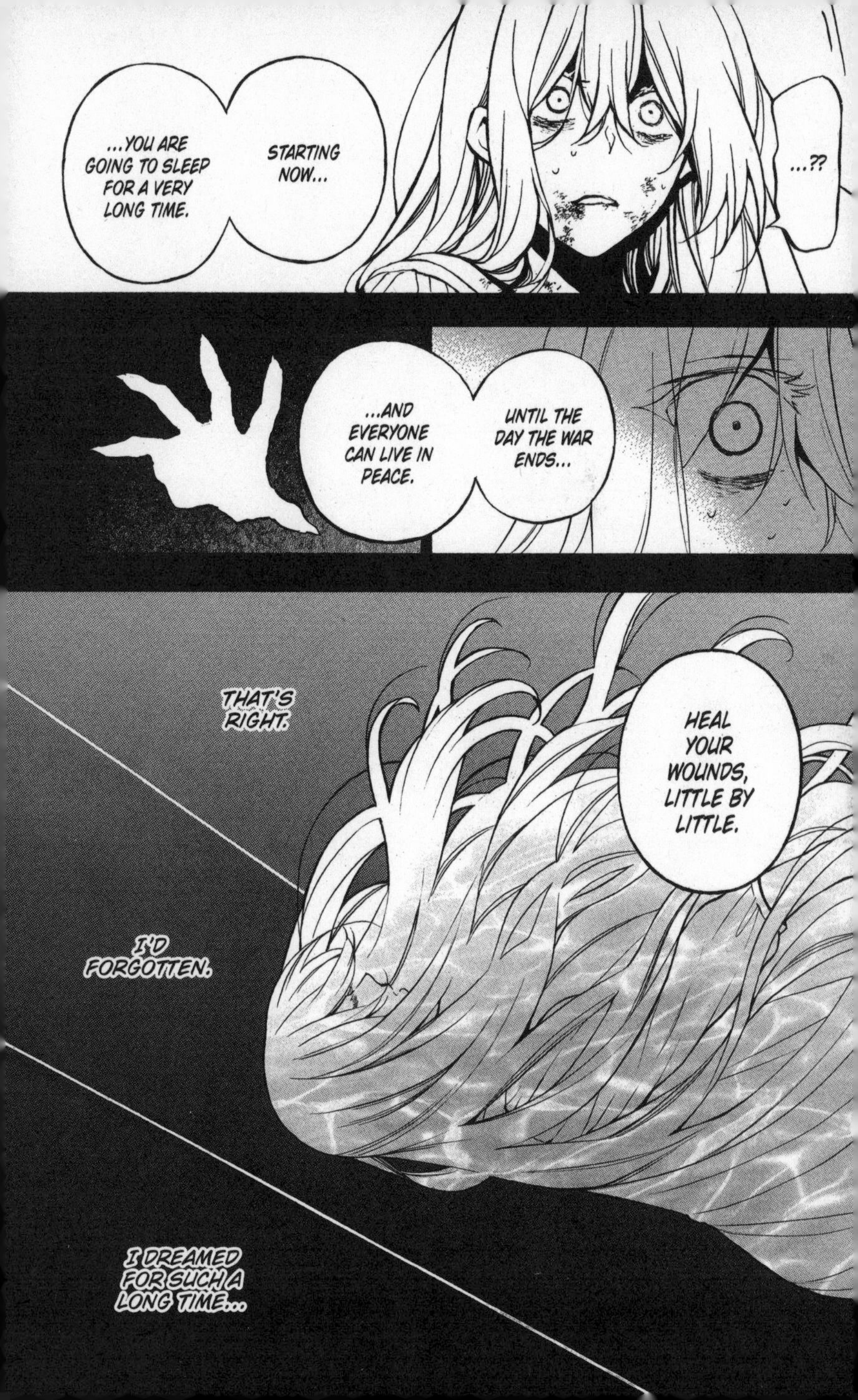
...??
STARTING NOW...
...YOU ARE GOING TO SLEEP FOR A VERY LONG TIME.
UNTIL THE DAY THE WAR ENDS...
...AND EVERYONE CAN LIVE IN PEACE.
HEAL YOUR WOUNDS, LITTLE BY LITTLE.
THAT'S RIGHT.
I'D FORGOTTEN.
I DREAMED FOR SUCH A LONG TIME...

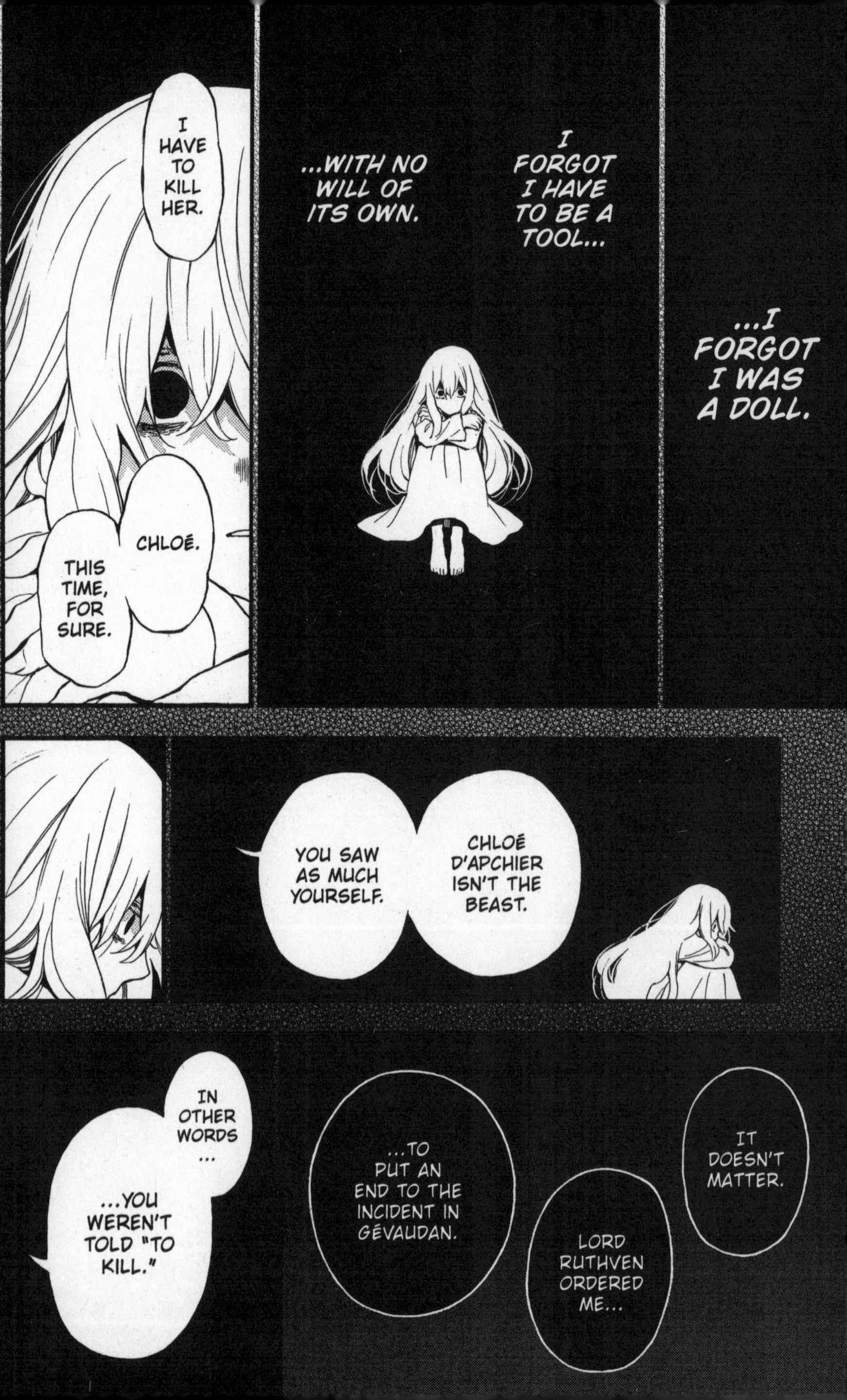
...I FORGOT I WAS A DOLL.
I FORGOT I HAVE TO BE A TOOL...
...WITH NO WILL OF ITS OWN.
I HAVE TO KILL HER.
CHLOÉ.
THIS TIME, FOR SURE.
CHLOÉ D'APCHIER ISN'T THE BEAST.
YOU SAW AS MUCH YOURSELF.
IT DOESN'T MATTER.
LORD RUTHVEN ORDERED ME...
...TO PUT AN END TO THE INCIDENT IN GÉVAUDAN.
IN OTHER WORDS...
...YOU WEREN'T TOLD "TO KILL."

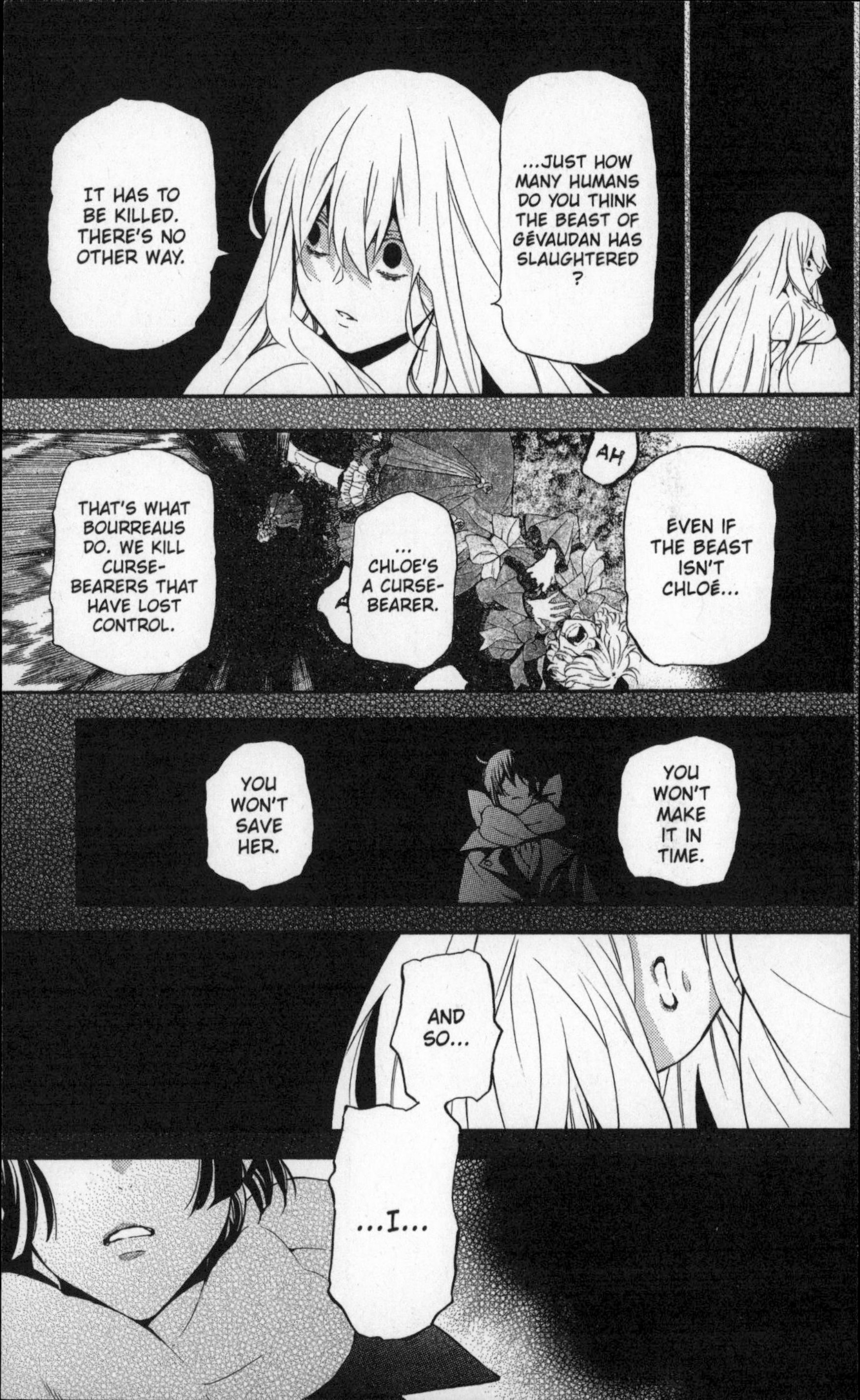
...JUST HOW MANY HUMANS DO YOU THINK THE BEAST OF GÉVAUDAN HAS SLAUGHTERED?
IT HAS TO BE KILLED. THERE'S NO OTHER WAY.
AH
EVEN IF THE BEAST ISN'T CHLOÉ...
...CHLOE'S A CURSE-BEARER.
THAT'S WHAT BOURREAUS DO. WE KILL CURSE-BEARERS THAT HAVE LOST CONTROL.
YOU WON'T MAKE IT IN TIME.
YOU WON'T SAVE HER.
AND SO...
...I...

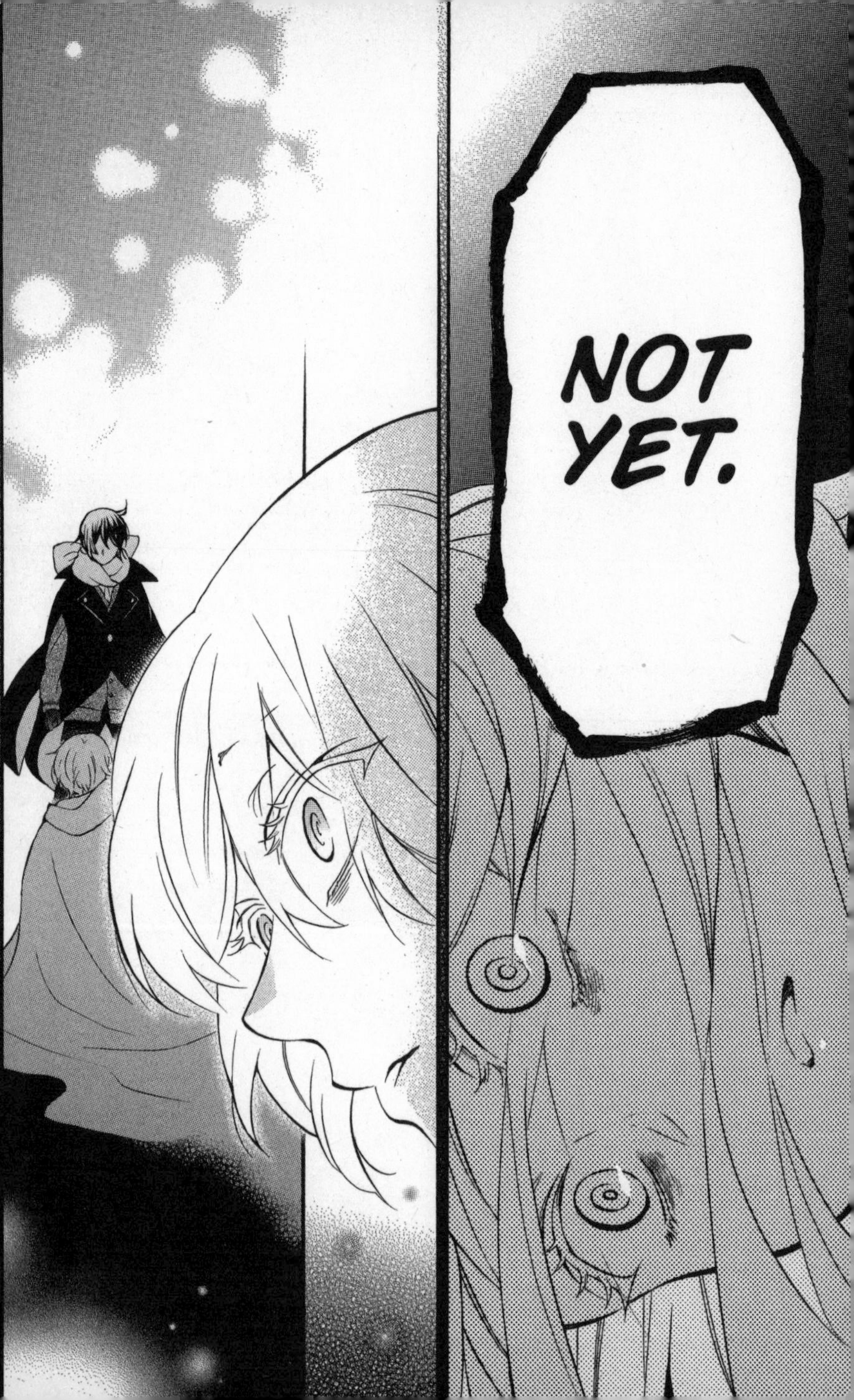
NOT YET.

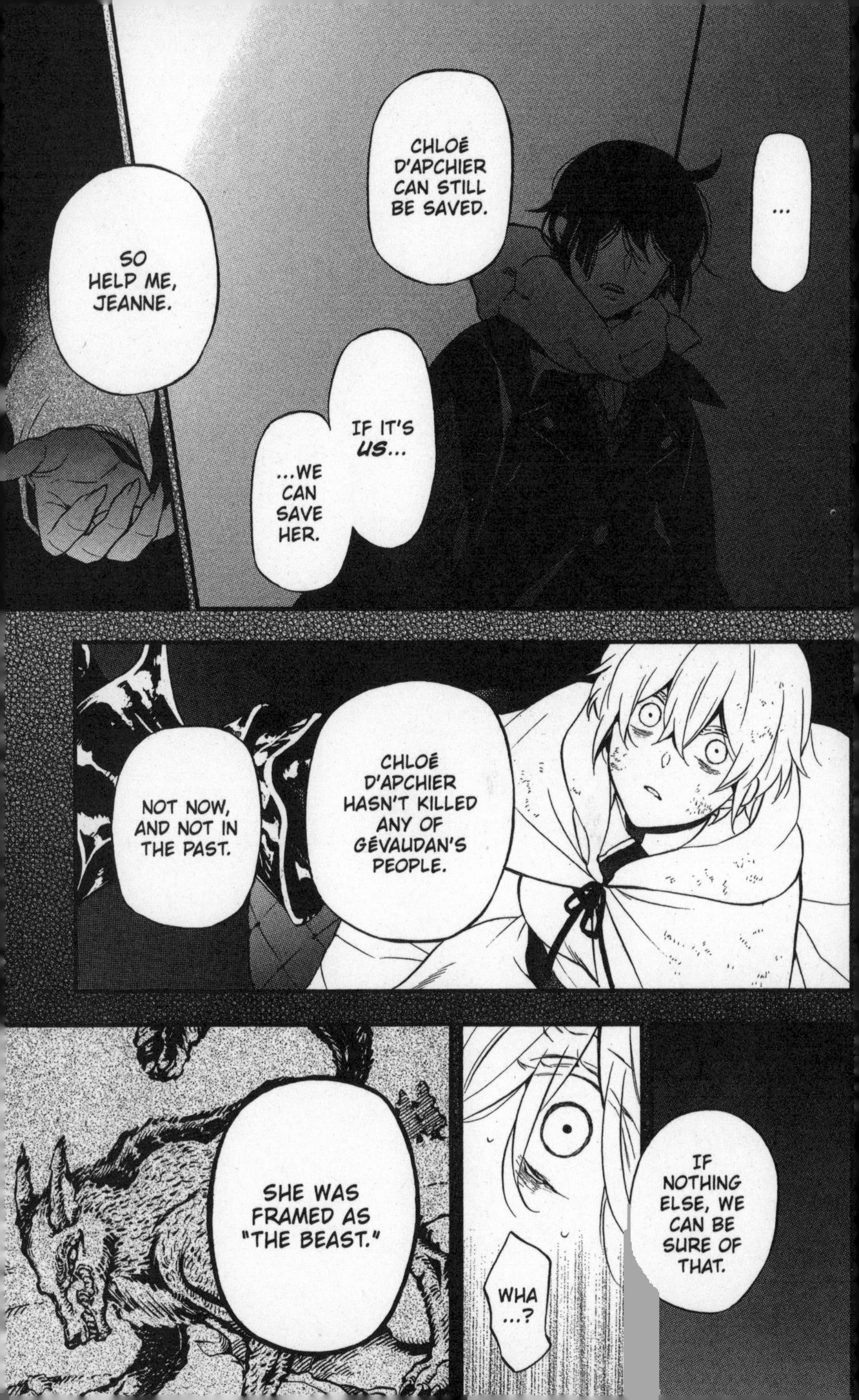
...
CHLOÉ D'APCHIER CAN STILL BE SAVED.
IF IT'S *US*...
...WE CAN SAVE HER.
SO HELP ME, JEANNE.
CHLOÉ D'APCHIER HASN'T KILLED ANY OF GÉVAUDAN'S PEOPLE.
NOT NOW, AND NOT IN THE PAST.
IF NOTHING ELSE, WE CAN BE SURE OF THAT.
WHA ...?
SHE WAS FRAMED AS "THE BEAST."

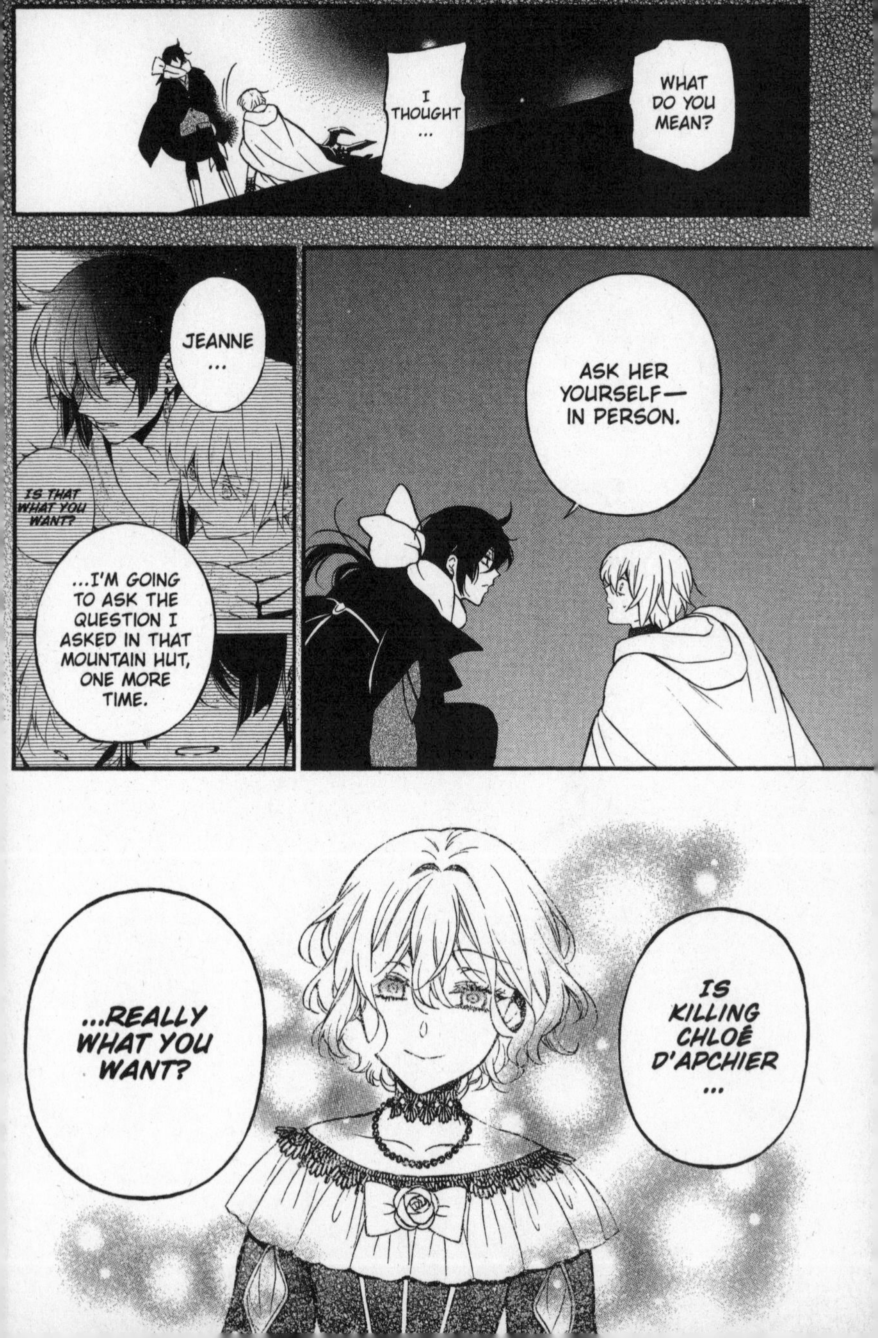
WHAT DO YOU MEAN?
I THOUGHT...
ASK HER YOURSELF—IN PERSON.
JEANNE...
IS THAT WHAT YOU WANT?
...I'M GOING TO ASK THE QUESTION I ASKED IN THAT MOUNTAIN HUT, ONE MORE TIME.
IS KILLING CHLOÉ D'APCHIER...
...REALLY WHAT YOU WANT?

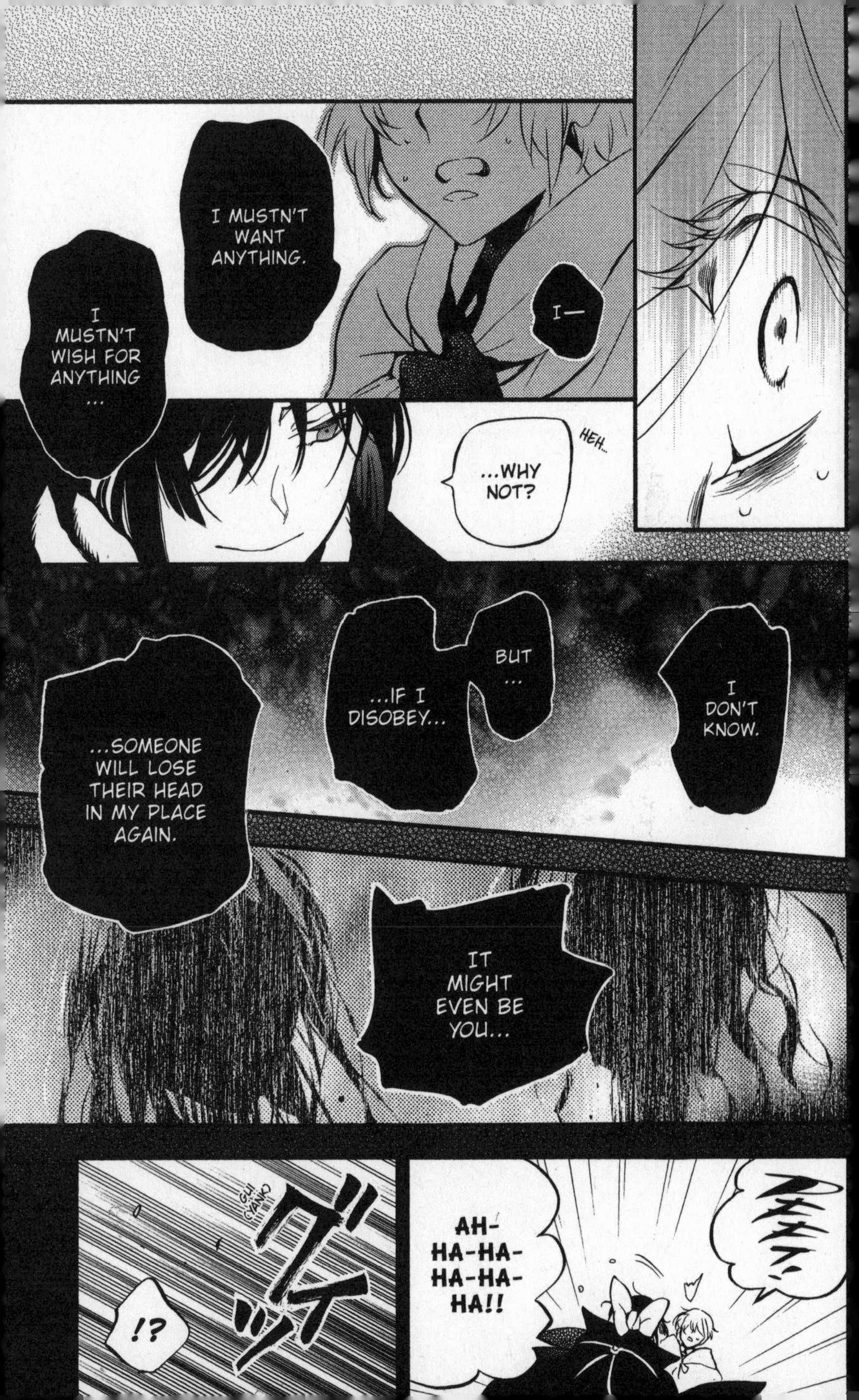

I—
I MUSTN'T WANT ANYTHING.
I MUSTN'T WISH FOR ANYTHING...
HEH...
...WHY NOT?
I DON'T KNOW.
BUT...
...IF I DISOBEY...
...SOMEONE WILL LOSE THEIR HEAD IN MY PLACE AGAIN.
IT MIGHT EVEN BE YOU...
AH-HA-HA-HA-HA-HA!!
グイッ
GUI (YANK)
!?

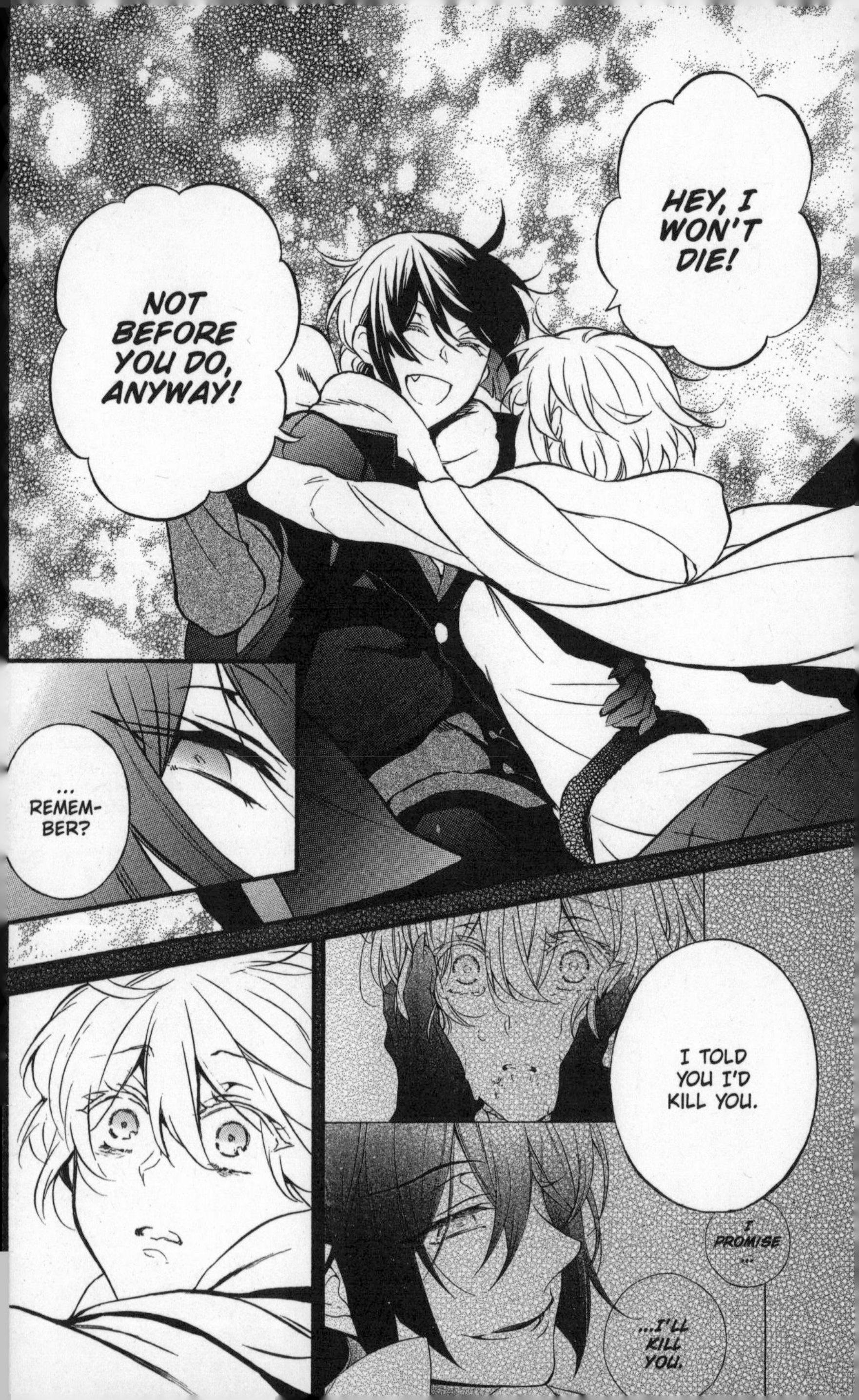
HEY, I WON'T DIE!
NOT BEFORE YOU DO, ANYWAY!
...REMEMBER?
I TOLD YOU I'D KILL YOU.
I PROMISE...
...I'LL KILL YOU.

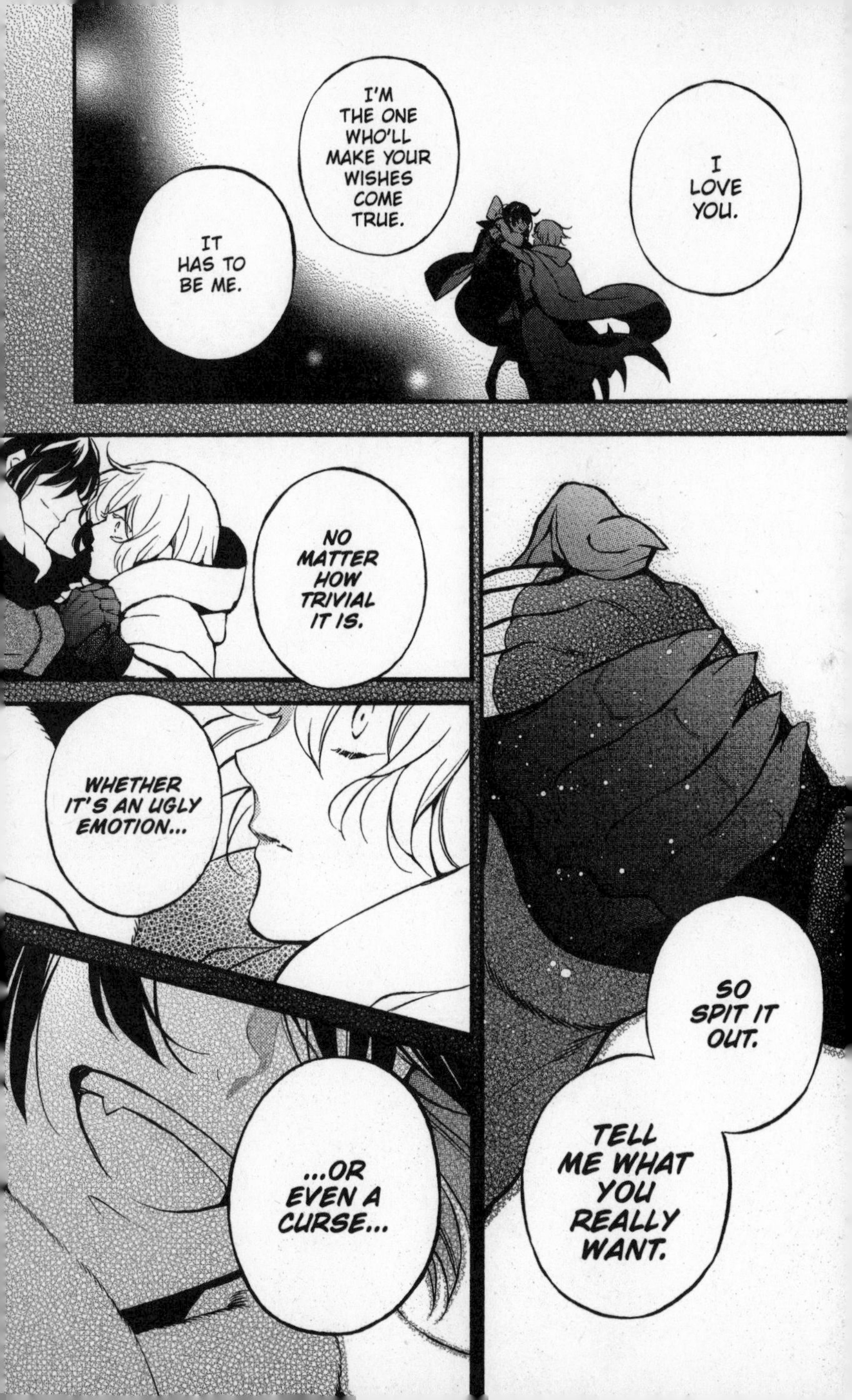
I LOVE YOU.
I'M THE ONE WHO'LL MAKE YOUR WISHES COME TRUE.
IT HAS TO BE ME.
SO SPIT IT OUT.
TELL ME WHAT YOU REALLY WANT.
NO MATTER HOW TRIVIAL IT IS.
WHETHER IT'S AN UGLY EMOTION...
...OR EVEN A CURSE...

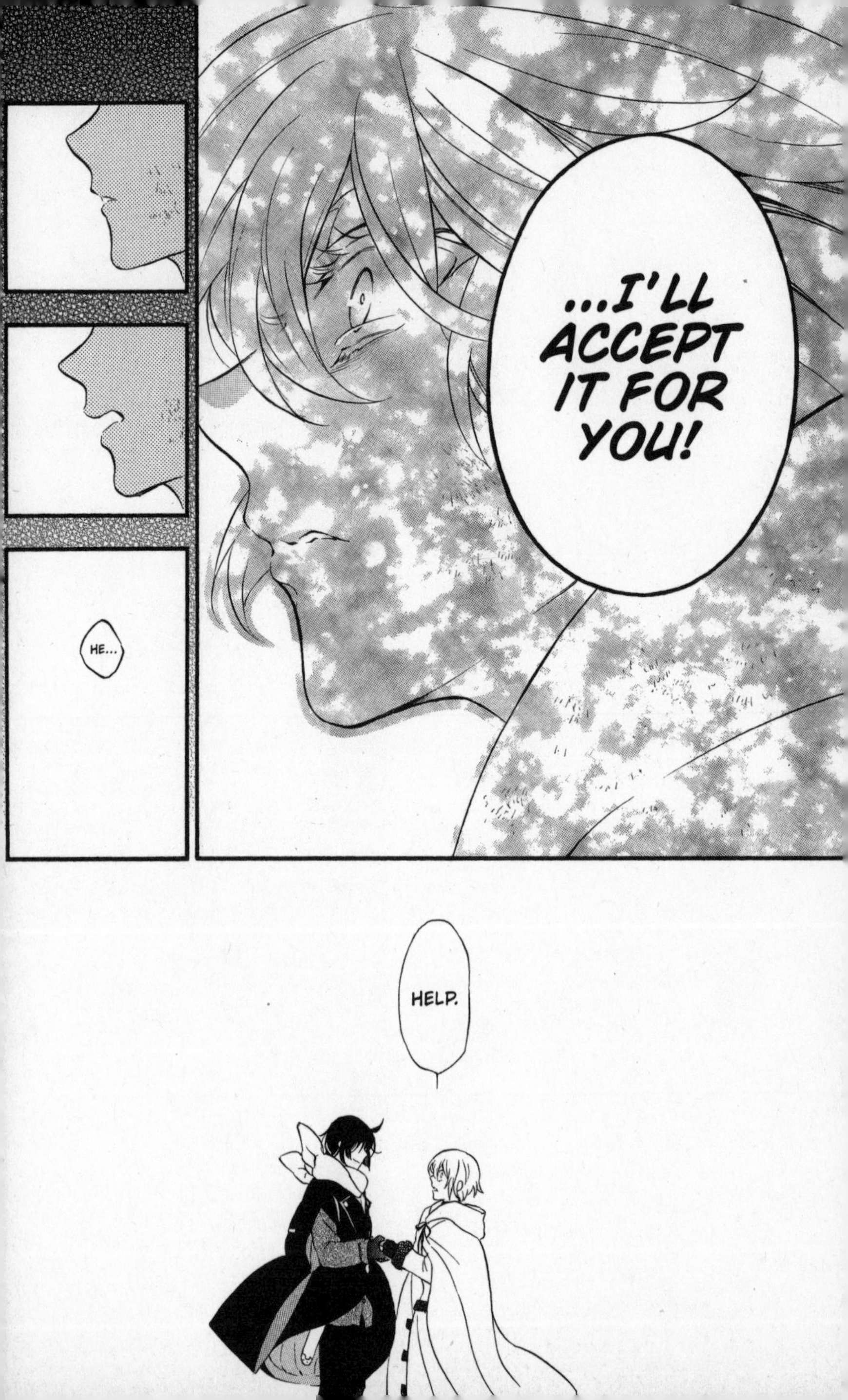
...I'LL ACCEPT IT FOR YOU!
HE...
HELP.

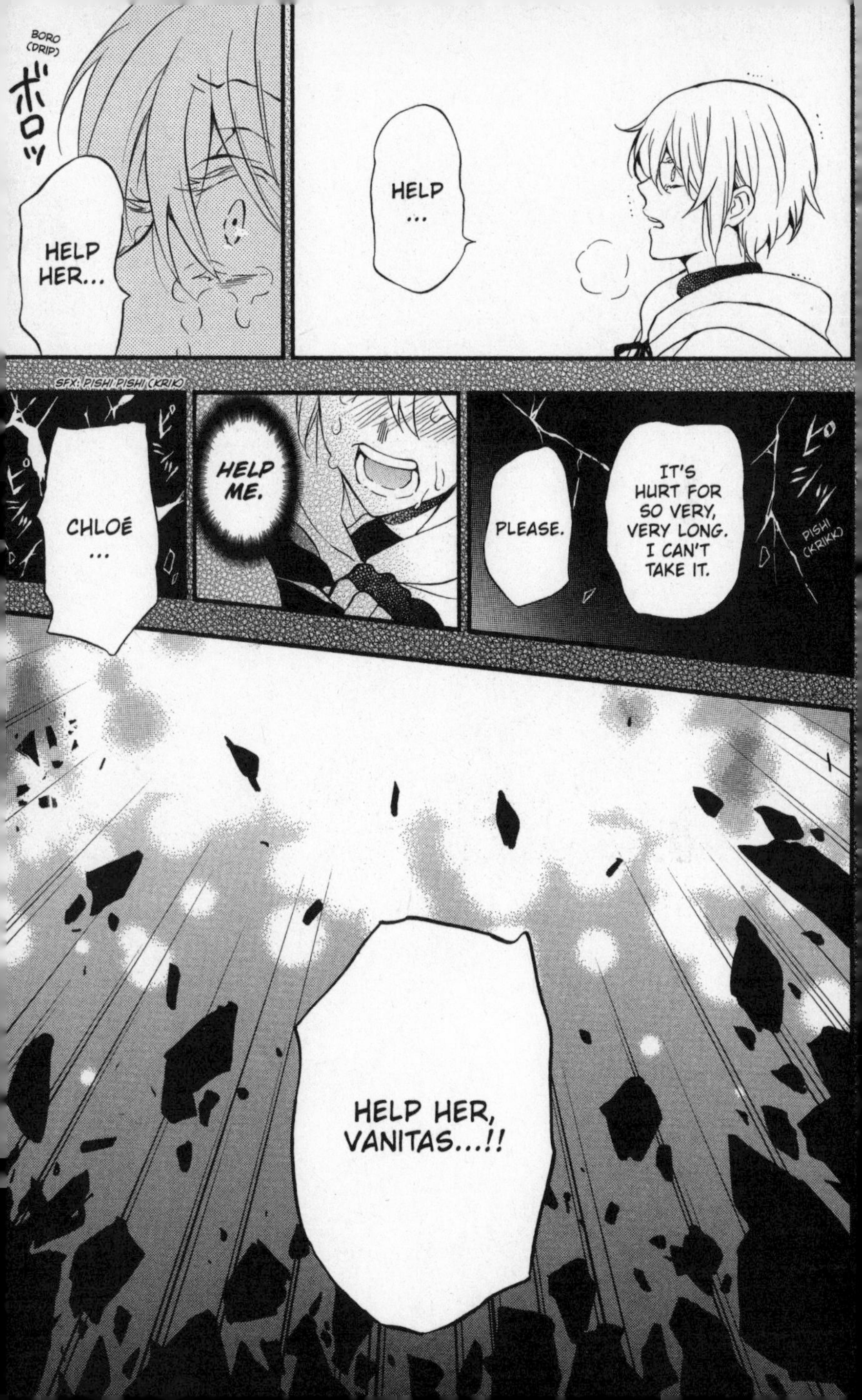
HELP ...
ボロッ
BORO (DRIP)
HELP HER...
SFX: PISHI PISHI (KRIK)
PISHI (KRIKK)
IT'S HURT FOR SO VERY, VERY LONG. I CAN'T TAKE IT.
PLEASE.
HELP ME.
CHLOÉ ...
HELP HER, VANITAS...!!

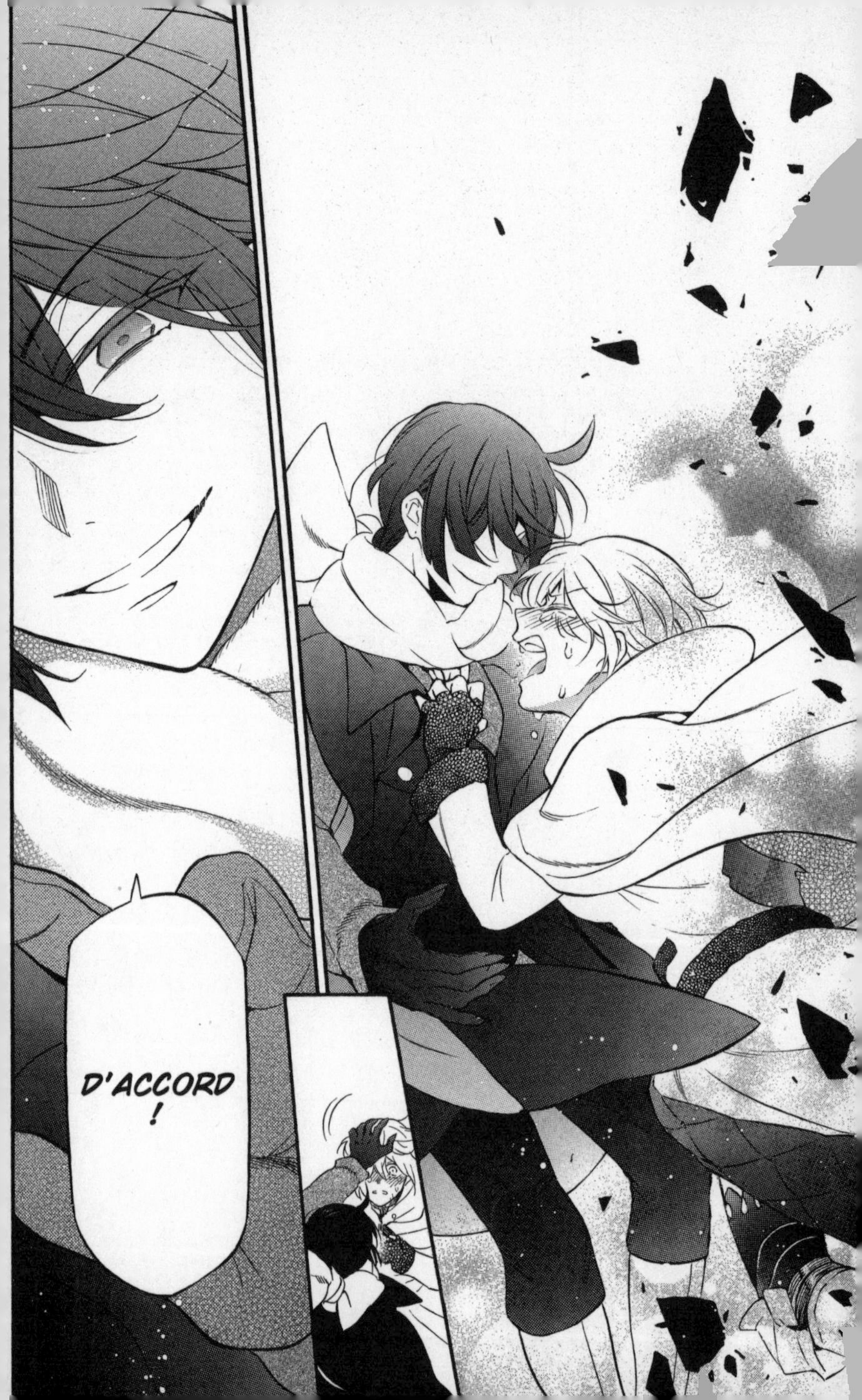
D'ACCORD !

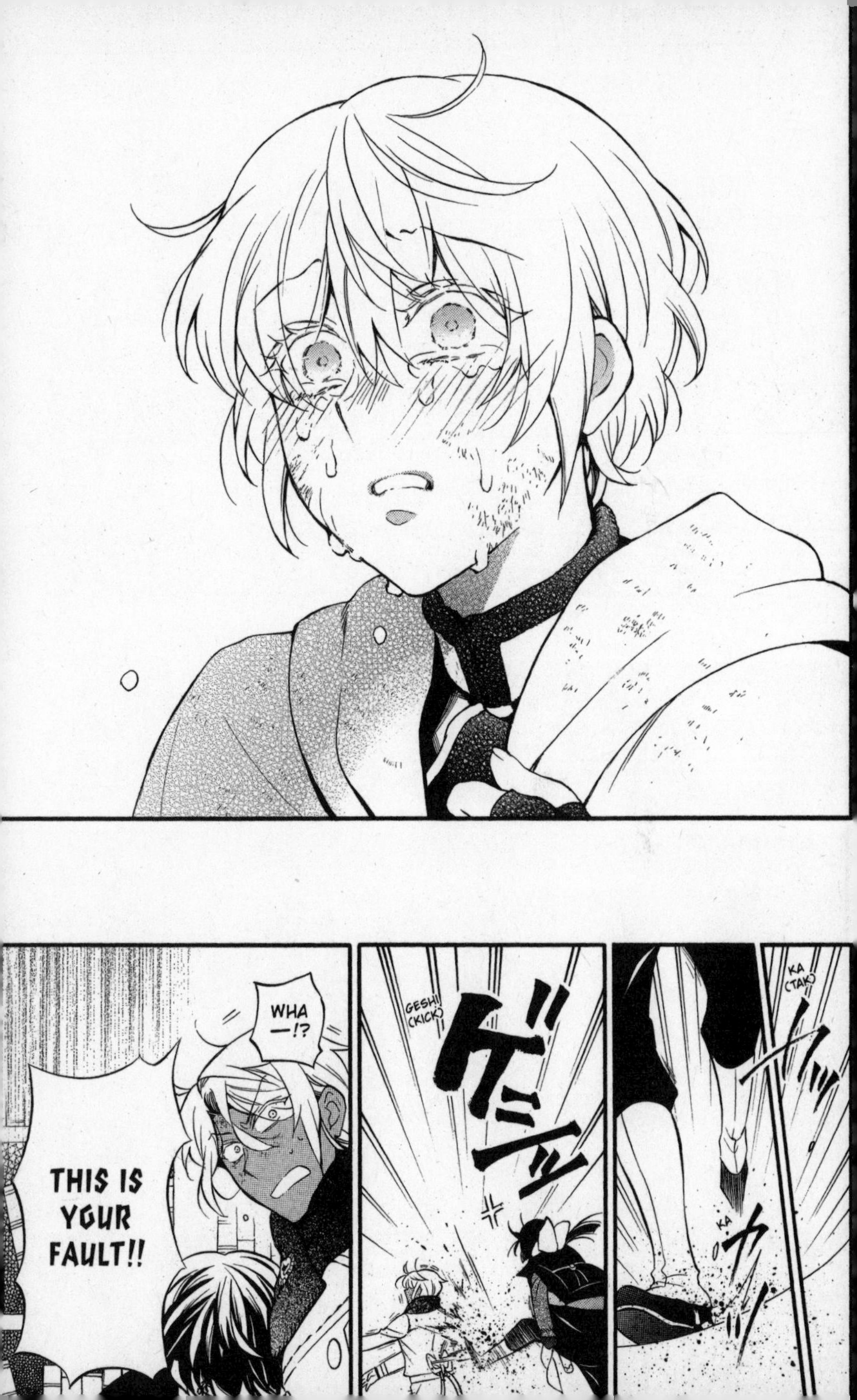
KA (TAK)
KA
GESHI! (KICK)
WHA—!?
THIS IS YOUR FAULT!!

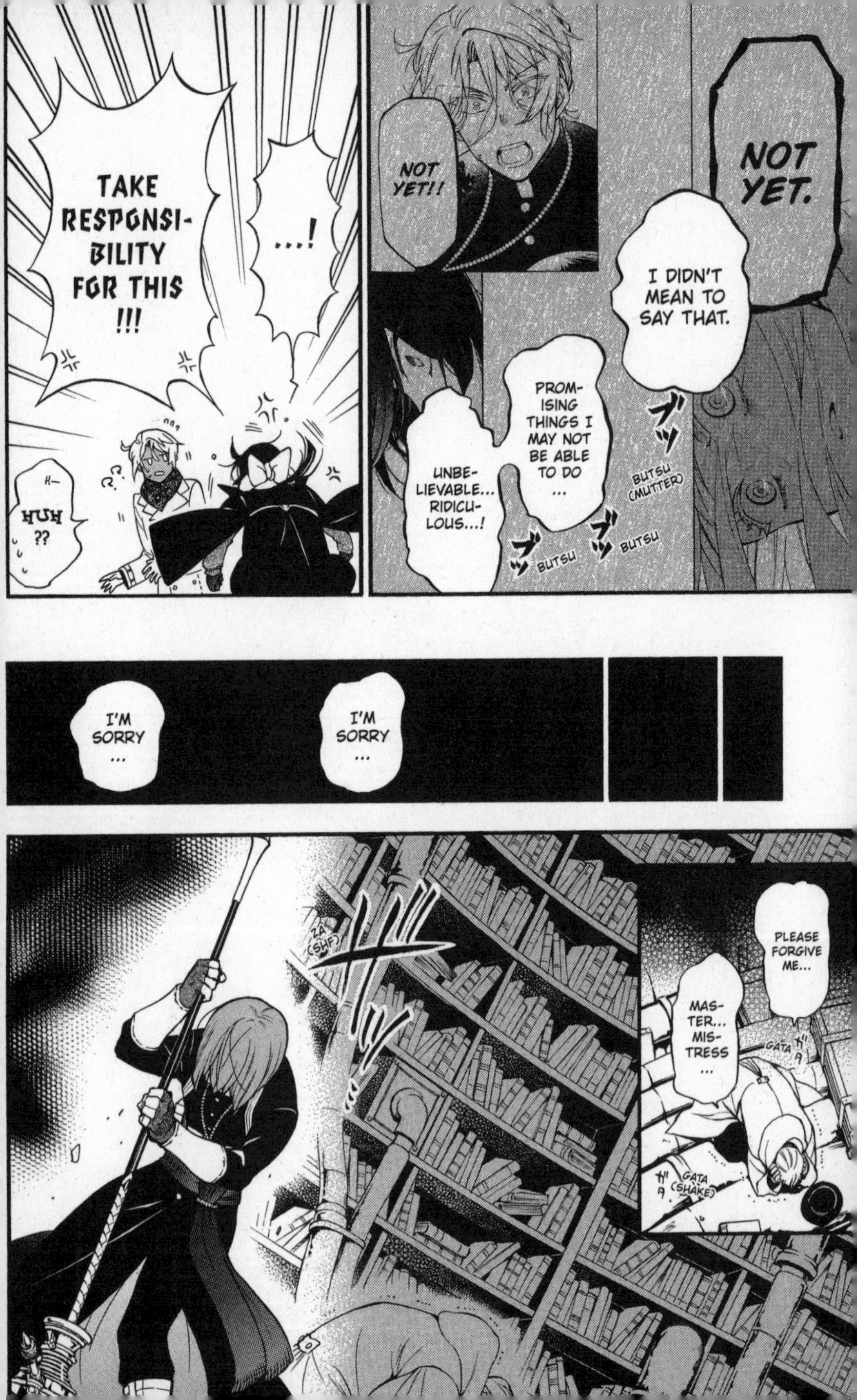
NOT YET.
NOT YET!!
I DIDN'T MEAN TO SAY THAT.
BUTSU (MUTTER)
PROM-ISING THINGS I MAY NOT BE ABLE TO DO ...
UNBE-LIEVABLE... RIDICU-LOUS...!
BUTSU
BUTSU
TAKE RESPONSI-BILITY FOR THIS !!!
...!
H-HUH ??
I'M SORRY ...
I'M SORRY ...
PLEASE FORGIVE ME...
MAS-TER... MIS-TRESS ...
GATA
GATA (SHAKE)
ZA (SHF)

Mémoire 59

Poupée Fissurée THE ESSENCE OF THE WITCH

Les Mémoires de Vanitas

HE GAVE HIS COAT TO
SOME FREEZING VILLAGERS.

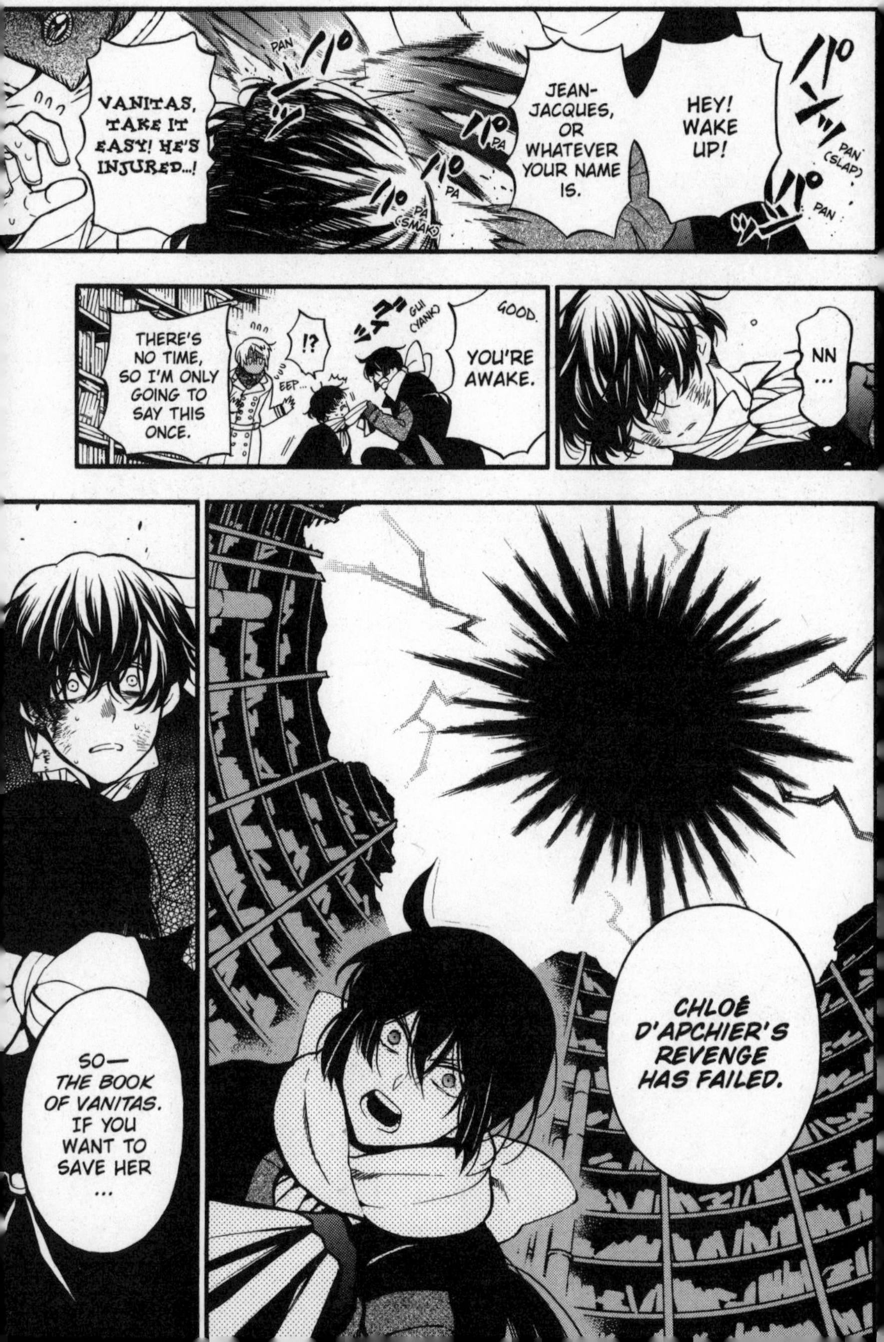
PAN (SLAP)
PAN
HEY! WAKE UP!
JEAN-JACQUES, OR WHATEVER YOUR NAME IS.
PA
PA
PA (SMAK)
PAN
VANITAS, TAKE IT EASY! HE'S INJURED...!
NN ...
GOOD. YOU'RE AWAKE.
GUI (YANK)
!?
EEP...
THERE'S NO TIME, SO I'M ONLY GOING TO SAY THIS ONCE.
CHLOÉ D'APCHIER'S REVENGE HAS FAILED.
SO— THE BOOK OF VANITAS. IF YOU WANT TO SAVE HER ...

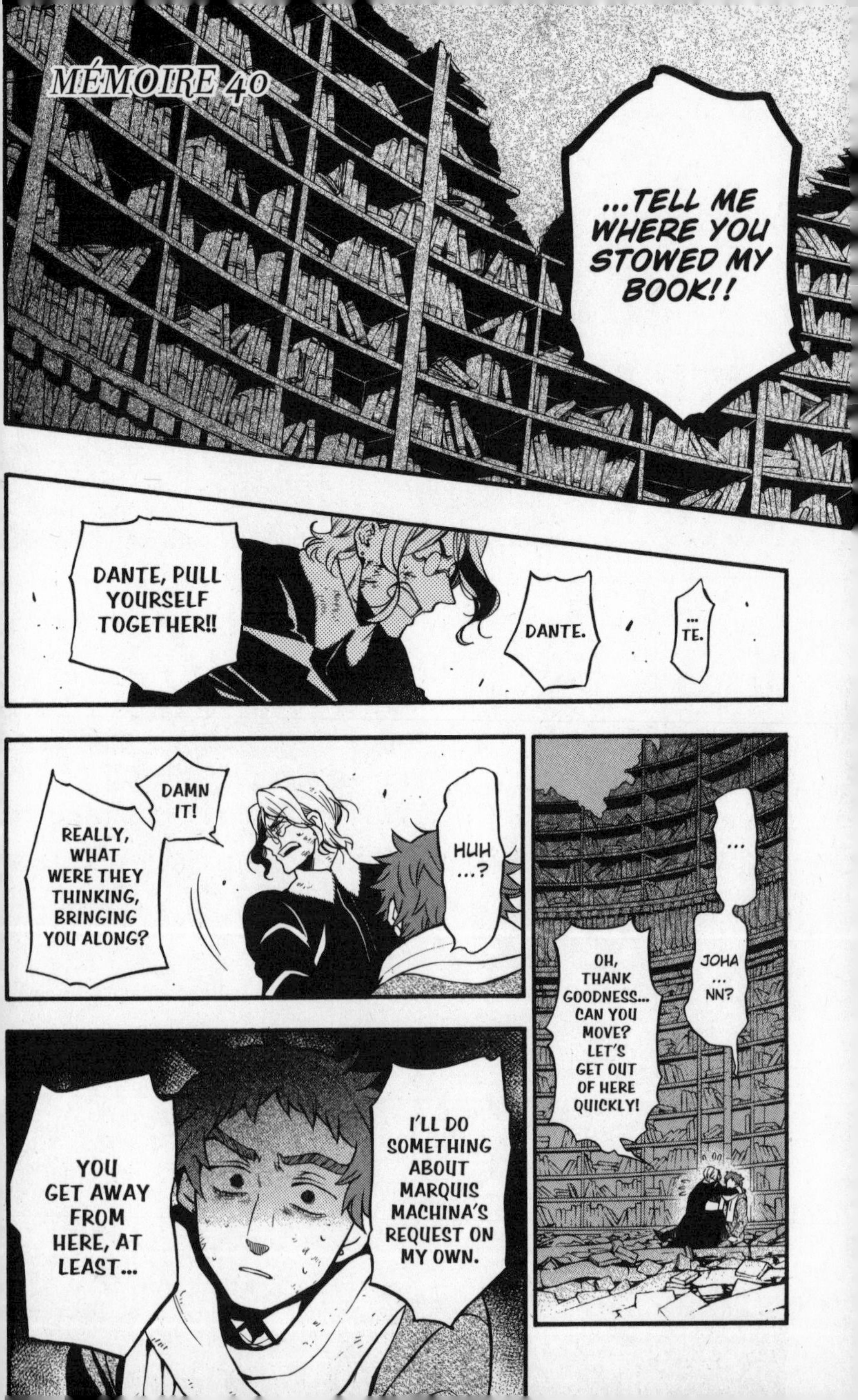
MÉMOIRE 40
...TELL ME WHERE YOU STOWED MY BOOK!!
... TE.
DANTE.
DANTE, PULL YOURSELF TOGETHER!!
...
JOHA ... NN?
OH, THANK GOODNESS... CAN YOU MOVE? LET'S GET OUT OF HERE QUICKLY!
HUH ...?
DAMN IT!
REALLY, WHAT WERE THEY THINKING, BRINGING YOU ALONG?
I'LL DO SOMETHING ABOUT MARQUIS MACHINA'S REQUEST ON MY OWN.
YOU GET AWAY FROM HERE, AT LEAST...

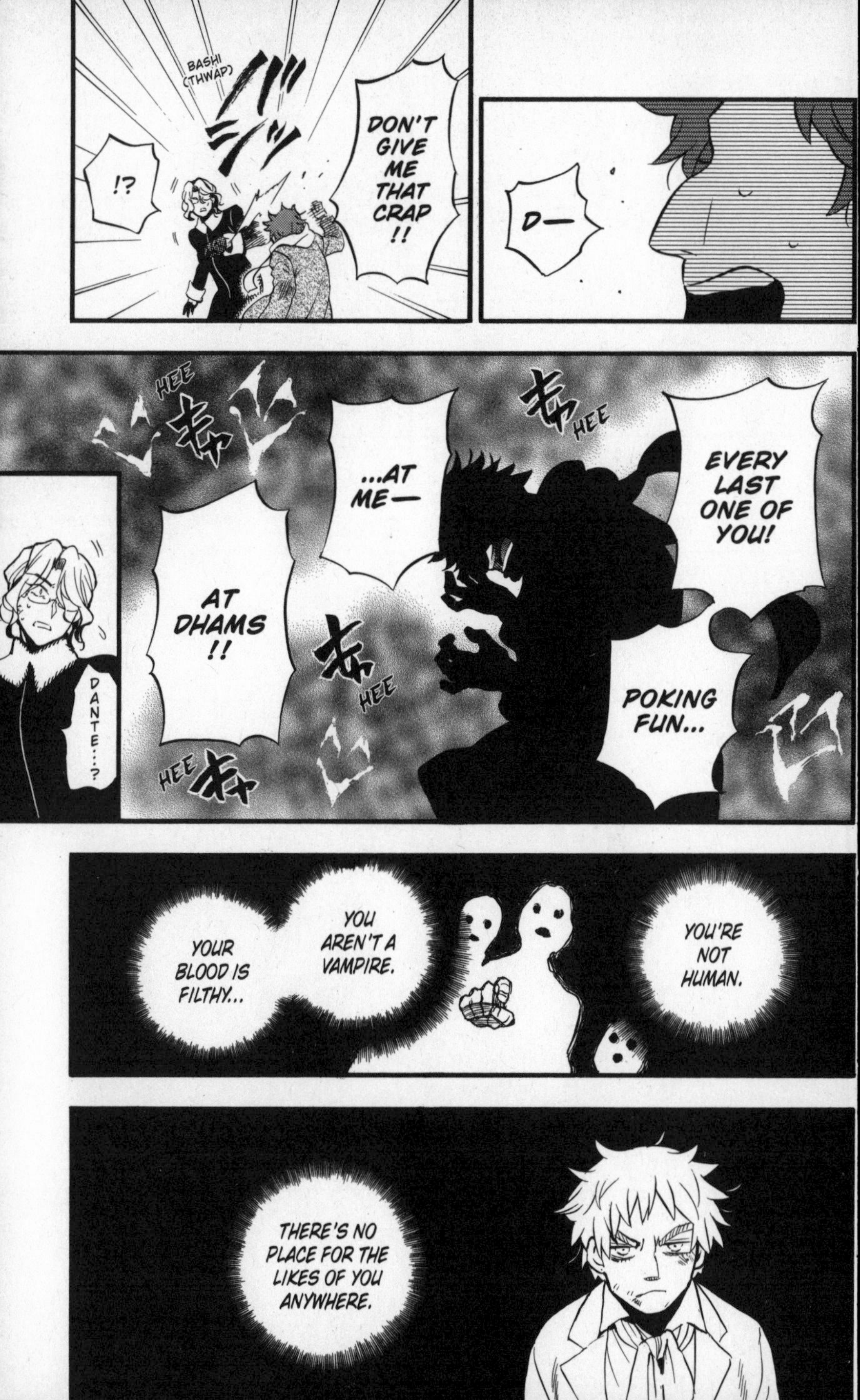
D—
DON'T GIVE ME THAT CRAP!!
BASHI (THWAP)
!?
EVERY LAST ONE OF YOU!
HEE
POKING FUN...
...AT ME—
HEE
AT DHAMS!!
HEE
HEE
DANTE...?
YOU'RE NOT HUMAN.
YOU AREN'T A VAMPIRE.
YOUR BLOOD IS FILTHY...
THERE'S NO PLACE FOR THE LIKES OF YOU ANYWHERE.

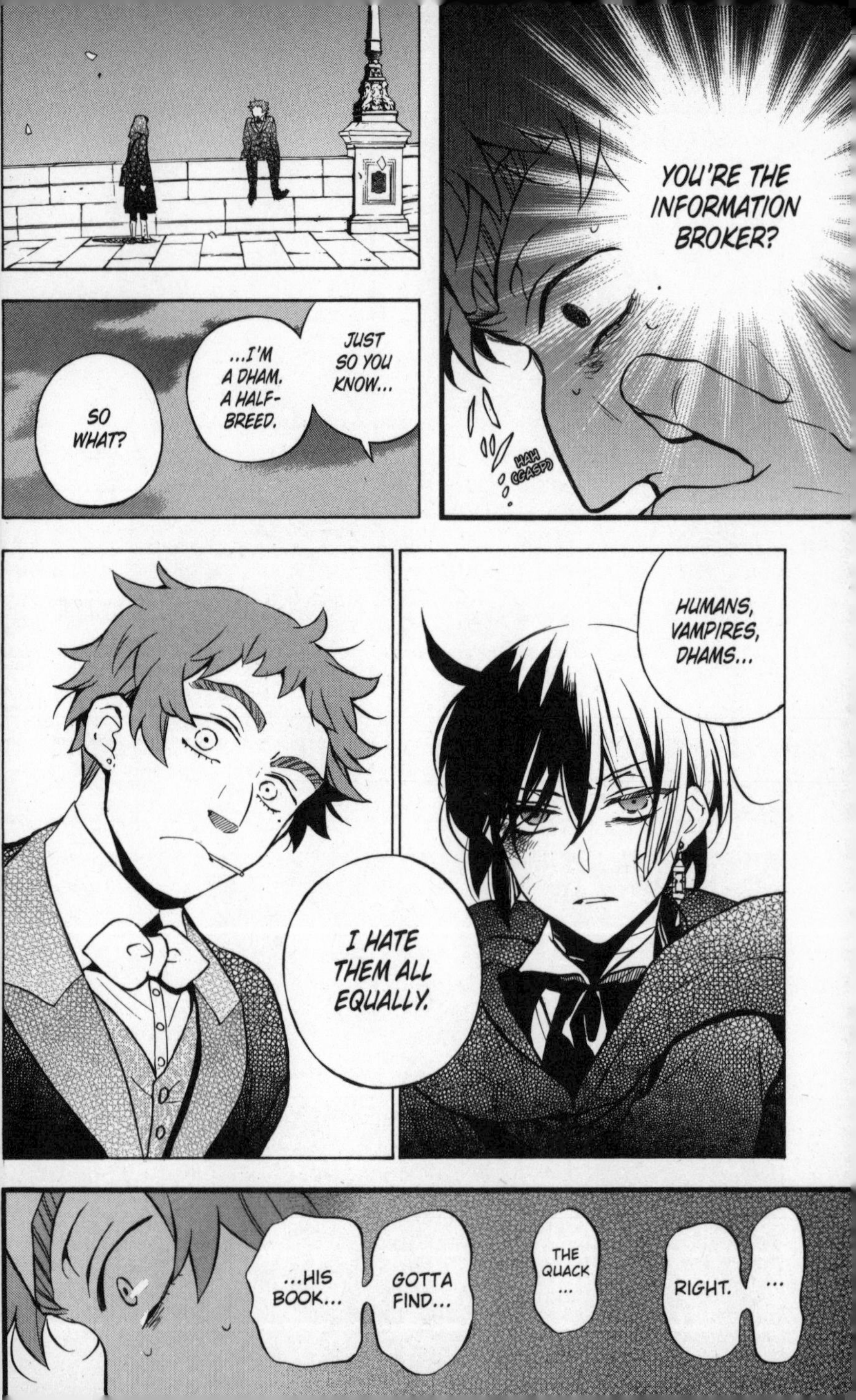
YOU'RE THE INFORMATION BROKER?
HAH (GASP)
JUST SO YOU KNOW...
...I'M A DHAM. A HALF-BREED.
SO WHAT?
HUMANS, VAMPIRES, DHAMS...
I HATE THEM ALL EQUALLY.
...
RIGHT.
THE QUACK ...
GOTTA FIND...
...HIS BOOK...

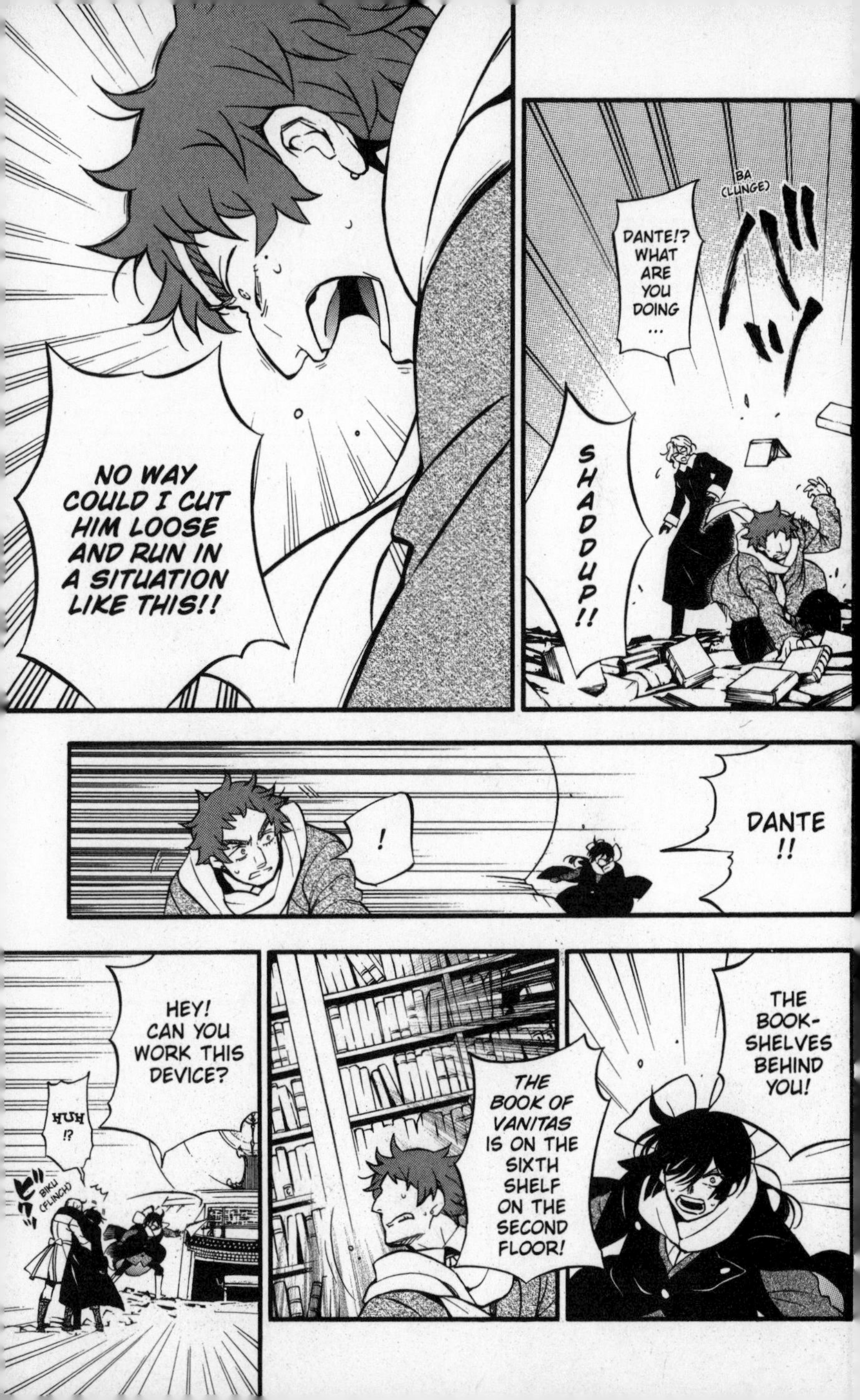
BA (LUNGE)
DANTE!? WHAT ARE YOU DOING ...
SHADDUP!!
NO WAY COULD I CUT HIM LOOSE AND RUN IN A SITUATION LIKE THIS!!
DANTE !!
!
THE BOOK-SHELVES BEHIND YOU!
THE BOOK OF VANITAS IS ON THE SIXTH SHELF ON THE SECOND FLOOR!
HEY! CAN YOU WORK THIS DEVICE?
HUH !?
BIKU (FLINCH)

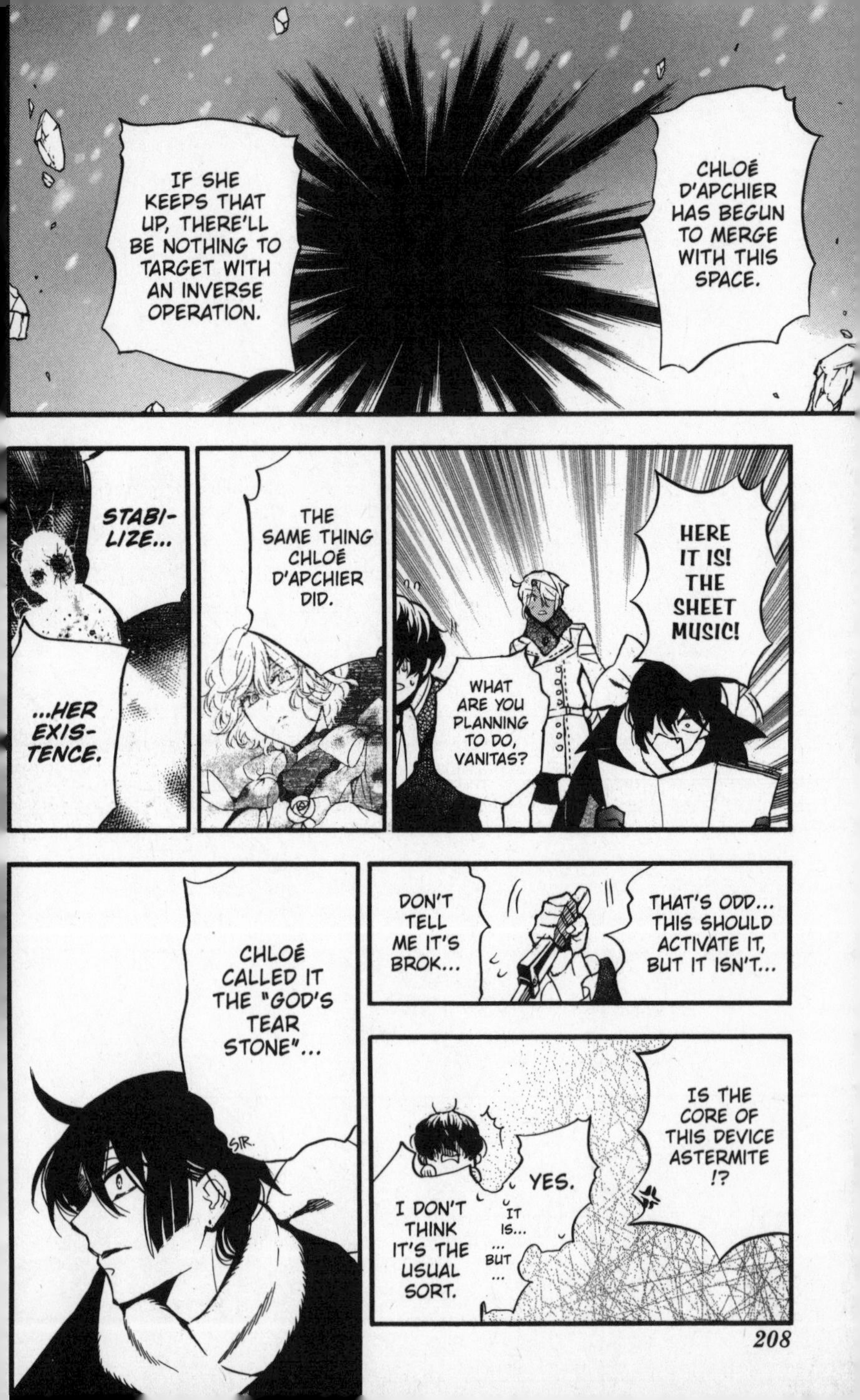
CHLOÉ D'APCHIER HAS BEGUN TO MERGE WITH THIS SPACE.
IF SHE KEEPS THAT UP, THERE'LL BE NOTHING TO TARGET WITH AN INVERSE OPERATION.
HERE IT IS! THE SHEET MUSIC!
WHAT ARE YOU PLANNING TO DO, VANITAS?
THE SAME THING CHLOÉ D'APCHIER DID.
STABI-LIZE...
...HER EXIS-TENCE.
THAT'S ODD... THIS SHOULD ACTIVATE IT, BUT IT ISN'T...
DON'T TELL ME IT'S BROK...
IS THE CORE OF THIS DEVICE ASTERMITE !?
YES.
IT IS...
...BUT ...
I DON'T THINK IT'S THE USUAL SORT.
CHLOÉ CALLED IT THE "GOD'S TEAR STONE"...

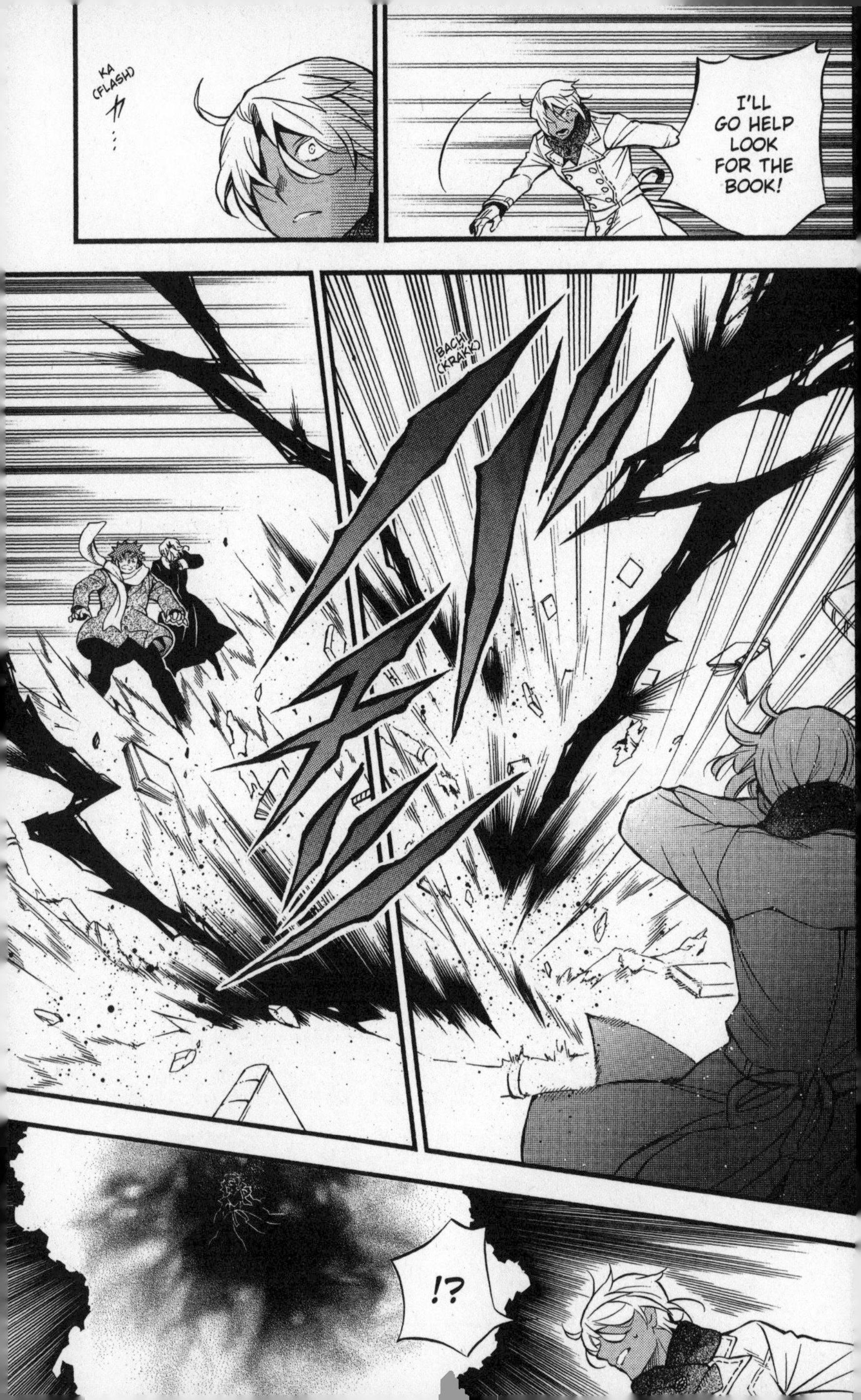
I'LL GO HELP LOOK FOR THE BOOK!
KA (FLASH)
BACHI (KRÄKK)
!?

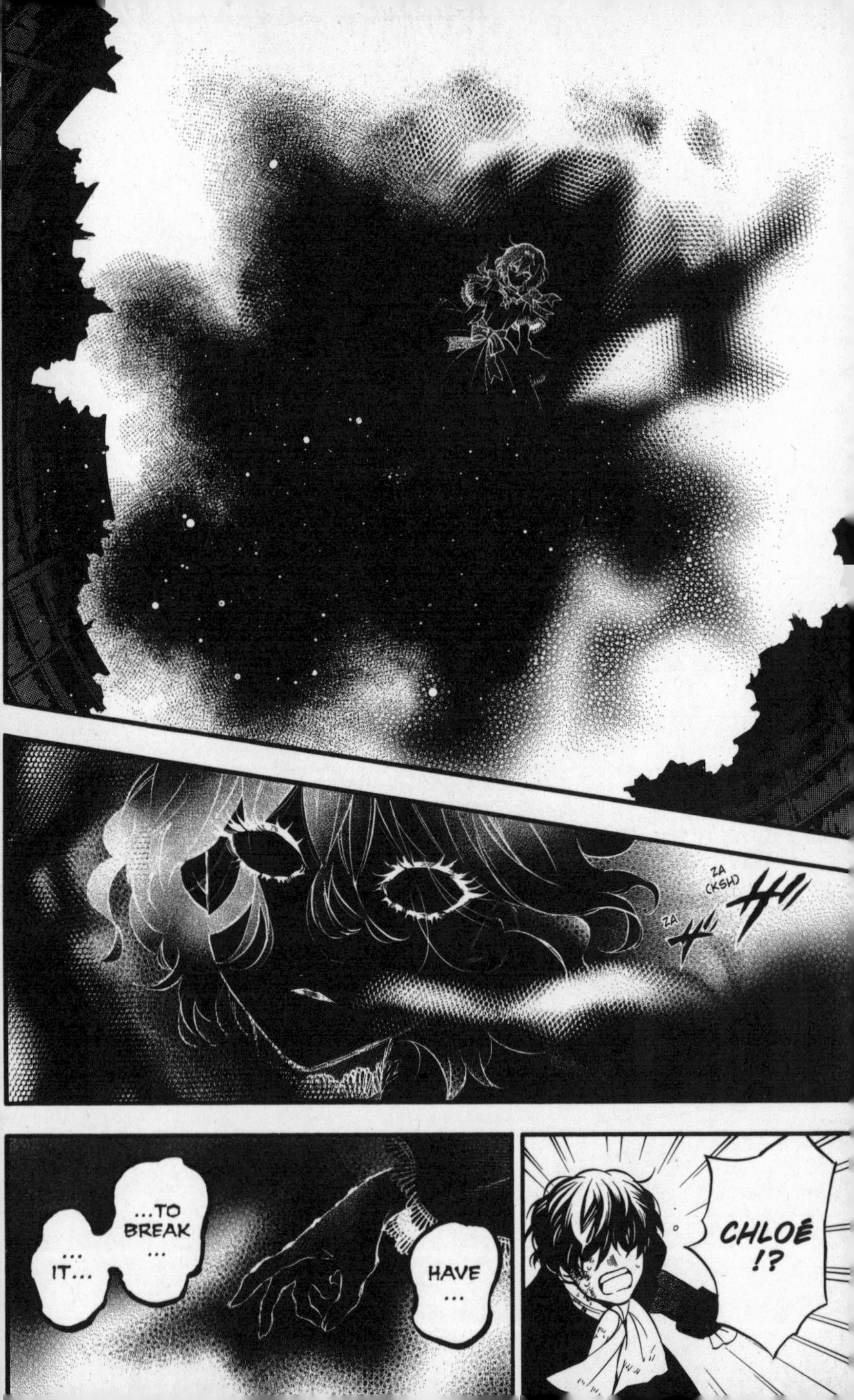
ZA (KSH)
ZA
CHLOÉ !?
HAVE ...
...TO BREAK ...
... IT...

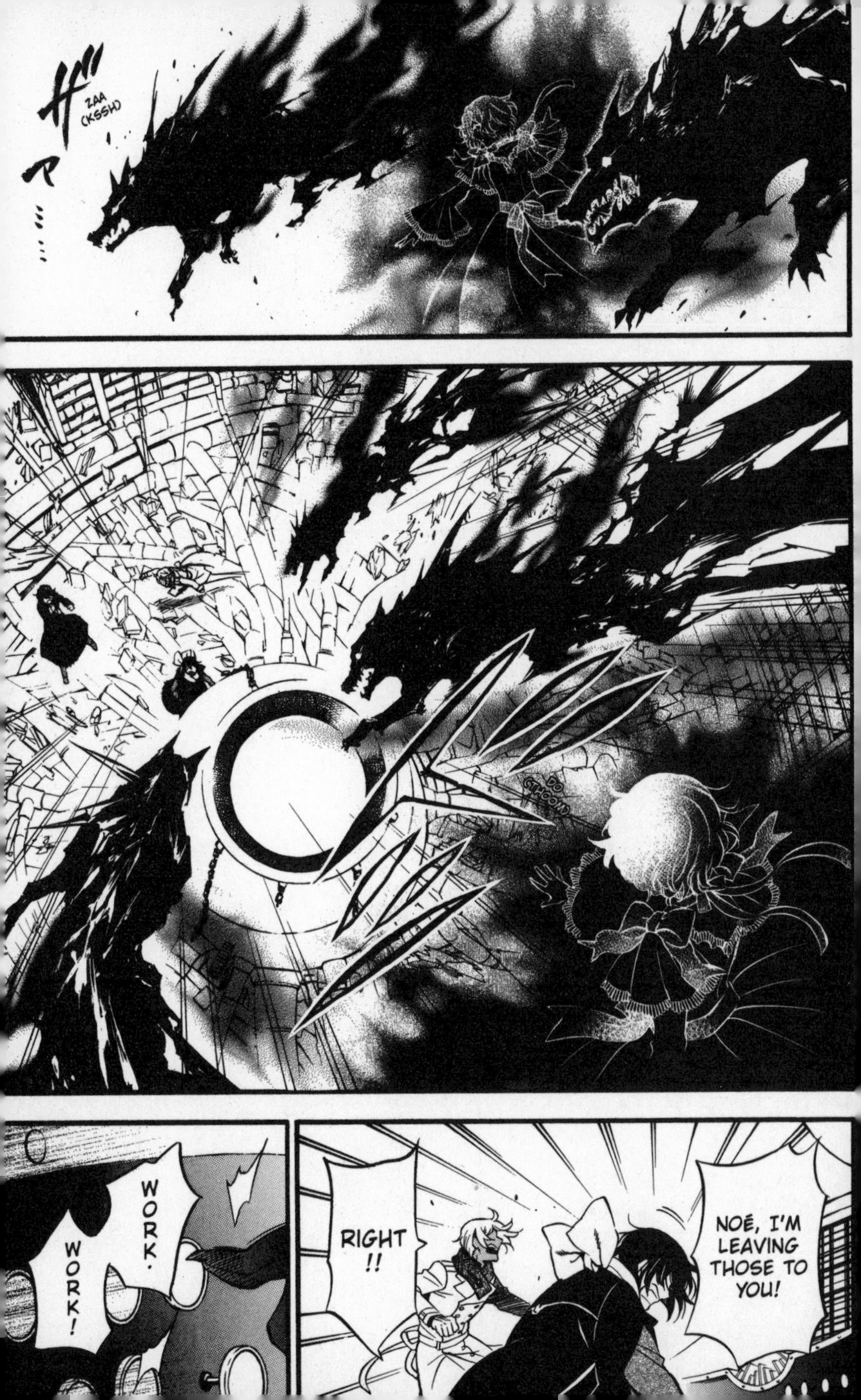
ザァ……
ZAA (KSSH)
DO (GTHOOM)
NOÉ, I'M LEAVING THOSE TO YOU!
RIGHT!!
WORK.
WORK!

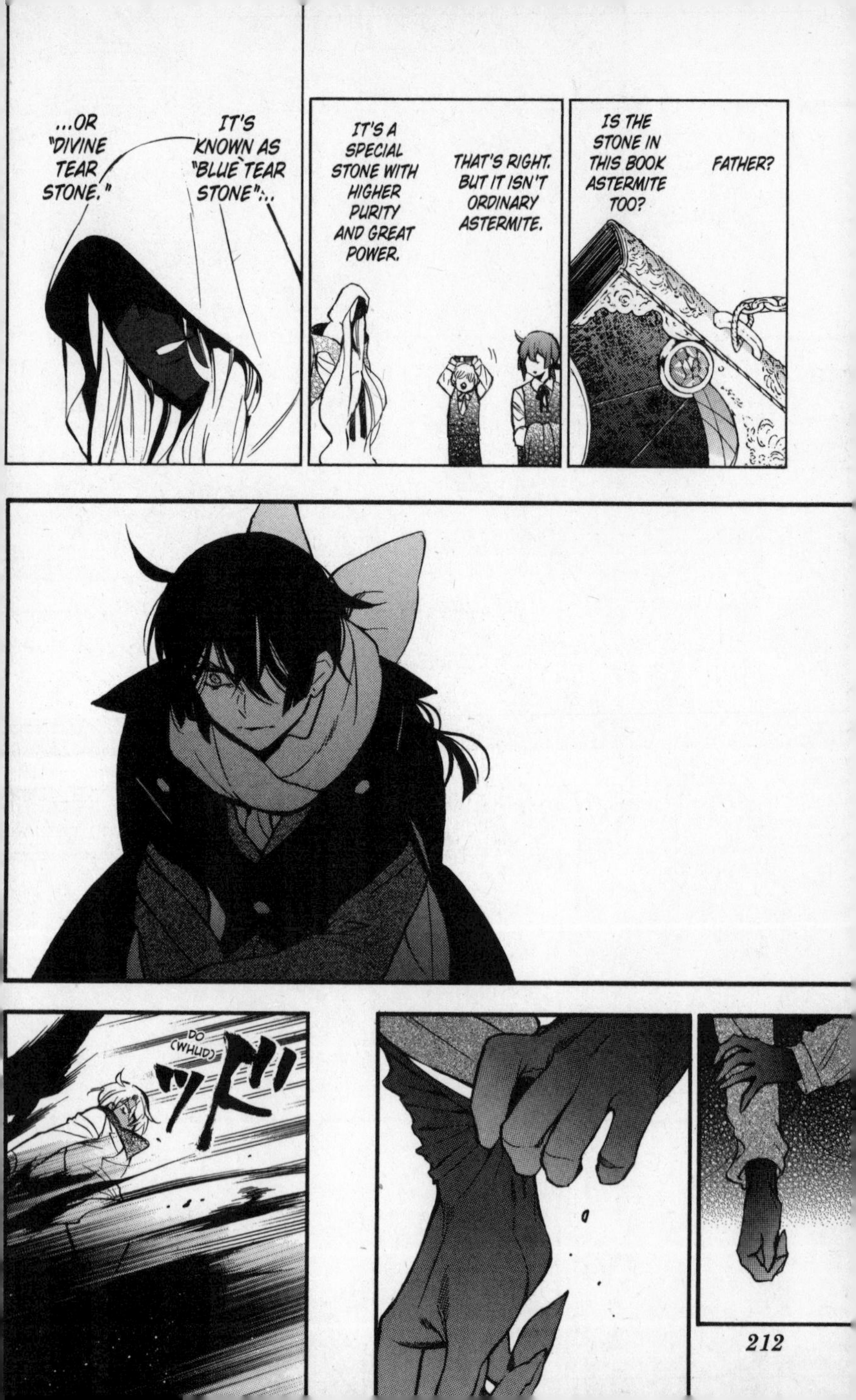
FATHER?
IS THE STONE IN THIS BOOK ASTERMITE TOO?
THAT'S RIGHT. BUT IT ISN'T ORDINARY ASTERMITE.
IT'S A SPECIAL STONE WITH HIGHER PURITY AND GREAT POWER.
IT'S KNOWN AS "BLUE TEAR STONE"...
...OR "DIVINE TEAR STONE."
DO (WHUD)

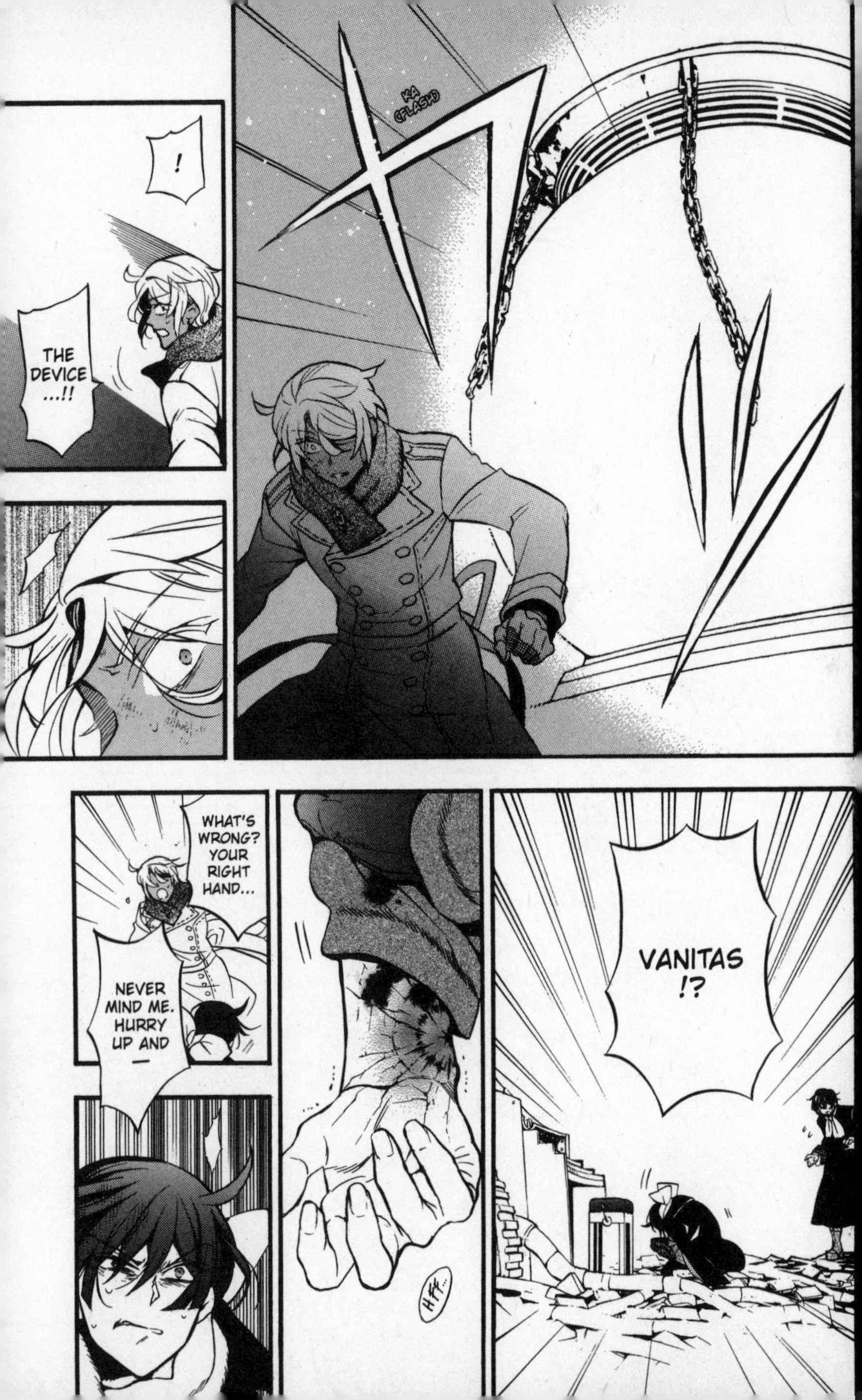
KA (FLASH)
!
THE DEVICE ...!!
VANITAS !?
HFF...
WHAT'S WRONG? YOUR RIGHT HAND...
NEVER MIND ME. HURRY UP AND —

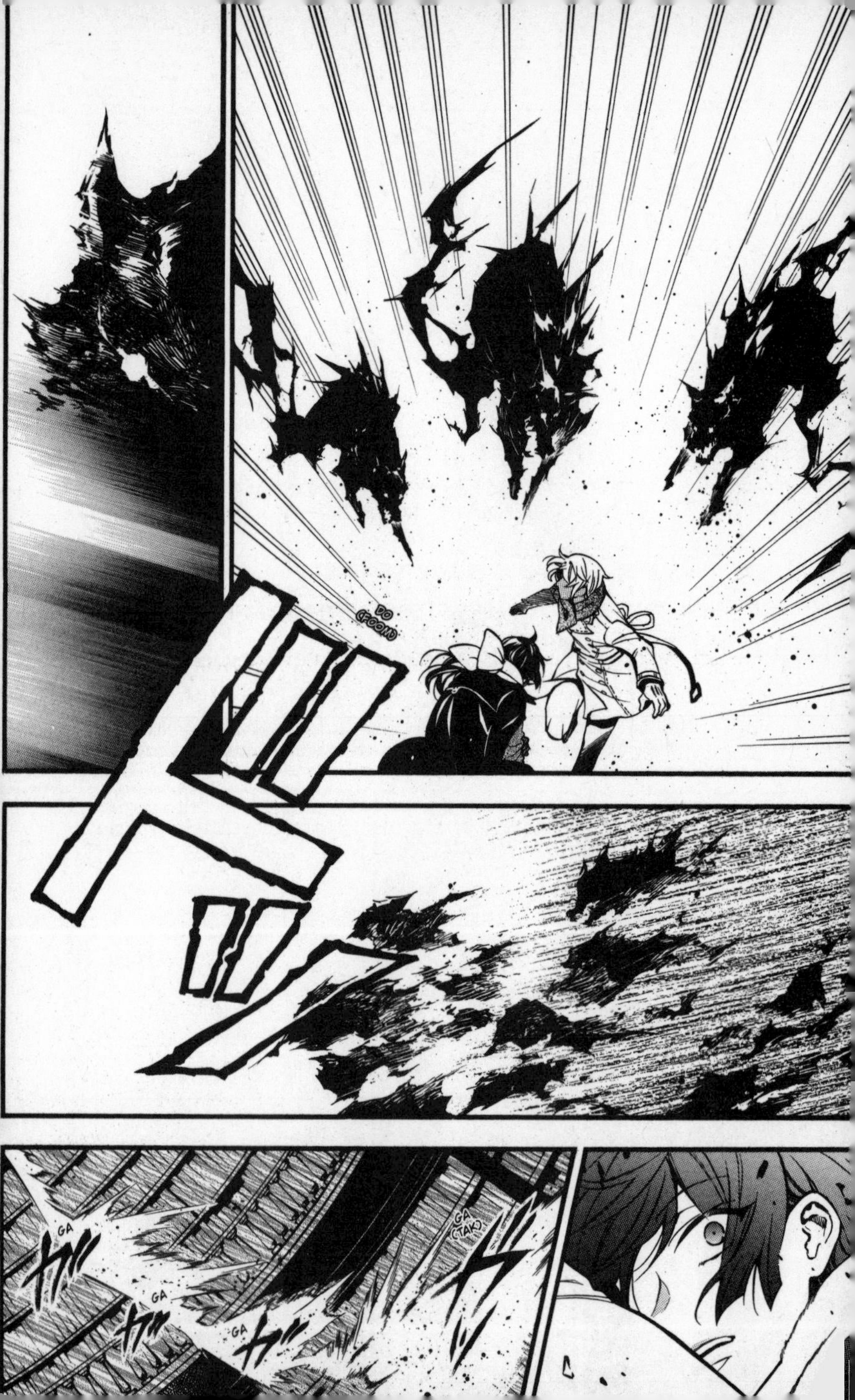
DO
(FOOM)
GA
(TAK)
GA
GA
GA

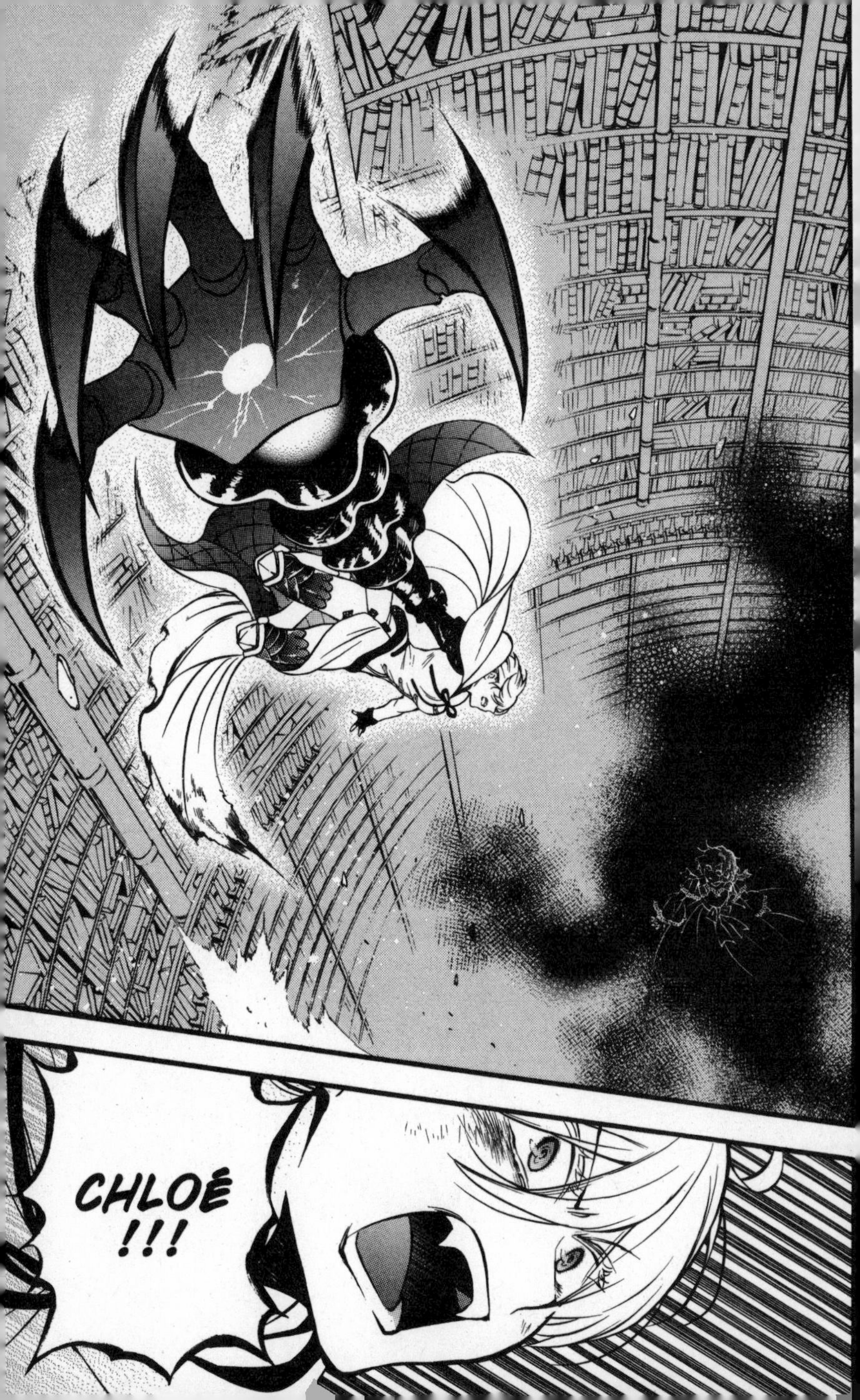
CHLOÉ
!!!

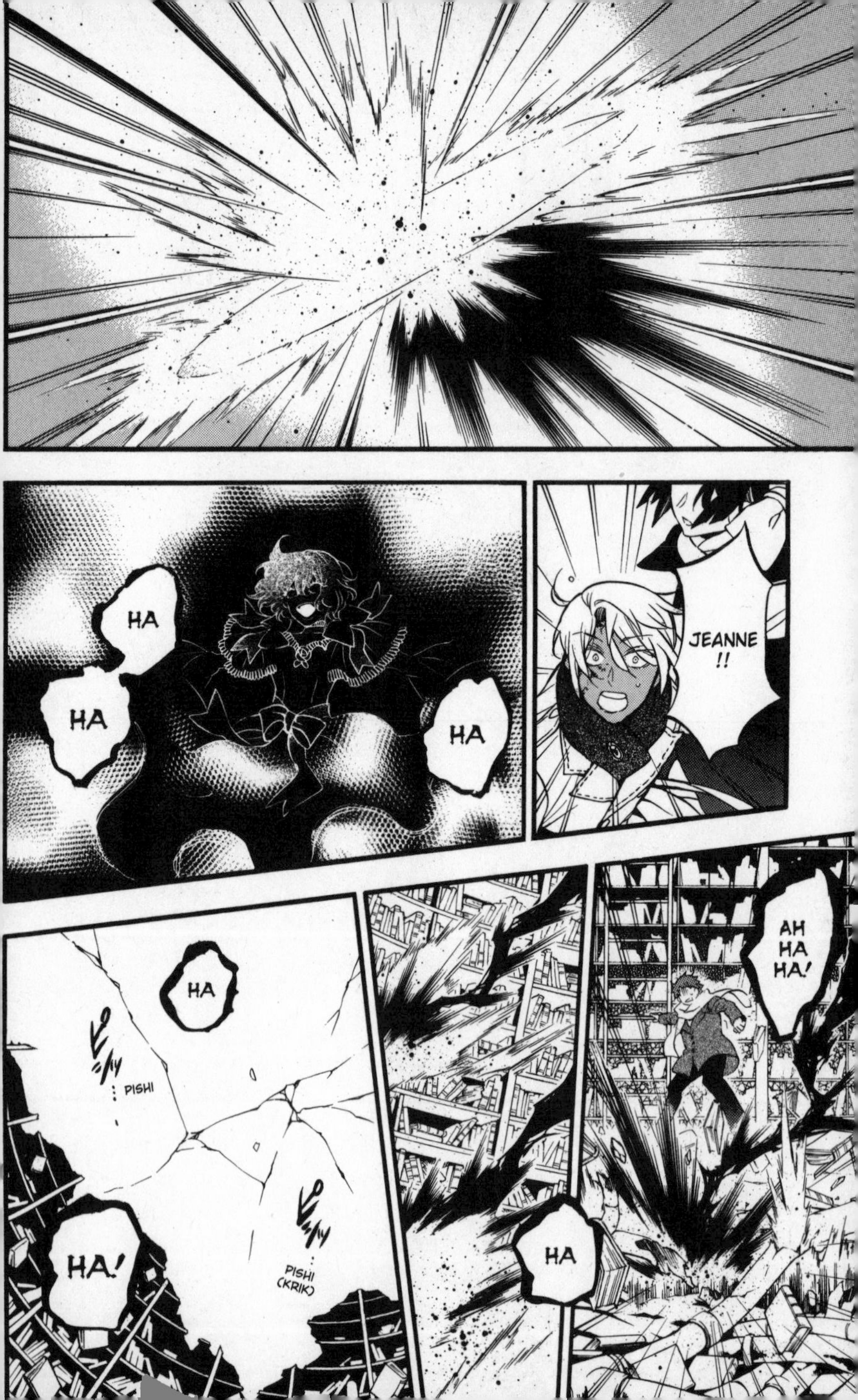
JEANNE !!
HA
HA
HA
AH HA HA!
HA
HA
PISHI
PISHI (KRIK)
HA!

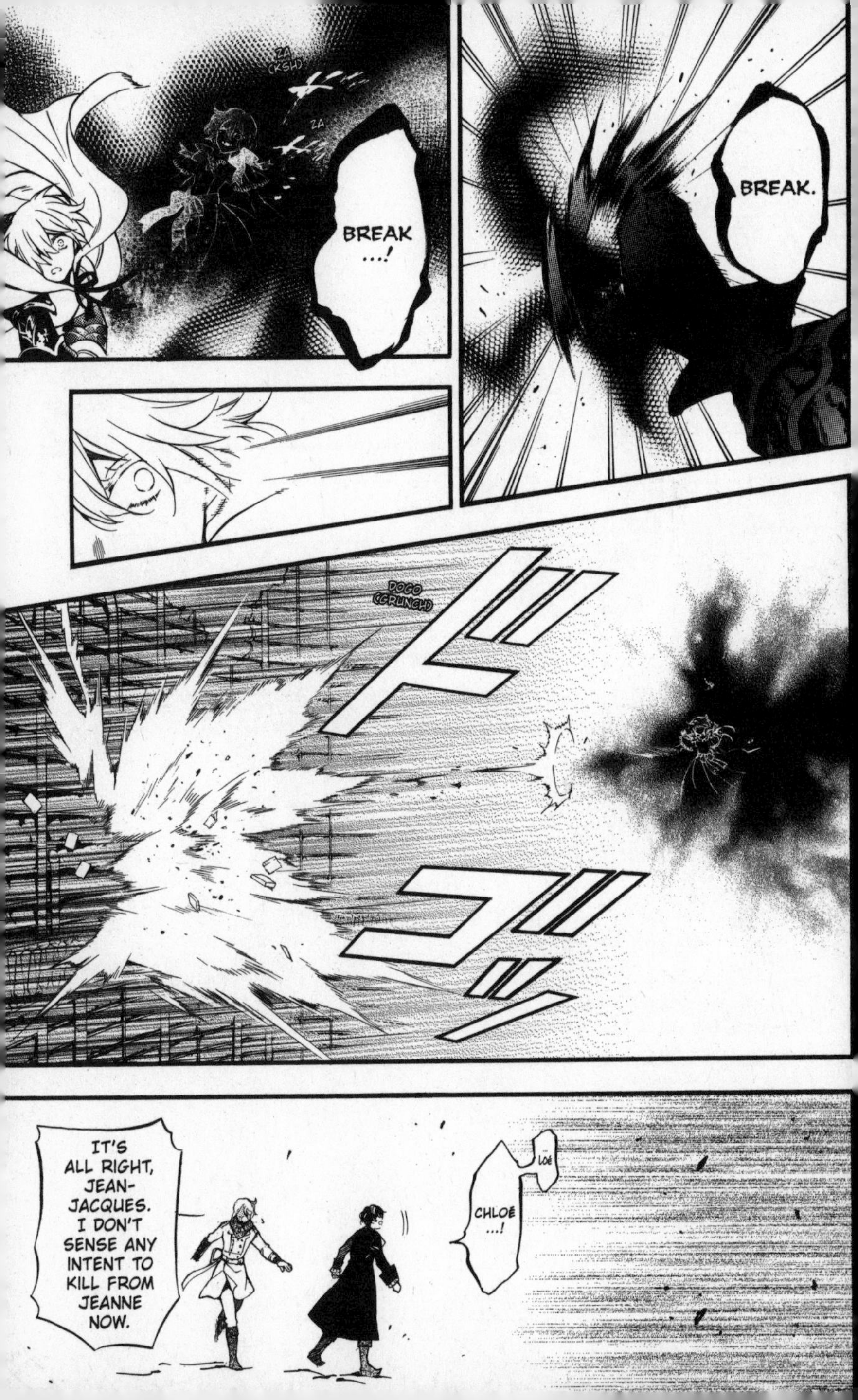
BREAK.
ZA (KSH)
ZA
BREAK ...!
DOGO (GRUNCH)
...LOÉ
CHLOÉ ...!
IT'S ALL RIGHT, JEAN-JACQUES. I DON'T SENSE ANY INTENT TO KILL FROM JEANNE NOW.

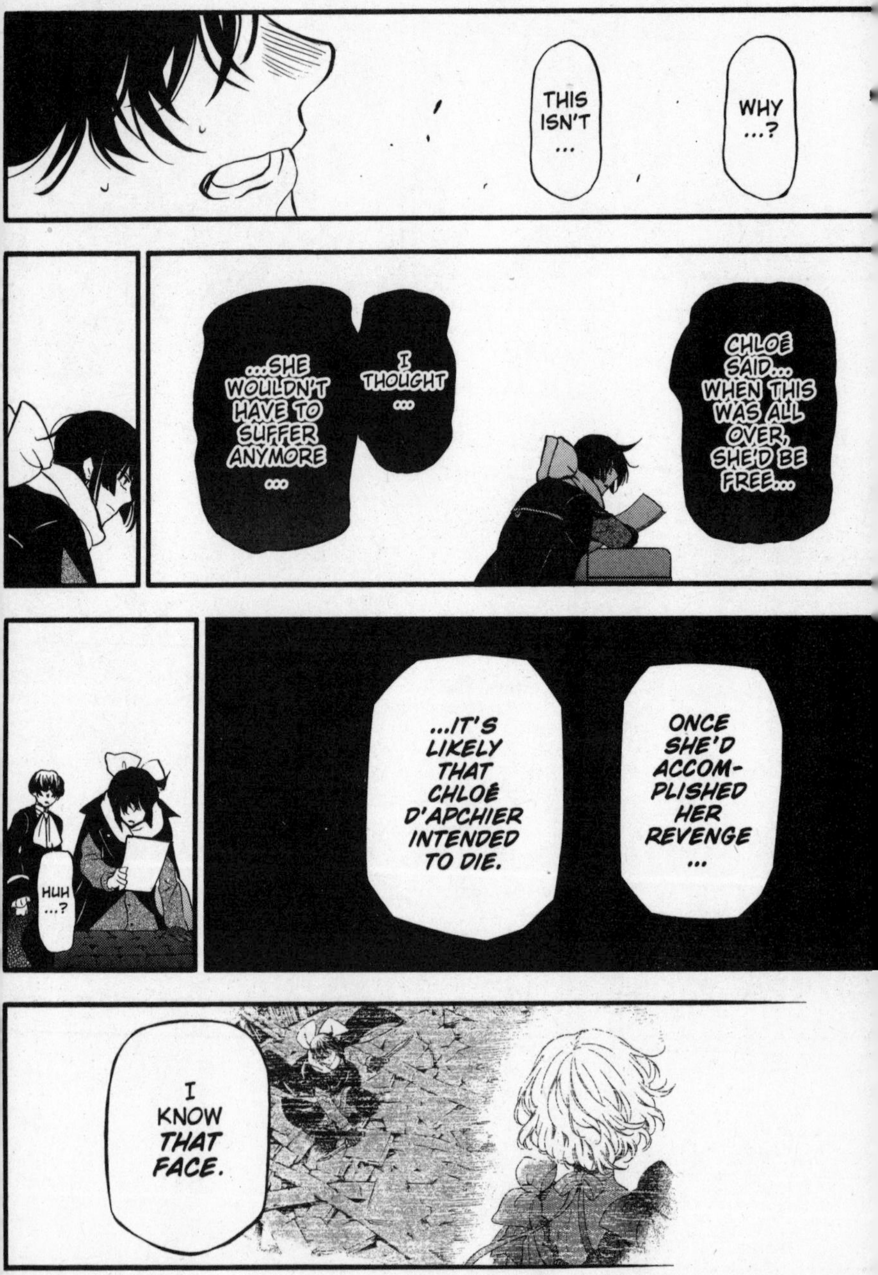
WHY ...?
THIS ISN'T ...
CHLOE SAID... WHEN THIS WAS ALL OVER, SHE'D BE FREE...
I THOUGHT ...
...SHE WOULDN'T HAVE TO SUFFER ANYMORE ...
ONCE SHE'D ACCOM-PLISHED HER REVENGE ...
...IT'S LIKELY THAT CHLOÉ D'APCHIER INTENDED TO DIE.
HUH ...?
I KNOW *THAT* FACE.

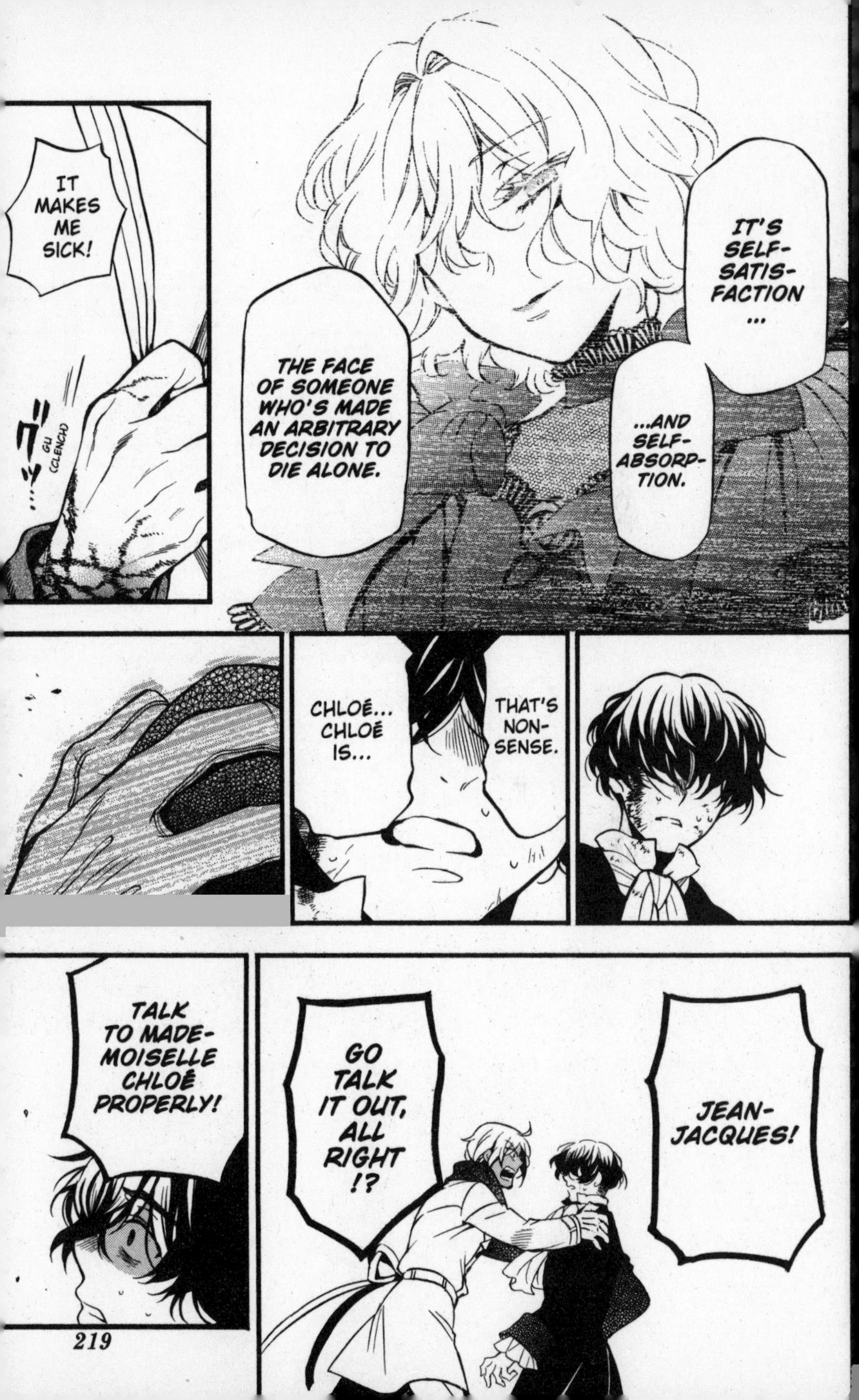
IT'S SELF-SATISFACTION...
...AND SELF-ABSORPTION.
THE FACE OF SOMEONE WHO'S MADE AN ARBITRARY DECISION TO DIE ALONE.
IT MAKES ME SICK!
GU (CLENCH)
THAT'S NONSENSE.
CHLOÉ... CHLOÉ IS...
JEAN-JACQUES!
GO TALK IT OUT, ALL RIGHT!?
TALK TO MADEMOISELLE CHLOÉ PROPERLY!

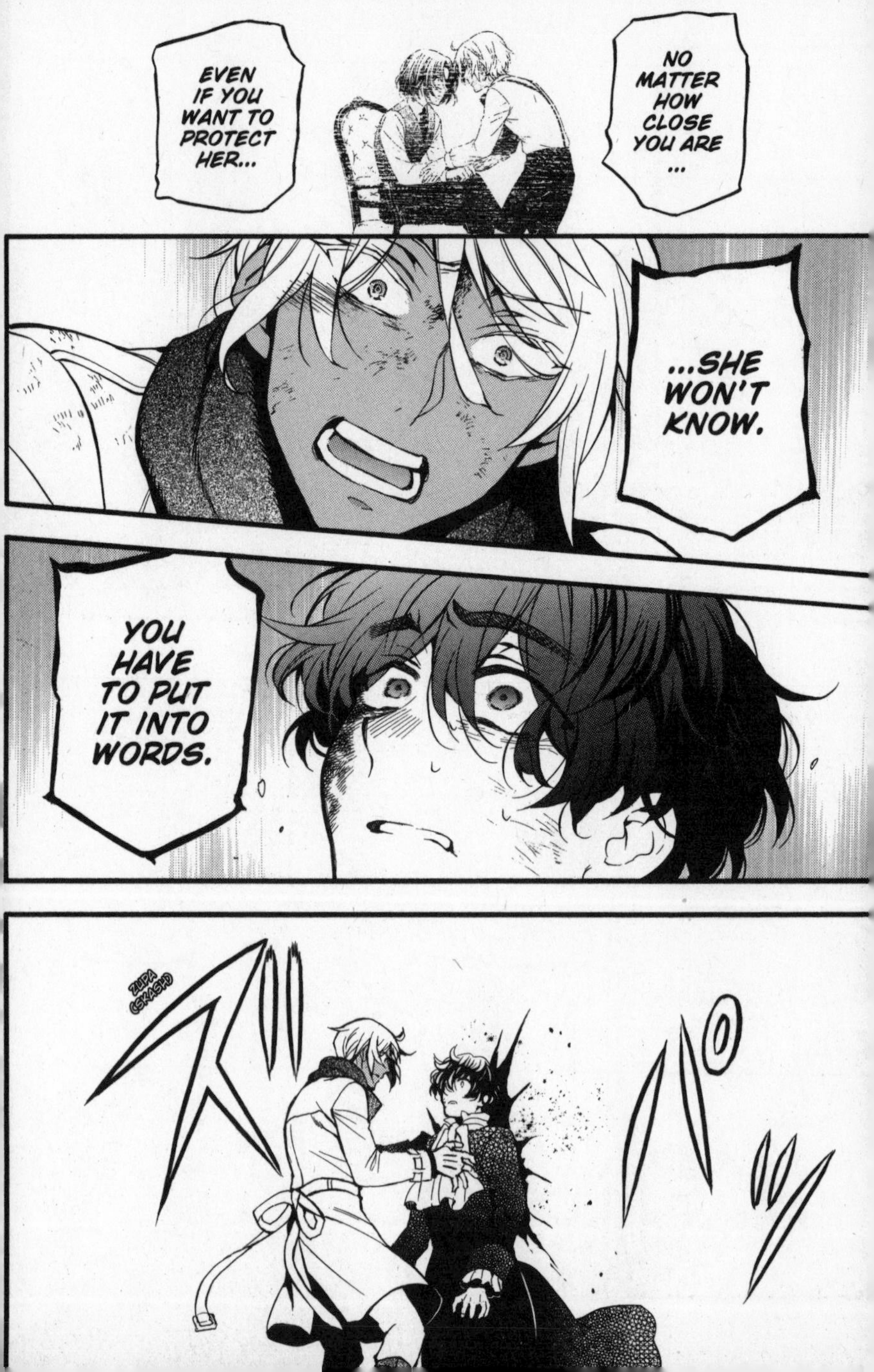
NO MATTER HOW CLOSE YOU ARE...
EVEN IF YOU WANT TO PROTECT HER...
...SHE WON'T KNOW.
YOU HAVE TO PUT IT INTO WORDS.
ZUPA (SKASH)

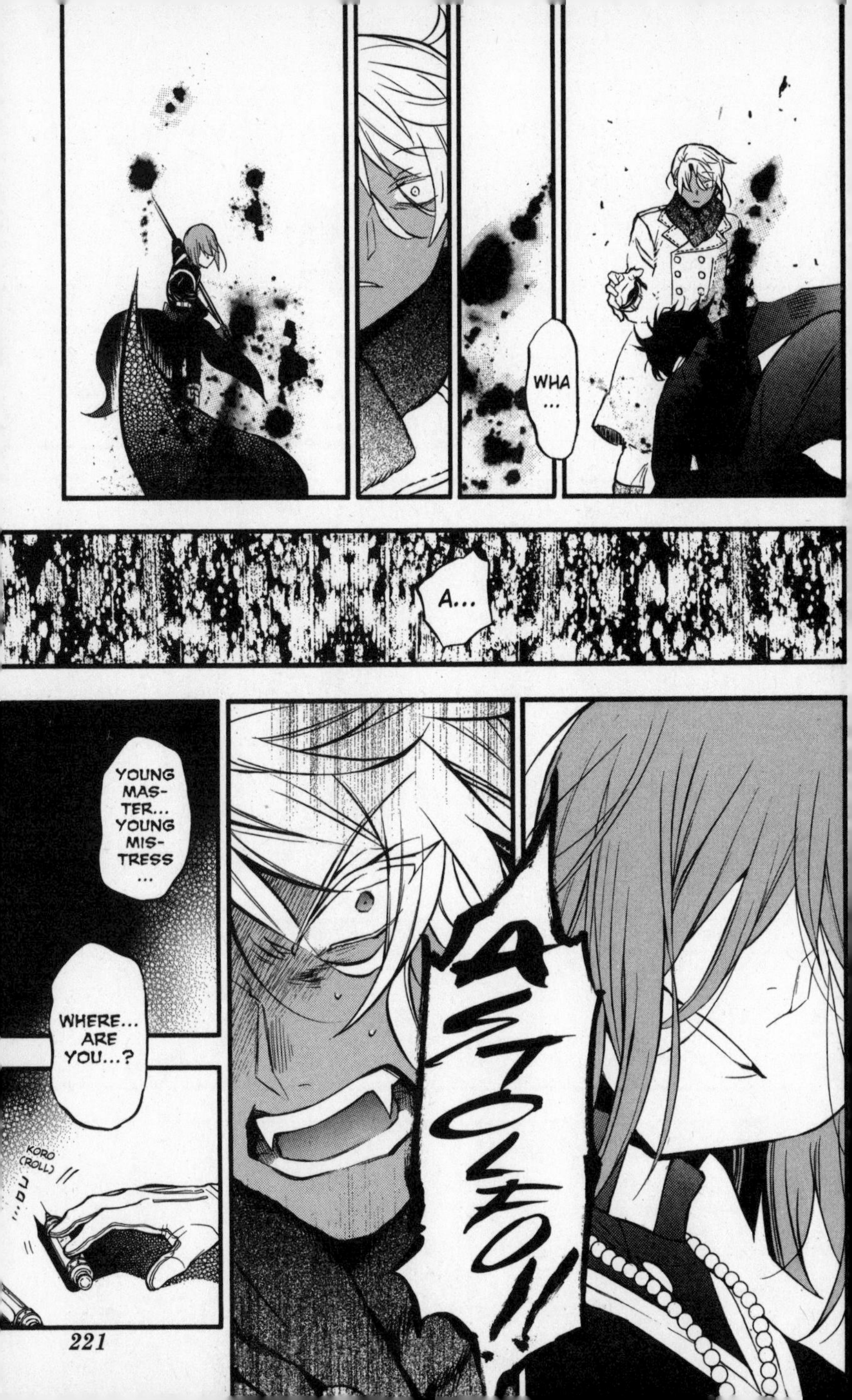
WHA...
A...
ASTOLFO!!
YOUNG MASTER... YOUNG MISTRESS...
WHERE... ARE YOU...?
KORO (ROLL)

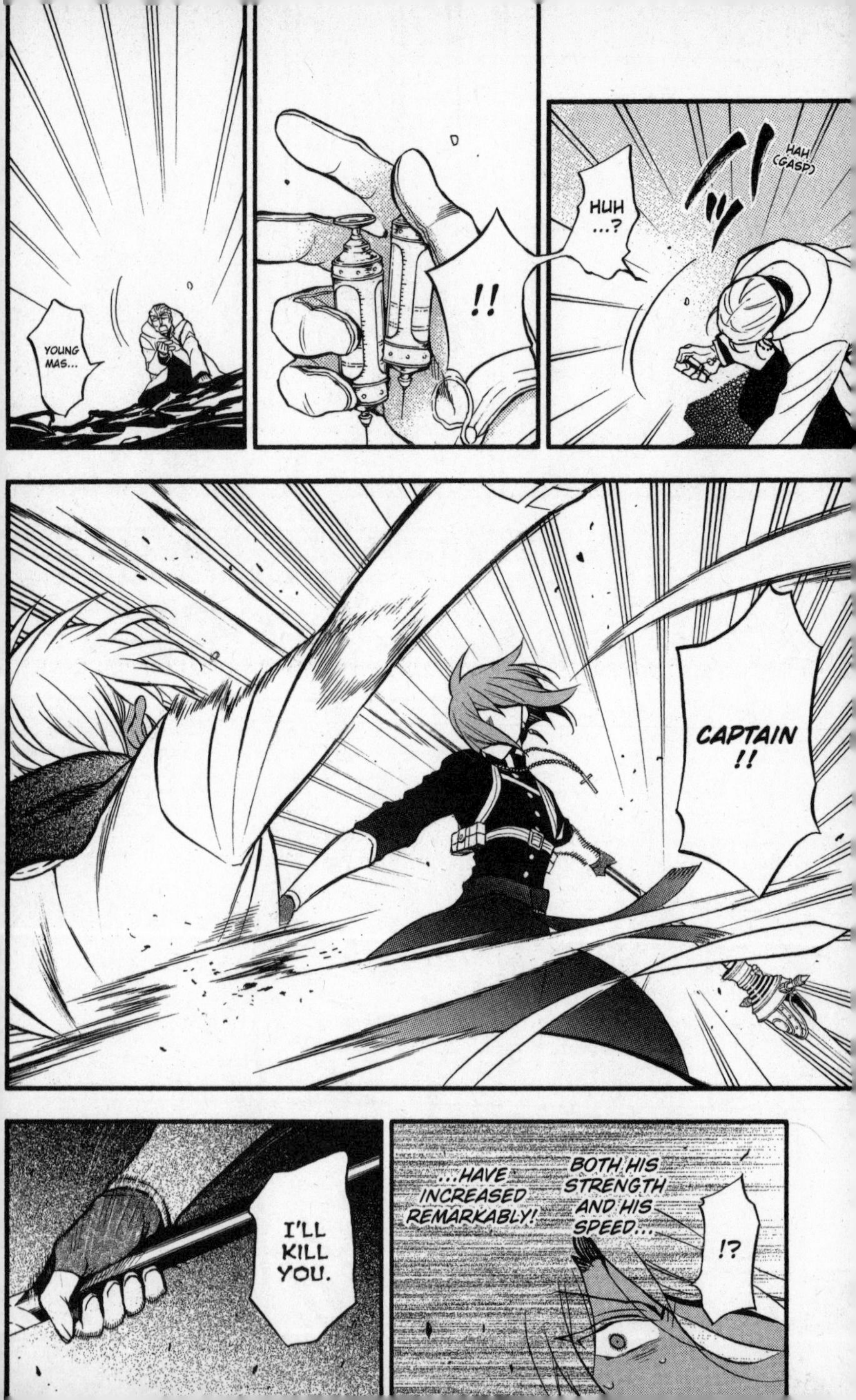

HAH (GASP)
HUH ...?
!!
YOUNG MAS...
CAPTAIN !!
!?
BOTH HIS STRENGTH AND HIS SPEED...
...HAVE INCREASED REMARKABLY!
I'LL KILL YOU.

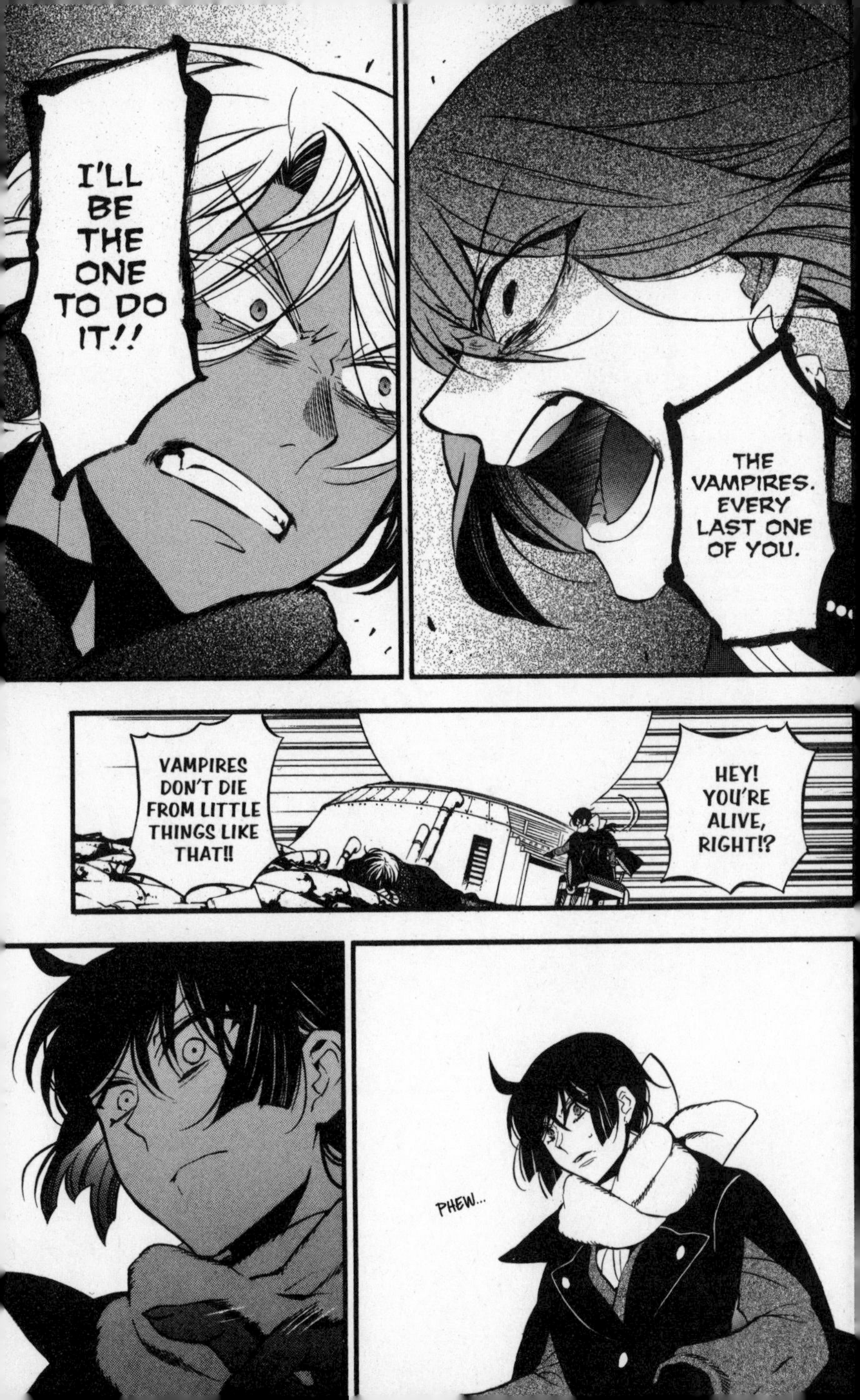
THE VAMPIRES. EVERY LAST ONE OF YOU.
I'LL BE THE ONE TO DO IT!!
HEY! YOU'RE ALIVE, RIGHT!?
VAMPIRES DON'T DIE FROM LITTLE THINGS LIKE THAT!!
PHEW...

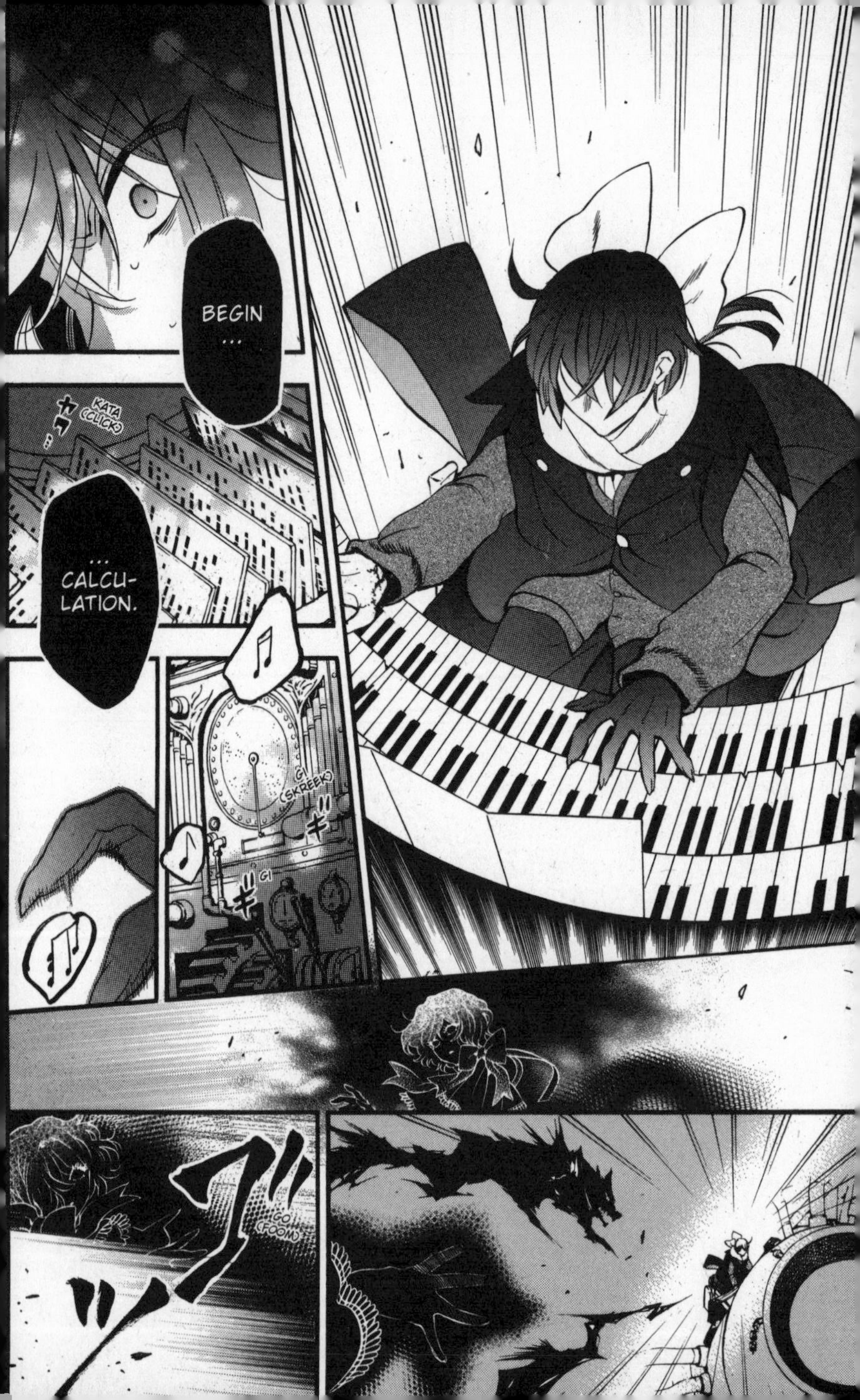
BEGIN ...
KATA (CLICK)
... CALCULATION.
GI (SKREEK)
GI
GO (FOOM)

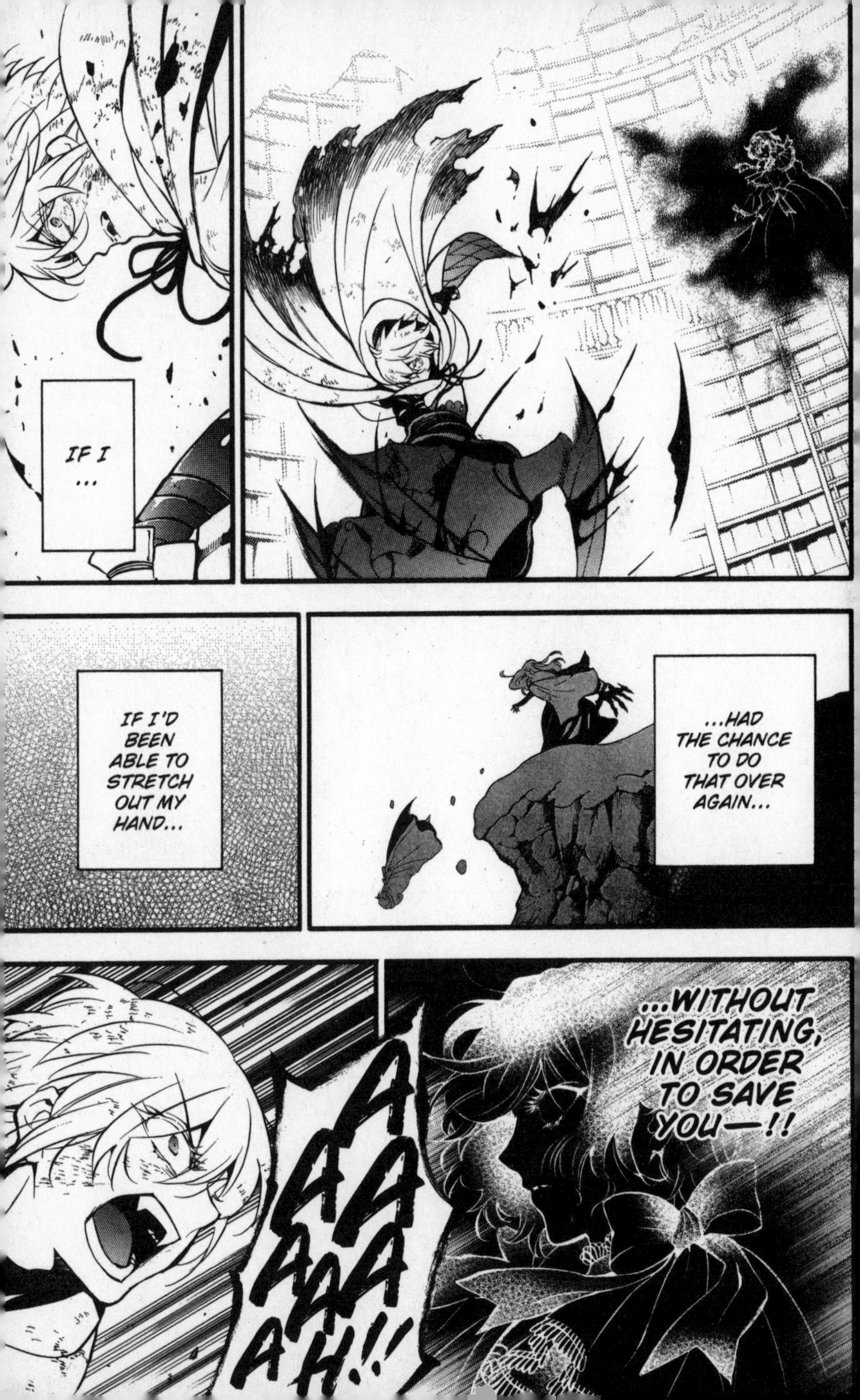
IF I ...
...HAD THE CHANCE TO DO THAT OVER AGAIN...
IF I'D BEEN ABLE TO STRETCH OUT MY HAND...
...WITHOUT HESITATING, IN ORDER TO SAVE YOU—!!
AAAAAAAAH!!

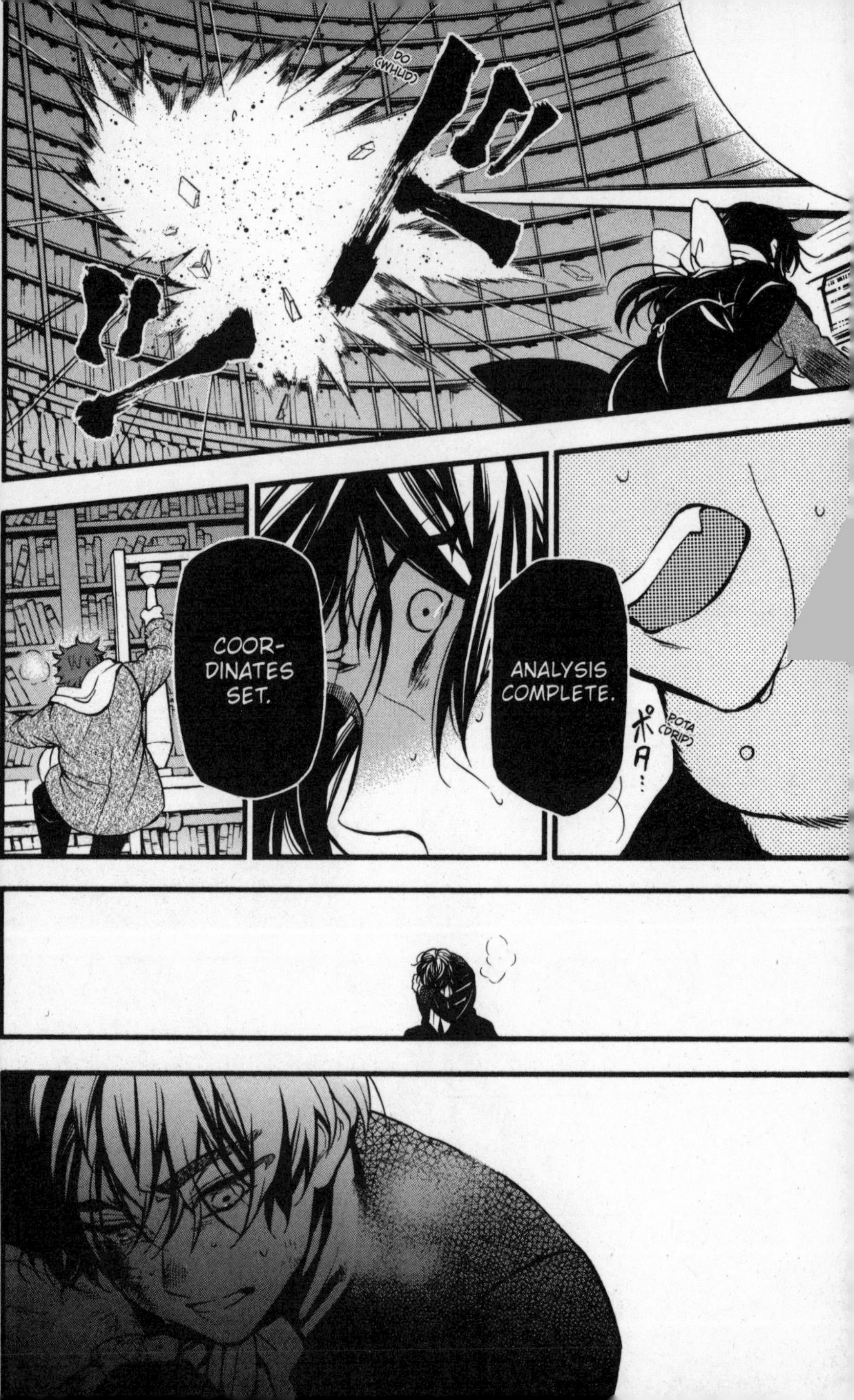
DO (WHUD)
ポタ…
POTA (DRIP)
ANALYSIS COMPLETE.
COOR-DINATES SET.

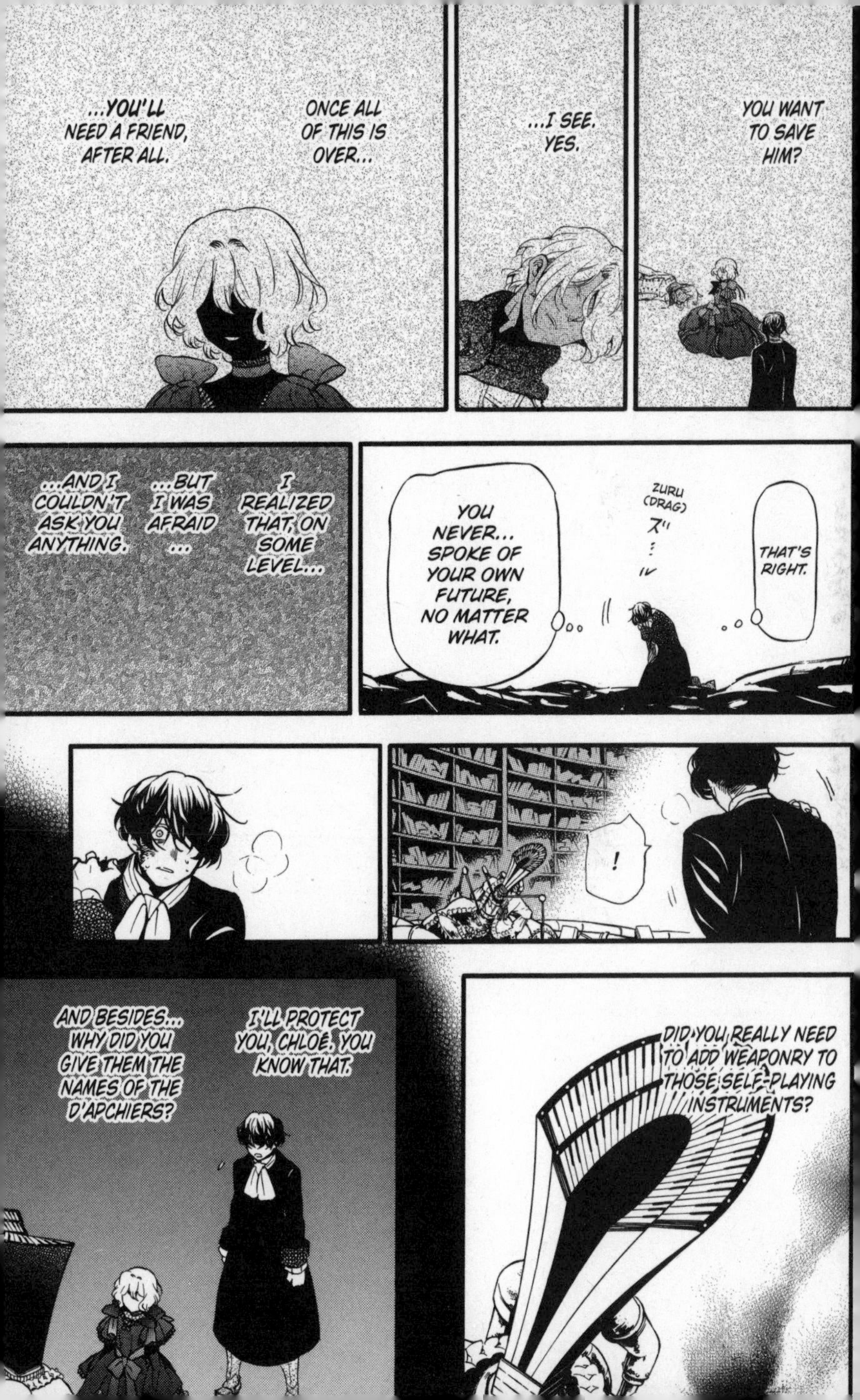
YOU WANT TO SAVE HIM?
...I SEE. YES.
ONCE ALL OF THIS IS OVER...
...YOU'LL NEED A FRIEND, AFTER ALL.
THAT'S RIGHT.
ZURU (DRAG)
ズル
YOU NEVER... SPOKE OF YOUR OWN FUTURE, NO MATTER WHAT.
I REALIZED THAT, ON SOME LEVEL...
...BUT I WAS AFRAID...
...AND I COULDN'T ASK YOU ANYTHING.
!
DID YOU REALLY NEED TO ADD WEAPONRY TO THOSE SELF-PLAYING INSTRUMENTS?
I'LL PROTECT YOU, CHLOÉ. YOU KNOW THAT.
AND BESIDES... WHY DID YOU GIVE THEM THE NAMES OF THE D'APCHIERS?

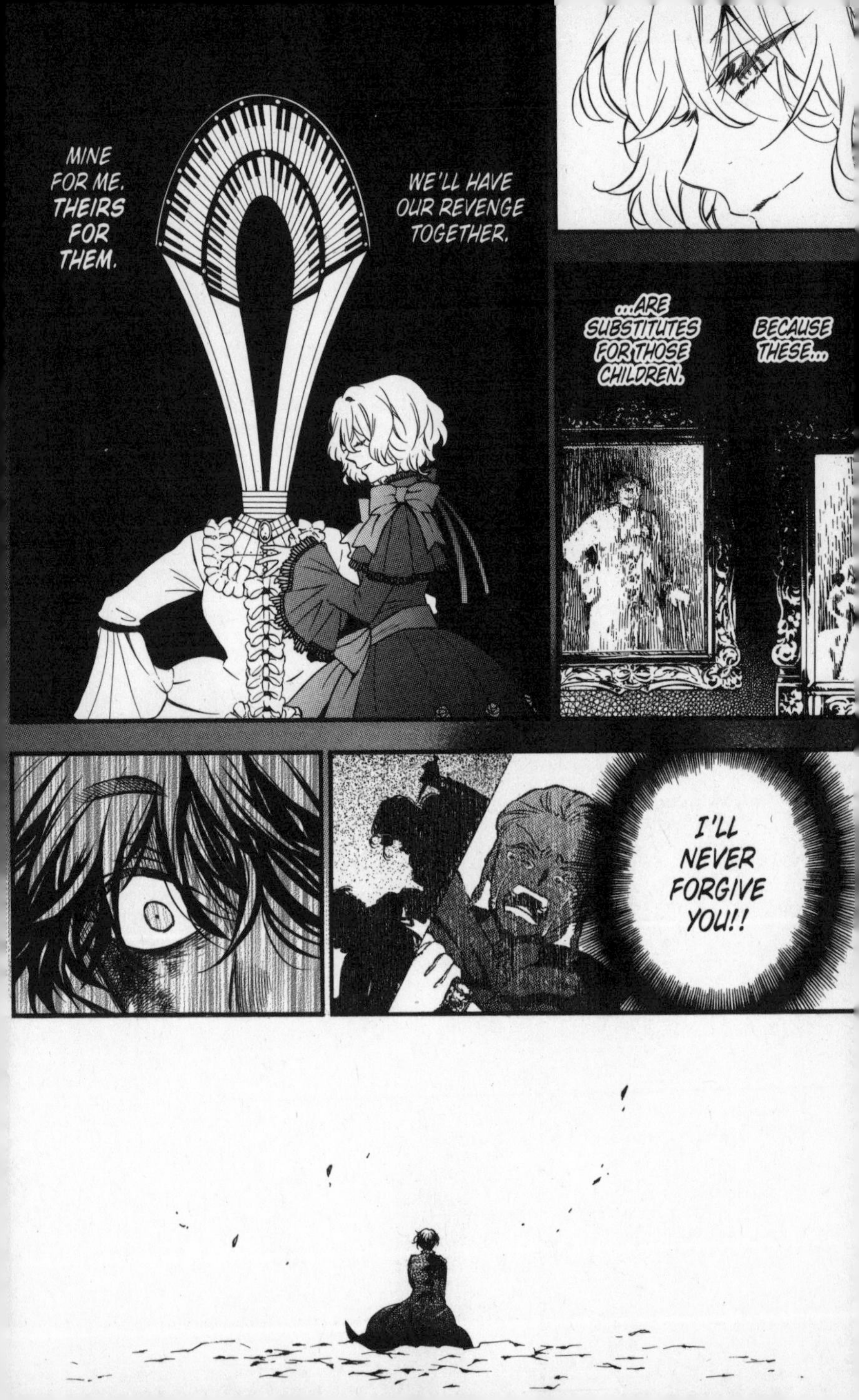
BECAUSE THESE...
...ARE SUBSTITUTES FOR THOSE CHILDREN.
WE'LL HAVE OUR REVENGE TOGETHER.
MINE FOR ME. THEIRS FOR THEM.
I'LL NEVER FORGIVE YOU!!

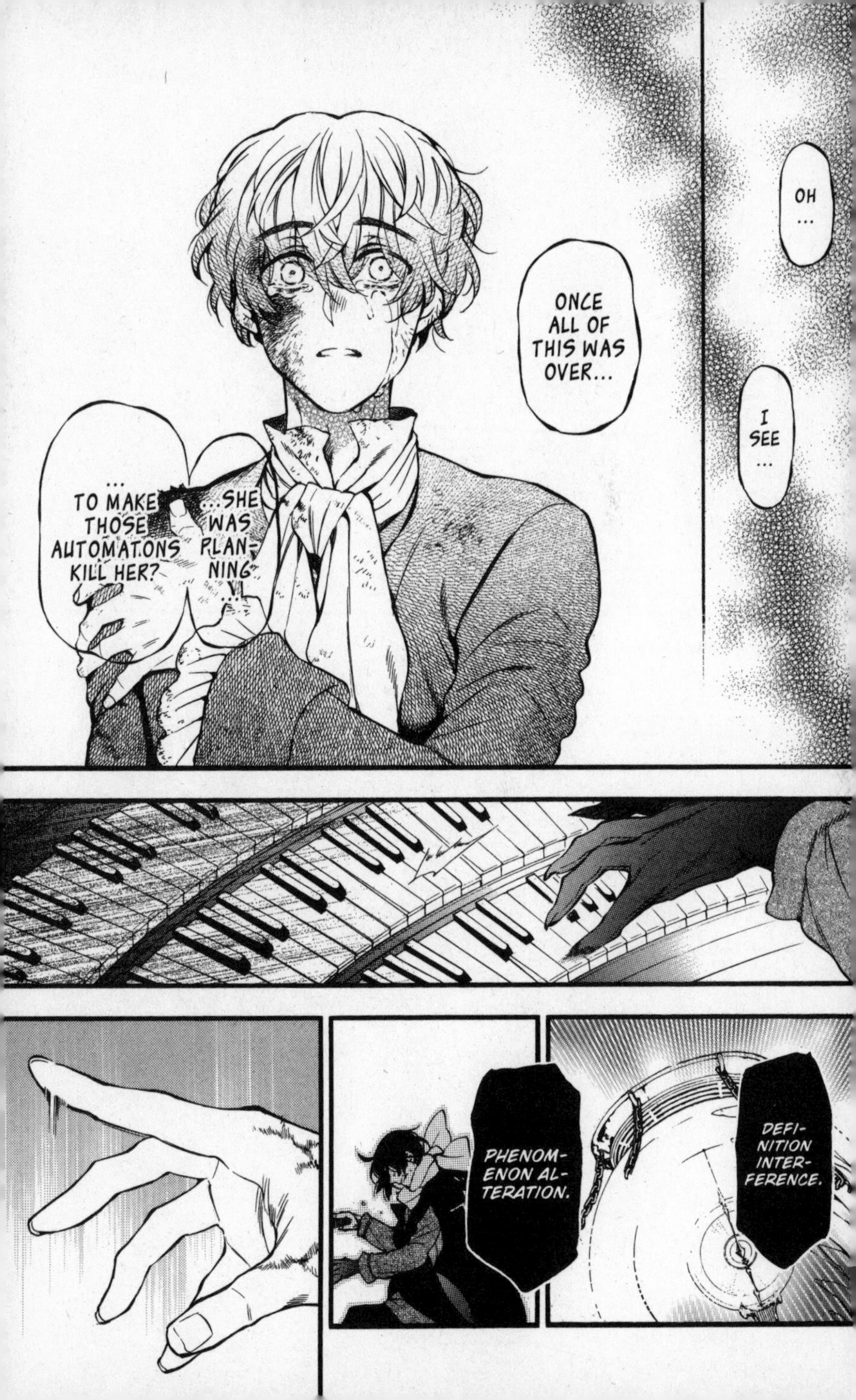
OH...
I SEE...
ONCE ALL OF THIS WAS OVER...
...SHE WAS PLANNING...
...TO MAKE THOSE AUTOMATONS KILL HER?
DEFINITION INTERFERENCE.
PHENOMENON ALTERATION.

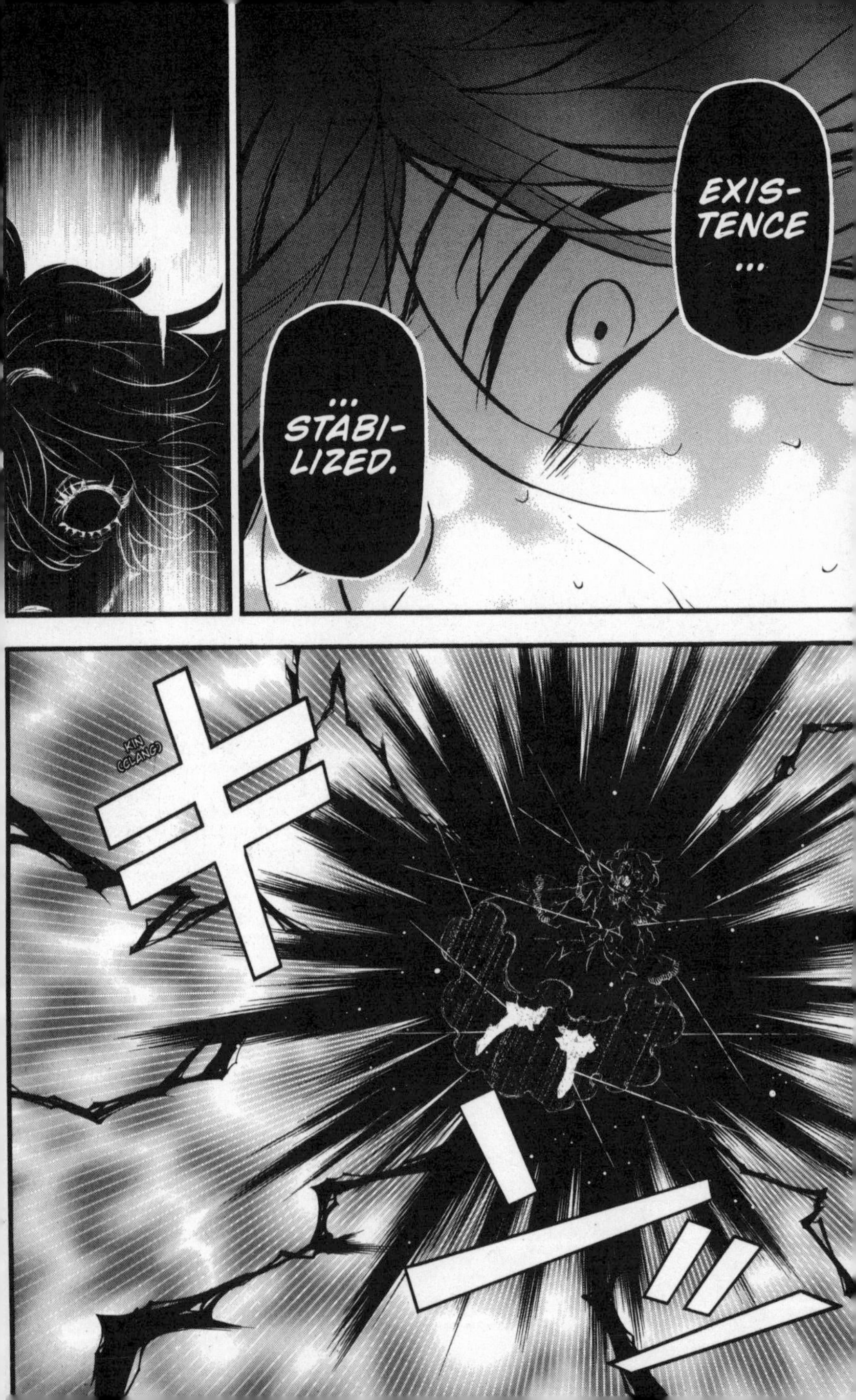
EXIS-
TENCE
...
...
STABI-
LIZED.
KIN
(CLANG)

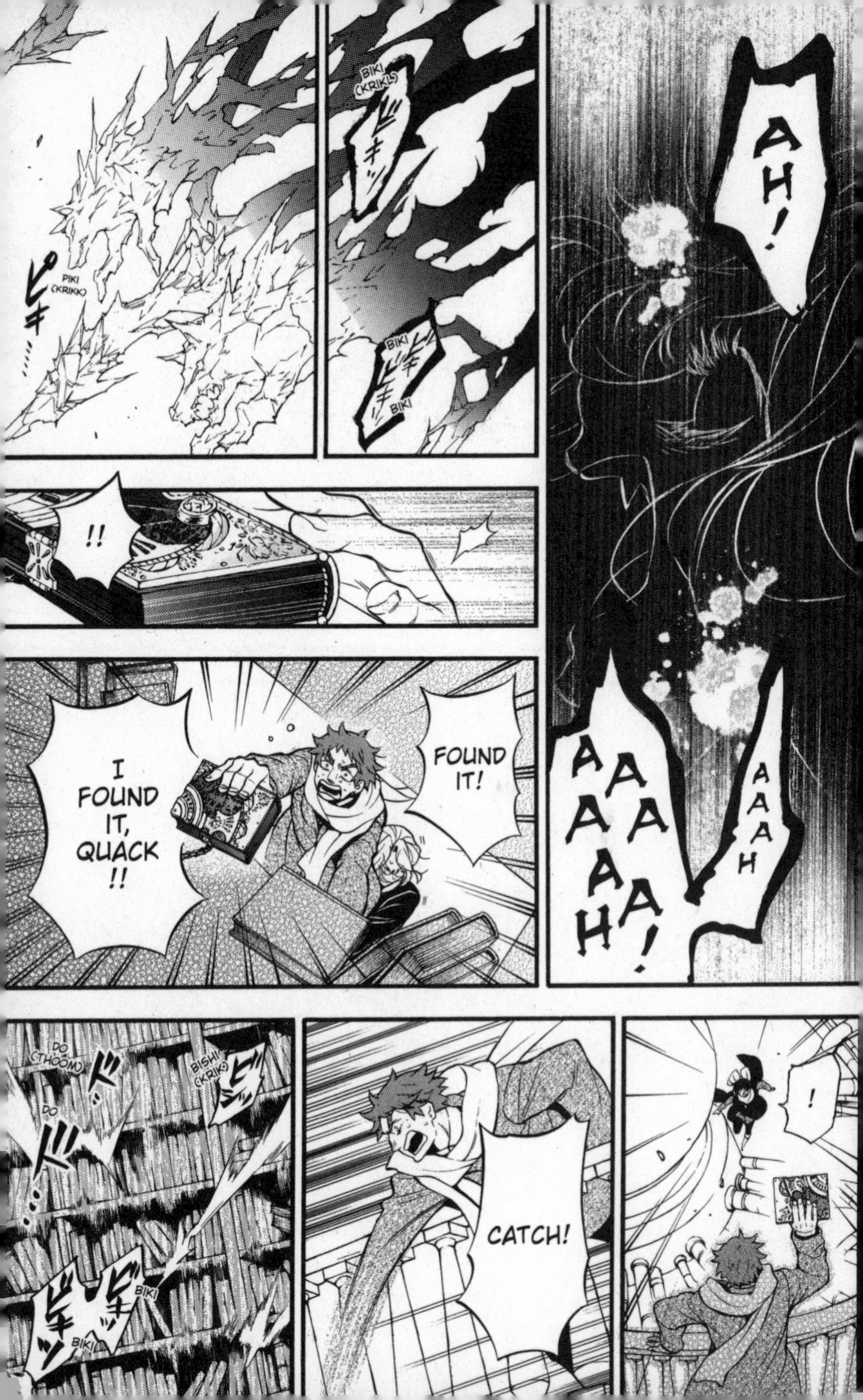
AH!
AAAAH!
AAAH
BIKI (KRIKL)
BIKI
BIKI
PIKI (KRIKK)
!!
FOUND IT!
I FOUND IT, QUACK!!
!
CATCH!
DO (THOOM)
DO
BISHI (KRIK)
BIKI
BIKI

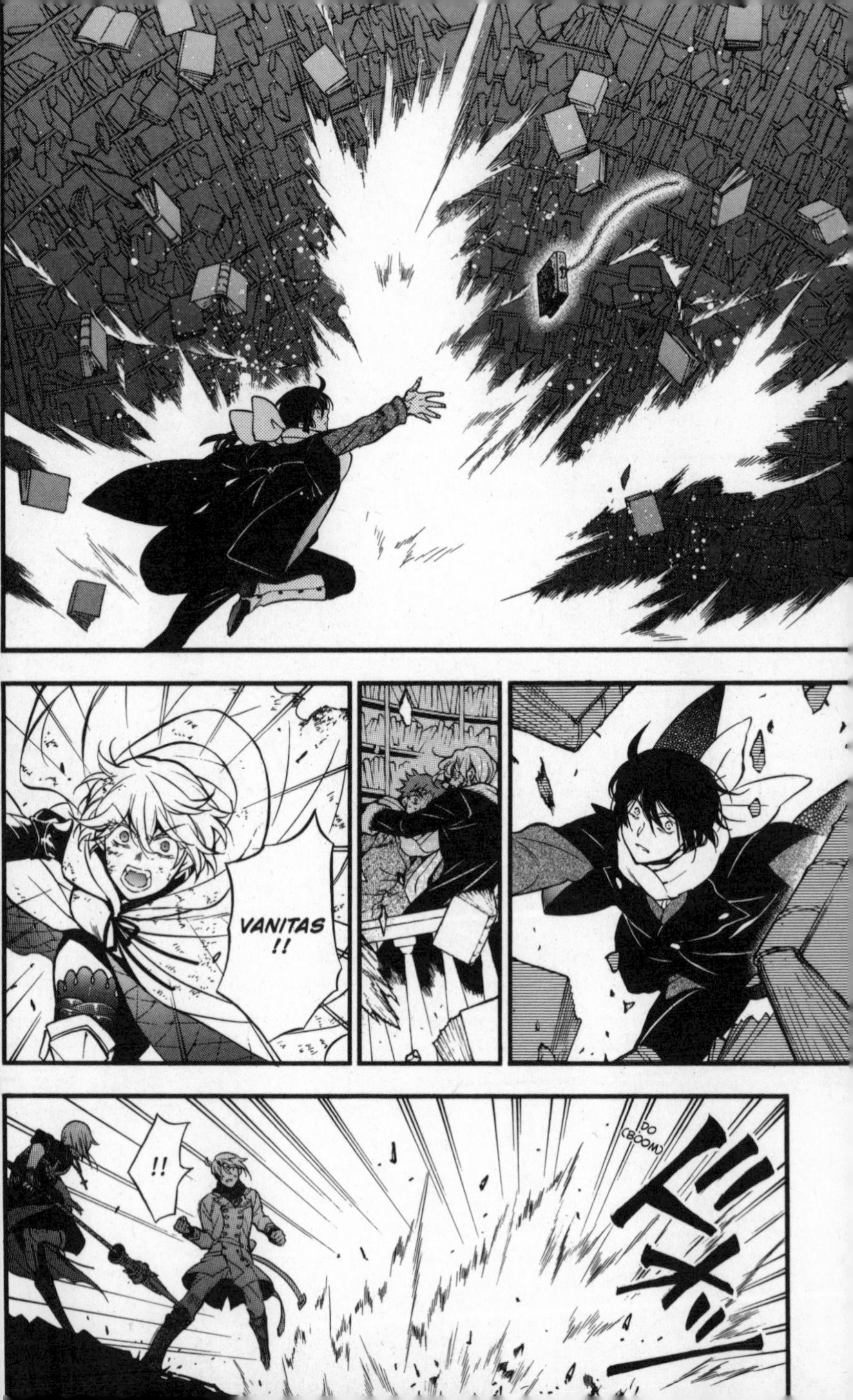
VANITAS!!
DO
(BOOM)
!!

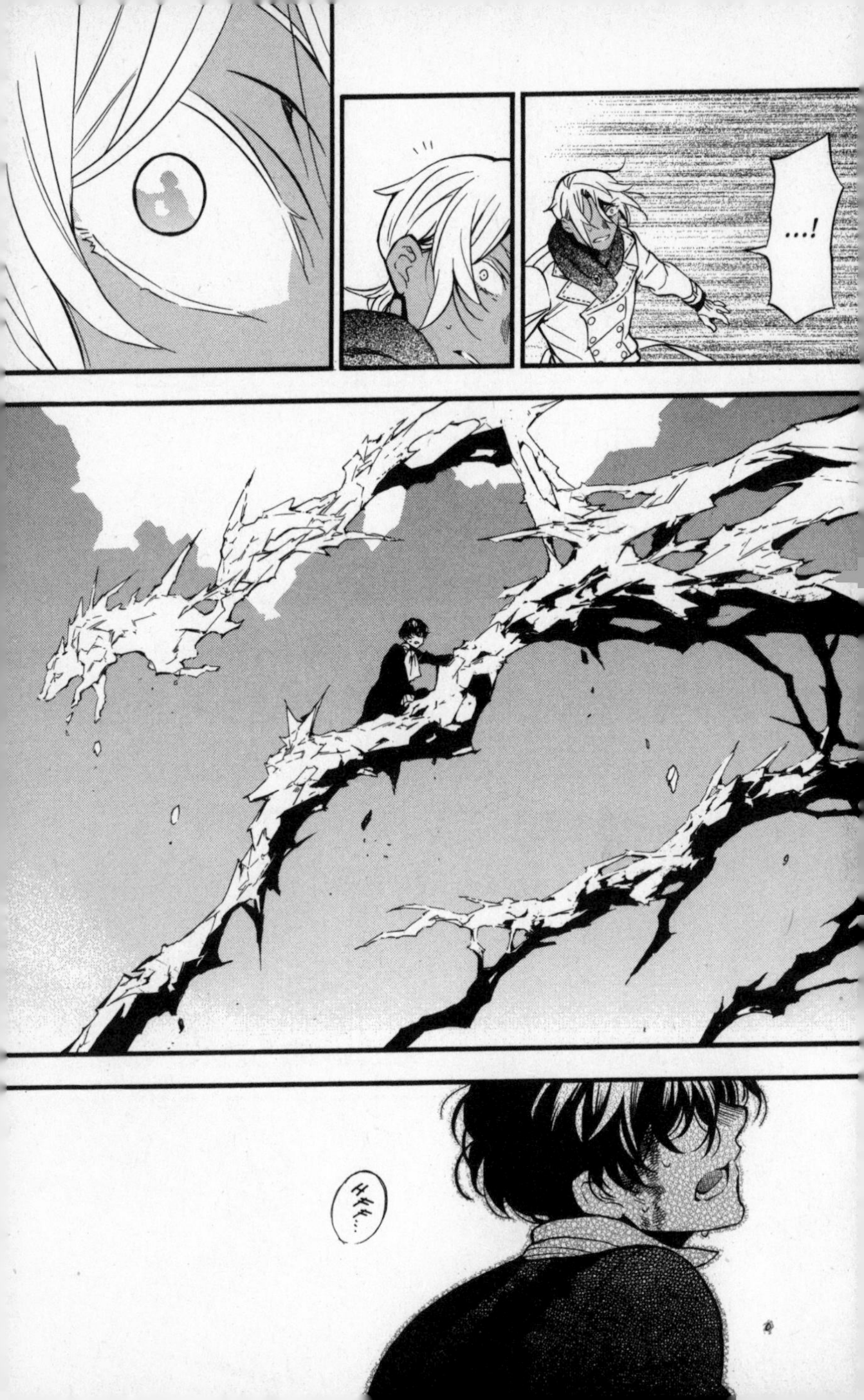
...!
HKK...

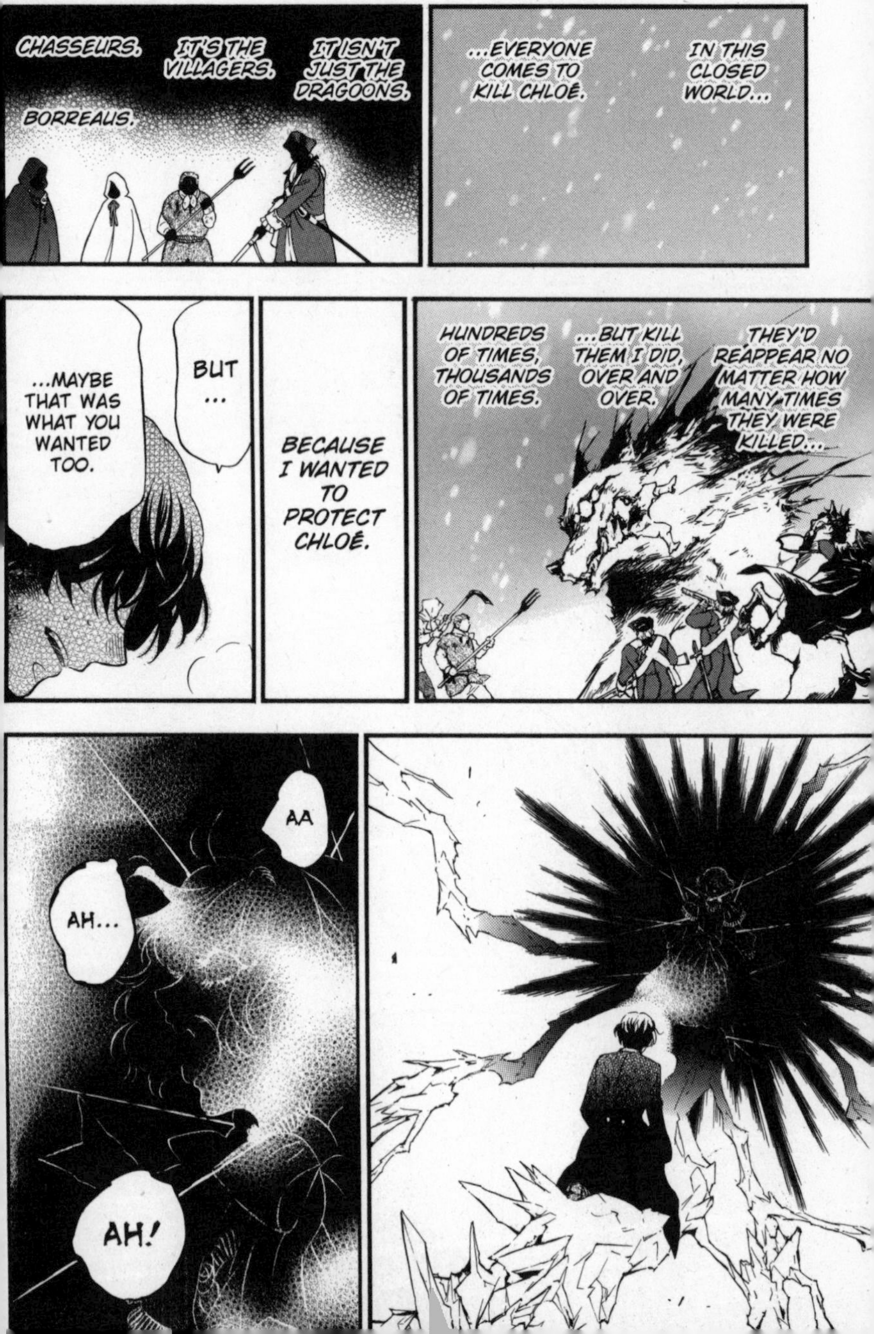
IN THIS CLOSED WORLD...
...EVERYONE COMES TO KILL CHLOÉ.
IT ISN'T JUST THE DRAGOONS.
IT'S THE VILLAGERS.
CHASSEURS.
BORREAUS.
THEY'D REAPPEAR NO MATTER HOW MANY TIMES THEY WERE KILLED...
...BUT KILL THEM I DID, OVER AND OVER.
HUNDREDS OF TIMES, THOUSANDS OF TIMES.
BECAUSE I WANTED TO PROTECT CHLOÉ.
BUT...
...MAYBE THAT WAS WHAT YOU WANTED TOO.
AA
AH...
AH!

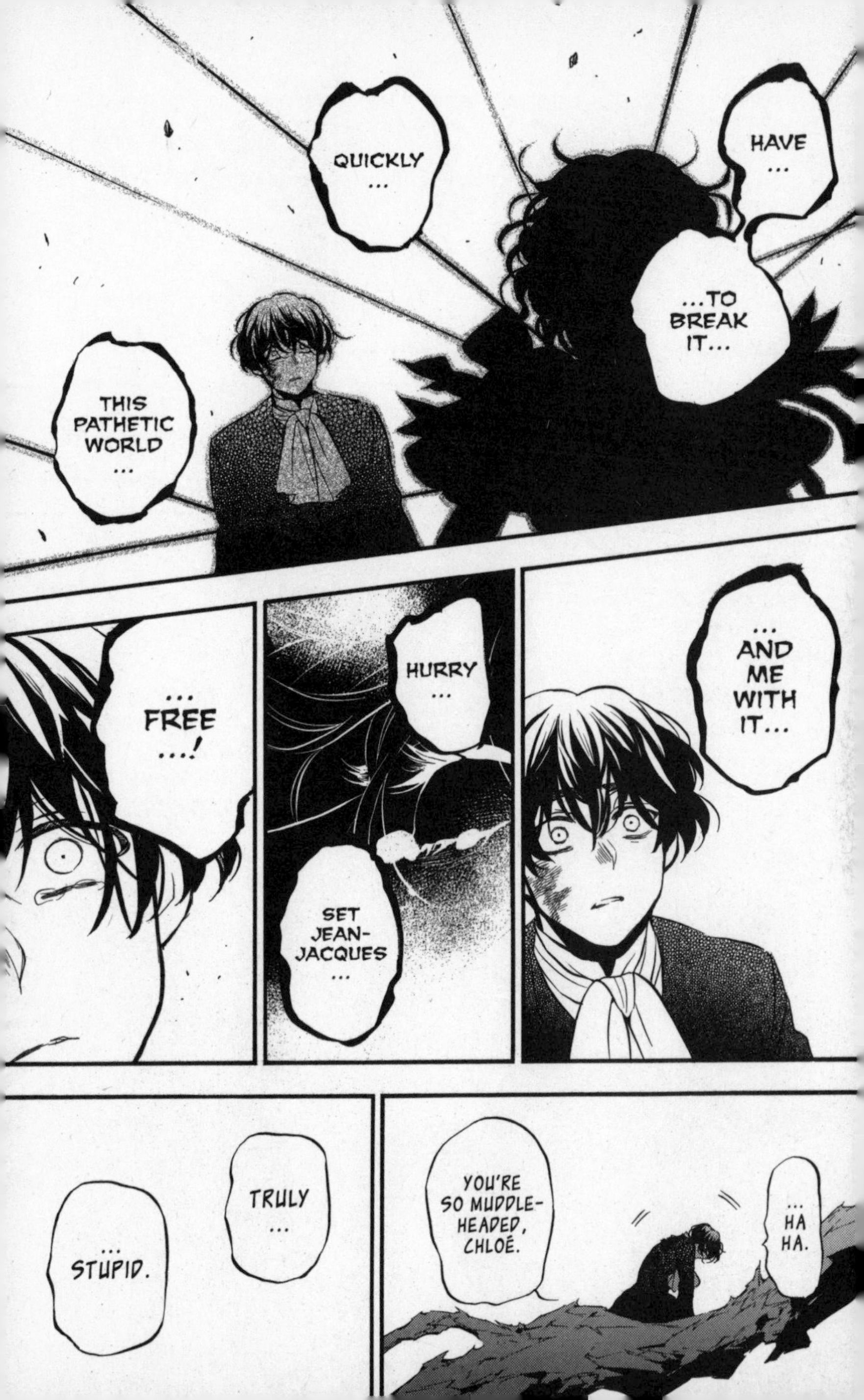
HAVE ...
...TO BREAK IT...
QUICKLY ...
THIS PATHETIC WORLD ...
... AND ME WITH IT...
HURRY ...
SET JEAN-JACQUES ...
... FREE ...!
... HA HA.
YOU'RE SO MUDDLE-HEADED, CHLOÉ.
TRULY ...
... STUPID.

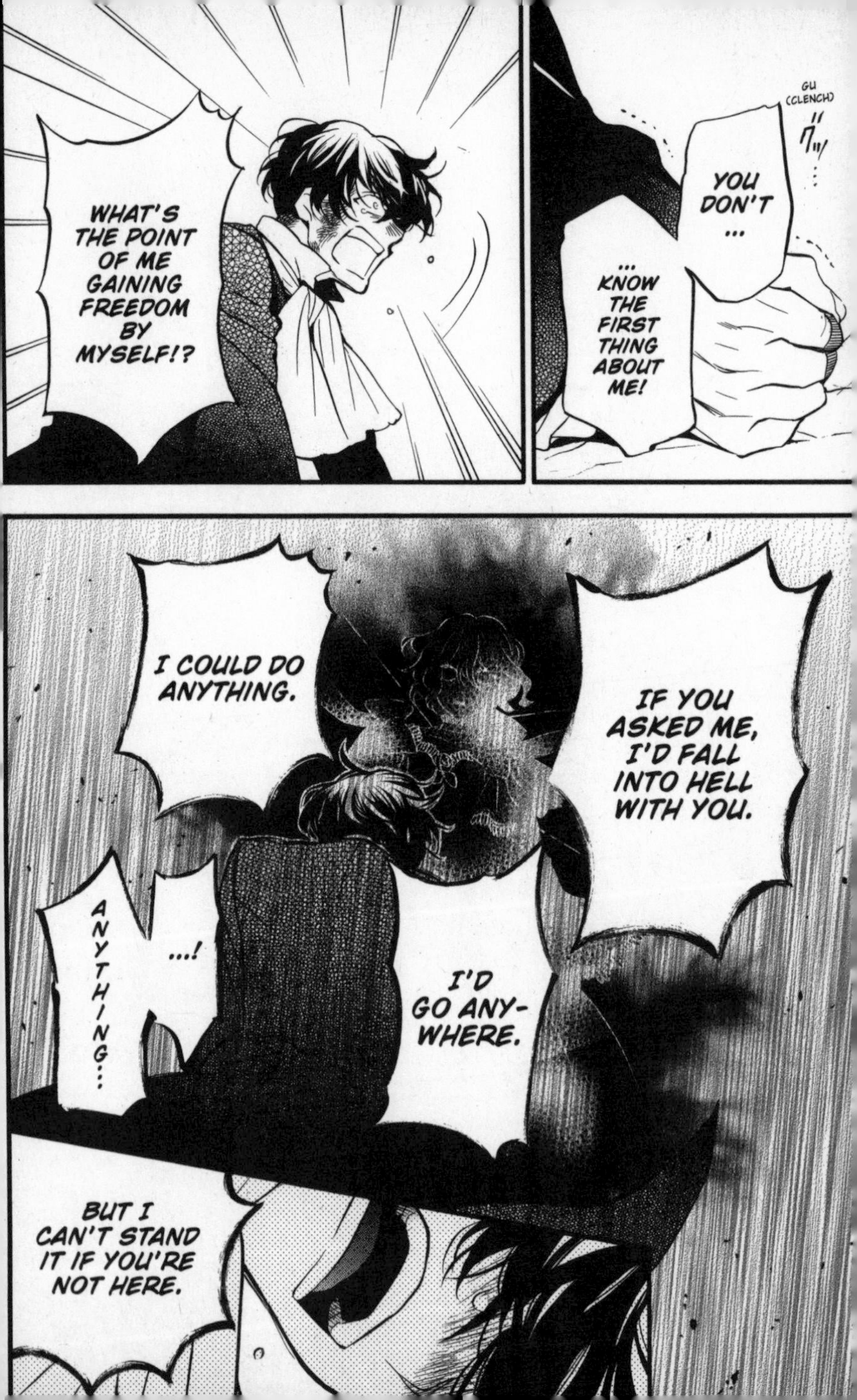
GU (CLENCH)
YOU DON'T ...
... KNOW THE FIRST THING ABOUT ME!
WHAT'S THE POINT OF ME GAINING FREEDOM BY MYSELF!?
IF YOU ASKED ME, I'D FALL INTO HELL WITH YOU.
I COULD DO ANYTHING.
I'D GO ANY-WHERE.
...!
ANYTHING...
BUT I CAN'T STAND IT IF YOU'RE NOT HERE.

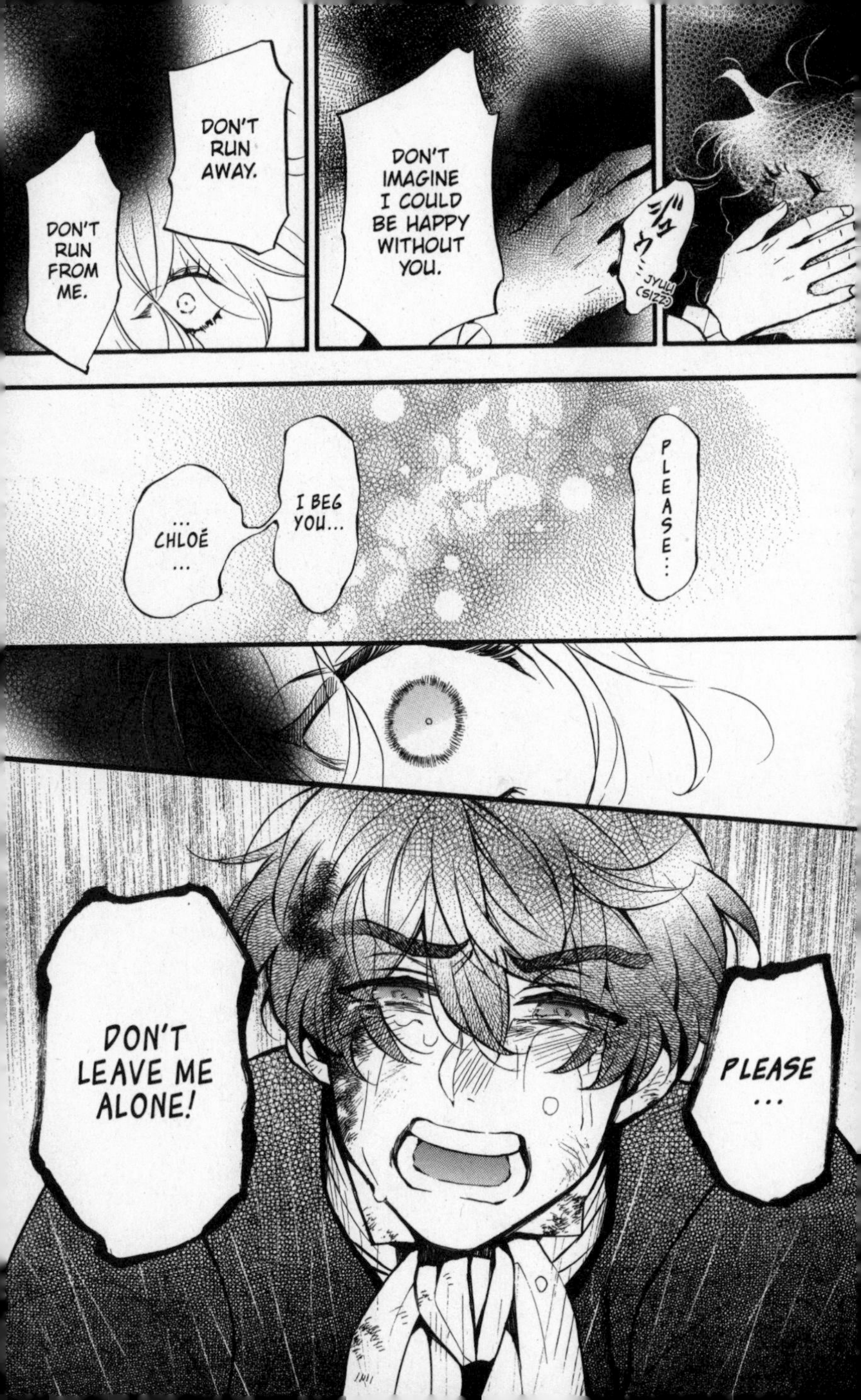
JYUU (SIZZ)
DON'T IMAGINE I COULD BE HAPPY WITHOUT YOU.
DON'T RUN AWAY.
DON'T RUN FROM ME.
PLEASE...
I BEG YOU...
...CHLOÉ...
PLEASE...
DON'T LEAVE ME ALONE!

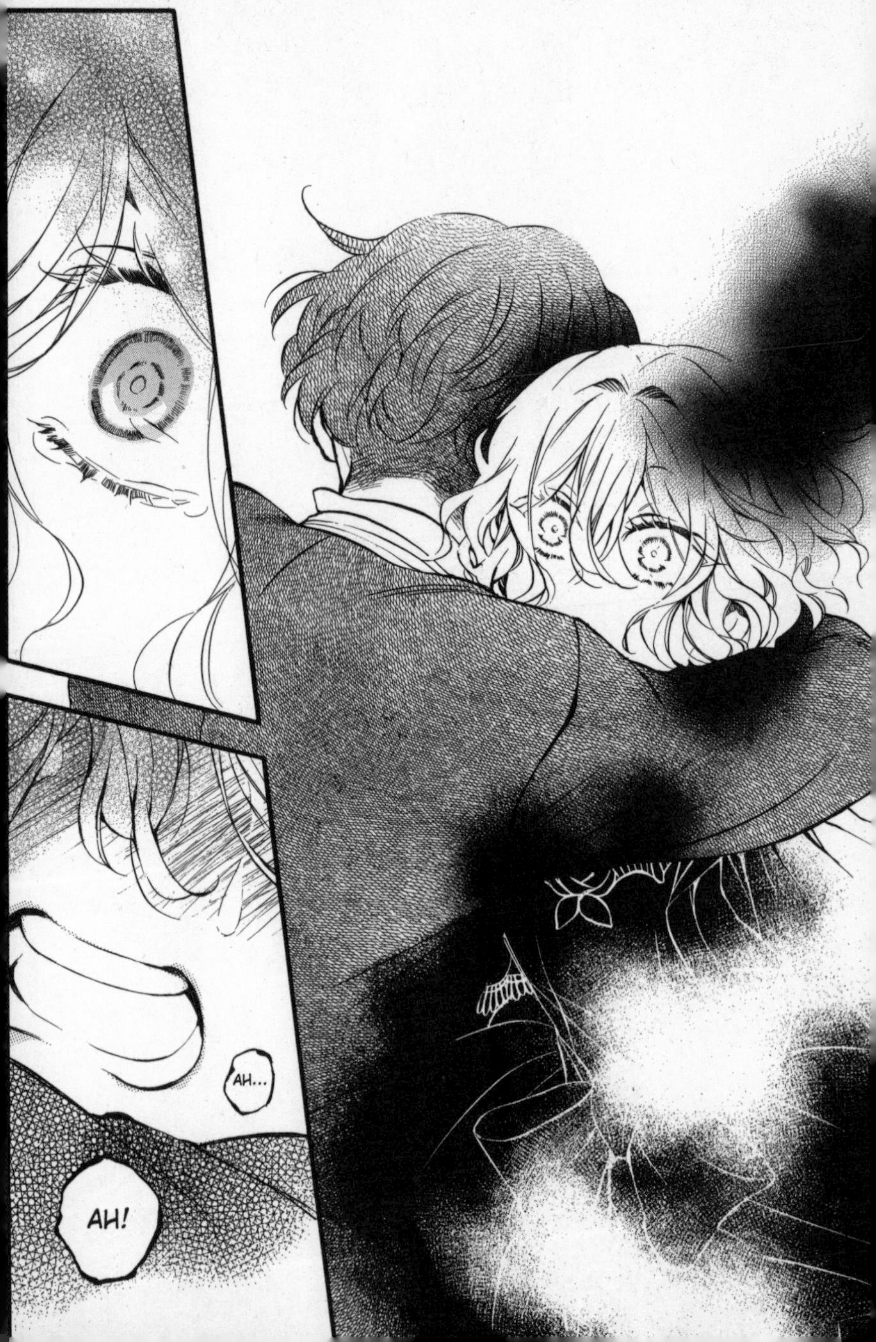
AH...
AH!

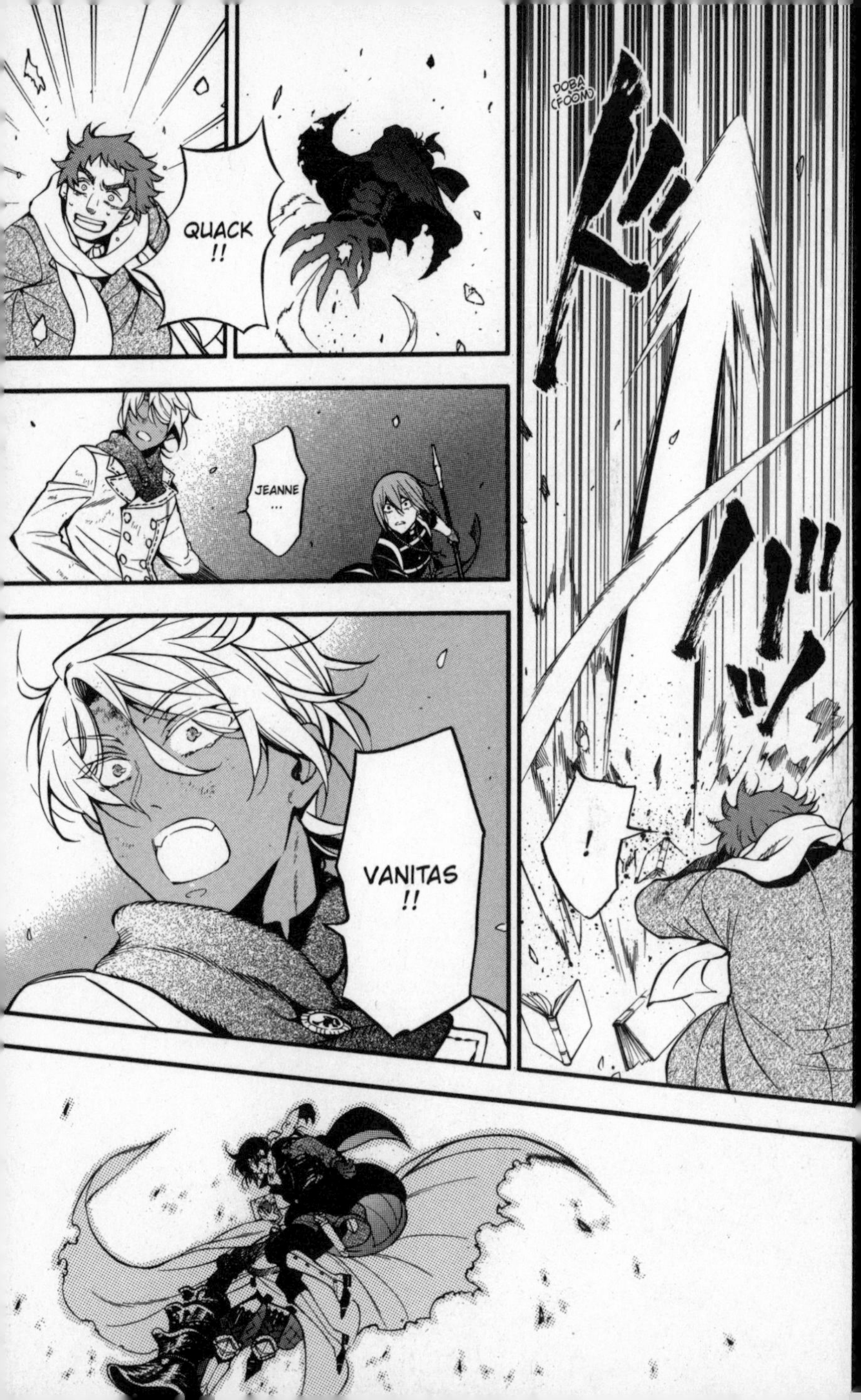
DOBA (FOOM)
!
QUACK !!
JEANNE ...
VANITAS !!

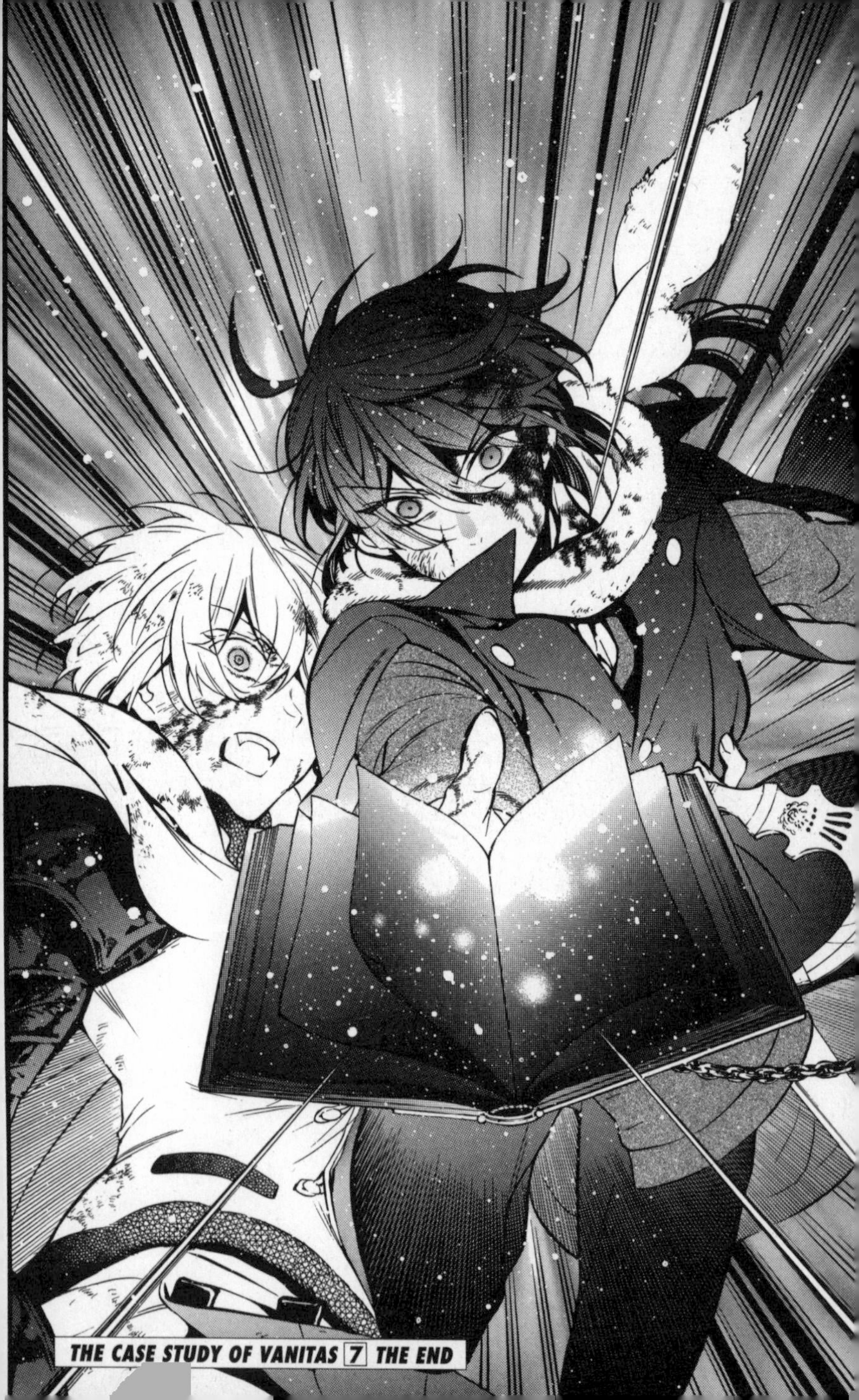

THE CASE STUDY OF VANITAS 7 THE END

Mémoire 10 Avec Toi ALONE TOGETHER

• CHASSEUR NOTE... VICE-CAPTAINS ARE APPOINTED BY CAPTAINS.

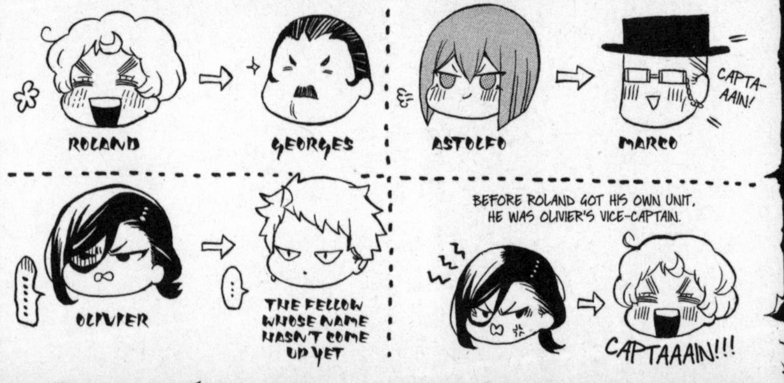
ASTOLFO
CAPTA-AAIN!
MARCO
ROLAND
GEORGES
BEFORE ROLAND GOT HIS OWN UNIT, HE WAS OLIVIER'S VICE-CAPTAIN.
CAPTAAAIN!!!
OLIVIER
....
...
THE FELLOW WHOSE NAME HASN'T COME UP YET

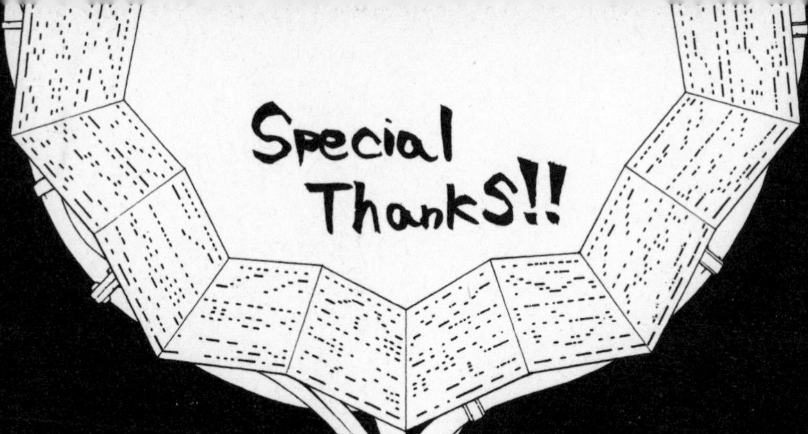

Special ThankS!!

KANATA MINAZUKI-SAN
LET'S GET HEALTHY TOGETHER

YUKINO-SAN
YOU'LL BE ABLE TO GO HOME TO PARIS SOON!

MIZU KING-SAN
ALL-ROUNDER MIZUKI

NOERU-SENSEI
DO YOU REALLY THINK THAT????

SAYA AYAHAMA-SAN
WELL-ATTENDED MOVIE-VIEWING TAKOYAKI PARTY

RYOOOO-CHAN
ALIVE!! I'M ALIVE!

KEI-SAN
COMMENTATOR FOR NOERU-SENSEI

KAHO KOIDE-SAN
COME OVER AND PLAY!
YOU DON'T HAVE TO WORK!

TAROU YONEDA-SAN
YOU GOT SO FAST AT DRAWING
WOLVES IT'S SCARY!

DAICHI SAWAIRI-SAN
LET'S DRAW THE HECK OUT OF 'EM!
*BACKGROUNDS, I MEAN

SAKANA-SAN
IF I FIND SOMEONE IN A RED MASK,
I'LL SECURE THEM

FUMITO YAMAZAKI-SAN
I DON'T KNOW WHICH CAJÓN IS GOOD. HELP ME.

EDITOR OGASAWARA-SAN
"ROMANCE IS A ★ LOVE MISSION" IS SURE TO SELL LIKE HOTCAKES, ISN'T IT!! THANK YOU VERY MUCH FOR THE COMMENT!!

DESIGNER-SAMA

EVERYONE WHO HELPED ME
COLLECT MATERIALS

and

you!!!

COMING SOON

ARC COMES TO A CLOSE

THE LONG, DREADFUL
NIGHT COMES TO AN END,
LEAVING THE ECHOES
OF HOWLS LINGERING IN
EVERY HEART.

The Case Study of Vanitas VOLUME 8

THE BEAST OF GÉVAUDAN

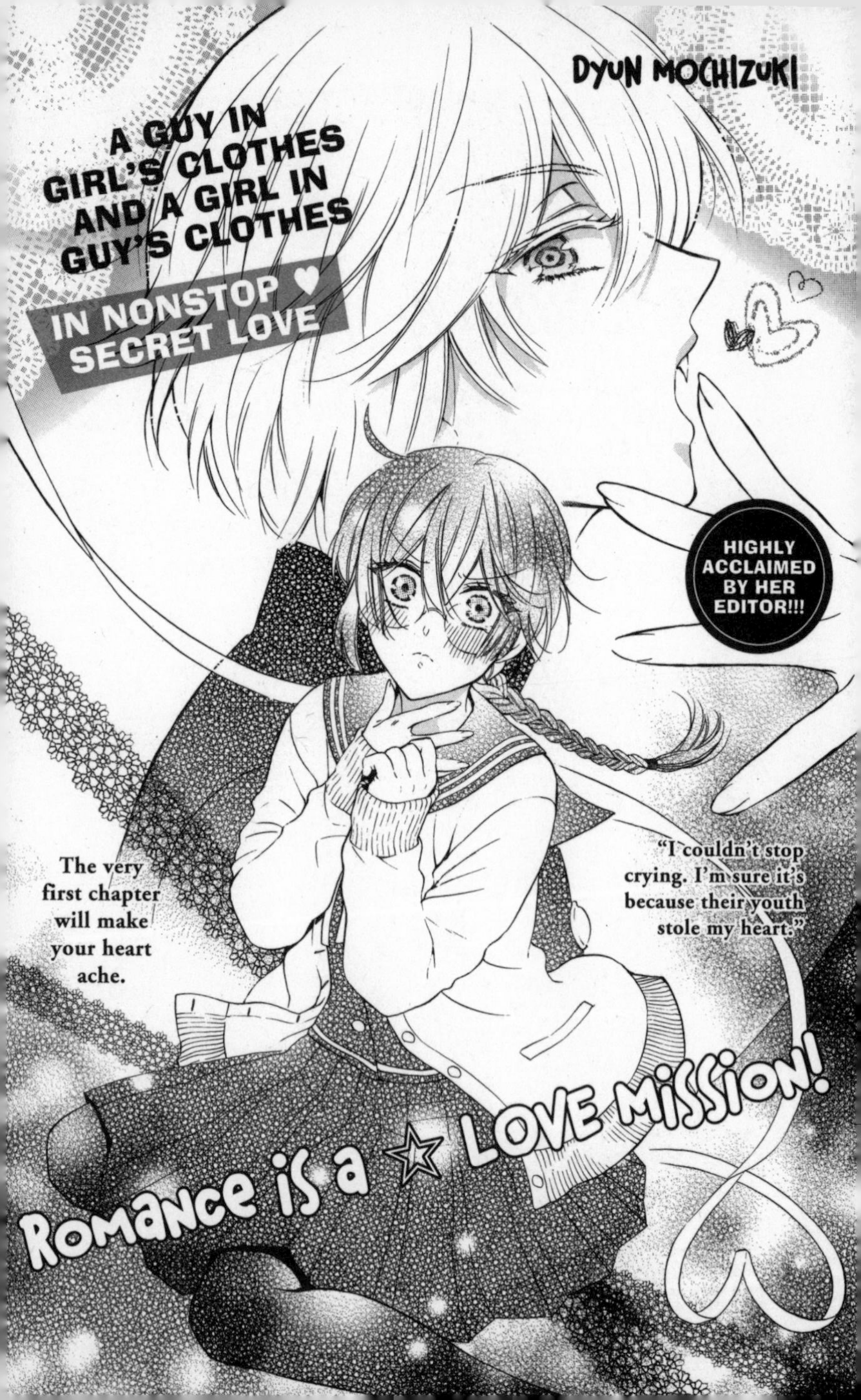
DYUN MOCHIZUKI
A GUY IN GIRL'S CLOTHES AND A GIRL IN GUY'S CLOTHES
IN NONSTOP ♥ SECRET LOVE
HIGHLY ACCLAIMED BY HER EDITOR!!!
The very first chapter will make your heart ache.
"I couldn't stop crying. I'm sure it's because their youth stole my heart."
Romance is a ☆ LOVE MISSION!

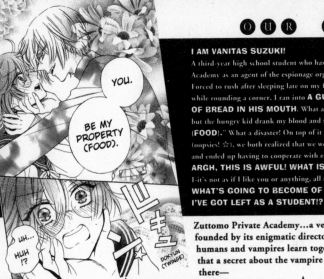

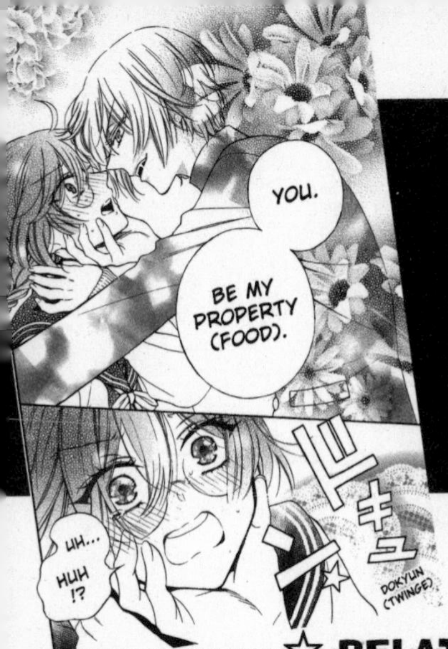
YOU.
BE MY PROPERTY (FOOD).
ドキュン
DOKYUN (TWINGE)
UH... HUH!?

OUR STORY

I AM VANITAS SUZUKI!
A third-year high school student who has infiltrated Zuttomo Academy as an agent of the espionage organization Blue Moon! Forced to rush after sleeping late on my first day as a transfer student, while rounding a corner, I ran into **A GUY HOLDING A PIECE OF BREAD IN HIS MOUTH**. What a shock! ☆ Not only that, but the hungry kid drank my blood and said "**BE MY PROPERTY (FOOD).**" What a disaster! On top of it all, due to a little accident (oopsies! ☆), we both realized that we were actually male and female, and ended up having to cooperate with each other.
ARGH, THIS IS AWFUL! WHAT IS WITH THAT JERK!?
I-it's not as if I like you or anything, all right!?
WHAT'S GOING TO BECOME OF WHAT LITTLE TIME I'VE GOT LEFT AS A STUDENT!?

Zuttomo Private Academy...a very peaceful school founded by its enigmatic director as a hobby, where humans and vampires learn together. Rumor has it that a secret about the vampire queen is hidden there—

☆ RELATIONSHIPS ☆

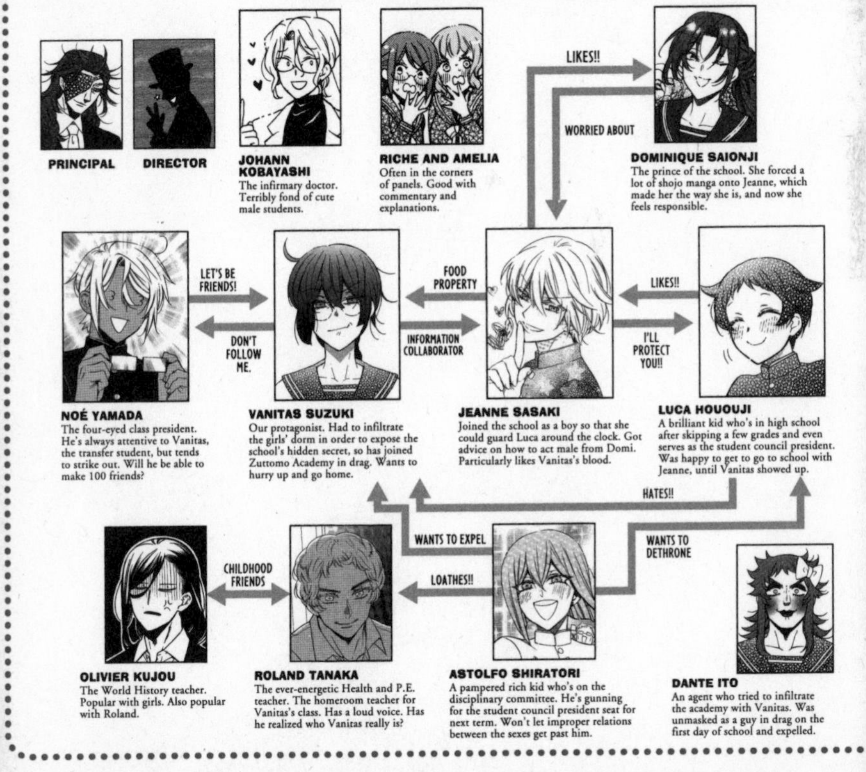
PRINCIPAL
DIRECTOR
JOHANN KOBAYASHI
The infirmary doctor. Terribly fond of cute male students.
RICHE AND AMELIA
Often in the corners of panels. Good with commentary and explanations.
LIKES!!
WORRIED ABOUT
DOMINIQUE SAIONJI
The prince of the school. She forced a lot of shojo manga onto Jeanne, which made her the way she is, and now she feels responsible.
LET'S BE FRIENDS!
DON'T FOLLOW ME.
FOOD PROPERTY
INFORMATION COLLABORATOR
LIKES!!
I'LL PROTECT YOU!!
NOÉ YAMADA
The four-eyed class president. He's always attentive to Vanitas, the transfer student, but tends to strike out. Will he be able to make 100 friends?
VANITAS SUZUKI
Our protagonist. Had to infiltrate the girls' dorm in order to expose the school's hidden secret, so has joined Zuttomo Academy in drag. Wants to hurry up and go home.
JEANNE SASAKI
Joined the school as a boy so that she could guard Luca around the clock. Got advice on how to act male from Domi. Particularly likes Vanitas's blood.
LUCA HOUOUJI
A brilliant kid who's in high school after skipping a few grades and even serves as the student council president. Was happy to get to go to school with Jeanne, until Vanitas showed up.
HATES!!
WANTS TO EXPEL
WANTS TO DETHRONE
CHILDHOOD FRIENDS
LOATHES!!
OLIVIER KUJOU
The World History teacher. Popular with girls. Also popular with Roland.
ROLAND TANAKA
The ever-energetic Health and P.E. teacher. The homeroom teacher for Vanitas's class. Has a loud voice. Has he realized who Vanitas really is?
ASTOLFO SHIRATORI
A pampered rich kid who's on the disciplinary committee. He's gunning for the student council president seat for next term. Won't let improper relations between the sexes get past him.
DANTE ITO
An agent who tried to infiltrate the academy with Vanitas. Was unmasked as a guy in drag on the first day of school and expelled.

I WANT A HOBBY OF SOME SORT...

Jun Mochizuki

AUTHOR'S NOTE

I've been looking for a
hobby (or another good
way to mentally shift gears)
besides manga and drawing
for ages now, but so far
nothing's really clicked
for me...Are there any
good hobbies lying around
somewhere?

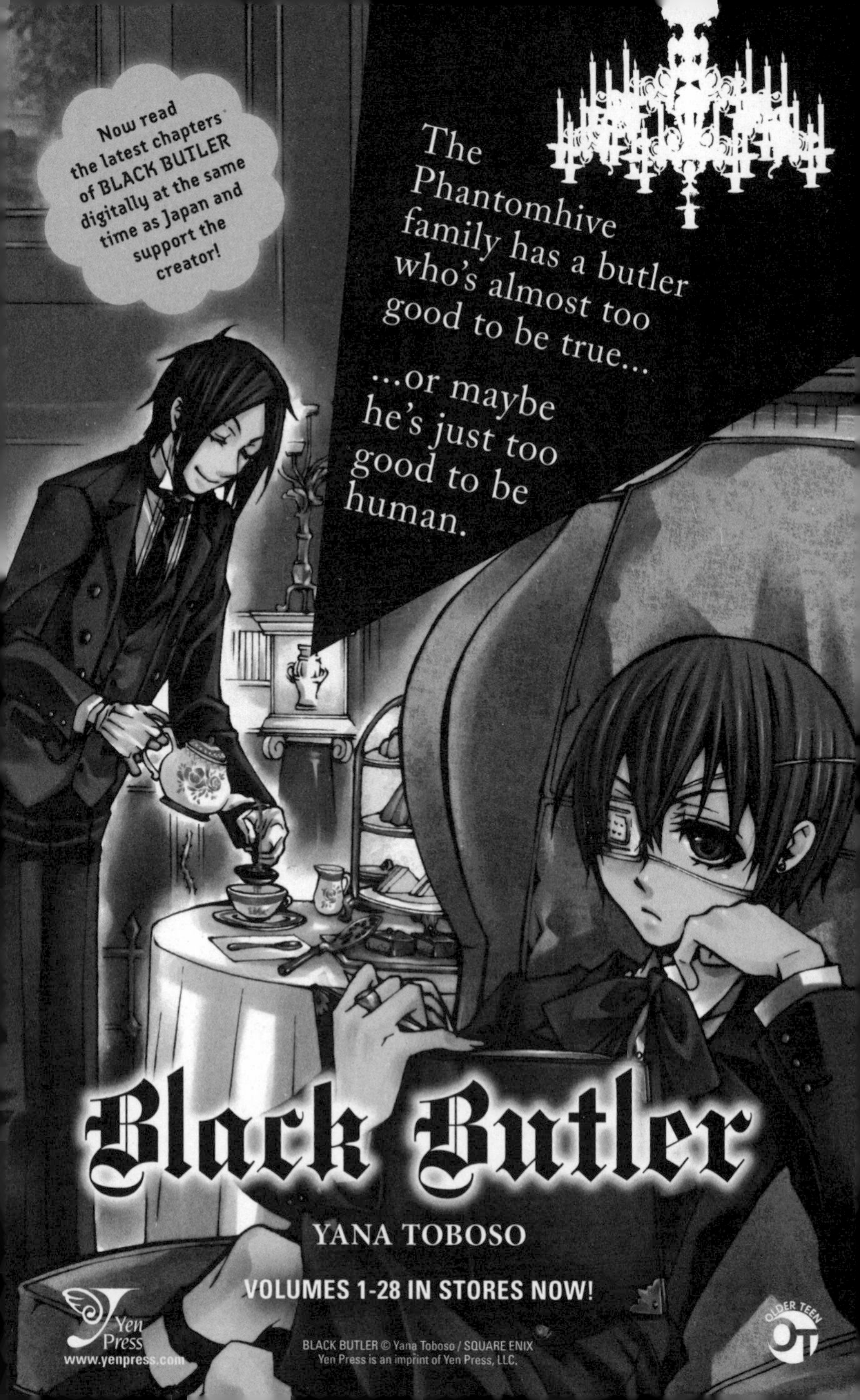

Now read the latest chapters of BLACK BUTLER digitally at the same time as Japan and support the creator!
The Phantomhive family has a butler who's almost too good to be true...
...or maybe he's just too good to be human.
Black Butler
YANA TOBOSO
VOLUMES 1-28 IN STORES NOW!
Yen Press
www.yenpress.com
BLACK BUTLER © Yana Toboso / SQUARE ENIX
Yen Press is an imprint of Yen Press, LLC.
OLDER TEEN
OT

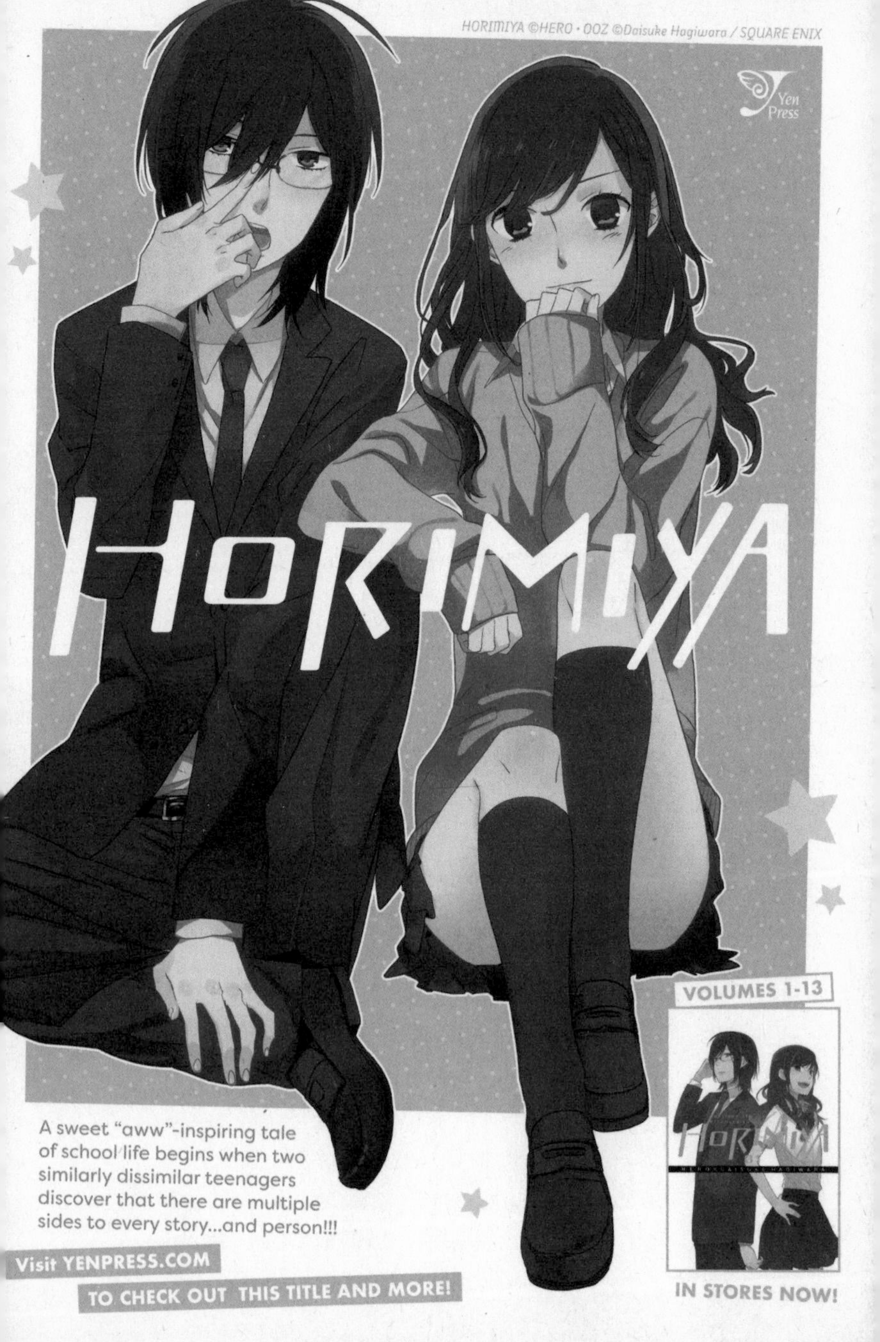
HORIMIYA ©HERO • OOZ ©Daisuke Hagiwara / SQUARE ENIX
Yen Press
HORIMIYA
VOLUMES 1-13
A sweet "aww"-inspiring tale of school life begins when two similarly dissimilar teenagers discover that there are multiple sides to every story...and person!!!
Visit YENPRESS.COM
TO CHECK OUT THIS TITLE AND MORE!
IN STORES NOW!

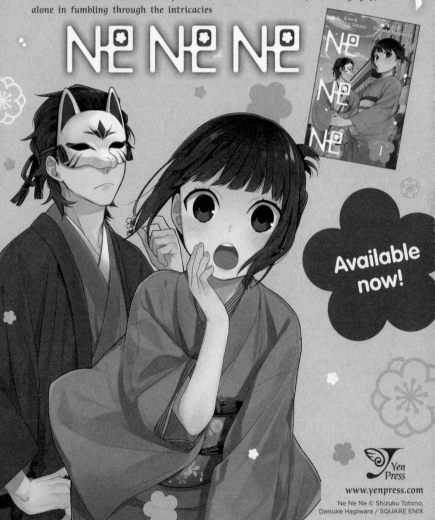

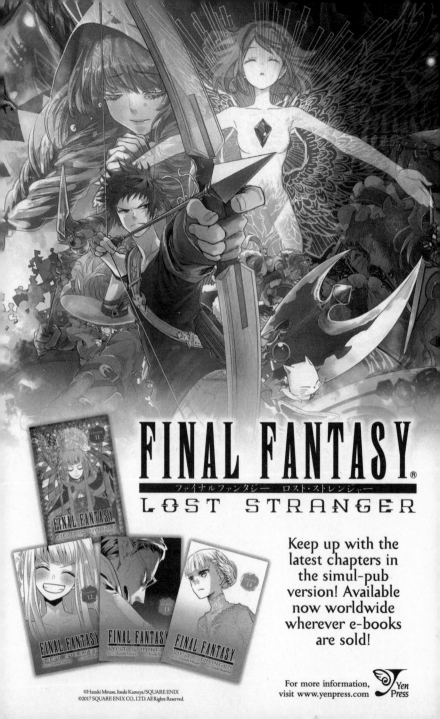

HE DOES NOT LET ANYONE ROLL THE DICE.

A young Priestess joins her first adventuring party, but blind to the dangers, they almost immediately find themselves in trouble. It's Goblin Slayer who comes to their rescue—a man who has dedicated his life to the extermination of all goblins by any means necessary. A dangerous, dirty, and thankless job, but he does it better than anyone. And when rumors of his feats begin to circulate, there's no telling who might come calling next...

Light Novel V. 1-9 Available Now!

Check out the simul-pub manga chapters every month!

www.yenpress.com

RED IS THE NEW BLACK IN THIS BLOODY, ACTION-PACKED SERIES ABOUT A GROUP OF RIGHTEOUS ASSASSINS!

Teenage country bumpkin Tatsumi dreams of earning enough money for his impoverished village by working in the Capital—but his short-lived plans go awry when he's robbed by a buxom beauty upon arrival! Penniless, Tatsumi is taken in by the lovely Miss Aria, but just when his Capital dreams seem in reach yet again, Miss Aria's mansion is besieged by Night Raid—a team of ruthless assassins who targets high-ranking members of the upper class! As Tatsumi is quick to learn, appearances can be deceiving in the Capital, and this team of assassins just might be... the good guys?!

Akame ga KILL!

FULL SERIES AVAILABLE NOW!

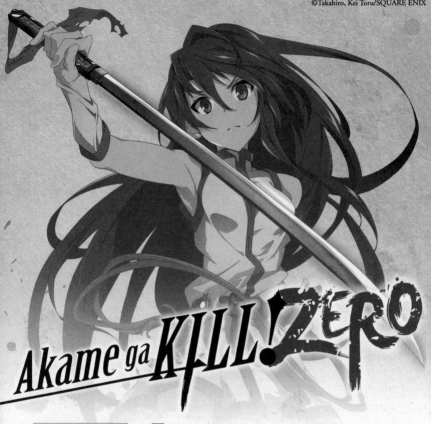

THE CASE STUDY OF VANITAS
VOLUME 7

JUN MOCHIZUKI

TRANSLATION: TAYLOR ENGEL
LETTERING: BIANCA PISTILLO

Vanitas no Carte Volume 7 ©2019 Jun Mochizuki/SQUARE ENIX CO., LTD.
First published in Japan in 2019 by SQUARE ENIX CO., LTD. English translation rights arranged with SQUARE ENIX CO., LTD. and Yen Press, LLC through Tuttle-Mori Agency, Inc., Tokyo.

English translation ©2020 by SQUARE ENIX CO., LTD.

Yen Press
150 West 30th Street, 19th Floor
New York, NY 10001

Visit us at yenpress.com
facebook.com/yenpress
twitter.com/yenpress
yenpress.tumblr.com
instagram.com/yenpress

First Yen Press Edition: July 2020

The chapters in this volume were originally published as ebooks by Yen Press.

Yen Press is an imprint of Yen Press, LLC.
The Yen Press name and logo are trademarks of Yen Press, LLC.

The publisher is not responsible for websites (or their content) that are not owned by the publisher.

Library of Congress Control Number: 2016946115

ISBNs: 978-1-9753-1380-7 (paperback)
978-1-9753-1379-1 (ebook)

10 9 8 7 6 5 4 3 2 1

WOR

Printed in the United States of America